OUR MINERVA

Our Minerva

The Men and Politics
of the University of London
1836–1858

F.M.G. WILLSON

ATHLONE
London & Atlantic Highlands, NJ

First published 1995 by
THE ATHLONE PRESS
1 Park Drive, London NW11 7SG
and 165 First Avenue,
Atlantic Highlands, NJ 07716

British Library Cataloguing in Publication Data
*A catalogue record for this book is available
from the British Library*

ISBN 0 485 11479 8

Library of Congress Cataloging in Publication Data
Willson, F. M. G. (Francis Michael Glenn), 1924–
  Our Minerva : the men and politics of the University of
London, 1836–1858 / F.M.G. Willson
     p.   cm.
  Includes bibliographical references and index.
  ISBN 0-485-11479-8 (hb)
     1. University of London--History--19th century.   2. Uni-
versity of London--Administration--History--19th century.
3. Politics and education--England--London--History--19th
century.   I. Title
LF412.W55   1995
378'.942'1--dc20   95-34751
                                                     CIP

Typeset by
Bibloset, Chester

Printed and bound in Great Britain by
the University Press, Cambridge

For

Judith and Terence Ball
Rosanne and David Townsend

Our Minerva cannot enter into the world without painful labour and throes. But when the new divinity or mortal is fairly in the world I hope she may be able to walk with less difficulty.

Thomas Spring Rice, Chancellor of the Exchequer,
to George Biddell Airy, Astronomer Royal, 16 August 1838

Wars and rumours of wars are evils everywhere and in no place more dangerous violent and I fear in few places are they more prevalent than in Universities.

Thomas Spring Rice to John William Lubbock,
first Vice-Chancellor of the University of London, 30 November 1838

Contents

Acknowledgements

I join with The Athlone Press in expressing thanks to the University of London, whose generous financial contribution has made the publication of this book possible.

For allowing me to draw on his deep and comprehensive knowledge of the history of the University and of University College London; for his offering of much expert guidance, encouragement and constructive comment; and especially for his contribution of a Foreword, I am most grateful to Negley Harte. Dr Ruth Richardson gave me very helpful advice on aspects of relevant medical developments in the 1830s. As in previous ventures, I owe great gratitude to my wife for judicious criticism, much patience and invaluable moral support.

The primary sources available for this study are less extensive than one would wish, but they are, nonetheless, spread over a wide range of collections. I am particularly grateful for the gracious permission of Her Majesty the Queen to make use of material in the Royal Archives at Windsor. The manuscripts of the University, and of University and King's Colleges London have been used with the blessing of the librarians and other authorities of the University and of the colleges: I am specially indebted to the staffs of the Paleography Room in Senate House, and of the Rare Books Room and Records Office of University College, for their willingness and efficiency in responding to my persistent demands.

For help received, access to and permission to quote from other archives, I am indebted to The Worshipful Society of Apothecaries of London; to the Royal Astronomical Society; to Baring Brothers & Co., Ltd; to the Trustees of the Broadlands Archives; to the Duke of Devonshire, the Trustees of the Chatsworth Settlement, and Mr Peter Day, Keeper of Collections at Chatsworth; to the Guildhall Library; to the Honourable Society of Gray's Inn Trust Fund; to Mr David Holland; to the Honourable Society of the Inner Temple; to the Council of Trustees of the National Library of Ireland; to the Honourable Society of Lincoln's Inn; to the Masters of the Bench of the Honourable Society of the Middle Temple; to the Royal College of Physicians and its librarian, Mr Geoffrey Davenport; to the Royal Society; to the University of Southampton; to the Controller of Her Majesty's Stationery Office; to the Royal College of Surgeons; to the Master and Fellows of Trinity College, Cambridge; to the National Library of Wales; and to the Wellcome Trust.

For advice and assistance with the choice and reproduction of portraits I am grateful to the staffs of the British Museum's Department of Prints and Drawings; of the Courtauld Institute of Art; of the Gordon Museum of Guy's Hospital; of the National Portrait Gallery; of the Royal College of Physicians; and of the Photographic Library of the Wellcome Centre for Medical Science.

List of Portraits

Numbers 1, 2, 7, 9, 13, 16, 17, 18, 22, 29 and 30 are reproduced by courtesy of the National Portrait Gallery; numbers 10, 15, 21 and 23 by courtesy of the British Museum's Department of Prints and Drawings;

numbers 4, 5, 6, 19, 20, 25, 26 and 28 by courtesy of the Courtauld Institute of Art and the University of London; numbers 3, 8, 14, 24, 27 and 31 by courtesy of the Wellcome Institute Library, London; numbers 11 and 32 by courtesy of the Royal College of Physicians; and number 12 by kind permission of the Dean of the United Medical and Dental Schools (Guy's Campus).

Foreword

The University of London has always been a very strange institution, barely understood by insiders, incomprehensible to outsiders, apparently characterised by continual internal conflict. Now in the 1990s an 'old' university among the total of nearly one hundred such institutions in the United Kingdom, it was historically the first in a succession of 'new' universities established since the early nineteenth century to break the monopoly in England of the medieval foundations at Oxford and Cambridge and of the very different ancient establishments in Scotland at St Andrews, Aberdeen, Glasgow and Edinburgh. The expansion of higher education in the 1960s saw a few other universities created in London, and since the further expansion of the 1980s, there have been several more universities in London besides the University of London.

The University of London in 1994, after years of wrangling, re-constituted itself – yet again re-constituted itself, that is to say as a streamlined confederation of effectively independent institutions, some of them famous multi-faculty colleges larger than most provincial universities or the other universities in London – University College London, King's College, Queen Mary and Westfield College, Royal Holloway, some of them large and internationally known specialised institutions like the London School of Economics, Imperial College or the School of Oriental and African Studies, some of them smaller and more specialised but not less distinguished like the Warburg Institute or the School of Pharmacy. The various fashionable ratings of teaching and research in higher education now rightly list the larger constituent parts of the University separately. This continues to bemuse insiders and confuse outsiders and confound foreigners. The University of London cannot readily be likened to any other institution, except it has been said perhaps the courts of Heaven, which notoriously contained many mansions.

Heaven and the University of London are however not easily confused. The conflict which has characterised the University of London has frequently been hellish. The strangeness of the University of London, and its potential for bringing together conflicting interests, were evident from the start in 1836. Even here the possibilities for confusion abound. The original start was in 1826, when the 'University of London' was first founded, opening its new building to students in 1828 on the model of the Scottish universities and of the universities of Germany. Students were admitted without religious restrictions and the range of subjects taught was expanded beyond what was smugly undertaken at the Anglican residential colleges of Oxbridge. King's College followed soon afterwards. Chartered in 1829 and opened in 1831, it offered a similar expanded curriculum to cater for the same expanding middle-class demand, but in an Anglican context. Both institutions had internal conflicts of their own, but they were new facts of life in London in the 1830s and it became evident that it was only the national government which could resolve the conflict between them, and the conflict with the various medical teaching hospitals in London, and the conflict with the two old provincial universities which hitherto had a monopoly of degree-giving powers in England,

This book throws new light on the origins of the compromise developed by the Whig government which created an entirely new University of London in 1836, turning the original 'University of London' into 'University College London', with consequent problems of identity and conflict which persist to this day. What was created in 1836 was a university that bizarrely had neither students nor teachers. It had no buildings of its own, and it had no capital of its own. The new University of London was an examining body appointed by the government and subject to the direct financial control of the Treasury. It examined and awarded degrees to candidates from UCL, King's, the London hospitals, and from a growing list of miscellaneous teaching institutions throughout the country, and indeed, as the century went on, throughout the empire. It lacked, however, any rigorous system of inspection or control over the structure of the teaching provided by any of these institutions, and they lacked any organic relationship with the 'University'. The University of London in the nineteenth century only asked questions.

In the later nineteenth century, the contradictions of the University of London became a prolonged issue of contention. Two Royal Commissions, in 1888–89 and in 1892–94, failed to resolve them, but produced documentation about the constitution of the University more voluminous than for any other organisation. After the eventual re-constitution of the University in 1900 as a federal university in London with an 'external' side, Sir William Allchin struggled for many years to produce *An Account of the Reconstitution of the University of London*, producing three fat volumes published between 1905 and 1912, covering 1825–88, 1888–91 and 1891–92 respectively. Allchin was the Dean of a medical school, and an expert (as symbolism would require) on indigestion. He died before completing the work, defeated by the quantity of minutes recording arcane but fraught business in the Senate, in Convocation, in the many pages of the proceedings of the Royal Commissions.

Professor Willson in this book is not attempting to do what defeated Allchin. He is not writing a history of the University of London. He limits himself to the period from 1836 to the major reforms of 1858, for reasons he identifies clearly. His focus is specific. He is concerned with the politics of decision-making about the University of London in this period. And what he writes is well digested.

The institutional records are sparse for this early period. Many key decisions are not explained in the archives of the University itself or in the archives of the government in the Public Record Office. Professor Willson has gone through these records with a toothcomb, and he has also combed through the surviving personal papers of the individuals concerned. The Senate of the University of London as established in 1836 was a quango, a non-elected government-appointed body of thirty-eight individuals, including a Chancellor and a Vice-Chancellor, offices originally held by Lord Burlington (later Duke of Devonshire) and Sir John Lubbock, tbemselves two strikingly important figures in British intellectual and scientific life. They did not play the roles later to be associated with their titles. Many of the other members of the original Senate of the University were also significant figures, and they represented various conflicting interests in early Victorian intellectual and professional circles. It is the conflict of interests as well as the conflict of personalities that Professor Willson carefully considers. Basing his work squarely on a wider range of documentation than has previously been deployed, he ably brings out the muddles as well as the battles.

For a task of this sort, Glenn Willson is ideally suited. He is a political scientist with considerable experience in his own lifetime of academic politics and university administration. He taught politics at Oxford in the 1950s and professed the subject at the then University College of Rhodesia and Nyasaland and at the University of California, Santa Cruz, in the 1960s. At Santa Cruz he became in 1967 Provost of Stevenson College, one of the innovative new colleges on that campus.

In 1974 he became Warden of Goldsmiths' College, an institution with a connection with the University of London of Byzantine constitutional complexity, and in 1975 he undertook the impossible task of succeeding the great and controversial figure of Sir Douglas Logan as Principal of the University of London, amidst yet another period of constitutional conflict and change within the University. Between 1978 and 1984 he was Vice-Chancellor of another new university, Murdoch University in Western Australia. Since retiring, he has written a painstaking and brilliant study of an extraordinary family, the Shaw Lefevres, several of whose members made significant contributions to public life and one of whom, Sir John Shaw Lefevre, was the second Vice-Chancellor of the University of London for the twenty years after 1842.

Glenn Willson thus brings a unique combination of qualities together, political, historical, administrative, practical, to inform this work. The potential relevance of what is carefully narrated is consciously left implicit rather than made jarringly explicit. Yet it is clear that the themes addressed here ostensibly for the 1830s, 1840s and 1850s are ones powerfully confronting us in the 1990s: What is the role of government in controlling the universities? What is the role of those managing universities in determining the syllabus or controlling the curriculum? What sort of degrees should be awarded and how should examiners be monitored? What should be the role of non-teaching 'lay' members of governing bodies? How should universities be financed? Some – by no means all – of the elements in the current debate were evidently raised by the beginnings of the expansion of the higher education system in the 1830s. This book will interest historians, but it will also have significance for others whose historical interests are less overt.

NEGLEY HARTE

Negley Harte, Senior Lecturer in Economic History at University College London, is the author of The University of London: An Illustrated History, 1836–1986 (The Athlone Press, 1986); *he was a member of the Senate of the University until its abolition in 1994, and is now a member of the University Council as well as being Public Orator of the University.*

Introduction

The beginnings of the University of London were entangled in the early traumas of two institutions. The first, launched in 1825 and taking students from 1828, was called the University of London, but in 1836 was renamed University College London, and has been known thereafter, more briefly, as UCL. The other, chartered in 1829, and opened in 1831, has always been King's College. The origins and growth of those colleges have long since been chronicled and assessed in the scholarly centennial histories by Hale Bellot and Hearnshaw. In 1986, Negley Harte celebrated the 150th anniversary of what he called, in a useful shorthand, the University of London Mark II, with his history of the institution which was created in 1836 as an entity separate from the two colleges.[1]

There is no need, therefore, to rehearse more than very briefly, and no cause to question, the major themes of what had transpired earlier and had increased in intensity in the decade from 1825 to 1835. The main relevant, social pressures were those of a rapidly growing professional and middle class, wanting additional channels of entry to higher education for their children; the impact of years of radical argument for political and administrative reform, largely spearheaded by Utilitarian thinkers; and the demand of Dissenters for educational parity. Alongside these was a manifestation of the scientific spirit – a turbulent medical world, in which the old categories of physicians, surgeons and apothecaries were overlapping and gradually producing, with much controversy, a more coherently structured profession, needing new kinds of medical education.[2]

Against increasingly flexible academic provision stood the closed Anglican communities of Oxford and Cambridge, with their monopoly of university education in England. Anglican fervour had ensured the appearance of King's College, next door to Somerset House, as a counterweight to 'The London University', which imposed no religious tests, attracted Dissenters, and had become known among the more combative Anglicans as 'The Godless Academy in Gower Street'.

Along the river, westwards, at Westminster, the Whigs had returned to power, after long years in the political wilderness, in 1830. By the spring of 1835 they had forced a fundamental constitutional change, had begun to introduce major reforms of social and political institutions, had been put out of office, briefly, towards the end of 1834, and were about to form another government. During those five fiercely political, near revolutionary years, no harmonious way of creating a university in the capital city had been found. Despite their teaching functions and their regulatory powers, neither the two recently founded colleges, nor the Colleges of Physicians and of Surgeons, nor the Apothecaries Company, nor the several hospitals and private medical schools in the capital were entitled to award degrees. Each institution and special interest group had fought its own corner, and by April 1835, the intense political and legal manoeuvring had produced something near deadlock.

The reforming Whigs, and the Radicals, had a natural sympathy for the first University of London, of which Lord Brougham had been and still was the leading spirit, and of whose council Lord John Russell had been an original member. But, notwithstanding that sympathy, their understandable suspicions of King's College and the constant pressure which Brougham and his colleagues kept up to achieve a charter for Gower Street, the Whig Government came to feel, by the end of 1834, that neither any one, nor all, of the existing institutions, should be endowed with full university powers. But the persistent attempts to bring about chartered status for 'The London University' led, in the new year, to a complicated row involving the Privy Council, the Monarch and Peel's short-lived administration: Peel suffered, as a result, one of the several heavy defeats in the Commons which led to his resignation in April 1835.[3]

The crucial objection to granting a charter to 'The London University' was not the hostility of Oxford and Cambridge nor, by implication, the existence of King's College; but the sense that, if such a charter was granted, not only King's but all the medical schools of London would be entitled to claim the same status. As Lord John Russell explained to Brougham eighteen months later, 'it was not advisable to give a power of conferring degrees to the London University, to the exclusion of all the Medical Schools and great Hospitals of London.'[4]

Lord Melbourne and his ministers cut through the claims of all the institutions to university status by ignoring them. They agreed, on 27 May 1835, to reject 'The London University's' application for a charter at the Privy Council on Friday 5 June, and to approve in principle a completely new scheme at Cabinet on Saturday 6 June. This duly happened.[5] Gower Street, to be renamed University College London, would receive a charter – as a college, without the power of conferring degrees. It, together with King's and other institutions to be approved subsequently, including medical schools, would present candidates for examination to a new body. That body's responsibilities would be confined to framing and conducting examinations for such candidates, and awarding degrees to those who took them successfully. When Thomas Spring Rice, Chancellor of the Exchequer, issued his first invitations to potential members of the new body, late in the following September, he referred to it as 'a Central Board under the Title of the Royal University of London'.[6] But when the first Charter was issued in November 1836, the prefix 'Royal' had been dropped.[7]

The idea of some kind of metropolitan authority which would award degrees had been raised in various forms for a decade but was only accepted, in 1835, as a solution of last resort. The details of the constitution of the new 'Board' need not detain us now, but its envisaged overall character and functions must have struck contemporaries as remarkable and peculiar, just as they did historians a century later. For here was a 'university' which would have no students to teach, no staff to teach them, no premises to call its own, and no money save what was granted to it by Parliament, yet it was to have a chancellor, a vice-chancellor and a sizeable senate. Small wonder that Hearnshaw wrote of it, with appropriate academic and collegiate scorn, as 'a body that was neither a university nor metropolitan, but a mere government department established to conduct examinations' or that Hale Bellot observed, with scrupulous accuracy, how 'grandiloquent language described modest proceedings', and how 'The University could not so much as print the Senate Minutes or increase its porter's wages by a shilling a week without Treasury approval.'[8]

The establishment of the University of London was a major innovation of educational policy, and its operation in the early years involved the taking of some significant educational initiatives. But this book is not a study of the academic and intellectual achievements of the new university – a task recently tackled by Professor F.M.L. Thompson and his colleagues.[9] The following pages are devoted to an enquiry into how its structure was put together and who actually ran what was, undoubtedly, a rather odd institution, and to an account of what might be called its micro-politics during the first twenty years of its existence.

Before beginning that enquiry, however, it is desirable to explain why it ends in 1858, for an on-going institution rarely makes a totally clear-cut change of direction at a particular point in time.

The University of London continued to be an examining, degree-giving, but non-teaching establishment until the end of the nineteenth century and it continued to work under governmental supervision. But by the mid 1850s there were several signs that the University could no longer be dismissed as 'a mere government department'. Its appeal as an authoritative source of degrees of good standing, and as the guarantor of reputable examining, was by then unarguable. By 1858, the University was matriculating over 250 students each year, some 130 were being examined annually for degrees and, since 1839, nearly 1500 degrees had been awarded. More than a hundred universities, colleges and medical schools had been approved by Government to certify that students had attended and been given instruction which entitled them to attempt London's examinations. Already, London degrees were the aim of colonial students. On its academic record, the University may be said, by the mid 1850s, to have 'arrived'.

In terms of its personnel, the Senate had been remarkably stable in membership, and a high proportion of the original nominees served throughout the first twenty years. The first large infusion of new blood – seven new members – did not take place until the end of 1849, and as we shall see, it did not make more than a modest difference to the core group who were the effective controllers of policy. But the addition of a further eight newcomers late in 1857–8, the cumulative effect of deaths and the decreasing attendances of several of the surviving originals meant that the profile of the Senate in the later 1850s showed clearly the onset of a new generation. In 1856, too, the founding Chancellor had resigned, though continuing his connection as a member of the Senate and the first Registrar had died.

A sense of the coming of age of the University and significant changes in the personnel of its governing body are, in themselves, good reasons for claiming that the mid to late 1850s marked something of a watershed. In addition, in 1855 the University moved away from the atmosphere of governmental administration by leaving its hitherto inadequate and infelicitous accommodation in Somerset House – a change reflecting increasing independence as well as increasing size. So, too, did two crucial modifications of practice then in the offing and which took effect in 1858. The first was a fundamental shift of educational policy: the restrictive rule whereby examinees had to produce certificates of attendance at approved institutions was abandoned, thus throwing the University's examinations open to all comers. The second was of major academic significance: science was accepted as a subject for a separate degree, and a Faculty of Science was established.

But of equal importance to these developments was a constitutional change which introduced a modicum of internal democracy and a consequent further growth of institutional independence. The principle of creating a convocation was mooted as early as 1840, but agitation for its introduction was not begun seriously until 1848 and the first formal acceptance was only achieved in the revised Charter of 1858.[10] But persistent pressure in the early 1850s led to the appointment to the Senate of three graduates of the University - William Withey Gull and Frederick John Wood in January 1857 and Charles James Foster a year later. They were Crown appointees, like all the earlier senators, but unofficially and symbolically, they were the vanguard of a guaranteed representation of graduates which, under the terms of the new Charter, would eventually extend to one quarter of the whole membership of Senate.

The Charter of April 1858 can be taken as marking the end of a period which (*pace* Hearnshaw), if not strictly definable as 'departmental', had certainly witnessed the operation of a tightly controlled, closed and wholly government-appointed academic corporation. In educational and in constitutional terms, after 1858, London University was moving into a different era.

CHAPTER 1

The Search for a Framework

The conversion of the decision made by the Cabinet on 6 June 1835 to set up a new University of London into the formal establishment of the institution took almost eighteen months. The first Charter, which included a list of the initial membership of the governing body, the Senate, was dated 28 November 1836. Subsequent progress towards setting and holding examinations and awarding degrees was also a slow business. The Senate held its inaugural meeting in March 1837, the first matriculation examinations were held in November 1838 and the first degree examinations in May 1839. The four preceding years were marked by much good intention and intense effort, but also by opposition, confusion, misunderstandings, quarrels and delays, as various interests and individuals clashed in the process of finding acceptable compromises.

The Cabinet's decision in 1835 was to award two charters; one to 'The London University', converting the Gower Street establishment into 'University College London', (King's College had been chartered in 1829) and another to set up a new University of London. It was agreed that Lord Brougham should be consulted about the UCL Charter, while the qualifications and appointment of the examiners who would operate under the banner of the new university was 'postponed for consideration'.[1] Such consideration – not merely of who should be appointed, but of the whole design of the new body – was entrusted, primarily, to Thomas Spring Rice, Chancellor of the Exchequer, who was created Lord Monteagle in 1839: he took a continuing interest in the University for the rest of his life, becoming himself a member of the Senate in 1850. But the more politically powerful Lord John Russell, Home Secretary, who had been a founder member of what was about to become UCL, was, especially at the outset, closely involved and, as will be seen, he was not averse to imposing his own ideas on his colleague. The cautious Melbourne, as Prime Minister, kept a shrewd watch on the major political implications of the exercise and on the selection of the first Senate. That body was to comprise a chancellor, a vice-chancellor, and 36 fellows. In what follows, the expression 'senators' should be read as being inclusive of all 38 members.

To the ultimately powerful ministerial trio of Melbourne, Russell and Spring Rice must be added the Radical MP for Bridport, the wealthy Henry Warburton, whose family fortune came from the timber trade. He was another original member of the Gower Street Council, and had made a reputation as a leading figure in moves to improve medical practice and to reform the medical profession. He had been the main force in the establishment of an Inspectorate of Anatomy to attempt to control the scandalous trade of bodysnatching, and recently he had been chairman of a major enquiry by a select committee of the House of Commons into medical education.[2] Spring Rice, Russell and Warburton, with some oversight from Melbourne, put together the University of London which came into being in the eighteen months from June 1835 to November 1836.

The essentials of the scheme which was produced during the second half of 1835 were not entirely new. The notion of some kind of comprehensive metropolitan university had been bandied about for some years and, as the obstacles to giving degree-granting power to any one, or to a host, of existing institutions became more obvious, the idea attracted more attention. Perhaps the earliest, and certainly the strongest and most consistent, lead came from and in response to some sections of the medical world, in no small part because they were particularly suspicious of the ambitions of Gower Street. As Hale Bellot put it, 'The medical profession was quite ready to see the erection of a non-sectarian metropolitan university, but was unwilling to invest with that dignity what it regarded as an upstart and unimportant establishment.'[3]

The *London Medical Gazette* had suggested the combining of Gower Street with the new King's College to form a London University as far back as 1828 and, in 1833 and 1834, spelt out the metropolitan idea in terms some of which would be found acceptable in 1835–6:

What is wanting to render London essentially an university, but to incorporate the several distinguished schools existing within it, thus rendering them so many colleges, and to vest in a particular body the government of the whole? This would be reform on a grand scale. The particular body should not be part or parcel of any of the subordinate establishments; no teachers from the different schools, much less than of a particular school, should have any part in the control of the general institution.

It may be that some official heed was paid to this idea in the latter part of 1833, because the possibility of establishing an independent board of examiners was mooted in the *Athenaeum* of December of that year. But it would seem that a specifically medical version of the idea was discussed by the Whig Government some time before Melbourne resigned in November 1834.[4]

The notion of an institution which would preside over all medical education in London and give its own degrees – a 'one faculty' organization – was canvassed and championed by *The Lancet*, that most scurrilous of journals, whose editor, Thomas Wakley, was to become MP for Finsbury in 1835. Well before then, however, such a scheme had registered with ministers, though it is unclear exactly when that happened, or who introduced it for governmental consideration.

Among Lord Melbourne's papers is an undated, unsigned, printed memorandum, marked 'Confidential'.[5] It begins with a straightforward political claim that 'the body of Dissenters are now more favorably disposed towards the measures of the Government than they were some months ago; [and] that they set the greatest store by some relief from disabilities connected with University education and degrees.' Then follow certain assumptions. First, that Oxford and Cambridge, backed by the House of Lords, will not 'agree to such relief as consists in meddling with subscriptions'. Second, that if one medical school is empowered to give degrees, all would have to be so empowered and the resultant competition would drive the standard of teaching so far down that the degrees 'must become lowered every day in estimation'. Therefore, no medical school should be given 'the power of granting degrees in Medicine, Surgery or Pharmacy'. Moreover, 'unless restrained, the London University will confer degrees in Medicine, as well as Arts and Laws,' because the law allows it and the House of Commons will not pass legislation to prevent it from happening. Third, that the ancient universities do not object to medical degrees and only want any London degrees in arts and laws to be distinguished from theirs by 'some slight variation in the titles of the Graduates'. And, fourth, the London University, 'for the sake of a regular charter and power of graduating, would consent to such restrictions, and to abstain from medical degrees altogether.'

The memorandum goes on to propose a plan,

which has this eminent advantage over any other, that it can be at once carried into execution, and thus secured from parliamentary risks of rejection or curtailment in one House, or extension in the other. Also it can be applied early enough to prevent the assumption of the general and unqualified power of graduation by the London University.

The format and language of the memorandum, its author's sophisticated and commanding feel for the political situation and the shrewd assessment of what positions the parties involved were likely to take surely indicate that this was the work of a senior politician, very likely a minister, and probably written in the autumn of 1834. It could have been the work of Melbourne himself – he had been Home Secretary for three and a half years before he succeeded Grey as Prime Minister in July 1834, and had been much involved in the unsuccessful negotiations for a charter for the London University in 1831. Perhaps it is more likely to have been written by Russell, whose enthusiasm for the dissenting cause was stronger than Melbourne's, and who had come to see the impossibility of giving Gower Street and the medical schools all that they were asking. But a case can be made that the author could have been Warburton, who was most knowledgeable about the medical world, and who was also in a position to have a close and direct acquaintance with opinion within the Council of the London University in Gower Street.[6]

Whoever put the paper together, though a fascinating question, is, in our context, less important than its timing and what it proposed. Shorn of a few details, the two major ideas speak for themselves:

It is proposed to constitute a Board, incorporated as an University . . . by Charter, with power of granting medical degrees only. . . . That it should consist of the Presidents of the London Colleges of Physicians and Surgeons, the Prime Warden of the Apothecaries Company, one delegate from the London University and King's College, Oxford and Cambridge; and one from the three great Hospitals, Guy's, St Thomas's, and St Bartholomew's. That all requisition of subscription, and all other tests be prohibited. That all certificates of attending medical courses be taken in common from the four Universities named; the three Hospitals, and certain others to be enumerated in the Charter; that full examination in medical science be also required by the Board, or by fit examiners appointed by them . . . that examinations in general learning and science be also had, but not of those candidates who have taken degrees in Arts of either of the four Universities named.

It is next proposed to grant the London University a Charter of Incorporation as a University, with a condition annexed, that no degrees in Theology be granted by it, nor any degrees in medicine, and that to the degrees in Arts and Laws there be annexed the letter L. . . .

It is conceived that this plan will, if adopted now, remove all difficulties, and effectually relieve and satisfy the dissenting bodies.

Although there was not to be such a medical university, the constitution suggested for it must surely be regarded as one of the antecedents of the governing body of the new University of London. And the assumptions on which the plan was based were proved to have been remarkably accurate. The London University in Gower Street, in its search for chartered status, was happy to escape the strongest opposition of Oxford and Cambridge by agreeing that no degree in theology would be part of its offerings. And when, by April 1835, it was clear that Government would not concede the giving of degree-awarding powers to each of the numerous medical schools, teaching hospitals and colleges of the metropolis, the Gower Street Council was willing – in vain, as it turned out – to abandon the offering of medical degrees, as it had degrees in theology, in order to gain its charter.[7]

It was quite reasonable, therefore, for the *London Medical Gazette* to claim, when welcoming the announcement of the decision to create a metropolitan university with degree-granting power, in the late summer of 1835, that 'this is precisely what we have been advocating for some years past.'[8] Neither in that nor other journals, nor in official records, however, is there evidence of any discussion of the details of the possible constitution of such a university. The one contemporary, non-governmental proposal which contained more than the merest outline appeared in 1835. It was published, probably though not certainly, in the latter part of the year – and may have reached Spring Rice early in 1836, by which time it would have been dismissed as politically unfeasible.[9] Its author was F.C. Parry, a barrister and graduate of Oxford, and his constitutional scheme was only part of a much larger argument, indicated by the pamphlet's title, *The Dissenters and the Universities*, sub-titled *The Civil Rights of the Dissenters most effectually secured by the Erection of a new University.*

It is worth summarizing Parry's basic scheme, if only to underline how what actually appeared as the University of London must have disappointed those with more ambitious visions; but also to show how 'natural' and widespread was the notion of a collegiate, teaching university - unsurprising among an elite overwhelmingly composed of graduates of Oxford and Cambridge. In some respects, too, Parry's plan echoes the framework of the earlier proposal of a medical university for the metropolis, which was also driven, as will be recalled, by concern to remove the disabilities suffered by Dissenters. But the vaguely federal form and the inclusion of teaching responsibility which he put forward were, as it happened, at least half a century before their political time in London.

Parry listed a number of existing institutions which should be 'considered as Colleges forming component parts of the proposed university.' The list included UCL and King's, Westminster School, Charter House, Christ Church, the Colleges of Physicians and Surgeons, the Royal Academy, Sion College, 'any institution of Engineers, or Mechanics, or Mathematicians, which can offer anything like a respectable permanency', 'perhaps Highbury', with a Roman Catholic college and a Jews or Hebrew college 'at some time ahead'. The heads, together with some professors, masters or governors of these institutions, should constitute an academical senate, to which 'the Inns of Court should be invited or permitted to send deputies from amongst their Benchers.' There should be a chancellor and a vice-chancellor, possibly 'annually replaced'. Students 'should enroll their names in one of the Colleges before they matriculate.'

The public records may not yet have yielded all the surviving documents which must have accompanied the earliest stages of the establishment of the University of London in 1835–6. What we think of today as position papers which set forth alternative ideas for the development of policy are almost totally absent – the only specimen is the confidential paper on a medical university discussed earlier. Perhaps there were no more such documents, and the whole of the debate was verbal and unrecorded, or contained in correspondence. But even the surviving correspondence in official and private collections, though sufficient to allow a reconstruction of the basic substance and chronology of the event, rarely does more than hint at discussion of structural forms and matters of fundamental principle. Fortunately, on matters concerning who should be involved, the story is more easily followed and is much more colourful.

The whole process was prolonged by insolubly difficult problems which arose in the medical context. But not a little of the long delay in producing the Charter was due to the fact that, however important the new University seemed to the academic and medical communities, it was a subject of relatively low political priority within the huge and controversial reformist programme of the Government. That Melbourne, Russell and Spring Rice were able to give as much attention as they did to the University of London is, perhaps, more remarkable than that, under the general political pressure, the affairs of the University were pushed aside, from time to time, and also suffered no small amount of muddle.

No doubt the majority of ministers turned away from the arguments about the desirability or otherwise of giving charters to any 'University of London' and to colleges with some relief, and left it to Spring Rice to pursue the apparently simple notion of establishing a new board of examiners. But it must have become apparent very soon to the Chancellor of the Exchequer and his colleagues, that a board of examiners which was also to have the power of granting degrees, and proclaimed as having the status of a university, posed new and strange problems, not susceptible of simple solutions: this would be no normal university. The ministers were Oxbridge men in whose minds the vision of a university had been set by their own experiences on Cam or Isis. Could you – or should you – they must have asked themselves, endow a mere government-appointed board with the dignity of their conception of a university – even a university without resident students? Were the models of Oxbridge, or even of UCL and King's, necessarily appropriate? Who would have any respect for a utilitarian group of examiners, however professionally expert, working from a prosaic government office? How many examiners would be needed? And how could the whole experiment be undertaken with absolutely minimum cost to the Government? Questions must have multiplied in their minds.

Primarily, they needed respected academic examiners, but they also needed men of administrative capacity, chosen with an eye to the special interests who would be watching the experiment with enthusiasm, anxiety or suspicion, and they needed leadership which would stimulate public confidence and be politically acceptable, particularly to the reformist camp, without offending their more moderate supporters. The search for a structure came first, logically enough, but it was soon running parallel with argument as to the provision to be made for medical education and with the search for senators. The final configuration, perhaps inevitably, was unoriginal, messy and never very satisfactory.

In a hard-hitting article which appeared in the *Irish Quarterly Review* in 1857, its writer deplored the fact that, in 1835 and 1836, Spring Rice

> most unfortunately fell into the hands and views of those members of University and King's Colleges, who were all for what may be called a third class Oxford and Cambridge, and thus the narrow terms of the Charter, confining the power of the University to the conferring of degrees on those only who should have spent the two years from Matriculation to the Pass Examination at some affiliated school or college.[10]

This reference to what was, from the start, one of the most controversial aspects of the new university, is most relevant to an account of the events of 1835–6 in its insistence on the close relations which prevailed between Spring Rice and his colleagues on the one hand, and University College on the other hand. The writer in 1857 may have been correct in his opinion about the thinking of King's in his particular context, but wrong if he was implying that Spring Rice had as equally close relations with King's as he had with UCL. There was, in fact, very little contact with King's, whereas most of the detailed argument about the shape of the new university occurred between Spring Rice and the UCL Council, represented mainly by two lawyers, William Tooke, MP, and John Romilly, with Warburton acting as a principal negotiator and conciliator.[11]

The long and sympathetic support of the reformist Whigs and the Radicals for 'The London University', and the traumas which had accompanied the Melbourne administration's abandoning of that institution's hard-fought original demand for chartered status, are sufficient explanation of the concern of Spring Rice and Russell, after 6 June 1835, to 'square' UCL, and of the touchy impatience of the UCL people to be the first to know what was in store for them.

It must have been early August before full agreement was reached among ministers on the essentials of the charters for Gower Street and for the new university, though an interim statement was made by the

Attorney General on 30 July in response to a question asked by Tooke, who had earlier accused Spring Rice of making communications which were 'dilatory or mysterious'. The Chancellor had replied, indignantly, on 19 July, that the Crown lawyers had received their instructions, that the results would be laid before both Houses of Parliament and that the Government was going ahead with the objective of making arrangements in the 'interests of religious freedom and the prospect of sound education.'[12]

The Attorney General, Sir John Campbell, in his answer in the Commons, merely told Tooke that two charters were being prepared, and that the new university would be empowered to grant degrees.[13] At that point, Spring Rice would not be drawn further, but within Gower Street the professors put pressure on the College's Council to send a deputation in search of more information to Russell and Spring Rice. Before any such deputation could be received – and perhaps to head it off - a much fuller statement was sent to UCL on 19 August, confirming that a charter was being prepared for 'London University College'; that the Government's over-riding concern was to 'provide a mode for granting Academical Degrees in London to persons of all religious persuasions, without distinction and without the imposition of any test or disqualification whatever' and that 'Another Charter will be granted to persons eminent in literature and science to act as a Board of Examiners and to perform all the functions of the Examiners in the Senate House of Cambridge; this body to be termed the University of London.'

The rest of the fundamental scheme provided that students from UCL and King's, and subsequently from any other 'Bodies of Education, whether corporated or uncorporated' which were named by the Crown, who had successfully completed a course of study at such establishments, could be admitted to examinations for degrees in arts, law and medicine. Spring Rice insisted on restricting candidates for degrees to those who had a collegiate preparation: he was, always, an enthusiast for the residential college.[14] But there was a significant difference between the provisions governing colleges preparing candidates for arts and law degrees on the one hand and the provisions governing medical schools on the other hand. Whereas the former had to apply to and be approved directly by the Secretary of State, the latter had to be recomended by the University and subsequently receive what became, in fact, the Secretary of State's practically automatic approval.

The Crown would have the power of appointing new and additional examiners from time to time. All by-laws and regulations for the conduct of the University of London would be submitted to the Secretary of State and thus made subject to parliamentary responsibility. The expenses of the examiners would be regulated and approved by the Treasury and paid for by 'Fees to be taken on Degrees'. And the King would be Visitor of the new university.[15]

That Spring Rice should turn to Cambridge as a model doubtless reflected his own familiarity with the system there, and his loyalty, as a graduate of Trinity College, then the most distinguished of the Cambridge academic institutions. Moreover he sat in Parliament for the Borough of Cambridge, which he represented from 1832 until 1839, and his correspondence reveals a close connection with the university's affairs throughout his career. There is no sign that anyone objected to his adopting the Cambridge system for London – it fitted the notion, however tenuous, that London would develop its own kind of collegiate connections, and that the new board of examiners would indeed be catering for candidates from various institutions, as were the Moderators in the Senate House at Cambridge.

This first sketch of a state-run university did not endear itself to William Tooke and, when it came before the UCL Council on 22 August, he moved its rejection. Warburton, however, put forward an amendment, which was carried, accepting the new university, but adding that:

> as the success of the plan depended on proper appointment of persons to the Board of Examiners, there should be another interview with the Chancellor of the Exchequer and Lord John Russell at which the views of Council on these matters be put to Ministers.

Warburton himself, with a single colleague, was to see Spring Rice and Russell 'to consider the details of the Governing Body'.[16]

In principle, therefore, Gower Street accepted the new order at an early stage of what was to be a long process, and never reneged on that decision, which removed a major possibility of embarrassment. Their acceptance also cleared the way for Spring Rice to turn his attention to what Warburton's tactic had apparently made the major concern of the college – the personnel of the new Senate. But UCL, having committed themselves to renouncing their ambitions and welcoming a different University of London, were not going to wait meekly to receive the draft of a further constitutional proposal from Downing Street. Throughout the autumn the college kept up the pressure, through deputations and correspondence, in which both governors and faculty were involved, and in which John Romilly was a major participant, to extract from Spring Rice his exact intentions on a whole list of topics. The minister agreed to answer in writing a string of questions which the college submitted, and the result was a letter containing a definitive statement, dated 22 November. Spring Rice told Romilly that he did not mind the substance of his letter being made public, but would be happy if the actual text was not reproduced. His hope was dashed, however, as the letter reached the press and was quoted extensively.[17]

The whole of the long list of questions put by UCL concerned important academic and administrative matters, but in a strictly constitutional context only three need be mentioned here. All three were highly significant for the future workings and jurisdiction of the new university. One related directly, in good professorial style, to personnel: it and the answer revealed the confusion and ambiguity between the concepts of 'Governing Body', and 'Examiners'.

> Are the members of the Governing Body to be limited in number? Are they to hold their offices for life or during pleasure? Will they all be required themselves to examine for Degrees, or will they be allowed to appoint Examiners? If they are themselves required to examine, will they be allowed to appoint Assistants?

To this the Chancellor of the Exchequer replied:

> It would be unwise in my mind to limit the number of Examiners or Members of the new University: their appointments should be during good behaviour, to secure their independence. In case of necessity, they should be authorised to have assistants for the *technical purposes of examination* when this is absolutely required: the examination papers and questions being, however, fixed by the Members of the University themselves, and the distinctions of honor awarded by them.

To the pertinent question of how fees for degrees were to be handled, Spring Rice considered that all fee income should be paid into a single fund, from which the remuneration and incidental expenses of examiners should be met; if more money was needed, there might have to be an application to Parliament.

The third question elicited a response which was to be of major constitutional significance, particularly for future medical examinees, for whom, under existing arrangements, a London degree would not be a licence to practise: 'Is it intended, either by Act of Parliament or otherwise to secure to Graduates . . . all the professional or other privileges (not connected with the Clerical profession) which are enjoyed by Graduates of the existing Universities?' Despite Spring Rice's straightforward, affirmative reply, this matter was to remain unsettled for nearly two decades; but his declaration was to be invoked at a crucial point later in the university's development.

In the last five weeks of 1835 the ministers may well have felt that they were making reasonably good progress with the preparation of their scheme. They assured both Gower Street and King's that special care was being taken to watch for any clashes or inconsistencies between College and University charters, and that the two Colleges would be treated impartially. Spring Rice told the suspicious Tooke that the drafts had been 'professionally through the hands' of Andrew Amos, Professor of English Law at Gower Street. Moreover, in a further gesture of goodwill, Spring Rice agreed that the original 'University of London', which had been renamed 'London University College' in the early drafting of the new charter, should be called instead, in response to Tooke's request, 'University College London', – a promise which was not fulfilled until late in the following year, after some further nudging.[18]

Nor could Spring Rice have been blamed for some complacency when he read the favourable initial comment of The *London Medical Gazette* on his leaked letter of 22 November: 'On the whole, we consider the arrangements to be at once conceived in a spirit of strict impartiality, and likely to afford a high degree of satisfaction to the public.'[19] But any comfort from such comment was to be short-lived, because the sketch of ministerial intentions brought anxiety, if not consternation, to the Colleges of Physicians and Surgeons, who saw that their control of entry to the professions would be weakened. Their opposition was to delay the drafting of a charter for several months.

CHAPTER 2

Medical Deadlock

Within six weeks of returning to power in April 1835, the Whigs had swept away the last chance of the London University in Gower Street, in its original form, receiving a charter as a degree-awarding institution, even if it excluded theology and medicine. At the same time, though the *Lancet* had not abandoned the idea of a one faculty university, there is no evidence that it was being considered seriously any longer in government circles, and it must have seemed that any future moves about an over-arching 'London' medical qualification were as uncertain as ever. When the administration's decision to include medical degrees in the awards of the new University of London was announced, it seems to have come as something of a surprise to the medical world, though there is no good reason why such a move should not have been foreseen.

Spring Rice had been a member of Warburton's Select Committee on Medical Education, and both men, doubtless with the support of powerful political and medical colleagues, must have seen the creation of the new university for London as a golden opportunity to impose some uniformity and comprehensiveness on the fragmented pattern of medical education. There is no record of exactly how or when the decision was made, or on whose initiative, but Spring Rice explained, a year later, that

> he had considered it desirable that all the arrangements by which the Medical bodies were to be affected should be settled by the Charter [of the new university]; and that the Degrees in Medicine to be conferred under the Authority of the Charter should carry with them the privilege of practising.[1]

In fact, the new university did offer medical degrees from the outset, though only after some major confrontations; but the hope that London degrees would be accepted as licences to practise was not destined to be fulfilled for nearly twenty years.

The profession of the time was at once a three-headed monster and a mass of fiercely independent hospitals, medical schools and private businesses. It was not yet ready for tidy solutions, nor were those who wished to pursue reform all of one mind. Moreover, the medical world had spawned, in recent times, a number of combative journals. Indeed, as two learned commentators have put it, with remarkable mildness,

> the history of medical education in London in the early nineteenth century is not all a record of disinterested men seeking only the public good. Several champions of invective were involved in the discussion, for which perhaps *melee* would be the more correct word.[2]

It is certainly a word very well suited to describe the in-fighting which attended the appointment of medical senators.

The nub of the minister's problem with the three leading medical establishments was, very simply, the latter's fear of and unyielding opposition to any loss of functions or influence. So far as physicians were concerned, by virtue of a statute of Henry VIII, an Oxbridge degree was 'a licence to practise medicine in any part of the kingdom, except within . . . seven miles of the City of London.' Since the time of Charles II, who acted under pressure to prevent Catholics from entering the profession, the Royal College of Physicians was allowed to admit only graduates of the Anglican strongholds of Oxford and Cambridge. Within the London area the Licence of the Royal College was required and, over time, it had become the rule that even those who chose to practise outside London needed an extra-licence from the college. In England, therefore, with rare exceptions, one could not be a physician without being an Oxbridge graduate, licensed in one way or another by the Royal College.

Physicians, however, were a small elite. The great bulk of those practising medicine were either surgeons or apothecaries, and 'those best qualified family medical men', who were beginning to be thought of as 'general practitioners', were a combination of the two. No higher educational qualifications were needed by surgeons and apothecaries: indeed, 'a university education was not thought necessary for a man who intended to become a surgeon.' But membership of the Royal College of Surgeons and of the Society of Apothecaries required the successful passing of examinations. Surgeons were expected to pass the Apothecaries' examination, and those apothecaries who intended to practise as surgeons were expected to pass the Surgeons' examination. However, there was no compulsion behind those expectations. The basis of training was essentially apprenticeship, walking the surgical wards and attending operations, and:

The chief function of the medical schools of London from 1815 to
1858 was to train young men to be good doctors with the status
given by the Licentiateship of the Society of Apothecaries or the
Membership of the Royal College of Surgeons, or better, by both.[3]

It was into the territories of the two colleges and the Society of
Apothecaries that the planners of the new university ventured, to be
greeted with a range of reactions from uncertainty and suspicion to
outright hostility.

Both colleges quickly sought reassurances after the nature of the
forthcoming University Charter had been revealed towards the end of
November 1835. By the following January the surgeons had drafted a
memorial asking whether 'it is intended that the proposed university
shall in any way interfere with the functions of this College.' More
directly, their president had asked the Attorney General if he would
find out from Lord John Russell 'exactly how the land lay.'[4] But their
anxieties were most probably relieved by the fact that negotiations
between Spring Rice and the College of Physicians reached an impasse
as early as mid February 1836.

The exact sequence of events in the negotiations with the Physicians
is unclear, and the official historian of the College, Sir George Clark,
gave the impression that the most important moves only occurred in
May 1836.[5] But from the Monteagle Papers there is clear proof that
the first – and as it turned out, the final – rejection of Spring Rice's
desire to have London degrees accepted as licences to practise came in
February. In an attempt to combine the College's wish to be involved
in the examinations, with the University's power to award the degrees,
Spring Rice suggested that two members of the College should be
appointed as examiners/senators of the University. But the president
of the College, Sir Henry Halford, insisted that the examinations for
the degrees should be left to the College. On 13 February, Spring
Rice wrote refusing to accept, and intimating that he would wait
until there was an opportunity to introduce legislation to enforce his
intentions.[6]

That Spring Rice and Warburton were in full agreement on this tactic
can be inferred from the latter's letter of about the same date to the
Edinburgh Town Council, in which he expressed the wish

to see instituted some uniform system of medical instruction and
examination, to serve as a basis for granting to persons properly

instructed and examined the enjoyment of equal professional immunities in every part of the United Kingdom. Whether such a plan could be carried into effect by means of any Crown charter, might reasonably be doubted. He thought the Government would scarcely be justified in delaying to constitute the proposed new University of London, for the purpose of maturing beforehand, and incorporating with the scheme of that university, a comprehensive measure of medical reform. The Government, he thought, should constitute the new University, investing it with all the privileges appertaining to such institutions, reserving to itself the power of modifying its laws and ordinances, so as to render them generally consonant to any general plan of medical reform that may hereafter be approved of. Except upon certain points, he was not informed of the details of the proposed plan.[7]

But, despite Spring Rice's firmness and Warburton's modest disclaimer of detailed knowledge of what was going on, both men seem to have been willing to listen to further attempts to bring the Physicians into line. The original documentation seems to have disappeared: we are largely dependent on Sir George Clark's interpretation of what happened, and he himself admits that it is impossible to identify many of those involved, or to be certain of the suggestions which were bandied about.

There was, first, a notable internal reform of College powers. In April, the Physicians abandoned their by-law which required a degree in medicine before entry to their Licentiate, and at the same time introduced a 'curriculum of education under the regulation of the College' to be taken successfully by candidates. This move constituted a direct challenge to the idea of the new university awarding medical degrees which would be recognized as licences to practise. Those supporting the College's tactic argued that:

as the Minister cannot put a stop to the arrangement . . . nor prevent the emanation of 'physicians' from the chartered body already in existence, his best and simplest course would be to come to some arrangement with them on liberal principles, so as to constitute the present College the medical branch of the new University.[8]

This idea, essentially leaving the College as the examining body, was to be no more acceptable to Spring Rice in May, than its earlier version had been in February. Nonetheless, early in May, Warburton took a group of Licentiates to see Spring Rice, apparently in the hope of finding a compromise. This is likely to have occurred on 7 May, for such an interview was reported in the Court Circular of *The Times* two days later. Those who accompanied Warburton were listed as Drs Arnott, Birkbeck, Clark, Clutterbuck, Holland and Sims, three of whom were to be among the first fellows of the new university. Their right to claim representative status seems to have been linked to an earlier attempt to establish an Association of Licentiates of the Royal College. However, because that attempt had been ignored by the great majority of Licentiates, this particular deputation was challenged by some of the medical press, who regarded its members as being 'gentlemen avowedly and actively at variance with their College.'

Clark suggests that Warburton was asked to lead the group 'because the radicals still regarded him as their most influential friend among the ministers.' However, the meeting was unfruitful. Spring Rice suggested 'that the College should grant licences without further examination to medical graduates of the new university, perhaps differing in some way for bachelors' and doctors' degrees.' This seems merely an embroidered repeat of the original proposal made to the president of the College, in February, and was considered by the Chancellor of the Exchequer's visitors to be incompatible with the College's charter.[9]

Very shortly afterwards, the College decided, formally, to send a deputation to Melbourne, consisting of Dr W.F. Chambers, Sir James M'Grigor and Sir Henry Holland, to complain that they had not been properly consulted and that there had been 'an unspecified suggestion made to Spring Rice by an unnamed fellow.' Melbourne was 'lukewarm' and passed them on to Russell, to whom they had nothing to offer and who gave them no satisfaction.[10]

It was, for both parties, the end of this particular road. Spring Rice explained to UCL, early in June, that the delay in making progress with the establishment of the Senate was due to:

the difficulty of arranging satisfactorily the Charter as it would affect the medical department . . . [and that while he recognized] that to obtain . . . [his] objects an Act of Parliament would be required . . . he had proposed . . . to procure the passing of such an Act, and to smooth the way for that measure he had been in treaty with the College of Physicians . . . [but] . . . that body were not reasonable in their propositions; he could not bring them to just terms; the mutuality they tendered was a mutuality all on one side; they had offered to examine the Candidates, and proposed that on their certificate the University should confer the degree; that he despaired of getting anything from them by negotiation and was prepared to proceed with the Charter giving the power of conferring degrees in medicine as well as in Arts; and allowing the law respecting the privilege to practise to remain as it is, until fitting time should arrive for the interference of Parliament in altering it.[11]

In 1842, however, a senior fellow of the College of Physicians claimed that a plan then being negotiated, whereby MDs of the University of London

at whose examinations the Censors of the College shall have assisted, shall be admitted Licentiates of the College of Physicians without further examination . . . was proposed to the Government at the time of the formation of the University of London and the reply given was, that such a plan, if it had been offered at an earlier date would have been favourably entertained, but that it was too late – the Charter of the University was already prepared and ready to be laid before Parliament.[12]

No manuscript has been found which would confirm or deny that claim.

Though there is not as much evidence of difficulty with the College of Surgeons, it is apparent that they, too, would not come to any accommodation with Spring Rice about licensing or common membership of the Senate. They would certainly have had no sympathy from Warburton, who had been engaged, in alliance with the editor of *The Lancet*, in a fierce agitation for a new and more democratic charter for the College.[13] In short, the leaders of both colleges were at loggerheads with the ministers, and it is not surprising therefore that in June, Spring Rice warned UCL that there could be trouble over the absence from the new University of some eminent medical men high in the hierarchies of the colleges, like Sir Astley Cooper, Sir Benjamin Brodie and Sir Charles Bell.[14]

At least one observer viewed the whole episode as a Machiavellian manoeuvre by Spring Rice to rid himself of unwanted people:

Mr Spring Rice's first endeavour was so far to consider the interests of the rulers of the Colleges of Physicians and Surgeons, that he invited them to have a share in the formation of the senate of the new institution. Selfish, fraudulent and debased as many of the individuals may be supposed to be, it could not have been expected, neither did the Chancellor the Exchequer anticipate, that any one of them would have had the courage to desert their profligate allies; there is a high moral feeling and sentiment of honour which is said to exist even amongst thieves; and on this the wily Chancellor of the Exchequer seems to have most judiciously calculated, so that by selecting the most *notorious* characters, those to whom he paid the high compliment of offering a place in the senate, they manfully rejected the office.[15]

Whatever was the truth about Spring Rice's strategy in connection with the Royal Colleges, those negotiations were not the only cause of delay in recruiting medical senators. Late in January 1836, the Council of UCL approved a motion opposing the appointment of any medical officers of London hospitals as examiners: Warburton was entrusted with the communication of this opposition to Spring Rice. He not only conveyed it to the minister, but stated publicly UCL's contention 'that no teacher of any medical school, and no medical or surgical officer of any hospital, shall be a member of the Board of Examiners.'[16]

In a long letter to Spring Rice, Warburton argued that the exclusion of teachers as examiners was widely accepted within the medical establishment. But he argued, further, that the medical officers of hospitals were also teachers, who took fees for the training of their students and were, as a result, much better remunerated than 'mere lecturers and professors at the medical schools.' He went on:

> It is not so much from an apprehension of partiality during examinations to their own pupils that a necessity seems to arise for excluding Teachers from the Board of Examiners, for that objection may be obviated, in some measure, by preventing any Teacher from examining or voting for his own pupil. But the chief objection appears to me to be this: that to this Board will necessarily be entrusted the framing the details of all such Regulations, as relate to the curriculum of study, and the conditions on which shall depend the recognition of Teachers and Schools: and past experience has shown, that whenever this minor kind of legislation has devolved upon Boards of which Teachers and Hospital Physicians or Surgeons were members (and, if Members at all, necessarily very influential Members) the regulations they have framed on such matters have strongly borne the stamp of the particular interests which they were calculated to serve.
>
> All teachers, without exception, are objectionable as Members

of the proposed Board. But if you maintain this objection against one class of Teachers, and abandon it, as against another class, the result is much worse than if, adopting no rule of exclusion whatever, you make all Teachers equally eligible. For in that case all interests being represented, the contention of rival parties secures a considerable degree of justice and impartiality: whereas by excluding all Lecturers and Professors, and the Teachers at Private Schools, while you admit Hospital Physicians and Surgeons, you are setting up just such another oligarchy of Hospital Medical Officers as has rendered the Council of the College of Surgeons so justly the subject of complaint.[17]

This proposal aroused considerable hostility in the medical press on the ground, mainly, that it was impracticable and potentially harmful to exclude teachers and practitioners from the examination process. But that exclusion was, in fact, largely though not completely implemented in the choice of senators, and the raising of the matter so strongly by Warburton and UCL must have added further obstacles to the appointment of well-known medical men as examiners.

CHAPTER 3

Choosing the Senators

Before following the progress towards the authorization of the Charter in November 1836, it is as well to see how Spring Rice and his colleagues had set about collecting the men who were, at this point in time, still being seen, primarily, as examiners, and whose number, he had suggested, should not be limited.

Even if every scrap of paper touching on the choice of members of the first Senate of the new University had survived, it is unlikely that they would reveal, in detail, all the influences and contacts which must have been involved. Those sections of the educational, intellectual, academic, literary, religious, artistic and scientific communities whose opinions were broadly sympathetic to the reformist attitudes of the Whigs and the Radicals, were small enough for their outstanding members to be well known, at least by reputation, to the leading politicians. Russell, Spring Rice and Warburton would each have been acquainted personally with many such people, and each would have had his own list. But as soon as the impending appointment of a new board of examiners was recognized, there would also have been no shortage of advisers, lobbyists and place-seekers. A great deal of the choosing would have involved discussion and argument, only a small proportion of which is likely to have been reflected in correspondence. And that choosing would have taken into account the awkward questions of political balance and the representation of special interests, quite as much as the relatively uncomplicated matters of academic competence.

There is, fortunately, a moderate amount of archival material from which a good deal of the chronological sequence of the search can be reconstructed, and from which some of its main features can be traced. It is clear, for instance, that Cambridge men – and especially Trinity College graduates – were a strongly preferred group, though there is no evidence that the College or University authorities in Cambridge were in any sense involved. It is clear, too, that there were reservations and disagreements over the inclusion of Church-men between those whose strongest concern was the pursuit of the interest of Dissenters and those, including Spring Rice, who were relatively orthodox Anglicans. In the scientific area, despite rivalries, there was a commonwealth of small, prestigious institutions like the Royal Society, the Royal Institution and the Linnean Society, whose members provided the ministers with ready-made candidates for office. In the medical context, however, one senses that the ministers were less sure of themselves, probably more amenable to Warburton's opinions, and certainly forced by controversy into more complicated diplomacy than had to be applied elsewhere. And despite the notion of remunerating examiners out of fees, it is obvious that, in general terms, appointment to the University was to be regarded as honorary. Even if heavy devotion to work was envisaged – which it certainly should have been but, apparently, was not – ministers did not want to pay for it from public funds: if there were any ministerial doubts on this score, they may well have made attractive the choice of some men who were already in government posts.

Late in 1836 the Prime Minister brought to Spring Rice's notice the name of a possible medical appointee, but did not push him hard, and remarked, 'I know not upon what principle you have selected the names.'[1] Whether, in fact, Spring Rice began the exercise with a clear notion of an exact combination which would meet his needs is unknown. But he had to exercise a lot of patience and political skill, during a period of some sixteen months, before the names of the first fellows were listed in the Charter.

Doubtless Spring Rice had some names in mind from at least the time of the Cabinet's decision of 6 June 1835, but the first written reference to the possible composition of the new group comes in a letter from him to Warburton, simply dated August of that year. It was on the eve of a meeting between Spring Rice and a deputation from UCL, and the College had obviously suggested that Churchmen should not be eligible for appointment. The Chancellor of the Exchequer replied:

> I think we shall satisfy you in all practicals, but the *exclusion* of any whether Churchmen or others is inconsistent with our first principles. And practically it would work ill. For instance, take Thirlwall, Sheepshanks, Dr Arnold and others are they the worse for being members of the Establishment and when everything else in their opinion is quite as we could wish their very position will advance our political views.[2]

It would seem, therefore, that Spring Rice must have taken at least Warburton into his confidence in mentioning a number of men he had already listed as potential senators and examiners. The three listed all became original members: the most famous, Dr Thomas Arnold, was Headmaster of Rugby, classical scholar, enthusiastic Anglican and a major force in the shaping of the nineteenth-century English public school tradition. The Rev Connop Thirlwall, Fellow of Trinity College, Cambridge, was a notably liberal classical scholar, soon to be Bishop of St David's. The Rev Richard Sheepshanks was another Fellow of Trinity, a barrister before being ordained, who had revealed political interest in 1831, when he was involved in the revision of borough boundaries, but primarily a man who subordinated his other interests to astronomy, in which he was a recognized expert.

It was not until 24 September 1835 that the first formal invitations were sent out, and there is no record of those to whom they were addressed. Spring Rice's letter, which was used both then and later, was copied into one of his personal letter books when he issued additional invitations in February 1836. But those who received it in September 1835 can only be listed, with some uncertainty, by using a system of elimination based on scattered references and letters of acceptance, mostly in various, regrettably incomplete, registers of Spring Rice's later correspondence, or elsewhere. The text of the letter was so designed as to make the invitation both flattering and provisional, though there is no evidence that Spring Rice or his colleagues took advantage of the flexible wording to withdraw any offer. After explaining the nature of the duties of 'the Royal University of London', he went on:

> His Majesty's Government are extremely desirous that the persons named in the Royal Charter should be such as to give to the public the fullest security for the effectual and impartial discharge of their new and most important duties, and it will be peculiarly gratifying to me if I am permitted to submit your name to my Colleagues as one of those who we may be enabled to recommend to the Crown as willing to undertake this important and most honourable trust. The duties will be confined to the period of the examination only, and therefore will not require any very considerable portion of your time, on which I am aware there are many other claims.
> But when it is considered how great is the object to be attained in

giving a useful direction, as well as affording new encouragement to the intellectual improvement of a numerous class of the King's subjects, who, without any distinction or exclusion whatever will be admitted under the proposed system to the honor of Academical degrees, I trust that you may be induced to give to the Government your zealous and valuable co-operation.[3]

Dr Arnold and George Biddell Airy, the recently appointed Astronomer Royal, previously a Cambridge professor, replied so promptly to the invitation that there is no doubt as to their having been approached at the outset. John William Lubbock, banker, scientist and Treasurer of the Royal Society, and Nassau Senior, the economist, were probably among the first group, though Senior did not reply until the following February. Lubbock's own correspondence includes the invitation, dated 24 September 1835, despite the fact that a record of its having been sent in February 1836, is entered in Spring Rice's register. The scientists John Dalton and Michael Faraday were not approached until February.[4] Nor was John Shaw Lefevre, the first Etonian to become Senior Wrangler at the end of his undergraduate years at Trinity College; subsequently he had turned to law and politics and was currently one of the three members of the highly controversial Poor Law Commission.

By the middle of February 1836, Spring Rice was able to indicate that he had either received acceptances from, or had made approaches to, all those mentioned in the previous paragraph and seven others. Sheepshanks and Thirlwall we have met already: to them must be added Edward Maltby, Bishop of Chichester, who was about to be promoted to the See of Durham. Then there were three more lawyers: Andrew Amos, who was already involved in scrutinizing the Charter exercise; John Austin, a previous Professor of Jurisprudence at Gower Street; and William Empson, Professor of Law at the East India Company's College, Haileybury. Empson was a close friend of Spring Rice and a future editor of the *Edinburgh Review*. Last came Warburton, listed by Spring Rice as being 'in Chemistry', though one might well believe that his membership was a reward for help with both UCL and the medical world which the ministers could scarcely withold. And while Spring Rice did not claim him as a member at this time, there is some evidence that he had also successfully recruited William Thomas Brande, who had succeeded Sir Humphrey Davy as Professor of Chemistry at the Royal Institution.

Thus Spring Rice had fifteen future senators and examiners enlisted or near-enlisted in the enterprise, covering in academic disciplinary terms classics, law and some of the sciences, notably astronomy and chemistry. It is notable that, five months after the search began, no medical men were named, though at least two of those eventually chosen had been recommended to Spring Rice.[5] This reflected the impasse which had developed in negotiations between him and the medical Establishment. But its problems were not allowed to interfere with the settlement of a major problem for the ministers – who was to lead the new University?

As with so many aspects of these earliest days of the University, there is no archival material which illuminates the discussions which must have preceded the choice of chancellor. One can well understand that a Whiggish sense of hierarchy, combined with a sound political realization of the desirability of endowing the new institution with a leader – or at least a figure-head – who commanded not merely political and social, but also intellectual respect, narrowed the field severely. The choice was one in which the Prime Minister must himself have taken a crucial interest, and it is unsurprising that it fell on a representative of one of the great aristocratic Whig families. William Cavendish, 2nd Earl of Burlington, who was to succeed to the Dukedom of Devonshire, as the 7th Duke, in 1858, had been a brilliant student of Trinity College, Cambridge. He had sat as MP for Cambridge University from 1829 to 1831, but lost his seat as a result of his enthusiasm for reform: thereafter, until he succeeded his father and moved to the House of Lords in 1834, he represented Malton and then Derbyshire. His political experience and loyalties, therefore, were impeccable from a Whig standpoint, and since he had abandoned politics in favour of taking a serious interest in scientific and industrial matters, he also met the criteria of intellectual respectability.

If there was any aspect of Cavendish's suitability which might have raised doubt, it was his age, for when Melbourne and Spring Rice wrote inviting him to be Chancellor, in the middle of February 1836, he was not quite 28 – and he was to preside over the first official meeting of the new Senate just a month before his 29th birthday. And Burlington himself shewed a graceful though confident humility when he heard the names of those who were expected to constitute the board. He told Melbourne that

I cannot help feeling that I am quite unworthy to be associated with them; if however you think it may be of any service to the Interests of the University, I shall be glad to undertake the Office, & will endeavour to discharge its duties to the best of my power.

There is no indication that Burlington was much involved in the remaining stages of establishing the membership of the Senate, or indeed of such forward thinking as may have taken place about the University, until after he received a formal letter of appointment and a copy of the Charter on 1 December 1836.[6] Unfortunately, he only began to keep his valuable diary in 1838.

Though sixteen might not nowadays be regarded as far short of a workable academic board in a very small institution, it was to be less than half the size of the final senate membership. Whether or not it ever occurred to the ministers, once they began to recruit people, that it might have been better to separate the idea of a governing body from the idea of a set of examiners, the fact is that throughout 1836 the number of 'Members' went on growing. Spring Rice's suggestion, in his letter of 22 November 1835 to UCL, that additional, non-senatorial examiners might be appointed, was the first hint that the concept of the board as a governing body, sufficiently representative of the various groups which had to be accommodated for political reasons, was beginning to take precedence over the notion of a narrowly-defined group of examiners. By February 1836, when Nassau Senior replied to the invitation to join, he warned that, 'If the division of labour is adopted and each examiner confined to his own subject, I hope to find time!' Spring Rice minuted: 'Not necessary for Board of Examiners to go through all the drudgery of examining. Power will be given them of appointing additional examiners.' And much later, as we shall see, when Russell was trying to ensure Brougham's membership of the Senate, he remarked 'You need not attend.'[7]

The first sixteen appointees had not fully covered the disciplinary ground, however, even without considering the needs of medicine, which were to account for the biggest extra block. Another six were deemed to be necessary to complete the nominally arts and law categories. Three of the six were scientists – for it has to be remembered that arts included science – chemistry, natural history and mathematics were integral and compulsory subjects in the London BA, alongside classics, moral philosophy, political economy, French and German.

Francis Beaufort, Hydrographer of the Admiralty, and James Walker, an eminent civil engineer, were added at uncertain dates in 1836. The Rev John Stevens Henslow, Professor of Botany at Cambridge, and the man credited with having facilitated Darwin's appointment to the *Beagle*, denied that he had ever been invited, when he found his name in the Charter, and was a reluctant recruit. 'I have received no communication from anyone on the subject, and know not to whom I am indebted for the mention of my name,' he protested to Russell.[8] His was only one of several examples of carelessness and muddle towards the end of 1836.

Joseph Henry Jerrard came to the attention of Spring Rice because he was either a friend, colleague or helper of the young Viscount Milton, heir to the Fitzwilliam earldom, and MP for North Northants, who died at the age of 23 in November 1835. Jerrard had been, since 1831, the first Principal of Bristol College, which Spring Rice described to Russell as 'a large preparatory school . . . which he has completely reformed.'[9] He was a Fellow of Gonville and Caius College, Cambridge, from 1828 until 1844, and was recruited for London as an examiner in classics. He was to become a considerable figure on the Senate: he was a strong and persistent spokesman for the Anglican interest, and was ordained as a priest in 1842. However, he joined the Church of Rome in 1851, only two years before his death.

Warburton was a prominent member of the Council of UCL, and it may well have been that fact which influenced Spring Rice to find someone who would be regarded as representing the Council of King's College. He offered a place to William Otter, who had been the first Principal of King's, and was just replacing Edward Maltby as Bishop of Chichester. Otter accepted in August, and Spring Rice may well have thought he had thereby balanced the sensibilities of the two colleges. But at the end of October, Lord John Russell, whose political antennae were particularly sensitive, wrote asking him 'whether there would be any objection to placing Brougham in the list – Otter is there already, and I fear the omission may be considered a slight.'[10] Brougham's name was accordingly added, but whether by accident or design, nobody told the mercurial Lord, who only learned of his inclusion from the publication of the Charter.

Throughout the ten months from December 1835, there was, on the basis of the records of Spring Rice's correspondence, almost certainly more lobbying and jockeying for places in the medical sector of the new

University than in all the other disciplinary areas. But because of the controversies already discussed, it is highly unlikely that any of the offers of appointment were made before the summer and autumn of 1836 – in the last week of July, the medical press listed, accurately, seven names of men who they claimed had been offered places recently, and added two more a month afterwards.[11] By November, no less than sixteen medical men had been added to the twenty-two arts and law people listed as Senators.

That the failure to bring the Physicians and Surgeons into harmonious co-operation was a serious embarrassment to the Government, is clear from both external and internal sources. The *London Medical Gazette* explained the reluctance of 'the patrons of the new institution . . . to launch it on the ocean of public opinion,' as being due to the 'extreme weakness of the medical department, as originally planned.' The journal also pointed out that the expected inclusion of 'some distinguished men,' in general science, would 'serve to give a character to the establishment, and, in some degree, counterbalance the weakness of the medical department.'[12] As late as September and October, the Prime Minister was taking Warburton's opinion into account in weighing the claims of medical candidates for places on the Senate, and remarked to Spring Rice that 'your list appears to be rather weak in surgery.'[13]

The one modest victory which the ministers could claim in their tussles with the medical corporations came when two prominent members of the Society of Apothecaries were persuaded to join the new University. Warburton was credited with having 'flattered the Apothecaries into acquiescence' by 'a piece of skilful generalship' - a not unreasonable attribution, though not capable of documentary proof.[14] John Bacot and John Ridout, both of whom were examiners for, and each of whom was to be, later in life, Master of the Apothecaries Company, suffered censure from their own Court of Assistants, however, because they were seen as having put themselves 'in the anomalous position of owing a divided allegiance' by accepting Spring Rice's invitation. The row within the Society of Apothecaries was to go on for a year: Bacot and Ridout stood their ground, and were later reinstated. They argued, successfully, that the Court of Assistants had exceeded its brief, and had no power to interfere with members' rights 'to belong to any scientific body they please.'[15]

Robbed of the chance of naming some of the most prestigious people in the Colleges, and restricted by the pressure to avoid appointing people holding positions in the medical schools, the ministers and

Warburton may well have been pushed into a rather desperate, late selection process. Further developments suggest that there were some stop-gap decisions, perhaps not least the probable dragooning of government-office holders like the Surgeon General for Ireland, Philip Crampton, and the military surgeon Sir James M'Grigor, Director of the Army Medical Department, as well as the listing of Richard Rainey Pennington, 'the fashionable apothecary who attends the present Premier and several of his colleagues.' Peter Mark Roget, Secretary of the Royal Society, insisted that he 'learned from the newspapers, and from that source alone' that he was appointed. Dr Charles Locock, a rising obstetrician who was to be *accoucheur* to Queen Victoria for all her children, accepted appointment only to have his name missed off the originally published text of the Charter - a cynical journalist suggested that Locock had a friend at court who had procured the omission of his name 'as an act of kindness.'[16]

The opposition to teachers of medicine and/or hospital medical officers had varying results. Six men who would seem to have been in one or other of the categories nonetheless became fellows. Cornwallis Hewett, Downing Professor of Medicine at Cambridge, was at least unlikely to teach London students. Archibald Billing of the London Hospital, a pioneer of practical teaching at the bedside, was apparently pressured into relinquishing his lecturership on accepting membership of the Senate.[17] John Sims, a Quaker who was Physician to Marylebone Infirmary, died before examinations began, but another Quaker, Thomas Hodgkin, Curator of the Anatomical Museum at Guy's Hospital, seems to have been a clear exception to any general rule of exclusion, as was Francis Kiernan, a controversial teacher of anatomy who had not been appointed to a Chair at King's, in part because he was a Roman Catholic who would not abandon his church. Jones Quain, Professor of Anatomy at Gower Street, had only recently retired.

The remaining three doctors were all in successful private practice: Neil Arnott, already established as an inventor, who would soon transfer his main interests from strictly medical to wider scientific matters; James Clark, who was to survive criticism of his part in the Lady Flora Hastings affair, and to be a major force in medical education; and Sir Stephen Love Hammick, Bt., Surgeon Extraordinary to both George IV and William IV.

The story of the adventures and misadventures of putting together the medical contingent in 1836 should not exclude the involvement of a man who was to be the cause of a major confrontation within the new University in its very early days. Dr James Craig Somerville was Inspector of Anatomy – the post which was the result of Warburton's parliamentary campaign to bring some order and constraint into the grisly business of supplying corpses to the schools of anatomy. Warburton regarded Somerville as having been

> the real author of the Anatomy Act, and . . . has undergone Martyrdom in his Profession as a Physician, in accomplishing [its] success. . . . By instituting a system of just distribution, instead of a scramble in which the wealthiest alone would win, he has exposed himself to the hostility of a numerous body of the most interested and powerful corporations and individuals in the Medical world.[18]

Somerville, like Arnott, Billing, Locock and Sims, had been a witness before Warburton's Select Committee on Medical Education. No doubt through Warburton's influence, Somerville was brought in to help Spring Rice with the organization of the medical faculty of the new University, and Warburton apparently implied to Russell that from Somerville 'was devised the plan upon which the Charter was founded.' This Spring Rice denied, insisting that the plan was settled before he met Somerville: but he readily admitted that Somerville had been 'of great use afterwards and as zealous and efficient as possible.'[19] Warburton spelt out what had transpired. Somerville, he claimed,

> has been freely consulted on the subject of the Medical Branch of the New University by the Chancellor of the Exchequer; and as Downing Street secrets will out, this is no mystery within the precincts of all the Medical Corporations. It was natural indeed to draw this inference, as the Members of those Corporations who conferred with the Chancellor of the Exchequer in Downing Street saw the Chancellor frequently admitting Dr James Somerville into his closet; and they afterwards found in the Charter the traces of Dr James Somerville's well known opinions.[20]

In December 1836, Warburton was primarily concerned to have Somerville considered as a strong candidate for the post of Registrar in the new University. He told Russell, in the letter just quoted, that

> The Medical Corporations are deeply incensed at the contents of the New Charter, and they will wreak vengeance, if they are able, on the heads of the advisers of the Government in this matter . . . will your

Lordship leave Dr James Somerville to be crushed, for the honest advice he has given to the Government.

Dr Somerville, as will be seen, was to be a fellow, briefly. And he was, indeed, to be 'crushed' in the context of the University of London – but by the medical men he had helped to have appointed to the Senate, rather than by the direct action of the medical establishments.

CHAPTER 4

The Team Assembled

Lord Melbourne's major anxiety about the new University lay not in the details of appointments, though as we have seen, he held up the final list to check some medical candidates, and had a hand in the nomination of both the Chancellor and Vice-Chancellor. He was particularly concerned, however, that the University's establishment and aims were not formally characterized as having been overwhelmingly conceived as a concession to the Dissenters. He had taken action to have the grievances of Dissenters investigated, and encouraged his ministers to find ways and means of relieving them,[1] but he was no radical, and was conscious of the political risks of going too far. When Lord John Russell, doubtless flushed with the success of having got the new University of London under way, wanted to force Oxford and Cambridge to admit Dissenters, Melbourne responded:

> Is this really necessary? Is not the charter of the new London University enough for the present . . . it is not prudent to stir this question. There is none upon which prejudice is stronger or more violent – many of our friends are in their hearts against it. It is also a very difficult question and one of which it is almost impossible to find a satisfactory solution.[2]

In the same spirit Melbourne had reacted to what was either an early draft of a statement of the basic intention of the University or, perhaps more likely, an early draft of the Charter. His note was undated: on a single sheet, headed 'Metropolitan University', the Prime Minister wrote:

> I have seen over this and it seems to me well conceived. But I would omit the points which I have underscored in the preamble and in the first enacting clause. There is no need to point so precisely to its being a measure for the benefit of the Dissenters. All persons will be entitled to take advantage of it under the words as they will stand after the omission.

The original is in the Monteagle Papers, where it is placed among the documents of 1834: conceivably it could refer to a draft circulated before Melbourne resigned in November of that year, when serious consideration was given to the possibility of creating a metropolitan university. But Spring Rice was not then at the Treasury, and the reference to the preamble and the first enacting clause makes it more probable that Melbourne was referring to a formal draft of the Charter, drawn up by the Crown lawyers. The words which the Prime Minister wanted to have deleted do not appear in any of the few advanced handwritten and printed drafts of the Charter in the Home Office records, but unfortunately they carry no date save that of the formal approval of the document in November 1836. The best guess may be that Melbourne's comment was written in response to an early draft, very late in 1835 or during the first half of 1836.[3]

By the beginning of August 1836, Spring Rice must have felt confident that the Charter was practically in its final form, and he may well have wanted to show all the interests concerned that he was not dragging his feet. On his own initiative, apparently, in the middle of the month, he laid a draft of the document, excluding names, on the table of the House of Commons.[4] Six weeks later, when writing to Melbourne, Russell complained that Spring Rice's action had been very improper.[5] However, no great harm seems to have been done: in October Melbourne received and cleared the list of appointees to the Senate, but mentioned that Warburton had raised 'some observations on the draft Charter itself, which must of course be corrected.'[6] And on 30 October Russell wrote a letter to Spring Rice which indicates, very clearly, *inter alia*, the relative power of the two men:

> I have this day countersigned the Charter for the London University on which I congratulate both you and myself. It was agreed to by the King last Wednesday but he wished to be satisfied on some legal points, on which he consulted the Chancellor. I have made a few alterations of little importance, to satisfy Warburton. One or two doubts however will remain on my mind. The first is, whether you intended any particular person for Vice-Chancellor. I have put in the name of Mr Lubbock, in which Melbourne concurs, but I can have it altered, if you have settled upon another person.[7]

There is no sign of the letter in which Warburton raised doubts, and no details of how far Russell had satisfied some or all of them. The Charter was dated 28 November 1836: it listed Lord Burlington as Chancellor, James William Lubbock as Vice-Chancellor – Lubbock did not know that he was to be Vice-Chancellor until he saw the appointment in the Charter[8] – and thirty five fellows. The carelessness which led to Dr Locock's name being missed out, and which probably accounted for the numerous mistakes made in giving senators wrongly spelled names, and in neglecting to include many of their honours and qualifications, was no doubt only carelessness. More serious legal incompetence may have lain behind the fact, discovered months later, to great embarrassment, that the Charter was only valid during the lifetime of William IV, which was fast ebbing away. And though it was to be passed off as a clerical error, the most important change in the printed version of the Charter from the declared intention of Spring Rice a year before, was the fact that the Senators were to hold their places at the Sovereign's 'will and pleasure' – which in practice meant that they had only political tenure and could be removed at any time by the government of the day.

Russell launched the Charter into the public realm with a provocative letter to Burlington, ensuring the new Chancellor of his support for

> an Institution, destined to confer the Distinction firstly due to proficiency in Literature, Science or Art without imposing a Test of Religious Opinions, or binding by the fetters of the Seventeenth Century the Talent, and Merit of the present Enlightened Age.

That letter, together with Burlington's tactful reply, and the new Charter, first appeared in the press on 12/13 December.[9] The defiant air of Russell's message, like the confusion and uncertainties and quarrels which had marked the eighteen months of the Charter's gestation, can be seen, in retrospect, as quite in keeping with the traumas which were to follow.

Whatever satisfaction and pleasurable apprehension was generated in those quarters of the population for which the new University was intended to provide exciting new opportunities was not reflected in the press. The immediate reception of the University and its Senate, in the editorial and correspondence columns of the London papers and the medical journals, was generally sceptical and lukewarm as to their institutional framework, and unbelievably scurrilous as to medical personalities.

Inevitably, the Tory papers took a partisan opportunity to throw cold water on the whole enterprise and to lay the blame for its alleged weaknesses on Lord John Russell – Spring Rice was scarcely mentioned. *The Morning Post*, for instance, predicted that degrees conferred by the Senate

> will scarcely be regarded by the world at large as distinctions of any considerable value. Had it been the intention of Lord John Russell to constitute a club of Whigs, capable of mingling science with liberalism in their *conversaziones*, the list . . . would have been unobjectionable. But, aiming at the formation of a permanent and influential national institution, he has certainly selected the Senate upon a principle much too narrow and exclusive to afford to the establishment the least chance of immediate success. This defect may be, and no doubt will be, remedied by some future Minister, who better understands the proper objects of such an institution, or is more sincerely desirous of promoting them. Then, but not until then, a fair chance will be afforded to the new experiment, in its own nature sufficiently doubtful, of distributing the honours of literature and science by the hands of men of heterogeneous habits and pursuits and linked together by no other tie than the piece of parchment on which their names are strung together.[10]

(It is worth mention, at this point, that neither Peel's Government, from 1841–6, nor Derby's short-lived administration in 1852 added any members to the Senate. Every member, from November 1836 to March 1858, was appointed while either Melbourne, Russell or Palmerston was Prime Minister.)

The Times saw the new University as the harbinger of a totally state-controlled system of education:

> This 'University,' as it is most absurdly miscalled, is as completely under the thumb of the Government as any of the clerks in the Treasury are; it consists of people removeable at pleasure; it must admit to examination for degrees all persons who present certificates that they have gone through a certain course of instruction at schools authorised to issue such certificates; the authority to issue those certificates is to be conferred on schools by the Crown – that is, by the Minister of the day; and the 'course of instruction' to be pursued

in these authorised schools is to be regulated by the Chancellor, Vice-Chancellor and Fellows, whose regulations respecting it must be submitted to the consideration one of His Majesty's Principal Secretaries of State, and to be approved by him, as also must all regulation touching the examination of candidates, and the granting of degrees.

And an Oxford correspondent wrote: 'Let things be called by their true names. This is a Government Education Board, not an University. Universities are bodies possessed of fixed privileges and rights, and of an independent internal government.'[11]

There had been criticism, as the Charter was being negotiated, of the requirement whereby candidates for degrees would only be accepted for examination if they had certificates of attendance at either UCL or King's, or at schools or colleges to be approved subsequently. When the Charter was published, this criticism was somewhat muted, partly, perhaps, because it was made clear that UCL and King's would have no monopoly. But the more radical view, which opposed any restriction on the freedom of people to apply to be examined, had by no means disappeared, and was given vigorous expression in the *Lancet*.[12] It was to continue to be a major focus of campaigning for two decades.

But if the Tories groused about another Whig job, and were on stronger ground in objecting to state control; if Oxbridge was contemptuous of a body without proper academic autonomy; and if the Radicals would have liked more direct access for examination candidates; none of these criticisms was backed by sufficient political clout to divert the Government from its chosen course. Moreover, though the size of the Senate caused a few eyebrows to rise, the membership of it, on all sides save the medical, was accepted almost without hostile comment save on its assumed generally Whiggish sympathies: there were no personal attacks on the non-medical men. But passions inside the medical world had run high, and the invective poured publicly on the list of medical Senators rivalled the sort of contemporary abuse usually levelled at politicians.

Spring Rice's warning about the absence of famous names was justified by the moderately worded letter of a 'Practising Physician':

in the list of fellows of the new Metropolitan University the names of many, I might almost say all, of the principal physicians and surgeons of the metropolis are wanting. We look in vain for the names of Sir Henry Halford, Sir Astley Cooper, Dr Chambers, Sir B. Brodie, Dr

Holland, Mr Earle, Sir C. Clarke, *cum multis aliis.* I can understand why . . . other physicians and surgeons of eminence who are actually engaged in the education of our youthful aspirants to medical honours should be excluded from a board which has to sit in judgement on their pupils' merits: but I should like to be informed . . . why the *magnates* of our Royal Colleges of Physicians and Surgeons have been, to all appearance, so studiously avoided.[13]

Far less inhibited were the denouncements of an Edinburgh MD. According to him, Arnott and Roget were 'more famed for scientific than medical knowledge. . . . Clarke has never been known as a teacher of eminence'; M'Grigor and Hammick 'are totally unfit for such an elevation in the face of the medical world'; the two Quakers, Hodgkin and Sims, had only been appointed in order 'to conciliate the broadbrims.' 'Mediocrity has hitherto been his [Billing's] lot.' Bacot and Kiernan 'are not at all entitled to such a distinction. They hold no place in the profession to warrant . . . so gross an exercise of patronage.' And 'though last not least, come up two of the ponderous old ladies of Rhubarb Hall, Pennington and Ridout, apothecaries. For what earthly purpose have these old draught vending pill gilders been made fellows and examiners.'[14] The *Lancet* was happy with only some of the appointments, and considered that the ministers

> have been earwigged . . . by some exceedingly *dishonest* advisers - by thoroughly *knavish* advisers. Otherwise, the several persons whom we could point out, and *will* point out, on another occasion, would not have been puffed into notoriety by disfiguring the Charter of a London University. . . . Two or three of the nominations are even of a disgraceful character.[15]

In the thick-skinned culture of politics and medicine, none of this probably disturbed unduly those at whom it was aimed. More worrying must have been the immediate and vehement rejection of membership of the Senate by a few of those listed in the Charter.

Brougham at once repudiated his inclusion. He told Tooke that he had no previous knowledge that he would be listed in the Charter:[16] he picked up the bad 'technical' errors in the document very soon after receiving his copy, and challenged Russell about the legality of the new University.[17] He must have confronted the Home Secretary about his doubts and about his inclusion, for he wrote to Russell on 21 December:

> I hope I expressed myself sufficiently clearly on the University

Charter to make you keep out my name in case you have occasion to issue a corrected Charter. I would do nothing on any account to mar the experiment, to which I of course wish all possible success. But I do not consider myself as having any kind of claim to a place among men of skill in their several departments and appointed to grant or superintend the granting of degrees. I am also connected with the London University [i.e. UCL] and so improper to belong to the General Institution – not because it has displaced and superseded ours in one very material respect, but on account of the bias which those connected with ours as I am very naturally be supposed to have. Furthermore – I know nothing of the constitution of the new body – not having to this hour read it and therefore I ought not to be represented as having approved of it – though for anything I know it may be the best of possible constitutions – as it may also be the very worst. The dilemma you have placed me in is this – that I must either seem to approve by being and continuing to be of it, or seem to be adverse by being withdrawn from it. So your busines is if a new charter is issued, to leave me quietly out.[18]

Russell admitted that the original Charter was flawed in minor ways and would be replaced: he told Brougham that being listed did not mean that he had to attend the Senate, and clearly hoped the matter would be forgotten. But his erstwhile colleague would not change his mind, though Russell tried three times, unsuccessfully, in the later months of 1837, to keep him on the list. Brougham in the meantime took no part in the work of the University, and his name did not appear when a revised Charter was issued on 5 December 1837.[19] The Earl of Burlington may not have been alone in his relief at this outcome: he admired Brougham's 'wonderful talents,' but felt that as a colleague he was 'not to be depended upon.'[20]

If Brougham had a sound political case for opting out, the Rev Richard Sheepshanks declined to serve out of good, timeless, academic petulance. He sent a letter of refusal to Spring Rice, and explained to Russell that:

When I first gave my consent to Mr Spring Rice's application, no persons were mentioned, nor could I well guess, until the list was published, that among gentlemen selected to direct a course of academical education and to ascertain the attainments of the students, I should find Capt. F. Beaufort, R.N., or even Mr H. Warburton, M.P.

Two or three years ago, those gentlemen occasioned me a great
deal of very unnecessary and very unpleasant trouble, about a matter
which to my understanding, was plain and simple enough. I lost
several months' time and temper, because they could not or would
not make out a question of ordinary grammar and of the lowest
possible mathematics, and yet would meddle, and I then formed a
resolution to avoid all future intercourse with either of them, which
was not absolutely necessary.[21]

There is no clue to the nature of the meddling which Sheepshanks
suffered from the Hydrographer to the Navy and from Warburton: but
the nature of his remarks tends to confirm a recent description of him
as 'a man of remarkably persevering vindictiveness.'[22] Neither Russell
nor Spring Rice seems to have tried to retain his services. His name, like
Brougham's, did not appear in the second Charter: he never put in an
appearance at the Senate.

To Brougham and Sheepshanks was added the 'fashionable apothecary,' one of 'the ponderous old ladies of Rhubarb Hall,' Richard
Rainey Pennington. Perhaps, for him, the public insults were too
much to bear: the *London Medical Gazette* reported, on the last day
of 1836, that 'he has had the good sense to direct that his name may
be withdrawn.' In fact, his name remained on the books until his death
in 1849; but papers were never sent to him, and he never found his way
to a Senate meeting.

Thus, within a month of the first publication of its membership, the
Senate had shrunk by three, to thirty five – but, as will soon be
apparent, that was a number of no particular significance. The first
sign of movement towards the setting up of an organization seems
to have been early lobbying for the post of Registrar – a story in
itself, for later examination. But at the end of January 1837, the new
Vice-Chancellor wrote:

All I know about the London University is that some time since
I received a copy of the Charter under a blank cover. I believe
Lord Burlington is out of Town, of course it is for him to take
the initiative.

He was still waiting a week later, and was *'very anxious to hear'* from
Lord Burlington, so that he could 'begin to see a little of his way about
it.'[23] But it was some three weeks later before Burlington called together
'a few of the members seven or eight in number who have . . . given
their consideration to the subject' to meet at his home 'for the previous

consideration of the course we ought to pursue.' Lubbock, Roget and Empson were certainly present.[24] There is no record of their discussions, and no scrap of paper to give any indication of how they thought the University should be organized. A week afterwards, on 4 March 1837, the Chancellor gave a dinner for the new Senate, which was followed by the first official meeting of the body, in rooms recently vacated by the Royal Academy, in Somerset House.

CHAPTER 5

An Oligarchical Tendency

This and the following chapter precede a chronological narrative of the University of London's progress from 1837 until the end of March 1858. In these two chapters an attempt is made to give some sense of the basic conditions in which the Senate worked, and a view of how the senators shared the load – or, to put it bluntly, which of them were really important. Because the membership of the Senate was only moderately extended, and because conditions of operation remained relatively unaltered for the greater part of the first twenty years, such a preview is quite feasible, and is in no danger of distorting the subsequent narrative. Moreover, while the archival material available generally is limited, there exist sufficient statistics of attendance at meetings, and of service as examiners, to enable a clear picture to emerge of which groups and individuals made the most significant contributions.

The Senate was, in practice, a large, working committee, subject to the supervision of the Home Secretary and the Chancellor of the Exchequer, who had to present a vote each year to the House of Commons to provide funds, and who were open to the questioning of MPs and peers about the operation of the institution. All the regulations which the Senate shaped, as well as every penny of their expenditure, had to be approved by Government. There was only one senior officer employed, the Registrar; he, a clerk of the Senate, and the whole organization, worked until 1853 in a few inhospitable rooms of that venue of numerous government offices, Somerset House, and then only moved temporarily to Marlborough House. Two years later it entered what might be called the first of its own homes, Burlington House. During the long spell in Somerset House there is no hint that there was any attempt made to provide even the most basic physical facilities in which some degree of social and collegial cohesion and warmth might be fostered. There was no common room, no dining facilities, and, though doubtless some new friendships were struck and many plots hatched in small groups over twenty years, the overriding impression is of a bleak utilitarian operation, made the more so by the high level of fragmentation of attendance and the strong pressures of sectional interests.

Two witnesses to the discomforts of the early years are worth quoting. Edward Maltby, Bishop of Durham, wrote to Russell in October, 1837:

> I cannot help observing, that our proceedings in the London University have been remarkably slow from the inconvenient numbers of those who have assembled to deliberate; and the little experience some of them have had in the actual conduct of Education. The place also where we assembled: the *bare walls* of Somerset House was both inconvenient and unhealthy – I caught a cold, when I first attended there which confined me nearly two months.

And in the summer of 1839, the Astronomer Royal, George Biddell Airy, complained that 'The attendance, with any degree of regularity, is most annoying: it gave me such dreadful pains in the face that I was obliged to give it up.'[1] One hopes that it was the physical atmosphere, and not the presence of his colleagues, which upset Airy.

The dignified nomenclature of Chancellor, Vice-Chancellor and fellows could not conceal the fact that the University of London was a small and vulnerable creature of Government and Parliament. But while it was a comparatively small operation, it involved far more effort and activity than was envisaged by Spring Rice when he wrote to prospective senators, that 'The duties will be confined to the period of the examination only, and therefore will not require any very considerable portion of your time.' It was so serious an underestimate of what had to be done in the first few years, that one is bound to wonder whether the ministers were naive, totally uninformed, or not a little sly. Perhaps, to give them the maximum benefit of the doubt, they had in mind how the University would work when the whole of its initial preparations had been completed, and when a regular pattern of examinations and an accepted allocation of duties had been established.

But to create a new examination system was the equivalent of creating a new academic curriculum. It could not be done without intensive academic debate, and that debate, added to all the logistical and administrative arrangements, had to be achieved by a totally new team, representative of a range of interests and attitudes not assimilated without prolonged negotiation and some bruising controversy. Moreover, as we have seen, it is not clear whether ministers thought, originally, that all the fellows would, or should, be examiners. There was internal disagreement about this in the Senate, but the terms of Spring Rice's invitation were interpreted to mean that at least some Fellows would be expected to participate directly in the examining process. Indeed, some were warned that they should give up certain posts which they held, in the light of their new duties. At least two of the appointees took this to heart: one, J.H. Jerrard, resigned the headship of a school, and as we have seen, Archibald Billing gave up a hospital lecturership.[2]

The extent of the effort which had to be made to get the new examination system working is easily demonstrated. From the first meeting in April 1837 until the end of 1839, there were 106 Senate meetings, more than 150 meetings of the faculties of arts, law and medicine, and 59 meetings of *ad hoc* committees. As the faculties and *ad hoc* committees were all composed of senators, those who attended regularly found themselves involved in detailed university business at least three times a week on average, for a period of over two-and-a-half years. They received no salaries or honoraria, and the small group of them who were paid as examiners were not paid their fees until after the first examinations were held late in 1838. The first non-senatorial examiners were only appointed a little earlier in that year.

Apart from the few fellows who were salaried government servants, and who may simply have regarded attendance at meetings as part of their official duties, the rest were clearly expected by ministers to devote a considerable amount of time without any expectation of material reward. As most of them were professional people already busy with their regular affairs, it says a great deal for their sense of public duty, and their general passion for higher education, that a considerable number of them were prepared to devote so much effort and time to the new University. It is, no doubt, also an interesting commentary on the relative affluence of at least some of the senators, and it would be only fair to accept that many fellows were particularly keen to pursue and promote their own professional concerns and to defend those concerns against the views of other parties. Nonetheless, it is hardly surprising that some of them grew painfully aware of the fact that they were being financially disadvantaged by having to spend so much time on unpaid duties, and it may well be that such discontent as did arise would have erupted more widely had not the pressure been greatly eased once the system of examinations was fully established.

After 24 full Senate meetings in 1837, 42 in 1838, and 40 in 1839, the body met only 19 times in 1840, 16 in 1841, and thereafter dropped to a range of 6 to 14 sessions per year until 1856 and 1857, when it met 19 and 16 times respectively. Full statistics of the arts and medical faculties are unavailable after 1839, but certainly they would have come together more frequently. *Ad hoc* committees were set up usually only a few times each year, though, in 1849, when a new Charter was in the offing, there were as many as 16 meetings of such committees. But it is clear that, once the great effort of settling the main lines of operation had been completed, the burden on the Senate became more like what Spring Rice had promised in 1835, though probably still appreciably more demanding.

All senators were appointed by the Crown and, though the 1836 Charter specified only tenure during pleasure, this was amended in 1837 so that, thereafter, they held office during good behaviour for indefinite terms. The Vice-Chancellor had to be re-elected, or a new one elected, annually, by and from amongst the fellows. It was also provided in the 1837 Charter that, if the number of fellows fell below 25, the Senate could themselves add new fellows to bring the number back up to 36. But during our period the complement never fell below 25 and, when a small injection of new blood was made in 1837, and larger ones in 1849 and 1856, they were made by the Crown. In other words, the Government never allowed the Senate to choose its new members.

With its membership of 38 – a Chancellor and Vice-Chancellor and 36 fellows, the Senate was one of many examples of the large and apparently unwieldy public bodies which had long been commonplace in British life. Perhaps they reflected some basic collegial instinct, certainly an ingrained distrust of undiluted specialists, and some inbred suspicion of the small group or the single, responsible functionary. There were plenty of precedents and, despite a difference of institutional role, the ministers were no doubt influenced to some degree by the examples of the two London colleges. UCL had a council of 24; King's was 42 strong. The Charter of the new University of London was not unusual, therefore, in listing as many as 38 names.

Ministers setting up this or any other such body were unlikely to be naive about the probable behaviour of so large a group. They would defend the length of the list of names by referring not only to the factors already mentioned, but also to the desirability of ensuring that there would always be a quorum available to transact business. They would be tactfully quiet about the need to have sufficient reserves to call up to meet any special challenges to governmental policies; and they would not welcome any suggestion that, with so large a number of senators, the possibilities of tactical voting and even coups could not be ruled out. What they would admit, privately, and what the world knew anyway, was that an oligarchical tendency would set in from the outset, and that the new institution would be run, effectively, by only a relatively small proportion of its membership. It is very unlikely, though, that they could have made accurate guesses about which of their appointees to the new University would make up that small proportion.

Professor Hearnshaw, in his history of King's College, revealed that:

> Of the forty two distinguished men who normally constituted the council, nearly half never attended at all, only a quarter were even moderately regular. The omnipresent and dominant triumvirate were the Bishop of London, the Dean of St Paul's, and the Rector of Lambeth. They were ably advised and supported by Archdeacon Cambridge, Dr Shepherd and Mr Lonsdale. They had, too, a little band of loyal and obedient lay followers, among whom Lord Bexley, Sir Robert Inglis, and Mr William Cotton were prominent.[3]

The examination of what happened in the case of the University of London's Senate yields somewhat similar results, though attendance overall seems to have been better. The major division was between those who attended less (most of them many less) than a quarter of the possible meetings, and those who turned up at more than a third. And, within the second group, there was a significant division between those who were present at between one and two-thirds of the meetings, and a small core whose attendance extended well beyond two-thirds. This general conclusion, however, reflects, simplistically, a mass of data, much of which is of sufficient interest to be given careful attention, and includes not only service on the Senate, but also service as examiners.

Thirty-eight Senators were appointed in the first Charter, in November 1836. Two of the original group were replaced by two new members in the revised Charter of November 1837. Seven new men who were named in the Supplementary Charter of 1849 only began to attend meetings in April 1850. At the end of 1856, a new Chancellor and six new fellows were gazetted, beginning their service, effectively, in January 1857. One fellow was appointed in February, 1858. The Charter of 1858 was signed on 9 April. Thus, from November 1836, until the end of March 1858, 55 men were appointed to serve on the Senate. Of the 38 initial appointees, 27 were still on the list 22 years later.

Although a considerable proportion of these 55 men were not to be significant members of the new University, it is as well to look at the whole group in terms of their national and social origins, their religious affiliations, and their educational experience, as well as at the way in which they were distributed between different disciplinary and professional specialisms. The overall pattern gives some idea of the balance of interests and the political impact which those who appointed them deemed desirable. Needless to say, most were strongly committed to support of Whig governments.

About a quarter of the nominees were either Scots or Irishmen, most of the latter being Anglo-Irish Protestants. At least eight of the medical men were among this Celtic contingent. A clear division between religious affiliations is difficult to draw: the bulk of them were Anglicans; there were at least two Roman Catholics and three Quakers, but the number of other Dissenters is uncertain. In the social context, those who were to preside over an educational innovation particularly aimed at making way for the children of a growing mercantile and professional class, were themselves strongly representative of that class.

Only the two chancellors – Earls Burlington and Granville – and one very late appointee – Lord Stanley, son of the 14th Earl of Derby - were landed aristocrats. Six fellows were the children of lesser landed gentry, some of whose families had entered that category only in the last one or two generations. Eight were the sons of clergymen, five of medical men, and another five were the offspring of lawyers, army officers, a schoolteacher, a private tutor and a collector of customs and excise. The largest contingent, however, well over a quarter of the whole group, were the sons of merchants, bankers, farmers, manufacturers and contractors. All those from the sectors listed so far had been raised in what would have varied from comfortable to wealthy circumstances. Only two or three had fought their way up from humble homes: of these, Michael Faraday was an important member of Senate; another, John Dalton, as we shall see, was struck down before he could make any contribution.

A good third of the first fellows had been sent to famous schools - ten were Etonians, and others in that group were mostly at Winchester or Charterhouse. A quarter were pupils of provincial grammar schools. A handful, from families both rich and poor, were given instruction at home. A few of the medicos were trained entirely at hospitals or in the Navy, but all save one of the doctors who had university degrees were initially at Aberdeen, Dublin, Edinburgh or Glasgow. The exception was a London graduate brought into the Senate in 1857. Almost half of the 55 senators were graduates of the ancient English universities; Cambridge provided most, including no less than 16 who had been students of Trinity College.

When we turn to disciplinary specialization, it is as well to stress how inappropriate it would be to think of subject groupings in late twentieth-century terms. By the 1990s we have long been accustomed to an unfortunately high degree of separateness and rivalry between the humanities, the social sciences and the natural and technological sciences. That there were some tensions between the Victorian versions of these categories could hardly be denied, but at the same time the great majority of the academic community was recruited from an intellectual elite whose common educational foundations were to be found in the classical languages, history and literature of Greece and Rome, in mathematics and in the ecclesiastical conformities of the Anglican Church. When the University of London was established, there was solid support for the traditional Classics and Mathematics, and for the addition of French, German, Political Economy, Chemistry and Natural History, within the syllabus for the BA. The Astronomer Royal, himself a man of quite modest social origins, wrote in 1839, that 'the University degree in Arts is intended to express that the person bearing it has the liberal education of a gentleman, and that this amount of education should therefore be indispensable for degrees in any Profession.'[4]

Despite this shared cultural background, and the less rigid division of academic disciplines, however, nothing is more striking about the first senators of the University of London than the sizeable contingent of medical men and scientists among them. Of the 55 members of the Senate between 1836 and 1858, 18 were medical practitioners and/or teachers of medicine; ten were unequivocally scientists or technologists; only seven were lawyers. Four were bishops, one of whom – Edward Stanley, Bishop of Norwich – had serious interests in ornithology, entomology, mineralogy and geology. The remaining 15 included three famous historians – Grote, Hallam and Macaulay; nine leading politicians, including Warburton, who had strong reformist concern for the practice of anatomy and medical education, and George Cornewall Lewis, who wrote scholarly works on philosophy, constitutional law and history; Arnold, a headmaster with classical and theological interests; a classics don, J.H. Jerrard; and a prominent financier, Lord Overstone.

Although the University's appearance on the scene reflected so much of the concerns of UCL and King's College – and perhaps because it did so – the new Senate included at the outset only six men who served on the councils or were professors at the colleges. As we know, Lord

Brougham, the most prominent founder and current President of UCL, was only briefly included in the new Senate and never attended; on the other hand, his fellow member of the Council, Henry Warburton MP, was to be an influential and controversial senator throughout. William Otter, Bishop of Chichester, had been the first Principal of King's College, but served less than four years with London University before his death in 1840. Three professors at UCL, Amos, Austin and Jones Quain, were not on the Council of the College but did become senators, though their attendance to the University's affairs was to be very slight. It was not until ten years afterwards that Warburton was joined by the conscientious George Grote, who had long been closely associated with the governance and the operation of UCL, and was to become in due course the third Vice-Chancellor of the University. In general, though the University's most numerous examinees were students of UCL and King's College and, though several of the University's examiners were on their faculties, at the governing level the colleges and the University kept each other at arm's length.

Though 55 men, from 1836 to 1858, were appointed to serve on the Senate, some of them did not serve at all, and many more attended so infrequently as to encourage the view that their influence was at best slight, and at worst, negligible.

It is tempting to take for granted the apparently only slight importance of the many nominal senators, and to concentrate on those who made substantial contributions of time and effort to the University's affairs. But not all the less constant attenders can be discounted, for a few made particular contributions in short spaces of time - for instance, in the very busy first two years – or raised issues of importance for the new institution, or were particularly important examiners. Moreover, in some cases there were significant reasons, worth considersation, for their failure to appear or to make any mark. In addition, many of them were colourful characters whose names on the University's scrolls should be cherished, even if their service was minimal. Let us turn, first, therefore, to those who, in the main, tended to be ineffectual and inattentive, before identifying the more consistently loyal, including those most persistently and aggressively involved.

We have seen that Brougham, Sheepshanks and Pennington never attended any session of the Senate or its committees. A fourth total absentee was the eminent scientist, John Dalton, who was a casualty of ill health. He was 70 in 1836, and suffered the first of several strokes within weeks of the Senate's initial meeting; he never recovered his full faculties, and died seven years later.

No less than 18 other fellows turned up at less than a tenth of the Senate's meetings and for a smaller fraction of the committee sessions which they were eligible to attend. A few of the original appointees, after contributing modestly during the first two or three very intensive years, seem simply to have lost interest or energy thereafter, so that over the whole of their often long tenures, they had, statistically, a very low level of attendance. Ten of these fellows always lived too far away from London to make regular attendance possible; two more were absent from Britain for longish periods and never paid any close, continuing attention to the University's affairs. It is difficult to find excuses for the few persistent absentees remaining outside these two categories.

Of those disadvantaged by distance, the most extreme case was that of Philip Crampton, who had a large medical and surgical practice, was Surgeon General to the Forces in Ireland, and lived in Dublin. He made one appearance at the Senate, in July 1838, and was seen no more. Dr Arnold of Rugby was at the centre of an early controversy over the religious content of examinations; he resigned in November 1838, and had attended only four Senates and a few committees. He was realistic about his situation as a person based outside London, and remarked to a colleague that, 'Living at such a distance as I do, I can be of no practical use.'[5] Cornwallis Hewett, Downing Professor of Medicine at Cambridge, no doubt suffered the same difficulties of accessibility; he died in 1841, so that his very small number of attendances were spread over only four years.

None of the four bishops was a frequent or regular participant. William Otter was appointed to the See of Chichester and the London Senate at almost the same time. By the time of his death, in August 1840, he had only attended one meeting in five. Edward Maltby, Bishop of Durham, was far more remote from London and, given that circumstance he did not do too badly to get to about one in seven meetings. Newell Connop Thirlwall, a famous classical scholar and Fellow of Trinity College, Cambridge, who was appointed Bishop of St Davids in 1840, managed only six Senates and four committee meetings in twenty years: he served as an examiner for a single session. Edward Stanley, Bishop of Norwich, appointed in the second Charter, was in a similar geographical difficulty and took his place at less than an eighth of the Senate meetings and even fewer committees in the twelve years before he died in 1849.

The Rev John Stevens Henslow, who held the Chair of Botany at Cambridge and the Rectorship of Hitcham in Suffolk throughout his tenure of the London Senate, was listed as present at no more then 5 per cent of meetings and committees in two decades, though he was also the sole examiner in Natural History for the BA, and in Botany for the MB and MD degrees from 1838 until shortly before his death in 1861. His biographer recorded that he 'thought well' of London University, as 'an institution . . . calculated to promote the study of the sciences and other branches of literature, among those classes of men, who seldom find their way to the ancient universities.' But he was not happy, apparently, with the instruction given to his London examinees, 'He complained of the methods of teaching botany adopted in London particularly . . . especially in the purely medical schools . . . "They are badly taught" was his constant complaint: "Botany has done them more harm than good."'[6]

The most articulate commentator on the problem which distance posed was George Biddell Airy, the Astronomer Royal, a plain-spoken and rather aggressive man who took up strong positions on University matters, and eventually resigned, after a row over procedure, in 1847. He lived at the Royal Observatory at Greenwich, only a few miles out of town, but complained bitterly that 'The late hour of meeting is a virtual exclusion of persons living so far off as myself,' and drew an accurate distinction between 'resident' and 'non-resident' senators.[7] Despite much concern for examining in hydrography and civil engineering, a genuine anxiety about the quality and operation of the examinations, occasional disputatious interventions, and a shrewd appreciation of the University's constitutional weaknesses, he attended less than 5 per cent of the Senates, though rather more committees, mostly during the early years of his tenure.

William Empson, Professor of General Polity and the Laws of England at Haileybury College and, from 1847 until his death in 1852, editor of the *Edinburgh Review*, had a rather similar level of concern as Airy. But he was based out in Hertfordshire, and came to only 30 of nearly 250 Senates, and to fewer committees, in fifteen years. He was, however, drawn in at short notice to be the single examiner in Law and Jurisprudence, in 1839, when the complex, under-confident John Austin, who had been Professor of Jurisprudence at the original University of London from 1826, resigned three months after accepting the appointment, on grounds of ill health. Empson was examiner for only two sessions.

Austin had, in fact, gone to Boulogne in the summer of 1835, and never lived permanently in London again. In the autumn of 1836 he was sent to Malta for nearly two years as one of two commissioners charged with recommending constitutional and legal changes. From 1841 to 1843 he spent the summers in Carlsbad and the winters in Dresden and Berlin, and from 1844 to 1848 lived in Paris. It is unsurprising that he never returned to the Senate after coming to half a dozen meetings in the initial years.[8] Andrew Amos, Professor of English Law at UCL, went even further afield. He was whisked off to India almost as soon as he had become a senator, and spent the next six years as the fourth ordinary member of the Supreme Council, replacing Macaulay. He returned in 1843, but in 1848 went to Cambridge as Downing Professor of Laws. He attended only ten times in twenty years.

Distance was not a problem for the remaining low attenders. Four medical men presumably found demands for their professional services too great to allow time to be spent on University business. Charles Locock, who was to be acclaimed as 'the leading obstetrical physician in mid-nineteenth century Britain,' played a significant role in a changing professional world by encouraging a linkage between medicine and obstetrics. He was a man of great charm and wit, whose friend and patient, the unfortunate Ada, Countess of Lovelace, daughter of Byron, called him her 'own dear *Old Arab Horse.*'[9] He was settled in London and was for the first two years as a senator also examiner in Midwifery and Diseases of Women and Infants. Later in life, like Richard Sheep-shanks, he developed an interest in national politics. He appears again in this narrative as a participant in an early medical controversy, but his concern for the University did not extend beyond very moderate attendance in the first years, and rare appearances thereafter.

Sir James M'Grigor, Bt, a high-ranking military surgeon and Physician Extraordinary to the Sovereign, concentrated most of his attendance into the first two years, 1837–9, during which he was present at roughly one meeting in five. Jones Quain, anatomist, squeezed his very slight service into the first two years. He had been professor at UCL from 1831 to 1835, but had retired because of a 'reluctance to endure some controversial hostilities which were incidental to that period and position.' He may well have thought that he had simply jumped from the frying pan into the fire; his appearances after 1840 were vestigial, for he passed most of his time in 'lettered and scientific ease, visiting the great capitals and centres of science, and enjoying communion with men of congenial tastes and acquirements.'[10]

In a very different category was James Craig Somerville, added to the Senate on the recommendation of Warburton in the second Charter, but cold-shouldered by his medical colleagues, who accused him of unprofessional conduct, though an inquiry failed to yield any supportive evidence: his virtual resignation came after only six stormy months, during which his attendance was minimal.

The last of the original London-based appointees who made only limited contributions were Sheepshank's enemy, Francis Beaufort, Hydrographer of the Navy; and James Walker, a distinguished civil engineer. Beaufort made his efforts mainly in the first two or three years, but Walker kept up a steady attendance at Senates and committees over the twenty years, at the rate of about one meeting in five.

Of the seven new senators appointed at the end of 1849, five failed to appear at as many as a quarter of the meetings. Indeed, only two of the five, Sir James Graham and Thomas Spring Rice, now Lord Monteagle, turned out for rather more than a fifth. In fact, this was no small achievement on the part of two busy political men. Graham, who, as Home Secretary from 1841–6 had been responsible to Parliament for the University's affairs, was in office as First Lord of the Admiralty from 1852–5: he found some time to come in the early 1850s. But the other three were disappointing: two famous historians, Henry Hallam and Thomas Babington Macaulay, attended respectively ten and four of the 77 possible meetings, and George Cornewall Lewis, with rather more excuse, especially from 1855 when he became Chancellor of the Exchequer, turned up at seven. None of the three is recorded as having been a member of any of the committees for which we have minutes.

Matthew Talbot Baines, who was in the Cabinet when he was appointed a fellow at the end of 1856, managed to attend only one out of the twenty meetings which occurred between then and March 1858.

One should make every proper reservation about particular events in which some of these members took prominent parts, and accept that some of them, like Airy, who left a useful private archive, Bishops Maltby and Stanley and James Walker, exercised some specific and possibly a little general influence in University affairs through correspondence or informal channels, particularly in the first two years. And Graham and Monteagle, though no great attenders as senators in the years from 1850 to 1856, were and had been in powerful political positions to supervise the University's affairs. Indeed, Monteagle played a significant role in the medical context in 1854, and was a strong attender in the fifteen months before the Charter of 1858 took effect.

Henslow's long service as examiner must make him a figure of importance in the development of teaching in Botany, but it is very unlikely that the short terms of office as examiners of Empson, Locock and Thirlwall were in any sense memorable.

Overall, judged on their willingness and ability to attend meetings, 28 of the 55 whose names appear on the senatorial list can scarcely be praised or blamed, individually or collectively, as fellows, for that shaping of the character of a new institution which comes from giving constant attention to its affairs: quite simply, they were not sufficiently involved.

CHAPTER 6

Those Who Served

The surviving records of attendance at Senate meetings are almost complete. Only the minutes of the first four sessions, in March 1837, do not list the members present, but that is not too serious an omission, as there were, altogether, 298 meetings up to the end of 1856, and a further 20 before the new Charter took effect in April 1858. Unfortunately, the records of meetings of the faculties of Arts and Medicine have only survived for 1837–9, and those of the Faculty of Law for 1837–43. The faculties were, effectively, standing committees of the Senate and were entirely composed of fellows: the Faculty of Arts was a Committee of the Whole, with 38 members. The faculties of Law and Medicine were each limited to those who were professionally involved in law or medicine, plus a small number of other senators chosen by the parent body. Medicine was 25 strong, but Law had only ten members. What is available is the record of 68 meetings of the Faculty of Arts, 77 of the Faculty of Medicine, and 12 of the Faculty of Law – the lawyers being far less addicted to coming together, formally, than their colleagues in arts and medicine.[1]

More fortunately, we have the records of most of the *ad hoc* committees. There are minutes of 156 meetings of 46 committees, of which four were Committees of the Whole on fundamental constitutional matters, while the others varied in size from four to twenty-one members, and were concerned with a wide range of topics, from abstruse legislative and examination problems, to the appropriate salary for the Registrar, to the arrangements for Presentation Day. These *ad hoc* committee minutes are spread over the whole twenty years, with a gap only in the early 1850s. They are, therefore, almost a complete record of committee activities other than those of the faculties. Regrettably, the records of one or two particularly crucial meetings are missing.

While it is disappointing that the faculty records are so restricted, what is available overall – minutes of over 600 meetings – constitutes a body of information about attendance at the full Senate and its standing and *ad hoc* committees whose patterns are unlikely to be more than marginally distorted by its incompleteness. That judgement is supported in part by the fact that a high proportion of the senators served throughout the twenty years and in part because a careful survey reveals a clear similarity in the diligence with which members of the Senate applied themselves by attending full Senate meetings, faculty meetings and other committee sessions. Moreover, the records of the first few, extremely busy, years are complete, and the patterns of attending then established can be seen to have survived, only marginally changed, throughout the period under review.

The possibility has to be faced that the mere figures of a person's attendance at meetings can be misleading. A board member with an impeccable record might in practice be a lightweight whose opinions counted for nothing, while the personal influence of someone who turned up only on rare occasions could have been always significant. And absentee members could still be important formulators of opinion by correspondence or through informal consultation. Nonetheless, over a period of twenty years, as the membership of the Senate was relatively stable, the overall pattern of attendance must be given due weight – it must certainly show who carried the main formal burden of the day, and whose contributions were minimal.

In an established English university there is no expectation that the Chancellor will be continuously and closely involved in the normal routine of the institution. He or she is a ceremonial figure whose special qualities are to be kept in reserve, as it were, for those hopefully rare episodes when argument with Government, or public controversy, or exceptional internal difficulty, call for an authoritative, independent exercise of negotiation, adjudication or conciliation. Such confidential influence is expected of those prestigious and experienced public figures who tend to become chancellors.

The second Earl of Burlington was not to enjoy such a relatively detached role during the first years of the new University of London, though by the early 1840s the character of the institution's life was beginning to produce and maintain the conditions in which the traditional expectations of a chancellor would apply. From 1836 until 1840, however, Burlington was – with some lengthy intervals - closely involved in the sometimes tumultuous in-fighting which accompanied the establishment of the University as a working organization. At the outset, almost alone, he had to tackle the most basic relations between the University, the Treasury and the Home Office; and subsequently he was the most important single channel of communication on various knotty problems between the Senate and the ministers.

At the same time, Burlington was a large and conscientious land-owner, and spent much of the year at Holker Hall, his home near Kendal, some 250 miles from London. He attended the Lords during the Parliamentary session, but liked to leave London as soon as possible. His marriage to Blanche Howard, a daughter of the sixth Earl of Carlisle, had brought him close to the society of Castle Howard. He was, and always was to be, much concerned with the affairs of the north of England.

From the outset until the middle of July 1838, Burlington presided at most of the meetings of Senate and threw himself whole-heartedly into tackling the problems of the University. On 14 July 1838 he left England with his family for the Continent. Some weeks later, at Baden, one of his sons became seriously ill, and Burlington, partly acting on the advice of Sir James Clark, decided to spend the winter months in Italy. He did not return to England until the following June. In the interim he had almost no contact with the University, and certainly took no part in the current complex business, which was handled by the Vice-Chancellor, John William Lubbock.

By the middle of 1839, when Burlington resumed his attendance at the Senate, the examination system had been inaugurated and Lubbock had a firm hand on the proceedings. The process of relieving the Chancellor of much of the detailed work had probably been advanced by Burlington's absence. The Chancellor presided at most of the meetings in late June and July 1839, but headed north for the rest of the year. He attended all the meetings in early 1840, and in March turned down a confidential approach from Cambridge to consider becoming Chancellor there.[2] Only a few weeks later, he suffered the greatest tragedy of his personal life when his wife died, leaving him a widower with young children at the age of only 32. It was an appalling blow to him. Throughout the following twelve months he kept in touch with Lubbock mainly by correspondence, but he was not keen to be in London, and he did not appear again at the Senate until May 1841.

Thereafter, Burlington rarely presided at as many as half the much reduced number of Senate meetings each year, though he ungrudgingly gave his attention to those matters of business which inevitably involved a call on the Chancellor's attention. Lubbock gave up the Vice-Chancellorship in 1842, and there was by then no need or likelihood that the kind of partnership which existed between the two officers in the heady days of 1837–8 would be re-created. And though there were constitutional episodes in which Burlington did his duty during the late 1840s and early 1850s, it is apparent from the absence of comment in his journal that the University was no longer a high priority in his life. Indeed, in June, 1856, he recorded:

> I had several members of the Senate of the London University at dinner - Ld Monteagle, Sir Jas Graham, Macaulay, Bp of St David's, Senior, Sir Jas Clark, Sir Stephen Hammick, Dr Roget, Dr Billing, Dr Arnott, Dr Hodgkin and Mr Walker. I have rather neglected them I fear for some years.[3]

Some weeks afterwards he tendered his resignation to Palmerston, and was out of office by the end of the year, though he continued as a fellow until his death in 1891.

Earl Granville, who succeeded him, sat in the Cabinet as Lord President of the Council during all but the last month of the period from January 1857 to March 1858. Thereafter he served until 1891. In the fifteen months of his service in the period covered in this book, he attended 60 per cent of the Senate meetings, and presided over the last stages of what had been a contentious progress towards constitutional change.

There can be no doubt that John William Lubbock, the first Vice-Chancellor, was a crucially important figure in the early years of the University. Drafted, as we have seen, by Lord John Russell, without consultation, his subsequent devotion fully justified Russell's choice. He was the heir to a baronetcy, to which he succeeded in 1840, and was the eldest son of a banker. He himself combined banking with a serious level of scientific enquiry: he became Treasurer and Vice-President of the Royal Society and, as his extensive correspondence shows, he moved in the highest circles of the scientific establishment. Presumably money was no problem for him, but he must have sacrificed no small amount of his other interests to the calls of the new University, and he did express to Burlington at the end of his term of office that he felt his successor should receive some remuneration. It was not a suggestion which was to receive any early attention, though Burlington was in full agreement and had pressed his opinion on Russell on several occasions.[4]

The first Vice-Chancellor held office from the end of 1836 until June 1842. During that period, his attendance at full Senate meetings and at the Faculty of Arts for the years for which we have records was almost 100 per cent, and his attendance at *ad hoc* committees was almost as good. In Burlington's long absences, he normally presided. When, after five-and-a-half years, he decided to give up the Vice-Chancellorship, the institution was in relatively calm waters – or, perhaps more accurately, was becalmed. By that time, the relationship of the Chancellorship and Vice-Chancellorship was what would be regarded as normal, and the Vice-Chancellor's role as the resident chairman and regular leader was fully accepted.

Lubbock followed Burlington's lead by retaining his membership of the Senate, but after 1842 he appeared only once more at a meeting, and there is no sign from extant manuscript sources that he was ever much more involved in University affairs. His successor, John Shaw Lefevre, came from a very different walk of life – a lawyer, politician and public servant in various guises, he had not been among the most conscientious attenders since his appointment among the original contingent of fellows. When Burlington approached him to take on the Vice-Chancellorship, he demurred and claimed that Nassau Senior had 'strong claims to be chosen.' But Burlington had doubts about the mercurial Senior, and told Lubbock that 'Lefevre would be more likely to attend to the affairs of the University.'[5] That may very well have been a shrewd judgement; but, as it turned out, Shaw Lefevre's service was not so concentrated, and his attendance not as frequent, as that of his predecessor.

Lubbock was a wealthy man, free to use his time as he wished, and he had devoted himself intensively to the University. Shaw Lefevre, when he took over, was the Joint Permanent Secretary to the Board of Trade. He promised Burlington that he would 'make such arrangements as respects my official attendance [at the Board] as will enable me to be present at the meetings of the Senate punctually and regularly, and to perform whatever duties may devolve upon me.'[6]

Given his remarkably busy public career thereafter, it speaks well of the respect in which Shaw Lefevre was held by fellow senators that he was re-elected Vice-Chancellor every session until 1861. From 1842 until March 1858, he attended over 80 per cent of the Senate meetings – a rather remarkable achievement in the light of the other calls on his time. During those years he was involved in one major commission of enquiry after another, sometimes as a single commissioner; he spent much time in Edinburgh on various governmental matters; he fought and lost a parliamentary election for Cambridge University; he moved from the Board of Trade to become Clerk of the Parliaments; and he was an important member of such administrative bodies as the Church Estates Commission and the Civil Service Commission. It was, of course, a different era from that of John Lubbock's tenure, and it is unlikely that a man as occupied with governmental business as Shaw Lefevre was, could have given the effort needed to get the examination system off the ground. The middle 1840s were quiet times for the University and, though the early 1850s brought a long struggle over graduate participation, it took place alongside settled and smoothly working academic procedures. Nonetheless, there was a difference of style as well as of circumstance between the first and second Vice-Chancellorships. Lubbock had been a private citizen with a driving concern to innovate; Shaw Lefevre was from the outset a salaried government servant, shy of publicity, a clever, conscientious and emollient adjudicator and administrator, and essentially a man of Whitehall and Westminster.

We should accept that Burlington and Lubbock from 1837 to 1842, Burlington and Shaw Lefevre from 1842 to 1856, and Granville and Shaw Lefevre in 1857–8, were at the heart of the University's affairs, though Burlington's attendances were, at times, unimpressive. We are left with 23 fellows who, it would appear from the statistics, formed, with the Chancellors and Vice-Chancellors, the working Senate. But six of these 23 fellows, along with Granville, served only in 1857–8, at a time of particular intensity in the University's constitutional context, and their strong attendance increased the 'active' pool beyond the usual level of the preceding 19 years. In fact, for those nineteen years, there were only 17 'active' fellows, and even that figure exaggerates attendance at any particular time.

We can divide the 17 in two ways – between those who appeared at from one third to two thirds of the Senate meetings during their membership, and those who were much more regular; and between the medical and non-medical fellows. It is also as well to take some note of attendance at different periods: 294 Senate meetings were held between April 1837 and the end of 1856, for which attendance records were kept. At almost two thirds of the meetings, only between six and 11 members were present; ninety-six meetings attracted between 12 and 17; only sixteen meetings were attended by 18 or more senators, and the largest turn-out was 26. But, despite the big proportion of small turnouts, the actual combination of members at each meeting was rarely the same. This encouraged a tendency, especially in the early years, for one meeting's work to be undone by the next, and this, in turn, annoyed and discouraged some senators.[7]

Most of the serious attenders were in office throughout, and a few who were not much involved at first made up their overall averages by greatly increased attendances in the 1840s and 1850s; while a couple of others started very strongly but fell away markedly in the later years of the period. And it is clear that attendance at the two years of faculty meetings which are recorded, and at *ad hoc* committee meetings throughout the period reviewed, does not alter the allocation of fellows to the categories of more or fewer attenders.

Because of the considerable variations in the size of turn-out in different periods, and because of the deaths of two especially loyal fellows – John Sims in 1838, and J.H. Jerrard in 1853 – the actual pool of active members of the Senate, excluding the Chancellor and Vice-Chancellor, at any one time before 1857 was only 14 or 15 strong.

From 1837 to the end of 1856, of the 17 active fellows, no less than ten were medical men. This was indicative less of medical dominance of the University – though there was some early concern about such a possibility[8] – than of the innate professional separatism of the doctors and, perhaps, their keenness to keep a watch on each other. Some of them had wanted a Faculty of Medicine exclusively manned by doctors, but that was defeated.[9] Nonetheless, in practice those who wanted to operate as a closed group were almost fully successful, if the extant records of the faculty's meetings for 1837–9 can be taken as typical of later years. Formally, the faculty was composed of all the medical men, plus four scientists, together with the Chancellor and Vice-Chancellor (both, initially, men of science), two bishops, one lawyer and the classicist, J.H. Jerrard. After the inaugural meeting, the Chancellor came only once more, while the Vice-Chancellor made very occasional appearances: the bishops never attended. Only Jerrard of the non-medical members went along regularly.

But the medical men did not confine themselves to their own faculty and to the Senate. They were full members of the Faculty of Arts, which was a committee of the whole senate, and they attended its meetings almost as much as they attended the meetings of the Senate itself. They were not represented, however, in the small Faculty of Laws. But they were more conscientious than any other category of senators: among the 28 poor attenders described earlier, only seven were doctors; and among the fellows who were present at more than half the meetings held during their tenures, six were medical.

The effects of so much built-in medical strength should not be overstressed. In a very important sense, it was not particularly relevant to the main internal controversies, which were not primarily concerned with arts/laws/medicine/science splits: some of the arguments, related to religious convictions, divided the medical men as much as the others, and most disputes were about constitutional and administrative, rather than disciplinary questions. Additionally, there were some very practical aspects of turn-out which dilute any notion of a Senate subjected to consistent medical steamrollering. Doctors' attendance was often of an uncertain and fragmented nature. When the first Vice-Chancellor resigned, the Chancellor told his successor that it was no good appointing a doctor to the post because of the likelihood that he would be called out of meetings to meet professional emergencies.[10]

Of the seventeen seriously attendant fellows, pre-1857, the non-medical contingent of seven included George Grote and Lord Overstone, whose service began only in 1850. Those who belonged to the original Senate were Henry Warburton; two professional scientists, Michael Faraday and William Thomas Brande; the Cambridge classics don, J.H. Jerrard; and the lawyer, political scientist and economist, Nassau Senior. The ten medical men were Arnott, Bacot, Billing, Clark, Hammick, Hodgkin, Kiernan, Ridout, Roget and Sims. But the 17 were also divisible into two different groupings.

Ten of the seventeen came to between one third and two thirds of Senate meetings, and all but one of them – Lord Overstone – served throughout the twenty years. Those ten men constituted what might be thought of as an outer ring of the working Senate: at an average meeting, two or three of them would be present, but not often the same two or three, and there was no discernible pattern to their appearances.

The remaining seven formed an inner core of regulars. Their individual attendances ranged from 71 per cent to 92 per cent. Four of them served throughout: one of them, John Sims, died in July 1838; George Grote only joined in 1850; and J.H. Jerrard, who was in at the start, died early in 1853. Thus the inner core was only five strong between the middle of 1838 and the beginning of 1850, and only six strong for the last three years of the period.

It is also interesting to consider the make-up of the outer ring and the inner core in terms of medical and non-medical members. Six of the ten medical men were in the outer ring, and all served from the beginning – Neil Arnott, John Bacot, Sir James Clark, Thomas Hodgkin, John Ridout and Peter Mark Roget. They were joined by four non-medical people, three of whom - the two scientists, William Thomas Brande and

Michael Faraday, and Nassau Senior – served throughout; the fourth was Lord Overstone, who was a senator from 1850. The doctors in the inner core were Archibald Billing, Sir Stephen Love Hammick, Francis Kiernan and, until his untimely death in 1838 at the age of forty-six, John Sims. Of the non-medical trio, only Henry Warburton, MP, served throughout; J.H. Jerrard died in February, 1853; George Grote joined the Senate in 1850.

If one is looking for the *apparatchiks* of the University of London in its early years, then they must belong to this group, and one must point in particular to Billing and Hammick, whose attendances over twenty years were, respectively, 83 per cent and 82 per cent; but even more confidently to J.H. Jerrard and Francis Kiernan, without whom any meeting must have seemed odd, and who turned out for 87 per cent and 92 per cent, respectively, of the Senate's sessions.

For the sake of completeness, one can add to this analysis of the 1837–56 period, a special comment on the months between January 1857 and March 1858. Of those who only joined in 1857–8, James Heywood, Sir Edward Ryan and Lord Stanley would take their places in the outer ring: William Withey Gull, Frederick John Wood and Charles James Foster in the inner core – but Foster, though he had been a formidable figure in University affairs prior to his joining the Senate, was only present at the two meetings which occurred between his appointment in February 1858 and the end of March. But in this last fifteen months, the attendance of three medical fellows – Bacot, Ridout and Roget, dropped considerably, while Lord Monteagle, spurred on by the intricacies of forthcoming constitutional change, appeared much more frequently than before.

From the attendance statistics, therefore, we now have the men who can be said to have been the active senators, responsible for the overall running of the fledgling University. Before making any final judgement, however, it is as well to remember that the original concept of the University was as a group of examiners. It is desirable to look at the senators who became examiners, and at those men who were appointed from outside the Senate, to see whether their work as examiners makes it necessary to add any names to those already listed as having influenced significantly the shaping of the new institution.

The records of who were appointed to be examiners, the minutes of examiners' meetings and the examiners' reports are, fortunately, almost fully preserved.[11] They augment and complicate the story. There were never more than 24 positions as examiners, save in Law where several additional examiners were appointed occasionally for single papers and the LL D. The regular posts were filled, over these years, by 41 men.

The propriety of having senatorial examiners was a matter of political dispute from the beginning, and the course of that dispute will be described in later chapters. In practice, it was quickly established that, while all examiners had to be elected, if fellows wanted to be examiners, they were always chosen or re-chosen, and fellows never competed with each other. No limit was put on the tenure of examiners. Posts not filled by fellows were advertised and, at the outset, each of the eleven vacancies attracted, on average, over eight candidates. But subsequently, competition was very limited. Once filled, annual re-election of the incumbents was very usual. In many cases, after the early years, very few men, and often none but the sitting examiners, put themselves forward. From 1840 to the end of the period, only a half dozen elections attracted more than five candidates, and those followed the resignations or deaths of previous examiners.

Only twelve fellows were examiners, not counting Amos and Shaw Lefevre: the latter gave a helping hand with law papers in 1842 and 1843, and Amos did a similar stint in 1843 and 1845. And four of the twelve served as examiners for only one to three sessions, all finishing their contributions by the end of 1841. Three served, respectively, for six, thirteen and fourteen years; and the remaining five were examiners from their initial appointments, in 1838 and 1839, for the subsequent eighteen or nineteen years – and then beyond the end of the period of this study. Three of the longest serving senatorial examiners were medical men, and a fourth a scientist who examined for both the Arts and Medical faculties. At no time were there fewer than five fellows actively engaged in examining – just over a quarter of the whole body of examiners needed in each year.

More than two thirds of the examiners, therefore, were not members of the Senate. Six lawyers were appointed from time to time on a sessional basis, to assist the single examiner in Law and Jurisprudence with specialist papers and LL D. candidates. Excluding them, thirty non-senatorial examiners were appointed during the years from 1839 until 1858.

Of these thirty, only one examined in Law. Eleven examined only for the medical degrees in Medicine; Surgery; Anatomy and Physiology; Physiology and Comparative Anatomy; Midwifery and Diseases of Women and Infants; and Materia Medica and Pharmacy. Four examined for the BA, MA, and medical degrees in Chemistry, Physiology and Zoology. The remaining fourteen covered the Matriculation, BA, and MA examinations in Classics; Moral Philosophy; Mathematics; Chemistry; French; German; Political Economy; and the optional papers in Hebrew and Greek Texts and Scriptural History.

As with the senators, the additional examiners gave very varied service. Nine of them were in office for four or fewer years – three of them at the beginning of the period, and the other six for short periods at the end. Another nine each put in between five and ten years. Three served throughout the period and nine others were examiners for periods exceeding eleven years. This distribution of service was roughly the same in both the medical and non-medical areas.

Examiners in charge of subjects uninterruptedly, over long periods of years, can fairly be supposed to have left some imprint on the content of what was taught. Whether such influence was intellectually sophisticated and enlightened or, at worst, a cause of distortion or inertia, or both, must be left to the historians of the subjects. But some such influence must have been exercised by the individuals, or very small groups, who dominated the lists of examiners between 1838 and 1858 – and some of those examiners went on for a few years beyond 1858. In order to suggest the men who were likely to have contributed most, in the context of examinations, it is as well to merge the senatorial and the non-senatorial office-holders.

It was for the medical degrees that the concentration of responsibility was most marked. Archibald Billing, a senator, and Alexander Tweedie, shared the examining in Medicine for all but one of the eighteen years of our period. Sir Stephen Love Hammick was examiner in Surgery for the same spell, and for the first six shared his responsibility with John Bacot – both were senators. Francis Kiernan, a senator, and William Sharpey, were together from 1840 to 1858 as examiners in Anatomy and Physiology. Edward Rigby took over from Charles Locock, a senator, as examiner in Midwifery and Diseases of Women and Infants in 1841, and retained the post until 1858. Jonathan Pereira was examiner in Materia Medica and Pharmacy from 1839 until 1852. John Frederick Daniell, Professor of Chemistry at King's College, who was a contender for the first Registrarship of the University, and William Thomas Brande, a senator, were the first examiners in Chemistry: Daniell died in 1845 and Brande, who had examined only for the BA in 1839, served the Medical Faculty for the rest of the period. Professor Henslow of Cambridge, a senator, was the sole examiner in Botany throughout - as, indeed, he was for Natural History in the BA degree.

Thus eight – or perhaps ten – men dominated the examining process for the medical degrees. There were, by contrast, only three regular examiners in Law, and only one of them was in office at a time. William Empson, a senator, served for only two sessions: his successor, John Thomas Graves, examined from 1841 to 1847; and then came Nassau Senior, a senator, who added Law in the LL B to his original, sole and long-standing responsibility for Political Economy in the BA degree.

Henslow's and Senior's contributions to the BA have already been mentioned. Daniell also doubled for the BA and medical degrees in Chemistry; he was succeeded for the BA by Thomas Graham, and then by Robert Dundas Thompson. Classics, Logic and Moral Philosophy were the preserve for most of the period of J.H. Jerrard, Senator; Thomas Borrow Burcham, Fellow of Trinity College, Cambridge; and the Rev Henry Alford, another Trinity fellow, later to be Dean of Canterbury. In the last five years, William Smith, Alexander Bain and Thomas Spencer Baynes took their places. G.B. Jerrard, brother of the classicist, was throughout an examiner in Mathematics, sharing for thirteen years with J.W.L. Heaviside, who taught at Haileybury and was a serious rival of William Benjamin Carpenter for the Registrarship of the University after Rothman's death in 1856. Carpenter himself was an examiner in Zoology from 1847 until 1856.

French was entrusted throughout the period to Charles Jean Delille, who taught the language at several London public schools. The first examiner in German was the Rev Dr Frederick Bialloblotzky, a scholarly but somewhat theologically controversial Lutheran from Hamburg, who taught at the City of London School. In 1848 he felt the call to undertake missionary work in East Africa and to seek the source of the Nile. He departed without notice, and simply wrote nominating a substitute examiner. For this the University dismissed him, and as his attempt to reach Mombasa was foiled by official obstruction in Zanzibar, he had to abandon his venture.[12]

The highly controversial examination in Hebrew and Greek Texts and Scriptural History, of which more later, was organized and marked by two clergymen. The Rev William Drake, who served from 1840 to 1860, had been a fellow of St John's, Cambridge and at the time of his appointment was Master of the Collegiate School, Leicester. The Rev Thomas Stone, who shared the duty for the first ten years, was the curate of St John's, Westminster.

As in the case of medicine, therefore, about ten men were prominent in the examinations for the arts and law degrees.

Of the non-senatorial examiners overall, those who have been listed by name must have had substantial influence on the shaping and conduct of their subject examinations and therefore on the teaching of those subjects in the affiliated colleges. But, in terms of influence on the major policies and decisions of the University of London, one must have strong doubts about all save, perhaps, a very few of them. There is practically no written evidence on which to base any assessment, and the absence of faculty minutes is particularly regrettable. But, because of the increasingly close knit nature of the medical world, and their long tenure of examinerships, it is possible that Alexander Tweedie, William Sharpey, Edward Rigby and Jonathan Pereira would have been heavily involved in the development of medical attitudes which would, in due course, be reflected in policy positions taken up by the medical senators. Despite the long service put in by several of the arts examiners, however, there is nothing to suggest that their influence extended beyond the limits of their narrow subject concerns. At the same time, it might be felt likely that of all the non-senatorial examiners, Daniell, Carpenter and Heaviside, as contenders for the Registrarship, must have been readily recognizable as active academic politicians.

So far as the twelve senatorial examiners are concerned, six were medical – Bacot, Billing, Hammick, Kiernan, Locock and Roget; two examined in Law – Empson and Senior; two were scientists – Brande and Henslow; and two were classicists – Jerrard and Thirlwall. Of these, Locock, Empson and Thirlwall all served as examiners for only the session 1839–40, and were poor attenders at the Senate: Henslow was a prominent and long-serving examiner, but took very little part as a member of the governing body. The other eight, however, were all among the conscientious senators: Bacot, Brande, Senior and Roget were within the outer circle, while Jerrard and three medical men – Billing, Hammick and Kiernan, were members of the inner core of attenders. Thus eight of the seventeen fellows who, together with the Chancellor and the two Vice-Chancellors, formed the working Senate from 1837 to 1856, were active and long-serving examiners, and five of them were from the Medical Faculty.

In any established British university today, the senior non-academic administrative officer, whether he be called registrar or secretary, is expected to have the same kind of capacity to oversee a complex organization, and to be able to offer expert advice to the Vice-Chancellor and the governing body on matters of policy, as is expected of a very senior civil servant in a government department. While there will always be argument about exactly how much influence such an official does or should exercise, there is no doubt that the exercise of some such influence is taken for granted.

The first Registrar of the University of London, Richard Wellesley Rothman, was not appointed until early in 1838, and was not involved in the controversies and manoeuvres which had attended the evolution of the institution during most of the two previous years. While his appearance on the scene must have provided enormous relief to Burlington and Lubbock, and enabled much faster progress to be made with the development of the examination system, there is no evidence to enable any assessment to be made of whether, and if so what, influence he brought to bear on major issues of policy which faced the Senate then or, indeed, during the rest of his tenure, which lasted until his death in 1856. As we shall see, he was no laggard in seeking the appointment as Registrar, but nothing in the surviving archives reveals him as a figure of any political stature. Under his supervision the examination system appears to have worked very smoothly, and the numerous volumes of his impeccably copied official correspondence bear witness to a highly competent and professionally discreet administrator, but do nothing to indicate how much his discussions with Chancellor, Vice-Chancellor and fellows were of any real significance for the subsequent policy making of the Senate.

Rothman, however, was primarily a man of some academic standing. He had been a fellow of Trinity College, Cambridge since 1825, and retained that office, becoming a senior fellow in 1843, until his death. He graduated in medicine, but then turned his attention to astronomy and wrote a 'learned and useful . . . *History of Astronomy.*' He was elected a member of the Astronomical Society in January 1830, three of his sponsors being Richard Sheepshanks, John William Lubbock and Charles Babbage. He served on the council of the Society and acted as its foreign secretary in 1840–1, and as its secretary in the following year. He gave up the secretaryship because his official duties made it difficult for him to pay sufficient attention to the Society's affairs.

Rothman must have been in close professional, scientific contact with several of the senior members of the Senate: he was certainly on easy and intimate terms with Lubbock. It is hard to believe that his opinions, both scientific and administrative, had no significance in the affairs of the University. But proof of any significant influence is not to be found in any of the official archives or in the private collections of correspondence available. His obituary in the minutes of the Astronomical Society declares: 'His retiring manners and silent temperament prevented his acquirements from making any show, but those acquirements were sound and extensive, and caused him to be held in high respect by those who knew him well.'[13]

William Benjamin Carpenter, who succeeded Rothman, was in office for only two years before the Charter of 1858 came into effect, and there is nothing to show, in that period, that his administrative capacity was significantly different from Rothman's. Subsequently, and in part no doubt because of the increasing size and visibility of the University, he cut a larger figure, and is credited with having made a greater impact. Comparison, however, would be difficult to make and almost certainly rather unfair to Rothman. Carpenter was a physiologist who had achieved a major professional reputation before becoming Registrar, and had been an examiner for the University since 1847.

During our period, therefore, it is difficult to regard either of the Registrars as important figures in the high politics of the young University of London. One has to suspect, though, that, on occasion at least, they must have given the Senate significant advice, while their efficient administration of an innovative examination system was a major contribution to the University's progress.

Just less than 100 men can be listed as having been, in one capacity or another, on the strength of the University of London during its first two decades of operation. There were 55 members of the Senate, twelve of whom acted, for varying periods, as examiners; 30 non-senatorial examiners, each of whom held office for at least one full session; a few specialist examiners of Law candidates, engaged only occasionally; two Registrars; a Clerk of the Senate – Mr Moore, the earliest employee; and a minimal number of porters, messengers, etc. But on the not insubstantial evidence available, it can be claimed with some confidence that the power, influence, responsibility and effort involved in establishing and consolidating the University as a working institution were exercised, overwhelmingly, by only 27 senators over the whole period, and by only 16 to 18 in the years before 1857.

In fact, in this context, the years from 1837 until 1858 fell into four periods. In each of them the most dominant people comprised a small, continuing core, together with one or two men who were equally regular

Table 1   The Working Senate

	Apr 1837 –Jul 1842	Jul 1842 –Mar 1850	Mar 1850 –Dec 1856	Jan 1857 –Mar 1858
Chan	Burlington	Burlington	Burlington	Granville
VC	Lubbock	Shaw Lefevre	Shaw Lefevre	Shaw Lefevre
INNER CORE				
Med	* Billing	* Billing	* Billing	* Billing
	* Hammick	* Hammick	* Hammick	* Hammick
	* Kiernan	* Kiernan	* Kiernan	* Kiernan
	Sims (to 1838)			
Non-Med	Warburton	Warburton	Warburton	Warburton
	* Jerrard	* Jerrard	* Jerrard (to 1853)	
			Grote	Grote
				Gull
				Wood
OUTER RING				
Med	Arnott	Arnott	Arnott	Arnott
	* Bacot	* Bacot	Bacot	
	Clark	Clark	Clark	Clark
	Hodgkin	Hodgkin	Hodgkin	Hodgkin
	Ridout	Ridout	Ridout	
	* Roget	Roget	Roget	
Non-Med	* Brande	* Brande	* Brande	* Brande
	Faraday	Faraday	Faraday	Faraday
	* Senior	* Senior	* Senior	* Senior
			Overstone	Overstone
				Monteagle
				Heywood
				Ryan
				Stanley

* = Examiner

in their attendance but who served for only part of one or more of the periods; and a slightly larger group whose attendance was not so constant but was always sufficient to ensure that its members were serious contributors to the work of the Senate. This pattern of service is shown as concisely as possible in Table I.

CHAPTER 7

Curriculum, Registrar, Charter

Most university teachers today would approach the task of framing a complete syllabus in their own discipline with both excitement and some apprehension. The personal vision would excite; the prospect of near endless argument would cause the apprehension. How much more exciting, and how much more bewildering, must have seemed the potential role of a new fellow of the University of London – to share responsibility for choosing what should be included in an entirely new curriculum suited to a new stratum of candidates for higher education. Only theology was to be excluded as a subject of examination.

There was, of course, no likelihood that what would come out of the exercise would exclude much of what was already taught elsewhere, saving theology – no small omission in the 1830s. Those who were involved had mostly been raised in the Oxbridge tradition, and a considerable proportion of the medical contingent had been trained in Scotland or Ireland and had experience of medical practice in Germany or France. But what they produced, in addition to an easily recognizable core of work in classics and mathematics, were some significant newcomers - the physical sciences, modern languages, and history – which made the degree scheme, in Professor Thompson's opinion, 'an innovation of outstanding audacity.'[1] And this more comprehensive curriculum was imposed, with no corresponding responsibility for teaching it, but only through an orderly series of examinations – for Matriculation, Bachelors', Masters' and Doctors' degrees, with appropriate distinctions of pass and honours.

Even if it were possible, it would be unforgiveably tedious to record the detail of the continuous and sometimes fractious discussion and correspondence which went into the production of the first examination syllabuses and regulations. Nor was there anything odd to comment on in the structure of the process itself – the usage of committees and sub-committees, the references backwards and forwards, and the submittal of final proposals to the full Senate, are wholly familiar to modern practitioners. The one unusual, ultimate requirement, the seeking of the approval of the Government, rarely raised any real difficulties.

What can be done, though, is to illustrate, first, so far as the archival material allows, the main lines of what was an extremely intensive exercise stretching over nearly two years, and to give credit to those who can be identified as having borne the major burdens of the day. Having done that, we should turn to a close examination of several major controversies and crises in the early life of the University which were experienced alongside, and to no small extent impinged upon, the exercise of creating its initial academic programmes.

If one looks for an early protagonist of a wider coverage of human knowledge in degree courses than was being provided in existing English universities, Nassau Senior is a candidate. He wrote, in an untidy scrawl, to Spring Rice, on accepting a place on the Senate:

> Will your Charter designate what are to be the studies called Arts and Law? I should try to have Political Economy included in Arts and real English practical law in law.
>
> I wish it were possible to re-arrange the heads of knowledge instead of these antiquated divisions so as to have distinct heads of
>> Pure Science – some by numbers [*sic*]
>> Physical Sciences – Geography, Geology, Chemistry, Mechanics, Optics, Natural History, Medicine, Surgery, etc.
>> Moral Science – Aesthetics – Poetics, Rhetoric
>>> Ethics – Morals, Jurisprudence, Pol. Economy
>> Intellectual Science – Logic, Metaphysics
>>> History, Law
>
> I do not mean that these should be good divisions – but merely as samples – of these heads Oxford and Cambridge give degrees in only one or two – could not the Royal University give degrees in all?[2]

The only comparable statement of any length which has survived is a long letter from Arnold, sent to Burlington for consideration by the Faculty of Arts because of Arnold's inability to attend a meeting - an inability which was very frequent, but which did not prevent the Headmaster of Rugby being at the heart of much early controversy in the University of London. The letter is interesting not merely because what Arnold proposed as the main content of degree examination requirements was largely accepted, but because it raised at the outset a basic question about matriculation.[3]

Arnold placed what he saw as the desirable offerings of the new

University in a context bounded by the practices of Oxford and Cambridge and the English public schools.

> Supposing us, then, to arrange our Examinations without considering the actual plan of study pursued at any other place, but merely on our own views of what is most desirable, it seems to me that at present we must be like a University without Undergraduates: that is, that the passing our Examination for the Degree of B.A. should be our act of matriculation; that this Examination should therefore be imperative on every one who comes to us, and that then it should be open to every man according to his own views, to go on either to a Degree in Law or Medicine, or to the higher Degree of Master of Arts; thus placing the Bachelors in Laws and Medicine on the same level with the Masters of Arts, according to the practice of the old Universities.
>
> If this be agreed to, it would follow that our Examination for the Degree of B.A. should not be more severe than persons of eighteen or nineteen may fairly be expected to pass. But then I would take a high standard of the capabilities of persons of such an age; that is, I would suppose them to have been well taught and to have taken fair pains: in short, I would take my standard from the highest classes of our present public schools; and would thus fix it higher than it is practically fixed for matriculation at Oxford at present, or I believe at Cambridge.

Thus Arnold seemed to be suggesting that the London BA should in effect be a school leaving qualification of a standard similar to that achieved by the best products of the public schools, and higher than the standard required for entry to Oxford and Cambridge. But it is clear that he did not expect a London BA to be the equivalent of an Oxbridge first degree. He seemed to envisage it, later in his argument, as intermediate between the best level of public school leaving achievement and the BA of the ancient universities. After outlining his notion of what the examination of a London BA should comprise, he went on:

> I would wish it to be remembered that what I have been here suggesting is merely the minimum to be required at matriculation. I have been also considering, as far as possible, that strong desire amongst professional men, that the strictly professional part of education should be begun early, in order to set a young man forward betimes on his particular career. It will be seen that, according to this plan, a young man *may* commence his professional studies immediately after his matriculation, that is, at the age when

he would naturally be leaving school. But I should be very sorry that any one should suppose that I think this the most desirable plan, or that I could propose it under any circumstances, unless the examination for the subsequent Degree, whether in Arts, Law, or Medicine, were to be made thoroughly efficient; and unless, even at our B.A. Examination, we showed by our system of classes and distinctions that we made a wide difference between the minimum that we would allow to enter amongst us and the proficiency which we deemed worthy of encouragement or reward. Our Master of Arts Degree must be what the B.A. Degree is at Oxford and Cambridge, the great object in a man's academical career, without gaining which no man can be considered to have gone through the University.

That those members of the Faculty of Arts who attended when Arnold's letter was presented (and it should be remembered that the Faculty was a committee of the whole senate) were not entirely happy with Arnold's structural proposals can be gathered from the fact that they resolved only on that occasion that 'a certain knowledge of Classics and Mathematics shall be an indispensable condition for the Degree of Bachelor of Arts.' But the idea of not having a separate matriculation examination must have been viewed with some concern and even alarm, for, on Empson's initiative, an immediate reference was made to the law officers of the Crown, for an opinion as to whether the Charter gave the University power to institute such an examination. An unequivocal opinion was delivered on 13 June 1837, stating that 'the Senate has full power to institute an intermediate examination, and to make the having passed at that examination an indispensable qualification for being admitted to the final examination on which the degree is to be granted.'

If there was much subsequent argument over whether or not to have a matriculation examination, it is not apparent from the minutes or from correspondence. A firm proposal that there should be a 'Previous Examination' was carried without division in a crucial committee in July, and the matter was settled in the spring of 1838, when the general circumstances of entry to the BA called for candidates to have passed a matriculation examination when they were at least 16 years of age, and to produce a certificate confirming that they had subsequently attended a course of study for two years at an approved institution. Thus, formally, it would have been quite possible for a young man to take his London BA in his 19th year. Readers of *Tom Brown's Schooldays* will remember that Tom, in the late 1830s, went from Rugby to begin his studies at Oxford at just that age.

The possible discrepancy did not go unremarked. Augustus de Morgan, the UCL mathematician, looking forward, in 1837, wrote: 'In all probability, the students who seek degrees in the University of London will be younger than those who go to Oxford and Cambridge, by perhaps a couple of years; an important difference at their time of life.'[4] But, in practice, the 16-year-old matriculants failed to materialize. Full statistics were compiled, and show that betwen 1838 and 1854 the average age of candidates for matriculation was never lower than 17 years and 11 months, and reached in one year 21 years 1 month. During the 1840s the average age of BA candidates ranged from 20 years 9 months to 23 years. London and Oxbridge were, in this respect, quite similar.

That London was willing to learn from elsewhere was clear from the suggestion, readily accepted by the Government, that the Foreign Office should ask for details of the constitutions and practices of some European universities. The exercise produced data from over twenty universities in France, Belgium, Holland, Russia, Prussia, Austria, Italy and Denmark. At least three analyses of the reports were commissioned, covering the Code Universitaire of France, and statutes of the Universities of Gottingen and Bonn. There is no record of any reference to them in Senate reports and debates, and it may well be that the influence of foreign example was rather marginal.[5]

The content of the BA was decided, with one notable exception, without major controversy. It is worth comparing Arnold's original scheme with Nassau Senior's ideas, thus giving some flavour of contemporary thinking, and then to describe the final outcome. Arnold suggested that:

> the minimum required for . . . the . . . B.A. would . . . be as follows:
> 1. A certain amount of Physical Science, all details of which I leave entirely to others. 2. The Elements of Euclid and Logic. 3. Some one Greek and some one Roman writer 'melioris aevi et notae.' 4. Some one treatise or work on Moral Philosophy, together with some one History or work of Poetry, to be taken from a list to be drawn up by the University. In point of fact, however, I would always require three books, as thus: If a candidate were to bring up, for instance, Cicero de Officiis and Homer, they might serve at once for his Philology and for his Moral Philosophy and Poetry. But then I would oblige him to take up some one work of History from our list, in the matter of which he should be examined in detail: but it might be an English history just

as well as a Greek or Latin one. The Poetry must of course be always read in a foreign language: an examination in an English poet would be absurd and impracticable. To these four things I would almost beyond all the rest add and insist upon, – 5. 'Exercises in Translation and in Composition.'

In the end, the matriculation examination comprised compulsory papers in Classics, Mathematics, Natural Philosophy and one of Chemistry, Botany or Zoology. The BA demanded the same width of subject matter. Again there were four compulsory subjects: Classics, which involved not only classic texts in Greek and Roman history, but also history of England to the end of the seventeenth century, and translation from and into either French or German; Logic and Moral Philosophy; Mathematics and Natural Philosophy, which included some mechanics, hydrostatics, hydraulics, pneumatics and astronomy; and Chemistry, Animal and Vegetable Physiology and Structural Botany. Thus, with the possible exception of French and German, the reality was extremely close to Arnold's plan of May 1837.

But, before there was agreement, there was an inevitable jostling for available space, and all parties were obliged to reduce some of their ambitions in order to produce an acceptable load. In Classics, at least, some of what was originally intended to be part of the BA syllabus was transferred to the Master's programme. But, outside the question of content, there were other struggles. A division of opinion about whether or not to restrict the whole examination procedure to the taking of printed papers was settled in favour of such restriction. There was considerable discussion about the desirability of giving Certificates of Proficiency in particular subjects to persons who had not taken a Bachelor's degree either at London or elsewhere. The Vice-Chancellor and Warburton were particularly desirous of allowing non-graduates to be eligible to sit for certificates. Warburton claimed that he had tried, unsuccessfully, to have such a power included in the Charter. Lubbock was especially keen to introduce certificates in navigation for sea captains – an interesting concern for the availability of more specialized vocational qualifications. But Airy, at least, was hostile to the idea, and counsel's opinion was that the University could only offer Certificates of Proficiency to graduates.[6]

Whatever debate there was within the small group of lawyers must have been conducted almost entirely privately, for the Faculty of Law met only three times in the first two years, and produced an examination syllabus which was accepted, formally, without challenge. Only candidates with a BA degree were eligible to take the LL B, and they had to be not less than 20 years of age.

In contrast, the Faculty of Medicine conducted a more intensive enquiry into what should be required of candidates than did the Faculty of Arts. The progress of that enquiry was seriously delayed because of controversies over the presence of Dr Somerville and over the question of payment of a Dean, to be described later. Unlike the lawyers, however, the medical men lived up to Arnold's view of professional people wanting to begin professional education early. The Faculty was not willing to limit entry to medical education to those who already had a BA degree, though such candidates would be welcome. It was agreed that some general educational qualification should be required of entrants to the MB examinations, and for many months a special examination in Arts for medical students was canvassed. But it became evident that there was substantial overlap with the matriculation syllabus agreed for BA candidates, and doubts were expressed as to the desirability of distinguishing between medical students and others. Augustus de Morgan advised Lubbock that the matriculation examination for prospective BA candidates was

> quite difficult enough, and probably a little too difficult. This being the case, even for youths educated at the best schools, I should be afraid that any addition would be found impracticable in the case of Medical Students, whose education has been hitherto, I believe, rather below than above the average, taking the whole body.[7]

Eventually, after much manoeuvring, and at the suggestion first of Cornwallis Hewett and then of Henry Warburton, the matriculation syllabus was slightly modified and accepted for candidates for both Arts and Medicine. Beginning medical students had to be at least 18 years of age, and for the London medical schools, Matriculation was the first 'defined general educational standard' required prior to embarking on the course of study.[8]

We have already quoted Thomas Arnold's view that without the BA at Oxford or Cambridge 'no man can be considered to have gone through the University,' and his suggestion that the equivalent for London should be the achievement of the MA, leaving the BA as a kind of matriculation. George Airy believed that having a BA degree was the indispensable mark of an educated gentleman and the essential starting point for professional studies and qualifications. Neither view represented what came out of the two-year-long negotiations for the first London degrees. Matriculation was, presumably, set at a lower level than Arnold had in mind for his BA *qua* matriculation, though the new BA was to be nearer the Oxbridge first degree level than he had anticipated. Matriculation was to be the universal basis for all London examinations, and Airy's idea that the BA should be demanded for all further professional study was put aside for medicine, though not for law.

When the different ages of candidacy, and the absence of compulsory examinations in theology, are taken together with the new content and structure of the London examination system, it is fair and accurate to consider that system *sui generis*. It was also regarded, by many experienced academics who were consulted, as probably too tough. Among several who demurred at one stage or another were the chemist, Daniell, from King's College London; G.W. Peacock, from Cambridge, who told Lubbock that the scheme was 'too extensive but . . . is a most creditable selection of subjects'; and de Morgan, from UCL, who admitted that his fear throughout had been

> that the University men on the Senate will mistake the character of the probable aspirants for degrees, and will apply maxims which, though true of the students at Oxford and Cambridge, will not apply to the heterogeneous compound which they have to deal with.[9]

The statistical treatment of attendance given in previous chapters is perhaps more readily assimilated and appreciated when we look at the concentrated effort put in by fellows during these two years of close involvement in producing the first examination syllabuses and regulations. For matriculation and the BA, the Faculty of Arts was the main workshop and was, of course, a Committee of the Whole Senate. Much use was made of other committees and sub-committees, and it is almost certain that a lot of the detailed work entailed correspondence and informal gatherings, only a small proportion of which is reflected in surviving documents. The smaller Faculty of Medicine used very few committees, and the attendances are almost certainly indicative of which fellows carried the intricate discussions of syllabus proposals.[10]

Because the Matriculation and BA examinations covered so wide a range of subjects, the scientists and medicos were as much involved as the lawyers and humanities people. The medical syllabuses were much more specialized but, even there, one member of the non-medical fraternity – Jerrard – was a constant attender at meetings. Interestingly enough, the scientists in the Faculty of Medicine appeared to take little part in discussions of the medical syllabuses. At one crucial stage, the drafting of the basic scheme of examination for the MB was carried by Arnott, Clark, Kiernan and Sims, a quartet not necessarily always in harmony.

But, in general, because there was so much essential give and take in the whole exercise, and because the same group of senators tended to turn up in initiatory and in subsequent mediatory committees, it is as well simply to list those who shared the detailed, heavy, constant work. The honours must go to the Vice-Chancellor, Kiernan, Jerrard, Billing, Arnott, Hammick, Clark, Warburton, Roget, Ridout and Sims. At a more modest level would come the Chancellor, Bacot, Faraday and Locock. Several others contributed in special areas, and by letters, and the lawyers were a small and unhurried group. The main burden, though, was undoubtedly taken by the first eleven men listed; eight of them were medical professionals, Warburton was heavily medically-oriented, Lubbock was a scientist; only Jerrard represented the humanities.

George Airy was largely a non-attender, but a good correspondent, and took no small part in arguing with Lubbock, particularly, about the BA syllabus, and in putting together the examination regulations for hydrography, navigation and civil engineering. He was an impatient man, very ready to take exception to human failings, and his comments are therefore perhaps doubtfully representative. But he was unsparing of confusion, and his outburst when faced with the idea of having, at a late stage, to change the matriculation syllabus to take account of medical wishes, gives a vivid impression of the atmosphere of weariness which must have burdened the hard-worked planners towards the end of a long and messy exercise:

> I know of but one compromise – that our University Arts Examination should be altered: but I am sick of alterations of this Examination. The faults of that examination arose in my opinion from its going through so many committees (one of which, as I mentioned at the time, altered it when as I think they had no business whatever to do so), till everything like the cool judgement of any individual upon it was quite lost.[11]

It is clear from the minutes, and from scraps of dialogue like Airy's, alone, that the whole process of putting the examination regulations together and accepting candidates for matriculation in November

1838 and for the first degree examinations in Arts and Medicine
in the following year, must have put all concerned, but perhaps
most especially the Vice-Chancellor, under considerable strain. The
strain would have been bad enough had it reflected only the lively
debate to be expected to accompany any major academic enterprise,
and had that debate taken place within a settled and widely accepted
institutional structure. But, as we must now see, the whole process
was bedevilled by political, constitutional, bureaucratic and personal
controversy.

If the seventh Duke of Devonshire and Sir John William Lubbock, third
Bt, contemplated, in their old ages, the beginnings of the University,
they must have pondered, perhaps with some wry amusement, how
they, alone for six months and with only a single clerk thereafter,
had to organize and preside over the production of a whole new
curriculum and scheme of examinations. They would have recalled
that the Charter, wrongly drafted in some respects, was valid only for
the reign of William IV: legally, it ceased to apply six months after his
death, and was replaced by a new document, imposed by Government
without consultation. Throughout the first year of the Senate, they
had to bring together and mould into workable order a collection of
mettlesome and, on occasion, irascible fellows, whose attendance was
markedly irregular. And all this was done without any senior, full-time
officer to provide a sound and continuous administrative base for their
operations. Henry Moore, the first clerk, was appointed only in June
1837, and the first Registrar, Richard Wellesley Rothman, was not
elected until April 1838. For the first few months, even on the most
paltry details, the Chancellor and Vice-Chancellor wrote all the official
letters, and Lubbock took the minutes of the Senate and its committees
himself.

It was not that the need to have a Registrar or Secretary was not
foreseen from the outset. Indeed, the prospect of a new and permanent
position of some seniority was not lost on politicians always on the
look out for patronage to satisfy the demands of their protégés, as
soon as the original Charter came into effect. And some of the
early moves in this particular game reflected a misunderstanding as
to whether the new post would be in the gift of the Government
or of the University. Lord John Russell enquired of Spring Rice,
in mid-December 1836, 'In whom is the appointment?' And, on
Christmas Eve, Peter Mark Roget wrote to Lubbock saying 'I trust

the appointment of a Secretary will be left entirely to ourselves.' Even six weeks later Empson raised the matter with the Chancellor of the Exchequer:

> If the Charter has left (as Dr Roget understands) the appointment of the Secretary with the Fellows there will be a stand made by many against taking out of their hands the use of their own discretion concerning – who is *the best obtainable man* – for a place on the filling up of which (with respect to qualifications, temper, acceptableness to the body) not only the comfort of the parties but the success of the institution may mainly depend.[12]

Whether or not they understood the legal position – which was that the University had full power to appoint its own officers – Russell and Warburton, and even Spring Rice himself, were not averse to pushing their own candidates, long before the Senate came together. Nor were several possible contenders for the job reluctant to enquire about it and to lobby their patrons. But even the nature of the post or posts to be created was unclear. Spring Rice reported to Russell that Burlington had thought of a single office of Secretary, rather than a Registrar: the Chancellor of the Exchequer himself felt that 'for the three Faculties of Arts, Law and Medicine there should be some fixed executive person and a general Secretary for the whole body, to be paid out of the Fees which the Treasury will fix on the examination for degrees.'[13] This financial notion was naive, unless it referred to the long term: for the immediate future the availability of early and sufficient fee income was grossly overestimated. But, in any event, as Empson had forecast, the Senate was to assert itself to no small effect in both the shaping and the filling of what became the single office of Registrar.

The first name to be bandied about was that of one Thomas Coates, a lawyer previously employed as Clerk to the original London University and currently Secretary to the Council for the Diffusion of Useful Knowledge. Coates claimed that Spring Rice had promised him the job, but when the possibility of his appointment was mooted, hostile advice poured in on Russell from Brougham, Warburton and Romilly, all recalling that the London University had complained of Coates' charges for professional business and that 'the displeasure of the Council' had forced his resignation. Russell was not wholly convinced, even though Warburton went so far as to write that Coates' behaviour, while 'not dishonest,' was 'yet very indiscreet and improper.' In any event, the Council of UCL would not give Coates a good recommendation, and

Spring Rice agreed that 'If Mr Coates turns out an improper person
. . . I think there is no reason why on such grounds he should not be
set aside.'[14]

Russell seems to have been the sponsor of James Hudson, who
had been for several years Assistant Secretary to the Royal Society,
and claimed the backing of many prominent figures in science and
medicine, including the new fellows, Beaufort, Brande, Clark, Faraday
and M'Grigor. Burlington, doubtless feeling the pressure, responded
diplomatically, telling the Home Secretary that, 'As far as I am
concerned, I should be very unwilling to refuse him my support
unless there should be strong reasons against him, with which I am
unacquainted.'[15]

But the third person to be pressed on both Russell and Burlington
was Dr James Somerville, the Inspector of Anatomy, whose candidacy
for the Registrarship and future appointment as a fellow were to cause
enormous disruption. His interests were championed, persistently, by
Warburton. On 16 December 1836, in the same letter to Russell in which
he expressed his disapproval of Coates, Warburton wrote, 'Poor Dr
James Somerville, who is starving, I commend to your Lordship's kind
consideration.' And on the following day, Warburton followed up with
a long recital of Somerville's success in administering the Anatomy Act,
his helpfulness in advising Spring Rice on the medical side of the new
University, his low salary, and his victimization by the establishment of
the medical profession. Warburton argued that

> It is on the Medical Branch of the New University that its success or
> failure, as a whole, principally hinges. Through corporation cabals,
> and tricks of every kind, it will have to fight its way. Great knowledge
> of medical details, good habits of business as an administrator, great
> firmness, impartiality, and above all zeal for the success of the work
> in hand, are required.

And it would make great sense, claimed Warburton, that Somerville
should hold both the Inspectorship of Anatomy and the Registrarship
of the University, in order to boost his position and prevent him from
giving up the Inspectorship, which event would endanger the whole
administration of the Anatomy Act.[16]

Russell passed this piece of special pleading over to Spring Rice,
who felt that Warburton's praise of Somerville was well deserved, and
that Somerville was 'greatly underpaid as Anatomy Inspector.' But he
was not enthusiastic about Warburton's plan. The latter had spoken

to him about Somerville, 'but not either as Secretary or Registrar but as Dean of the Medical Faculty – or some such office, and in that department I cannot conceive that there could be a better public servant.' However, Russell admitted to Spring Rice just after the New Year that 'I have proposed to Lord Burlington that Mr Hudson and Dr James Somerville should be the two officers of the University.'[17]

At the end of January 1837, the new Vice-Chancellor confided to a colleague that he was 'very anxious that we should be careful and judicious in the selection of Officers, of the Registrar more particularly. I fear injudicious promises have been made.' He was almost certainly correct in that surmise, but in fairness it is necessary to stress the sheer uncertainty which still prevailed about the nature of the new institution. In the same letter, Lubbock, who was to be its working head, went on to say, 'I think we ought to have a Library and Professors. If we do not we shall be the only university in the world without.'[18] But he was soon to become fully aware of the narrow scope of his institution, and if, by then, he, Burlington and the ministers had not previously appreciated the true situation, they must all have come to realize that nobody could be casually ushered into the office of Registrar behind the backs of the Senate.

In all probability, Burlington and Lubbock imagined, when they made the definition of the Registrar's position one of the first items on the agenda of the initial meeting of the Senate on 4 March 1837, that such definition, and a subsequent search for candidates, would be completed in a couple of months. Their worst scenarios could not have included one which entailed a delay of thirteen months before the first Registrar was installed. But the exercise proved to be controversial from the beginning: the major point of contention was the salary to be offered, which matter was involved with and inflamed by Warburton's known wish to see Somerville appointed. The arguments divided the fellows and brought them into sharp confrontation with the Treasury. A settlement was not reached until the following February.

It is as well to stress, again, that the names of those who attended the first four meetings of the Senate were not recorded, and that thereafter, while those who attended were listed, neither the numbers nor the names of those who voted in divisions were normally included in the minutes. But in committees, as the result of a close vote, it was decided that the names of those voting in divisions should be recorded. To add to the complications, the difficulties of pinpointing exactly who was present at committees – including the Faculties of Law and Medicine – are compounded by a rule which the Senate adopted, only after some disagreement, whereby any fellow could attend committee meetings, but only those appointed as members of the committees could speak and vote. If the recording of members present is to be trusted, it seems that such additional attendance was rare. But given the distinction between the rules for full Senate and for committees, any attempt to suggest who supported what in the Senate must often only be an informed guess, as consistency cannot always be guaranteed in the attitudes of fellows.

A committee was set up at the first meeting to consider the duties to be required of the Registrar, how much he should be paid, and whether he should be a member of the Senate. A week later they suggested a list of orthodox functions, and a salary of 'at least £1000' per annum, 'until the University shall be in the receipt of an income to be derived from fees.' They also recommended a ban on the Registrar being a member of the Senate and a requirement that he be not actively engaged, while he held his post, in any profession, business or office. Non-membership of the Senate was the only one of these provisions to be agreed at the meeting on 18 March, though subsequently the list of functions and most other conditions were never big problems.

But almost immediately the salary question took precedence, with the opposition to £1000 coming mainly from George Biddell Airy, the Astronomer Royal, and Warburton. Airy exchanged spiky letters with Lubbock, and presented a hostile memorandum, arguing that the holder of the new post was not worth so much because he would not carry a level of responsibility for advising on policy, planning and public relations, nor any professional 'care of the literary or scientific reputation of the country or the University in regard to any subject whatever.'[19] Warburton's motives were much less straightforward and were embedded in medical politics. Those politics being particularly public, it is unsurprising that the medical press was quickly, though often inaccurately, informed of the controversies over filling the post of Registrar.

Immediately after the second meeting of the Senate, the *London Medical and Surgical Journal* approved its understanding that the new post would be advertised and opened to competition:

This looks well as a commencement, and it is the more necessary as, for some time past, a good deal of jobbing has been going on to seek the office, and a certain individual has even vaunted of his success. We must sincerely hope, that no member of the Medical Profession will be appointed to such a situation, as the habits and pursuits of men of any eminence or character, totally unqualify them for the appointment.

But a week later the same journal claimed, without qualification, that Somerville was 'about to be appointed,' and that the idea of advertising the post was being 'stubbornly resisted by Mr Warburton, an *ultra liberal* member of the senate, who is anxious to provide for one of his private friends, on the plea of having actively assisted him in the parliamentary medical enquiry.'[20]

Far from having either appointed Somerville or altered their committee's salary proposal, the Senate, at their fourth meeting, on 22 March, defeated a motion that the salary should be £700, by thirteen votes to eight, and approved a further motion that it should be at least £1000, by fourteen to seven. This was conveyed, triumphantly, to a colleague in Edinburgh by the Professor of Anatomy and Physiology at UCL, Thomas Sharpey:

the New University have had several meetings and have at last decided on the salary of their Registrar or Secretary. Warburton and Somerville's other friends wished to fix it disgracefully low and thus keep worthier men out of the field – they proposed £200 a year to begin with, a sum for which you can scarcely procure a common clerk in London: but they have been victoriously beaten and £1000 a year is fixed on, if the Government will give it.[21]

The Government, in the person of Spring Rice, however, took only two days to reject £1000 firmly. Inevitable Treasury parsimony no doubt played its part, and Airy's objections may well have been representative of a sense that £1000 was simply too much by the standards of the public service. At the time, salaries of about £1000 were paid, for instance, to such people as the Librarian and the Principal Clerk in the Journal Office of the House of Commons, the Secretary to the Ecclesiastical Commission and senior clerks in the Home Office. In his formal reply to the University, however, the Chancellor of the Exchequer restricted himself to arguing that, while £1000 would be appropriate when the institution was 'in full activity,' at this initiatory stage the duties 'cannot be so onerous and engrossing as they must become hereafter.' Moreover, Spring Rice believed that to ask the House of Commons to approve the suggestion would damage the University, and stated flatly that, if it was attacked on the floor of the House, he 'could only defend it on the authority of those from whom the recommendation came, and not from a concurrence of opinion in the measure recommended.'

This first exercise in senatorial politics excited strong feeling. It raised from the outset the issue of how much independence of, and support from, Government the University was to enjoy: but it also revealed internal divisions based on differing professional interests and personal ambitions. One can only speculate on how much, if any, collusion there may have been between Spring Rice and Warburton. The Chancellor of the Exchequer had not warmed to Warburton's plan to have Somerville hold both the Registrarship and the Inspectorship of Anatomy, but he may have been sufficiently sympathetic to Warburton's claims for Somerville to have thought that a lower salary would deter stronger opposition. The strong case made by the Treasury as to the real, initial worth of the post, though, was persuasive in itself – and very much more respectable. But, whatever the pressures and manoeuvres, Spring Rice and Warburton moved in the same direction. At the next meeting of the Senate, on 5 April, when Spring Rice's letter was read, Warburton gave notice that he would propose a salary of £500 at the following session.

When he did so, however, three days later, his motion was defeated by thirteen to eight, and by a vote of fourteen to six it was agreed to appoint a commmittee to draw up a statement in support of the higher salary, to be sent to the Chancellor of the Exchequer. As there is no indication of dissent in the compilation of the statement, we can assume that the members who put their names to it were among those in favour – the Chancellor and Vice-Chancellor, the Bishop of Durham, Arnott, Beaufort, Jerrard and Roget. But their statement came under severe internal review. At successive meetings, on 15 and 22 April, its arguments in favour of a high registrarial salary were reduced by the excision of comparisons with official and commercial posts, and by other changes which were made in a whole series of contested amendments, some of them the result of close voting. George Airy kept up an unrelenting protest against making any statement of reasons in favour of the higher figure.

By this time the medical press was not only fully aware of the general nature of the controversy, but was able to add other names than Somerville's to a list of potential candidates. The *Lancet* had carried a vicious attack on Brougham, Warburton and Somerville on 15 April, and a week later, on the same day that the Senate finalized the version of its recommendation to be sent to Spring Rice, there appeared in the *London Medical and Surgical Journal* an article worth quoting at length, as it gives something of the curiously shabby flavour of the row:

The appointment of a Registrar to the Metropolitan University has become a stumbling block to the progress of the new Institution, and it is with pain we have now to state that *intriguing* is busy at work by different parties, each of which is endeavouring to serve a selfish purpose, by getting the important office filled up by a *friend*, in place of selecting some well qualified individual who might have come forward, had it been thrown open to competition. We are not, however, without hope, that as the appointment will not immediately take place, some person will come forward with pretensions of a much higher order than any of the present candidates, and thus leave no excuse for controversy and *jobbing* amongst the senate. Mr. Warburton has not yet, nor is it likely that he will, relinquish *his* favourite protege. Certain representatives of the corruptionists, who became necessarily elected among the senate, are using all their praiseworthy endeavours, to provide for Mr. Daniell, the Chemical Professor of King's College; whilst Dr. Forbes of Chichester has met with an able advocate and place hunter in Dr. James Clark. The general impression at present is, that neither of these jobbings will succeed. The *fame* which the Inspector of Anatomy has acquired in executing the functions of his office, and the transactions that have lately taken place at the Home Office, are such as, in all probability, to induce the government not to part with so valuable a servant as Dr. James Somerville; and however well qualified Mr. Daniell may be to lecture to the empty benches of the high Churchmen's College, we have no right to suppose that such talents would render him a competent Registrar of the University. The claims and pretensions of Dr. Forbes are of an order which no one can so well appreciate as his friend Dr. James Clark, and though the mutual feelings of regard and friendship which these two individuals entertain towards each other, so fully exemplified in their works, (we allude to dedications and compliments,) may be highly praiseworthy, it is not a time for Dr. Clark to evince it, at the expense of an important national institution. Without any unkindly feeling towards Dr. Forbes, we cannot help expressing our hope, that the Senate should not make choice of a medical practitioner, more particularly of one, whose humble position in early life, must have deprived him of those advantages of early education and polished habits, which will be so very desirable for the Registrar to possess; but also, because the habits and avocations of all medical practitioners are very different from those which the duties of the office will necessarily require. An individual ought certainly to be chosen, who, in addition to the education, manners and habits of an accomplished gentleman, has a talent for what is usually called the business of life.[22]

Daniell and Forbes were both to be candidates when the election of a Registrar took place many months later, and Daniell was to be a very serious contender, who ended as the runner-up. Exactly when he was first approached, or himself became interested in the possibility of standing, is unclear, but at some stage he did consult Dr Otter, Bishop of Chichester and former Principal of King's, about it. The Bishop was supportive, but also warned Daniell of the danger that he might be unpopular with some his colleagues at King's, who were 'very sensitive' about any connection with the new University. Chichester admitted that he himself had suffered criticism by such people as a result of having accepted a position on the Senate.[23]

The insistence of a majority of the Senate – albeit a small one – in proposing a salary of £1,000 led Spring Rice to adopt a reluctantly acquiescent attitude. He agreed to put forward a salary of £1,000, but went on, in his letter to Burlington:

At the same time, in the same spirit of frankness which Your Lordship's indulgence and the candour of the Senate will, I hope, justify me in using in my intercourse with you, I must add, that the difficulties to which I originally adverted, do not appear to me to be diminished, and still less removed.

This message, read to the Senate on 29 April, led to a motion, almost certainly drafted by Warburton, that the Chancellor of the Exchequer should be informed that

the Senate, retaining their opinion that it would be expedient to give the Registrar a salary of £1,000 a year, yet, under all the circumstances of the case, they are willing to yield their assent to the proposed salary of £500 for the first year.

But while the number attending was reduced and doubts had crept in, there remained present just enough of those who were willing to insist on the original proposal: the motion was lost by nine votes to eight.

Towards the end of May, Spring Rice decided to meet the expenses of the University for the financial year which had begun on 5 April from the Civil Contingencies vote, and only bring in a formal, separate estimate for the University for the year beginning in April 1838. He did not define exactly what he would agree to as a salary for a Registrar appointed during 1837–8, but told the Senate that he would include a salary in the estimates for 1838–9, and went on, 'when I go to Parliament I hope you may be already in action, and thus some of the objections . . . may be mitigated, if not wholly averted.'

Whether Spring Rice was merely buying time and hoping to reach some compromise agreement with the Senate, and what might have happened had the normal procedures of Treasury and Parliament been followed, are questions which were made irrelevant early in June when William IV died and was succeeded by the young Victoria. In accordance with current constitutional practice, Parliament was dissolved and a General Election followed. The upset and consequent long delay in routine government business led the Senate, unable to make progress with finding a Registrar, to appoint a clerk – Henry Moore – in June, for one year, at a salary of £200. And in mid-July, with the summer well advanced, they adjourned until the beginning of November.

So exiguous is the surviving, or available, official material, that it is impossible to say precisely when it was discovered that the original Charter had died with his late Majesty. According to Lord John Russell, writing a year later, the Charter did not cease to be effective until six months after the death of the Sovereign: in any event, it does seem clear that the drafting and presentation of a new document was being considered by mid-August 1837.[24] That some changes to the original were desirable had been accepted, as we have seen, as soon as it had appeared, but Russell had been in no hurry.[25] Those changes related particularly to the tenure of fellows, but what almost certainly focused ministerial attention was the need to replace the names of the unwilling Brougham and Sheepshanks, and pressure from Warburton to enhance the status of Dr Somerville. The whole operation was kept strictly within governmental circles, and Warburton was the only member of the Senate who was able to influence the ministers. Certainly neither Burlington nor Lubbock was consulted. At the end of November Russell told Brougham that,

We have altered the Charter for the London University. It is no longer during pleasure – and if the numbers fall below twenty four they may themselves elect new members. I have left your name out but the instrument is not yet completed.[26]

The new Charter was dated 5 December 1837: it included two new fellows - Edward Stanley, recently appointed to the See of Norwich, and Dr James Somerville.

The appointment of Somerville removed him from the registrarial context, but in other respects it was to prove to be calamitous, arousing immediate consternation in the medical faculty. That story takes its place a little later, but the inclusion of Somerville in the Senate was only one aspect of the anger and disillusion which was felt over the high-handed ministerial action and the consequent slight to the fellows and, particularly, to their Chancellor. And, for some at least, the villain of the piece was Henry Warburton. Jerrard wrote to Airy

> The circumstances connected with the issuing of the new Charter have given great offence to nearly all the Members of the Senate. Our Chancellor heard nothing about it until it was prepared and on the point of being sent to him – and the only individual consulted about it (as I am informed) was Mr Warburton who recommended one of our new Fellows. This appointment has excited very great dissatisfaction, not only on account of the strong prejudice existing against the individual in question among his medical brethren, but also as it was *known* that he was not popular with the Senate, on the occasion of his application for the Office of Registrar.[27]

Some time later, Roget told Burlington how, after the new Charter had been issued,

> We learned to our great surprise, that the Second Charter had been drawn up and actually signed without any previous communication to your Lordship of any such Charter being contemplated, or intimation of the changes intended to be introduced into it, and without the slightest inquiry how far those changes might meet with the concurrence of the Senate. One of our members, as it appears, availing himself of his private influence, has prevailed on the government to appoint as Member of the Senate the very individual who, in consequence of the strong feeling manifested by that body, had deemed it advisable to withdraw, after having been so prominently brought forward as Candidate for the subordinate station of Registrar.[28]

The revised Charter, therefore, was not received with any great enthusiasm, and arguments for further changes were to flourish in the coming years. But bad feeling about the manner of its introduction, though it added to the discontents of the Senate, was less traumatic than the row which had set in during the autumn of 1837 and was at its height for the first six weeks of the New Year, which revolved around that contentious figure, the Headmaster of Rugby.

CHAPTER 8

Dr Arnold and the Scriptural Examination

Thomas Arnold accepted Spring Rice's invitation to join the Senate in September 1835; he resigned at the beginning of October 1838. His early death, in 1842, was followed a few years later by the publication of his letters, which tell of his hope that, by working within the new University, he could give 'a religious influence to its proceedings,' in order to realize his vision 'of a great institution of national education, which . . . should be Christian, yet not sectarian.' The story of his internal struggle over the defeat of his cherished wish for a compulsory examination in the Scriptures, and his eventual inability to accept the compromise of a voluntary examination, is well known.[1] But it is a story which has been told almost entirely from Arnold's perspective, and his arguments need no further special analysis. Here we are examining the impact of his concern on his colleagues and on the early working of the Senate.

The crucial proposal for the inclusion of a Scriptural examination in the requirements for the BA degree was recommended by a sub-committee which had been appointed by the Faculty of Arts on 24 June 1837 to draw up the first scheme for the syllabus in Classics. That report did not reach the Faculty, formally, until November 1837. The sub-committee had only three members – Arnold, the Bishop of Chichester (Dr Otter) and Jerrard. Arnold's biographer claimed that Arnold 'gave notice of his intention of recommending the introduction of the Scriptures as a part of the classical examinations for every degree,' but did not indicate how, when or in what circumstances the notice was given. Unfortunately, too, there are no surviving minutes and only a little relevant correspondence to clarify how much the proposal was debated within the sub-committee.

It is highly probable, though, that Arnold did take the initiative, and it is very unlikely that Otter and Jerrard – and several other members of the Senate – could have been unaware that Arnold would make a strong bid for the inclusion of some religiously oriented subject matter in the examination curriculum. He had haggled with Spring Rice when first offered appointment to the Senate. The minister, who later recalled having 'discussed at great length' with him some of the political difficulties which would arise from trying to meet his wishes, apparently persuaded him to 'join . . . without insisting on a Scriptural examination; on the alleged ground of fact, that such an examination was not practicable on account of the objections of different classes of Christians; and on the hope . . . that the Christian character of the University might be secured without it.'[2]

In the long interval between accepting a fellowship and coming together with his new colleagues in the University, however, Arnold consulted his friends, became convinced that there was 'a very great necessity for avowing the Christian principle strongly, because Unbelief was evidently making a cat's paw of Dissent,' and shifted his ground on the question of a Scriptural examination. Henry Crabb Robinson, at UCL, recorded in his diary in January 1836 that Arnold had 'required that he shall be at liberty to refer to Christianity as a system of divine truth, not a mere scheme of philosophy. But he says Christianity shall be referred to in a way that shall offend no sect whatever.' A month afterwards, Arnold wrote to Crabb Robinson:

> I am glad to hear that we are in a smooth course with the new University. No man in England, I believe, more wishes to be able to go on with this cause than I do; no more believes it to contain the elements of great good, if saved from one fatal, and I cannot think most needless, taint. Meanwhile I will be patient, and wait, and comply with anything in my power, with anything save the abandonment of that which is more than all besides.

But a year later, just before the first meetings of the Senate were to be held, he told Crabb Robinson of his expectation that 'individually I shall have to leave the new Ship on account of their no-Christianity notions.' After only another few weeks, rumour of his unwillingness to remain a fellow unless 'more were done in the examinations as to Theology,' reached Crabb Robinson, who challenged Arnold about it. Arnold replied that he would 'do nothing hastily,' that he had 'no wish to have Degrees in Divinity . . . or to have a Theological Faculty,' and was 'quite content with Degrees in Arts.' But he went on to argue that 'moral studies not based on Christianity must be unchristian, and therefore are such as I can take no part in,' and declared that it would be 'an experiment undoubtedly worth trying . . . for the sake of upholding the Christian character of our University,' to examine every Christian candidate for a degree, except Roman Catholics, 'in one of the Gospels and one of the Epistles out of the Greek Testament.'[3]

On 30 April 1837 Arnold approached Otter, whom he apparently did not know previously, and laid out in a long letter some possible ways of meeting what he clearly felt to be unarguably essential – 'our Bachelor of Arts' Degree must imply a knowledge of the Christian Scriptures.' He suggested that 'there might be members of the Senate of different denominations of Christians to examine the members of their own communions.' Alternatively, he thought of requiring from 'every candidate for a Degreee in Arts, a certificate signed by two ministers of his own persuasion, that he was competently instructed in Christian knowledge as understood by the members of their communion.' And thirdly, he outlined a procedure of individual examination of candidates who would each 'bring up at his own choice some one Gospel, and some one Epistle in the Greek Testament,' and who would 'declare, on coming before us, to what communion he belongs.' Whichever method was chosen, he insisted on the indispensability 'to every plan of education, or for the ascertaining of the sufficiency of any one's education in a Christian country, – that Christian knowledge is a necessary part of the formation and cultivation of the mind of every one.'[4]

The first outline of the subjects to be included in the BA syllabus was laid before the Faculty of Arts on 17 June 1837, and in it no mention was made of Scriptural studies. Arnold, Otter and Jerrard were obvious enough choices to form the sub-committee on Classics which was set up a week later to define the content and to undertake the detailed work of shaping the scheme of examination. Whether, by then, Arnold had communicated his ideas to Jerrard, as well as to Otter, is unknown. But it is as well at this point to say something about Otter and Jerrard, and the peculiarly important role the latter played in the whole episode.

Arnold had approached the Bishop of Chichester in part because Otter 'had practical experience of education' and because he was 'one of the few members of our profession who happen to belong to the University.' Jerrard was not a 'member of our profession.' He was an ex-headmaster and a devoted Anglican who was to be ordained some years later and, ultimately, to leave the Church of England for that of Rome. For the present, however, he was clearly not 'one of us' in Arnold's view. In 1837, Otter was 69; he had been a friend of Malthus and, despite his six years as Principal of King's, was markedly sympathetic to the Whigs.

Jerrard was 36, some five years younger than Arnold. It is unlikely that Otter and Arnold were too far apart in matters presently in dispute within the Church of England, but, given his ultimate destination, one may assume that Jerrard's sympathies lay with the Tractarians, with whom Arnold quarrelled as much as he did with the secularists - he remarked on one occasion that 'after having undergone my share of abuse for being a Radical, I am likely to be abused by the other party as a bigot.'[5] While there is no overt sign of friction between Arnold and Jerrard, it could well be that they were, temperamentally, a little distant from each other.

We have already seen that Jerrard was one of the most conscientious attenders and participants in the Senate's affairs throughout his tenure of office, which only ended with his death in 1853. He had given up the headmastership of Bristol College in response to Spring Rice's invitation and, though he held a fellowship at Cambridge, clearly thought of himself as a professional fellow and examiner of London University, entitled to remuneration as such. There are hints that Burlington found him somewhat tiresome, and that Lubbock doubted his judgement, while Rothman complained that he always procrastinated 'to the last moment.' But he was a man of genuinely liberal educational ideas, as can be seen from his evidence to a select committee on education in 1836, notable for his strongly reasoned disapproval of corporal punishment in schools. His sheer regularity of service and his tenacity earned him recognition by colleagues as the spokesman of the Church in the Senate and its committees.[6] Without doubt, he was a willing workhorse, but he certainly hoped for tangible reward: in trying to obtain Church preferment, in 1845, when both Otter and Arnold were long dead, he cited his

> exertions in getting Scriptural Examinations established at the University, in the face of a large and influential Party by whom all such Examinations were, at first, violently opposed. My two colleagues on the sub-committee that proposed those Examinations (the late Bishop Otter, and Dr Arnold of Rugby) requested me, as being, at that time, a layman, and thus free from much of the obloquy to which *they* were exposed, to bear the brunt of the battle on that occasion. This I cheerfully did – although the unceasing anxiety and labour in which the agitation of the question for some months involved me, were such as severely to try my health.[7]

There can be no doubt that Jerrard had to carry much of the load, and it was he who framed the original proposal of the sub-committee to include Scriptural studies, which first came officially before the Faculty of Arts on 29 November 1837. On that occasion neither Arnold nor Otter was present. Discussion was postponed until 2 December, when the proposal was accepted, by the narrowest of margins. The crucial meeting was held on 7 February 1838, when the first proposal was withdrawn and a compromise arrangement was imposed. At both those meetings all three members of the sub-committee were present.

In the interval between the meetings of 2 December 1837 and 7 February 1838, however, Jerrard was left alone in London to struggle with an extremely awkward situation. His memories of those two months were not a little bitter towards Arnold:

> No opportunity for a meeting of the Sub-Committee had been afforded from the 3rd of the preceding December until the very day (February 7th) appointed for the meeting of the Senate: for although the writer [i.e. Jerrard] had not considered himself at liberty to leave London during the agitation of this momentous question, his Colleagues were both detained, throughout that period, by their respective duties and engagements in the country. But soon after the commencement of the Christmas holidays, he wrote a very urgent letter to Dr. Arnold, stating the exceedingly anxious and harassing nature of the contest in which he found himself engaged, and the painful sense of responsibility which he felt in being called upon, day after day, to answer the most minute and searching questions relating to the proposed Examination, without the power of immediate communication with either of his Colleagues; and as *two* discussions, to which he had been invited, and on the issue of which he thought *much* depended, were then at hand, he entreated Dr. Arnold to come up to town, if possible, and be present on those occasions; for fear that the cause which they both had so much at heart should suffer from the insufficient nature of the advocacy which it might receive, or from want of a perfect agreement, on all points, between them; (for although there was a general understanding amongst the Members of the Sub-Committee as to the method of conducting the Examination, no formal scheme for that purpose had yet been drawn up). Dr. Arnold wrote back to say that he was then in Westmoreland, and had made arrangements for devoting his time during the vacation to his History of Rome; and mentioned the extreme inconvenience and sad interruption to his labours which

would arise from complying with the writer's request.[8]

Thus did the fascination of research and writing conflict with other academic interests, even in 1837. But it is unlikely that Arnold's rigid advocacy would have been modified by his presence in London. The opposition which the sub-committee's proposal aroused centred far less on the detailed content of the syllabus than on two fundamental objections to the whole exercise. There were those who were simply antagonistic to any examinations in religious subject matter; and there were those who were not averse to having examinations to test knowledge of Christian Scriptures, but who could not stomach any idea of requiring expression of religious belief or of imposing tests on candidates who were not Christians. Much depended, therefore, on the legal interpretation of the University's Charter, whose relevant passage declared that the institution's purposes included

> the advancement of Religion and Morality, and the promotion of useful knowledge, to hold forth to all classes and denominations of Our faithful subjects, without any distinction whatsoever, an encouragement for pursuing a regular and liberal course of Education.

By the time when the sub-committee's proposal was known, though before it came before the Faculty of Arts, Otter and Jerrard had become very well aware of the difficulty of carrying Arnold with them. All three seemed to agree – and subsequent events proved, after a noisy argument, that they were correct – that they could produce a syllabus which would be sufficiently acceptable to Dissenters. But the point of no return for Arnold was the notion that compulsory examination could not be forced on Jews, other non-Christians and unbelievers. As he saw it, in correspondence with Empson,

> The whole question turns upon this; – whether the country understood, and was meant to understand, that the University of London was to be open to all Christians without distinction, or to all men without distinction. . . . Now, are we really for the sake of a few Jews, who may like to have a Degree in Arts, – or for the sake of one or two Mahomedans, who may possibly have the same wish, or for the sake of English unbelievers, who dare not openly avow themselves – are we to destroy our only chance of national education?[9]

What the sub-committee put to the Faculty of Arts (in effect to the Senate) at this stage was not a detailed syllabus, but a brief statement of principle: 'That, as a general rule, the Candidates for the B.A. Degree shall pass an Examination either in one of the Four Gospels or the Acts of the Apostles, in the original Greek; and also in Scripture History.' Jerrard, the draftsman, admitted later that 'The great difficulty from the first was the case of the *Jews*,' and he had hoped to meet it by inserting the phrase 'as a general rule'. Once the battle was joined, however, he was quickly disillusioned.

The debate in the Faculty of Arts on 2 December 1837, on the sub-committee's recommendation, went on for four hours. Twenty-one members were present and, when the question was put, the recommendation was carried by ten votes to nine. It was then agreed that the names of those who voted in the division should be recorded, and we know, therefore, unequivocally, that the winners were the Bishops of Durham and Chichester (Maltby and Otter), Arnold, Bacot, Beaufort, Jerrard, M'Grigor, Ridout, Roget and Senior; while on the losing side were Airy, Arnott, Billing, Clark, Henslow, Kiernan, Lubbock, Sims and Warburton. The Chancellor was entitled to cast a vote, but did not choose to do so; and the other member listed as attending, Hammick, must either have left the meeting earlier, or abstained. Nobody present could have had any doubt that the close decision would be challenged. Indeed, before the meeting broke up, a resolution was carried asking that the law officers be consulted as to the legality of the recommendation.

Because the vote had been in favour of a proposal which would have been sympathetically received by the majority of religiously orthodox, politically conservative people, no great notice was taken by the Tory press. An article in the *Morning Chronicle* late in January was dismissed, privately, by the Earl of Burlington, as 'very heavy and stupid'. Perhaps because the nature of the argument, as it developed, was rather esoteric and relatively short-lived, public debate was not extensive – the only exchange of any note was in the *Globe*, which printed, in response to expressions of concern, a long letter from the Archbishop of Dublin, Dr Whateley, expressing confidence that what had been achieved in the way of non-sectarian religious instruction in Irish schools could be envisioned for the University of London.[10]

But, while the circles most immediately concerned were understandably agitated, real anxiety did extend far beyond the Senate. Informed people in the wider world recognized full well the potential delicacy of the situation. Empson's and Crabb Robinson's correspondence with Arnold reflected the concern with which the proposal to require a Scriptural examination was greeted. Empson had sketched the problem for his father-in-law, Lord Jeffrey, the eminent Scottish critic and former Lord Advocate, just before the first debate on the matter took place in the Faculty of Arts. Jeffrey responded:

> I am very sorry about your London University schismatics; and am rather mortified that Arnold should be so sticklish. But if he means only that your classical graduates should know the unclassical Greek of the N.S., as well as that of Plato and Xenophon, I think you should not hesitate to indulge him. If the examination is to be in the *doctrine*, as well as the *language* – and truly an examination in the *theology* rather than in *classics* – the difficulty no doubt will be greater, and his unreasonableness more surprising. Yet even then (though I feel that the advice may seem cowardly), seeing the ruinous, and even *fatal* consequences that would follow from the secession of all your *clerical* associates, I believe your better course will be to comply – making the best terms you can for tender consciences and special cases. I do not much like the counsel I give you, and shall be glad if you find you can do justice to the institution by following an opposite one. But I do not see how.[11]

And the Earl of Burlington, at the eye of the storm and yet a little detached from its fury, recorded Brougham's comment that 'we are out of our senses . . . in introducing Religious examinations.' He also admitted, to himself, that Spring Rice's hopes of a compromise were impracticable. 'The question having been mooted,' he wrote, 'it must be carried, or smash goes the University.'[12] As for Arnold, his published letters during the interval between the meetings of 2 December 1837 and 7 February 1838 refer only briefly to the affair, but he had no illusions as to the opposition, which he characterized towards the end of January as 'very fierce'.[13]

Not only was the opposition fierce, but it moved with remarkable speed, no doubt in part because Warburton was directly involved at UCL and was also close to the United Committee of Dissenters which operated from Dr Williams' Library. By mid-December a deputation of Dissenters and another from UCL had been received by the Home Secretary who, along with other ministers, was not pleased. Nassau Senior wrote to Whateley:

> You have heard I suppose of the result of Arnold's motion for a Scriptural examination in the University of London. I seconded it, and we carried it, by a majority of one – 10 to 9. But it will have to be discussed several times before it is finally adopted, and may

be defeated, where numbers are so balanced, in any one of them –
or may finally be disallowed by the Secretary of State. My Radical
friends are furious, and Lord Lansdowne and Lord John and P.
Thompson shake their heads. But absolutely to reject so important
a branch of knowledge seems a disgraceful concession to that most
unreasonable of all parties, the Dissenters.[14]

On 18 December, Lord John Russell wrote to Burlington a letter
which demonstrated a smooth political technique and the sheer confidence of ministerial power. He had avoided referring the matter to the
law officers, arguing that 'this question can hardly be made a dry point
of law, and that its solution depends not less upon the manner in which
the Examinations are conducted, than upon the letter of the regulation
itself.' He accepted the possibility of framing examinations which might
not offend any class of Christians, but feared that 'such Examinations
. . . might be so pursued as to force the scholar to a defence or apology
for his religious faith,' and did 'not think that these apprehensions would
be allayed by the exemption of such as should plead religious scruples,
from the proposed examination,' because 'Such a plea might probably
be misconstrued, and the grounds of the refusal would leave a wide
scope for malignant rancour and personal attack.'

Russell then hinted at a compromise without committing himself to
it. 'Whether it might not be possible to frame a rule which should leave
it to the Candidates for Degrees to be examined in the Greek Testament
and Church History at their own express desire, I am not prepared to
say.' But he followed this by making very clear his wish for serious
modification of the original proposal, and the likely consequences of
the University not complying:

> It would be most unfortunate if a rule were established which should
> make the University an object of suspicion instead of a means of
> increasing the just distinctions to be conferred upon Learning and
> Science. It would scarcely be less of a calamity were the authority
> of the Secretary of State to interpose a bar to regulations deemed
> essential by the Senate. I must therefore request Your Lordship to
> bring this matter again before the Senate, and to state to them
> fully the difficulties which I feel must arise should they persist in
> requesting the opinion of the Law Officers of the Crown on the
> proposed regulation.[15]

Faced with this peremptory command, but aware of Arnold's difficulty in attending, arrangements were made for the Faculty of Arts

to meet on 7 February for a 'discussion . . . on the subject of the recommendation of the Sub-Committee in Classics respecting an Examination in part of the New Testament and in Scripture History.' Thus there was, altogether, a gap of almost two months after the first debate, and that gave time for a good deal to happen apart from the heavyweight interventions by UCL, the formal group of Dissenters and the Government. Almost certainly, there would have been far more written exchanges than have survived, and innumerable conversations which have gone unrecorded. But what we have is evidence of strong support for the possibility of an agreed syllabus from the principal and three professors at King's College; an exercise in tapping Dissenting opinion undertaken by the Quaker, Dr Sims, which led in particular to correspondence with Dr Pye Smith, the formidable Congregationalist tutor from Homerton College, whose replies were much quoted in subsequent discussions; and extensive efforts by the indefatigible Jerrard to debate with all parties in a search for an acceptable compromise.[16]

But the extent to which compromise seemed to be in the air should not be allowed to conceal the degree of animosity which was felt towards the original proposal. The ailing Cornwallis Hewett, who rarely appeared, assured Lubbock from Cambridge that he would certainly attend and vote down a resolution which he felt to be 'not only perfectly irreconcilable with the Spirit of the Charter but also calculated to produce irreparable mischief both to the previous fair fame and future prospects of the University.'[17] Burlington gave a dinner party on 3 February for Lubbock, Roget, Locock, Kiernan, Arnott and Jerrard. While he thought Lubbock would be 'a little more favourably disposed' if the complaints of the Dissenters could be met, Arnott was 'very much against' the whole proposal. Burlington felt that from what he heard, 'the decision on Wednesday next will be adverse to the proposed Examination,' but also confided to his diary that he had 'some idea intrigues are going on to prevent two members from attending who formerly voted for it.'

An account of the whole episode, written by Jerrard in 1846, showed that, to a very considerable extent, he succeeded, both within and without the Senate, in finding a way which could be followed by all Christians. But he was aware throughout that the main problem concerned the position of Jewish candidates, and he described the relevant objections expressed strongly in the meeting of 2 December 1837. If Jewish candidates were to be compelled to take an examination in the New Testament, 'to the study of which it was alleged that many of them, from the nature of their education, entertained a *peculiar repugnance*,' it would be 'a great hardship, or rather . . . a species of persecution.' And if they were not so required,

> it was argued that before any Candidate could claim a special exemption from the Examination, he must declare himself to be a Jew; and thus, that a 'distinction,' invidious in itself, and contrary to the Charter, would be made between Candidates.[18]

Russell's hint at the possibility of offering choice was probably the earliest written suggestion of a solution, but on New Year's Day 1838, Dr Pye Smith sent to Jerrard

> a plan which would . . . answer every desirable purpose. . . . It is, that any Candidate for a degree . . . shall be at liberty to profess a readiness to be examined in the Hebrew text of the Old Testament or in the Greek of the New, or in both; and in the Antiquities, Natural Civil History, and Chronology of the Holy Scriptures; that the Examiners be authorized to comply with such a request; and that this examination shall not be taken in substitution for that in any branch of philology or science.[19]

In the development of his own thinking on the subject, Jerrard did not acknowledge anyone else's contribution. But he prepared for the forthcoming discussion a scheme which adopted Pye Smith's ideas, and included specific safeguards which reflected the concern which had been expressed that there should be no testing or required expression of religious belief. The most crucial parts of his draft regulations declared

> That all Candidates for the B.A. Degree shall be examined either in one of the Books of the Pentateuch in the original Hebrew, or in one of the four Gospels or the Acts of the Apostles in the original Greek; and also in Scripture History. . . . That none of the questions fixed upon be of a doctrinal character; and that no question be so put as to require an expression of religious belief on the part of any Candidate.
>
> That a printed paper be placed before each Candidate, having on *one* side the passages selected from the *Hebrew* text, with questions relating to the old Testament only; and on the *other*, the passages selected from the *Greek* text, with questions relating to the New as well as to the Old Testament; and that the Candidate, without being asked any *viva voce* question on the subject, be allowed to choose whichever side of the paper he may think proper.

> That no answer or translation given by any Candidate be objected
> to on the ground of its expressing any peculiarity of doctrinal views;
> provided always that it be decorous in tone and language.

Jerrard discussed this new direction with Otter, who signified 'cordial
approval', and with many 'friends of the University, representing a
great variety of religious opinions,' and found that 'the prospect of
the alternative in favour of the Jews produced in a very short time a
remarkable re-action of feeling with regard to the whole question.' The
new scheme gained 'the zealous support of many influential persons,
who had regarded the original measure with doubt and uneasiness; it
removed or greatly softened the jealousy of others, and evidently took
from the hands of those who continued hostile to it, their favourite and
most formidable weapon.'[20]

But it did not convert Arnold, who said so in a letter to Jerrard
which does not seem to have survived. The latter, nonetheless, took
his proposal to the last meeting of the sub-committee, which was held
immediately before the full meeting of the Senate on 7 February,
apparently convinced that Arnold would then fall in with it. As
Jerrard recorded, ruefully, many years later, he had never for a moment
suspected that Arnold's 'views on this subject would be pushed to the
length to which they were then carried.' In what must have been a
painful and stressful meeting, Jerrard and Otter found themselves faced
with an intransigent and immovable colleague. Arnold

> could not consent to give up the *principle* that *every* Candidate should
> pass an Examination in the *New* Testament; and he very strongly
> objected to the recognition of the admissibility of Jews, *as such*, to
> Degrees in Arts. On being reminded of the language of the Charter,
> he stated his reasons for understanding that language as meant to
> apply, exclusively, to Her Majesty's *Christian* subjects; said that
> under *that* impression he had joined the University; and added, that
> had he thought that Degrees *in Arts* were to be avowedly conferred
> on Jews, or persons of any other 'Class or Denomination' who were
> 'not Christians, even in name,' he never would have accepted a seat
> in the Senate.

The whole of the three-man argument is described in fascinating
detail in Jerrard's account. Doubtless with their eyes on the clock - for
the discussion 'continued up to the very moment of the assembling' of
the Faculty of Arts – Otter and Jerrard insisted that, since the previous
December,

A considerable change of opinion had taken place in the Senate. Few, it was presumed, would *now* attempt to justify the exclusion of the Bible from the Examinations of the University; and, on the other hand, if the original rule should be proposed by Dr Arnold (especially with the declaration that it was not to admit of any exception whatsoever), it would not probably find a seconder. In fact, the alternative was now *known* to be between the modified measure and an *optional* Examination.

Dr Arnold was . . . entreated to consider what *must* be the consequence of his vote on this occasion. In voting *against* the modified measure, he would in fact be voting *for* the optional Examination (for if the former were negatived, the latter *must* be adopted).

It was in this divided state that the sub-committee attended the Faculty meeting, along with twenty-two other members, which made it one of the largest gatherings recorded. Of those who had been present on 2 December, only the Bishop of Durham and Roget were absent. The six newcomers were Brande, Empson, Faraday, Hewett, Lefevre and Walker. But the session was rather anti-climactical. Jerrard and Otter, in view of 'the extreme disadvantage of its being opposed by their colleague, Dr Arnold,' did not deem it advisable to bring the new scheme before the Faculty, and also withdrew the original proposal.

> There was consequently no motion before the Senate [actually the Faculty of Arts]. Whereupon it was proposed, and after some conversation agreed to by nearly all present, that Scriptural Examination, to be followed by Certificates of proficiency, should be instituted at the University; but that the submitting to it or not should be left to the option of Candidates.[21]

No vote was taken and no names of mover or seconder were recorded in the minutes, but a relieved Empson reported to Napier that 'The papers will tell you how cleverly we got out of our London University religious difficulty. The proposition made will hold, as it is Warburton's own.' To Spring Rice, Empson claimed that the successful motion was 'adopted unanimously'. He also revealed that

> Lord Burlington read a strong letter from the Bishop of Durham in favour of the original recommendation and a still stronger one from the Bishop of Norwich, in which he speaks of Candidates for

infidelity, etc. . . . It is an awful beginning for your new Bishop [Norwich] to write language which, if he had used in the presence of one minority ought to have cost him a pull of his nose. His son was a favourite pupil of Arnold's; and so he pays Arnold back his debt in this fashion.[22]

The original letters from the two Bishops are among Burlington's papers, and the passage by Norwich to which Empson took understandable exception, reads:

no christian ought for a moment to sanction, for the mere purpose moreover apparently of accommodating I trust and believe a very limited number of candidates professing any of the various shades of infidelity which in proportion as they predominate cannot fail of unhinging those ties of social union, which constitute the moral worth of an enlightened population.[23]

Warburton, a few days after the meeting of the Faculty of Arts, was well pleased:

All those who were opposed to the examination as a compulsory pre-requisite for passing the degree of B.A., to whom I have spoken, approve of the examination on the footing on which it now stands, and consider, even, that it will be advantageous to the University, by removing the imputation that it is an infidel one, without forcing the conscience of a single individual.

But at the same time he supported the notion of having voluntary examinations available in various subjects, with certificates of proficiency awarded for success in them, and warned the Vice-Chancellor that if the Scriptural examination was unique in this respect, 'greater objections' would be taken to it than if it were one of a numerous class.[24]

Arnold told a friend that

Every single member of the Senate except myself was convinced of the necessity, according to the Charter, of giving the Jews Degrees; all were therefore inclined to make an exemption in their favour as to the New Testament Examination, and thus to make the Examination not in all cases indispensable. Most were disposed to make it altogether voluntary, and that was the course which was at last adopted.[25]

He did not resign, however, for several months, during which he took an occasional part in discussion of the syllabus and regulations for the voluntary examination. But he remained troubled by the rejection of his own convictions, and particularly by the fact that his fellow Anglicans on the Senate, and in King's College, had not and would not follow his line. There were many rumours of his impending departure, and at the beginning of October 1838, he wrote a long letter of resignation to Spring Rice, which seems to have been passed to Lubbock in Burlington's absence from London. The Vice-Chancellor was non-committal, merely noting Arnold's contention 'that the University does not satisfy the great principle that Christianity should be the base of all public education in this country.' The final, official notification of resignation was sent to the Earl of Burlington on 7 November.[26]

Spring Rice, however, spoke his mind, privately, to both Lubbock and to Whately, who had been trying hard to persuade Arnold to remain on the Senate. The minister was careful to ensure that the details were not given any undue publicity – 'The motives for the act are as far as third parties are concerned very immaterial, but yet they would not be communicated to the public without leading to much vexation and angry controversy.' Of Arnold's behaviour, however, Spring Rice wrote with the impatience of the politician who finds an inability to compromise unforgiveable:

> I have come to the conclusion I regret to say that with all his talent and all his high and honourable principle he [Arnold] is a wrong headed man. At least I am certain that he wants that practical discretion without which neither abilities nor good intentions can produce useful results.

And interestingly, as a pointer to Spring Rice's basic sympathy with the Churchmen's viewpoint, he told the Archbishop of Dublin that Arnold's resignation was

> very provoking every way. It provokes me because it diminishes my confidence in his practical wisdom, and because a resignation on principle exposes other members of the Senate who do not resign to much of obloquy and animadversion. I think he has at once committed a fault and made a blunder and all Irishman though I am the blunder does not enable me to justify or to excuse the fault. No doubt if all men could be brought to a really catholic and philosophic spirit it might have been possible in my judgement to have made a compulsory theological course of examination a part of the curriculum of study at the University. But in the times and with the opponents we have to struggle with was this so practicable

an undertaking? To make the best of the elements in our profession seems to me the duty of every one and establishing our voluntary examination . . . did appear to me as near an approximation to what I should have abstractedly have preferred as we could have ventured on it at least at the outset.[27]

From participants with very different views of the controversy there were confident predictions that the voluntary examination in Scriptural studies would be taken by a sizeable majority of the candidates for the BA.[28] No forecast was ever so wrong. Eight years later, in the knowledge that only 7 per cent of candidates had chosen to sit the examination hitherto, the persistent Jerrard was to try again to change his colleagues' minds.

CHAPTER 9

Enter Rothman: Exit Somerville

By the middle of February 1838, the score or so of members who had shown themselves to be committed to the task of establishing the University had been working together for almost a year. The serious consideration of the real academic tasks involved in creating a new examination system had been under way, if rather haltingly, from the second half of 1837 onwards. It was a process which, inevitably, made the conscientious members of the Senate more familiar with each other. The dimensions of what they were expected to do became more clear, and professional interests and controversies set in which no doubt kept the arguments over the Registrar, and over the Scriptural examination, and even the indignation over the new Charter and the controversial appointment of Dr Somerville, within a realistic and at the same time a dynamic perspective.

It is almost certain that, as the curriculum-building exercise had developed, so had a natural tendency for fellows to fall into like-minded groups, however untidily defined at the margins. The Arnold affair certainly delineated a division within the Senate between what Burlington found himself referring to, 'by way of distinction,' as the Religious party, clustering around Jerrard, Arnold, Senior and the three bishops; and their non-Anglican or secular opponents, who would have looked to Warburton as their main spokesman, and included, among the list of major attenders, the Vice-Chancellor, the Quaker Sims, the Roman Catholic Kiernan, Arnott, Billing and Clark. It was a division which may well have cast its shadow over the process of choosing a Registrar.

It is also very likely that the ability of the Vice-Chancellor to keep some business moving, even with the help of only one clerk, may have impressed on some fellows the possibility that the earlier claims about the probable extent of the administrative load on a Registrar had been somewhat exaggerated. And it could well be that the reappointment of Spring Rice as Chancellor of the Exchequer and the knowledge of his continuing strong doubts as to the acceptability of a high registrarial salary, combined with all the other factors which were moulding the

Senate's attitude and behaviour, to prepare that body for a moderate compromise.

At the very beginning of the argument, Airy had wanted to suggest a salary of not more than £600, and a motion for £700 had been defeated at the fourth meeting of the Senate. An undated letter from Empson to Lubbock, probably written late in 1837, hinted that Spring Rice was thinking of a regular annual government contribution of £500, it being understood that the University could raise the salary to £1000 when its own resources allowed - and that Empson, Arnott and Clark felt this to be a possible way forward. But with Burlington out of town until the end of the year, it was not until February 1838 that the subject was raised again formally.[1]

After a committee meeting on 3 February, Burlington recorded that 'A strong opinion was expressed as to the necessity of a Registrar, and I think an almost universal agreement that it is advisable not to insist on the larger salary.' Confidence about the Senate's reaction seems to have grown steadily, and Burlington and Lubbock, with 'a few others' agreed on 14 February to raise the matter of the Registrar at the next meeting. A week later, Burlington wrote:

> Saw Spring Rice on the subject of the salary of our Registrar. I asked him whether he would object to £600 a year. He at once acceded, and said he would readily increase it at the end of the year if we desired it. ... The University met this afternoon. The question of the Registrar's salary was settled in five minutes and an advertisement calling upon candidates to announce themselves was agreed upon.[2]

Spring Rice confirmed his acceptance of £600, with the cautionary proviso 'until the future increase of the University . . . shall afford an adequate sum for defraying this charge.'

Applications for the Registarship were to be submitted by 24 March, and a week before that Airy wrote to Lubbock, expressing the hope that the selection 'will not be made an affair of private friendship with anyone and that no vote will be engaged.' It was an unworldly and possibly hypocritical comment, for Airy himself – like so many of his senatorial colleagues – was heavily lobbied, not least by the successful candidate, who pressed on him lunch or dinner just before the final poll.[3] But there was certainly no lack of applicants – 63 in all – and though many of them were 'young men . . . mostly in the profession of the law,' none of whom 'would be for a moment countenanced by the Senate,'[4] the list included several senior contenders, whose interest confirmed the extent to which the new University was seen as having a potentially significant and prestigious future.

Among the candidates were several men whom we have already met: Thomas Coates, who had been black-balled by Brougham, Warburton and Romilly; James Hudson, Assistant Secretary of the Royal Society; John Frederick Daniell, the distinguished Professor of Chemistry, and strong Anglican, from King's College, who would be an examiner for the University from 1839 to 1844; and R.W. Rothman, the eventual winner, whose career was sketched in Chapter 6. Other notable contenders were Charles C. Atkinson, Secretary of UCL; Dr John Forbes, of Chichester, founder and editor of the *British and Foreign Medical Review*; Samuel Laing, a fellow of St John's, Cambridge, who had been Second Wrangler in 1832; Dr McChristie, Secretary of the London College of Medicine; a well-established barrister, John Thomas Graves, a future professor of Jurisprudence at UCL and an examiner for the University from 1841 to 1848; and William Thomson, fellow of the Royal College of Physicians and Surgeons of Edinburgh.

There is some evidence to support the view that Lubbock wanted Rothman, that Burlington shared Lubbock's enthusiasm, and that Rothman's principal rival was Daniell. Lubbock and Rothman had discussed the tactics necessary to achieve the latter's election before the end of 1837. Rothman kept up the pressure on Lubbock, writing in the late stages of the selection process that:

> You could do me the greatest service by saying a word in my favour quietly to Mr Walker: if he votes for me, it is *impossible* for Daniell to get a majority, even giving him the three Bishops, Bacot, Ridout and all the doubtfuls. Walker told me he should vote for whoever the Chancellor and Vice-Chancellor supported.

And Rothman had asked Airy whether his vote was going to be cast for anyone else, as long ago as October 1837! He certainly regarded Airy as a supporter, and wrote to him just before the final selection meeting - 'May I most earnestly request your attendance at the ballot . . . as I have reason to believe the contest will be very close.' But Airy was unable or unwilling to attend.[5]

On 28 March the Senate agreed a voting procedure to choose a short list of five, providing that all candidates who received an equality of votes should be included. The result was four clear-cut candidates - Daniell, Graves, Laing and Rothman, and four others all receiving the same number of votes and taking the fifth place – Atkinson; C.P. Roney,

Secretary to the Royal Literary Fund and manager of the Polytechnic Institute; Thomson; and Hensleigh Wedgwood, youngest son of Josiah, a fellow of Christ's College, Cambridge, a barrister and currently Police Magistrate for Southwark. The final choice was made on 7 April when, on the first ballot, Daniell and Rothman tied for first place. On the second ballot, Rothman won by a vote of fourteen to twelve.

Twenty six members, including Burlington and Lubbock, attended the meeting. The ballot was secret, and even the number of votes cast was not recorded officially – we know the bare, numerical result only from Burlington's diary.[6] It is almost certain that Daniell, as a King's man, would have received the votes of the three bishops and probably the vote of a strong Anglican like Jerrard, while Rothman had listed Bacot and Ridout as Daniell's people. The two chemists, Brande, who had been Daniell's tutor, and Faraday, were probably also in his camp. Lubbock may well have been joined by Warburton and Walker in plumping for Rothman, and it would not be surprising if Hewett and Henslow, as fellow Cambridge dons, also supported him. Though in the Chair, the figures show that Burlington must have cast a vote, almost certainly for Rothman. But this leaves in question the loyalties of half of those who voted in the final ballot.

We cannot know how most of the medical men divided. And, indeed, without Somerville among the candidates (though he was present as a fellow on this occasion and would almost certainly have voted with Warburton), it may well be that professional academic rivalries were of much less than crucial significance. Even so, Daniell, a King's man and a devout Anglican, could well have suffered through an antagonism - intensified by the recent row over the Scriptural examination – of those opposed to any further shadow of religious influence falling across the new University. While the voting lists for the division on the Scriptural examination of 2 December 1837 and for the election of the Registrar on 7 April, 1838, cannot be known exactly, there are some strong similarities between them. In a long perspective of educational and social history, however, it is more significant that the last two candidates were both men of science – an astronomer and a chemist – and that Rothman's election meant that the University's chief official and his two superiors, the Chancellor and Vice-Chancellor, were of the same intellectual persuasion.

Rothman was elected on 7 April 1838. He took up the office not more than a couple of weeks later, for the first official letter over his signature was dated 25 April. He arrived on the scene when the Senate was sorely troubled by the next major problem – Dr James Somerville.

Thomas Arnold left the University voluntarily and, despite the considerable controversy he had aroused, to the regret of many of his
erstwhile colleagues. James Somerville was simply frozen out by the
fierce hostility of a majority of the medical fellows, and departed
amidst the bewilderment and indifference of the rest of the Senate,
who never had much chance to find out what kind of man he was.
And while his work as Inspector of Anatomy has been the subject of
various commentaries, no rounded picture of him emerges from them
or from the scattered reports and correspondence in public and private
records. He had been appointed Inspector of Anatomy in 1832, after a
seemingly orthodox early career. He was born at the turn of the century,
qualified as an MD from Edinburgh in 1820, and then spent eighteen
months studying in Paris before beginning to practise in London and
later to lecture at St George's Hospital.

Somerville enjoyed the support of Brougham;[7] in the University
context, more significantly, as we have seen, he was the candidate
of Henry Warburton for the Registrarship and then for a place on the
Senate. Russell admitted, after major trouble over Somerville set in,
that 'the appointment was at Warburton's earnest request.' Burlington
felt that the Home Secretary had 'acted very unwisely in placing
[Somerville] in the Senate,' adding that the minister's 'conduct in being
led so much by Warburton is unaccountable.'[8] But Russell claimed that
he had no knowledge of any of the imputations which were levelled at
Somerville, and if Burlington had heard of any special problem when
Somerville's name had been put forward for the Registrarship, he makes
no mention of it in the quite numerous passages which he devoted to the
affair in his diary.

In any event, the task of trying to establish exactly what it was that
Somerville had done to arouse the implacable opposition of many
colleagues is an impossible one. None of the documents which contained
the details have survived, and no public statements were made, almost
certainly because of indications that action for libel was considered
highly likely. And this uncertainty about Somerville's responsibility
in the context of the University of London is only part of the greater
uncertainty which hovers over all his ten-year stint as Inspector of
Anatomy, which ended with his sudden dismissal by the then Home
Secretary, Sir James Graham, in 1842. The author of the most scholarly
review of the contemporary struggle to control the unseemly jostling for

corpses, concluded that 'Somerville's own probity was questioned on more than one occasion, and whether he was in fact above suspicion of complicity in breaches of the [Anatomy] Act may never be known.'[9]

However, though the full story cannot be told, the nature of the controversy over Somerville is clear enough. The new Inspector's attempts to abolish the worst evils of the trade in human bodies were only partly successful, and within the system which he created, 'maldistribution apparently persisted.' Whether or not Somerville's necessarily secretive dealings involved irregularities on his part, he was placed in a most vulnerable position.

> The marketplace competition which governed the anatomy business at this period was antipathetic to the co-operation Somerville perhaps hoped for in his term of office. . . . He was increasingly beset by difficulties, probably the most important of which was that he had made few useful allies. He suffered the hostility of the powerful hospital anatomists, who deeply resented his intervention in their business affairs, and who believed his 'general distribution' was weighted in favour of London University, [i.e. UCL] to the other hospitals' detriment. The Royal College of Surgeons, dominated by the hospital men, still nurtured designs upon the control of the distribution itself. On the other hand, the smaller anatomy school proprietors seem to have felt a grievance that the 'general distribution' benefited the hospitals.[10]

Within days of the release of the revised Charter, which included Dr Somerville in the list of fellows, the Chancellor was made aware of the displeasure of several of his medical colleagues. Among the earliest to make his hostility known was Dr Locock, who was to be an implacable enemy of Somerville throughout. But close behind was Dr Roget, who called on Burlington on 25 January 1838, 'to explain . . . that after Dr Somerville's appointment . . . it would be impossible for him to act as Chairman of the Medical Committee or to attend its meetings.' Somerville's character, in Roget's opinion, was 'exposed to much attack in a pecuniary point of view.' And a day later came Arnott, whose views coincided with those of Roget, though he was less 'angry and bitter' about the affair. Much worried by these signs of more trouble brewing, Burlington took himself first to see Russell – who pleaded ignorance of any of the imputations against Somerville and hoped they would be disproved – and then to Spring Rice, who

shared the Chancellor's fear that the appointment 'was a heavy blow
to the University,' regretted that Somerville had been nominated, and
agreed that 'if the allegations against him are true, he must be made
to withdraw.' A discomfited and apprehensive Burlington wrote in his
diary, 'I foresee great difficulties.'[11]

The only formal mention of Somerville, in the immediate aftermath of
his appointment, were his recorded attendances at the Senate for 17 and
31 January 1838. At the first of these he was made a member of both the
Faculties of Arts and Medicine. It is some measure of the care which was
taken to conceal the progress of the whole episode from public attention
that, thereafter, his name appears only once in the minutes of the Faculty
of Medicine, on 28 May, and that, though he was listed as present at the
Senate on 7 April, there was no recorded discussion of the controversy
over his membership until meetings held between 27 June and 18 July.
In fact, controversy raged and escalated, with only a few weeks' respite
while an enquiry was taking place, from the end of January until the
middle of July.

Roget and Locock brought Clark with them to Burlington on 30
January, and the first non-medical fellows to be drawn in – the
Vice-Chancellor and Beaufort – joined them, while the Bishop of
Durham wrote expressing 'discontentment' with Somerville. Roget
claimed he had a list of twelve fellows incensed by the appointment,
and of the whole group, only Lubbock was willing to try to find a
compromise: Burlington thought Roget 'rather unreasonable' but felt
that all the rest, though more moderate in their sentiments, nonetheless
wanted Somerville removed.[12]

Burlington kept Russell in touch with developing attitudes, and the
Home Secretary called in Warburton, who was 'extremely surprised
at the accusations against Dr Somerville.' They turned to Dr Sims,
who was to be one of the very few supporters of Somerville, and
asked him to act as an intermediary between the accusers and the
accused. Russell, understandably, was eager to know exactly what
were the charges against Somerville, but by 6 February Sims and
Warburton, though they had been in touch with Locock, had not
been able to produce a clear picture of the dispute. Russell accepted
their notion that an enquiry was needed, and proposed a committee of
three, including the Chancellor and Vice-Chancellor and either of the
two lawyers, Empson and Shaw Lefevre. Russell, no doubt influenced
by Warburton, was suspicious of the enemies of Somerville, and made it
clear that he wanted an assurance that 'the gentlemen who bring forward

the charges will abide by the result of the enquiry, and not subsequently state other grounds of objection, should those charges be disproved.'[13]

Lubbock wanted to be sure that Somerville himself approved this procedure, rather than preferring to leave the matter to the Senate as a whole. Warburton, whether he consulted Somerville or not, took a stronger line with Russell and objected to having the case referred 'to any Members of the Senate who . . . have all more or less heard stories connected with the charges.' That there was some truth in this is borne out by a letter Empson wrote to a friend on 11 February in which he said, 'The MDs hate James Somerville so intensely that they threaten, I hear, none of them to continue their attendance in case he comes. I trust they will modify.'[14]

Russell responded by suggesting that 'the case should be referred to Mr Samuel March Phillipps, the Under Secretary of State [at the Home Office]. He has no personal acquaintance with Dr J.S. beyond seeing him occasionally on official business.'[15] In conversation, Russell confided to Burlington that he thought Somerville 'must retire,' from which the Chancellor presumed that the minister had 'reason to be satisfied the charges are not unfounded.'[16] Burlington then approached Locock to find out whether Russell's proposed procedure was acceptable. A week afterwards, on 17 February, Burlington wrote:

> Heard from Dr Locock respecting Dr Somerville. He and the others who agree with him decline to come forward and go into an investigation of the charges before Mr March Phillips, but they make a statement of what they believe to be the facts, and think Dr Somerville should deny their truth if he is able. Called upon Mr Phillipps – he does not quite approve of this mode of proceeding, but having now in his possession the nature of the charges and the authority upon which they rest, he will satisfy himself as to their existence and then call upon Dr Somerville for an explanation. I trust the matter is now in a train for being cleared up. It has been suffered to impend over us much too long.[17]

For a little over two months there was silence, while March Phillipps pursued his enquiries. Somerville kept away, and if there was continued argument, none of it 'leaked'. But after a meeting of the Faculty of Medicine on 24 April, a major crisis developed. It is difficult to reconstruct the exact sequence of events, but clearly Somerville, whether on his own initiative or spurred on by others, may have decided to try to force the issue by appearing at a meeting of the Senate on 7 April, before the report on him had been completed. This appearance was clearly made known, informally, to the Faculty of Medicine, and when they met next, on 24 April, his opponents were so outraged that they refused to attend thereafter. No business was done at meetings called for 30 April and 28 May. Somerville is listed as having turned up on 28 May, along with Billing and Sims - the single record of Somerville's attendance at the faculty – but there was no quorum. The faculty did not come together again until 20 July.

Meanwhile, the Home Secretary decided to ask Shaw Lefevre – a trusted Whig politician and administrator – to work with Phillipps on collecting and assessing the evidence about Somerville. Their report reached Russell by mid-May, and he sent it on to Burlington with his opinion that

> while the rumours alluded to were founded on circumstances calculated to excite suspicion, no fact has been substantiated which ought to deprive Dr Somerville of the station which his talents and labours have enabled him to maintain.
>
> Trusting you will agree with me in opinion I hope it may be in your power to restore harmony in the Medical Branch of the University.[18]

The Chancellor was not fully satisfied with Somerville's defence, but agreed, as did Lubbock, that 'no case of dishonesty is substantiated.' By 22 May Burlington had held a meeting with several of the medical men and judged that 'all except Dr Locock seem reasonable about Dr Somerville, and will consent to go on.' But it was too optimistic a judgement. In the next week, Arnott, Bacot, Clark, Kiernan and Ridout indicated that if Somerville continued to be a member of the Senate, they would not attend; Jerrard was unconvinced by the evidence in favour of Somerville; Roget offered his resignation as Chairman of the Faculty, and Locock sent his resignation from the Senate to Russell. By 28 May, Burlington felt that it was 'clearly impossible to go on while Dr Somerville continues to be a member,' and told Russell so.[19]

But Russell was not to be easily convinced and, while apparently accepting that Somerville might have to go, was also prepared to let Roget and Locock depart, perhaps seeing them, through Warburton's eyes, as being basically antagonistic to the Government's – or at least to Russell's – interests. Burlington saw 'no prospect of going on well from this course,' and also told the Bishop of Chichester that Somerville could not be induced to withdraw quietly, as the Bishop hoped. Spring Rice was 'very civil as usual, but one never can reckon on his fair words,' wrote Burlington, who was bemused by the difficulties involved, but determined 'to do my best.' In the second week of June he was using Kiernan to find out whether Arnott and Clark would remain if Roget and Locock left, though he did not think they should. It was the response to this move which led Russell to capitulate.

On 12 June, Arnott and Clark called on Russell and told him that 'it would be impossible for the others to remain if Roget and Locock were omitted.' The minister then agreed that Somerville would have to be made to retire: but it would be made clear that while the retirement was necessary 'in order that the University may resume its labours,' it was not required 'on account of the imputations against his character.' But neither Russell nor the senators had reckoned with the hostility and persistence of Henry Warburton, who, on 14 June, sent the following letter to Russell:

> Dr James Somerville has received no official information from your Lordship in what manner the enquiry into his conduct has terminated, and it is only through me that an extract from a letter on the subject, addressed by your Lordship to Lord Burlington, and amounting to an acquittal, has been made known to him.
>
> If the matter had here ended, or been likely to end, it might not have been necessary to request your Lordship to make any direct communication to Dr James Somerville; but his accusers, as your Lordship is aware, refuse to acquiesce in your Lordship's decision, and renew the charges they had previously made.
>
> The Report of Messrs Phillipps and Lefevre, and a copy of so much of your Lordship's letter to Lord Burlington as expresses your Lordship's decision, ought then to be communicated to Dr Somerville, in order to enable him to consider, with his Counsel, what further measures may be necessary to his justification.
>
> I have seen the Report of Messrs Phillipps and Lefevre only under restrictions which Lord Burlington has imposed upon me, and have not felt myself at liberty to inform Dr J.S. or his Counsel what the nature of that Report is. Dr Sims has not yet seen it; but it has been read, under your Lordship's directions, to the gentlemen who preferred the charges.
>
> I think it right to inform your Lordship that according to the view at present taken of this matter by the advisers of Dr J.S., there remains only one course for him to pursue, and that is to bring an Action for Libel against Dr Locock, when Dr Locock may state what facts

he pleases, in justification: and seeing that Dr S's accusers do not think proper to acquiesce in your Lordship's verdict, it is much to be regretted that this mode of adjudication was not had recourse to in the first instance.[20]

The threat of a libel action certainly seems to have stopped Locock and his colleagues in their tracks, but it also caused both Russell and Burlington to conclude that there was no way to avoid the business becoming public.[21] At the same time, by accident or design, both Parliament and press showed an awareness of the row. A motion to lay the Senate's minutes on the table was made by Thomas Milner Gibson on 14 June and was successfully resisted by Russell:[22] but a day or two later the *Medical Gazette* asked,

> Can the rumour be true, that the disgust excited by the domineering spirit of a certain member of the Senate has now risen to such a height as to threaten the very existence of this embryo university? Or is the cause of the dissensions which exist to be found in the conduct adopted with respect to the appointment of a gentleman to a seat in the Senate who, when candidate for an inferior office, had been almost unanimously rejected? However this may be, we understand that nearly all the members of the medical faculty have resigned; while from the denial of this fact, and the endeavours made to induce them to resume office, it is evident that the patrons of the Metropolitan University are in great alarm.[23]

It is not unreasonable to see the whole of the Somerville affair, from the first meetings of the Senate in March 1837 through the attempt to have him as Registrar, his appointment to a fellowship, and his ultimate departure from the University scene, as a contest of will between Warburton and the more conservatively inclined senators, medical and non-medical. How much Somerville may have been coerced into following Warburton's lead for the latter's political advantage, how much he may have been a constant suppliant for promotion, or simply fanatically ambitious for the cause of medical reform, must remain matters for mere speculation. But there is little doubt that by the middle of June 1838 Somerville was beginning to want to escape from his tortuous connection with the University of London, and that Warburton either acceded to his wish or accepted, as a practical politician, that this particular game was up. The threat of libel was enough to prepare the way for a compromise settlement, which Warburton pursued thereafter with professional skill, but without much ultimate success.

On 26 June, Burlington learned from Warburton that Somerville did not wish to remain on the Senate, but could not withdraw because to do so would 'destroy his character'. Nonetheless, Warburton promised that Somerville would not try to attend the Faculty 'if the others would consent to go on.' On the following day Warburton gave notice that at the next meeting of the Senate he would draw attention to the 'non-presentation of any Report of the Committee of the Faculty of Medicine.' Armed with this, the weary Burlington went back to Russell on 'the everlasting Somerville business,' warned him of what was to happen, and then persuaded the hostile Arnott and Roget to come to the Senate.

The Senate met on 30 June, and the Chancellor's description of it in his diary seems, in the light of such other, meagre evidence as there is, to be a fair account:

> We have had a most unpleasant meeting at the University to-day. The whole of the recent unfortunate circumstances connected with Dr Somerville's appointment came into discussion. Warburton complained that the Senate was not made acquainted with the state of the Medical Committee. I stated that my reason for not having brought the subject before the senate was that I hoped the business would be settled without dragging the University into a most painful discussion. Warburton found fault with the course I have pursued – most of the other members of the senate seemed to approve. A long conversation took place as to whether the proceedings on the Investigation should be printed in our minutes it was however finally agreed as I thought pretty generally, that such a course would not be advisable and no one moved that they should be printed. Warburton threw out as a suggestion that the Medical Committee should meet again for business, promising he would do his best to prevent Dr Somerville from attending the Senate until the legal proceedings which he thought probably might be instituted were brought [to a] close. I think this suggestion might very reasonably be acted upon. However no positive agreement was come to and I fear Dr Roget and some others are still averse to it but I hope finally they may be brought to agree to it. Dr Roget insisted on a letter of his being read and printed in the minutes. It is a foolish and most injudicious one and will I fear do him no credit.

Burlington was correct in his gloomy estimate of the probabilities.

He wrote at length to Roget, trying to persuade him and his colleagues to go back to work on the Faculty, but at the next Senate, on 9 July, he found that 'the medical gentlemen are obstinate and will not attend the meetings of their Committee.' An 'ill-advised letter from Locock' had been printed in the minutes, to Burlington's dismay, and when the question of the annual reappointment of the Medical Committee was raised, it was agreed that before this was done all the medical members except Somerville should be asked whether they would attend if appointed.

The results of the consultation were revealed at the meeting two days later – 11 July – and the minutes of that meeting include the texts of all the letters received. Only Billing and Sims were willing to attend if Somerville was a member. Brande pleaded ignorance of the whole affair; Hewitt said he lacked the time to come, any way; Hammick felt he could come in view of Warburton's promise that Somerville would not attend for the present, but thought it useless in view of his colleagues' attitudes. Arnott, Bacot, Clark, Kiernan, M'Grigor, Locock, Ridout and Roget all simply refused to serve so long as Somerville was a member. After some argument, it was agreed that the whole affair should be put, formally, before the Home Secretary. Russell called for a delegation, and on 13 July Burlington was to take with him Chichester, Lubbock, Arnott, Clark, Shaw Lefevre and Sims. However, Sims fell seriously ill – he died only days later – and Billing took his place. It was a nicely balanced group.

Russell had hinted to Burlington on 9 July that he was 'disposed to a new Charter.' He told the delegation that he would issue one, but would first consult Warburton, who 'desired an interview.' That interview, with a delegation led by Warburton, was held the next day.[24] No more detail is available, and there is no record of what passed between the minister and Warburton's group. Unfortunately, for the narrator, Burlington and his family departed for the Continent on 14 July, and were not to return to England for eleven months, so that we have no more relevant diary entries for the ensuing weeks. But the outcome of the Somerville affair was a complete victory for the majority medical group. Russell wrote to Lubbock on 16 July saying that Somerville had tendered his resignation, but that he (Russell) had not yet received the letter. Whether he did receive it, whether he and Warburton managed to find some face-saving formula which enabled Somerville to abandon his threatened action for libel, or whether Somerville was simply bullied into giving up without any further fight, may never be known, for there is, at present, no documentary evidence.

Russell's promise to produce a new Charter was not fulfilled. In 1837–8, and indeed later, 'a new charter' was a kind of shorthand for possible, limited changes to the personnel of the Senate and to the conditions under which fellows were appointed. As we know, the first Charter had provided for appointment during pleasure, while the 1837 revision had changed this into appointment during good behaviour, and had added the possibility that if the number of fellows fell below twenty-five, the remaining senators could elect new members to fill the vacancies. It is clear that the secrecy with which the revised version had been drafted and approved was resented by many members of the Senate, and it seems certain that, when Russell met the delegation to discuss the apparent *impasse* in the Somerville affair on 13 July 1838, the possibility of some other way of appointing senators in future was raised. But any early hopes of change were quickly dashed, for Russell's letter to Lubbock, three days later, declared, flatly, that 'I do not propose to renounce by any new Charter the power of the Crown to name Members of the Senate.'

The presence of Dr Somerville had disrupted, seriously, the attempts of the Faculty of Medicine to put together a syllabus for the medical examinations. The process of getting rid of him had split both the Faculty of Medicine and to a lesser extent the Senate as a whole, and had demonstrated how separate a world the medics inhabited. The episode had also reflected the strains which existed between the established medical men and the Whig Government, and made relations between Government and University rather more delicate. The call for a new Charter was to be repeated and widened in 1839–40, but, by mid-summer of 1838, in the light of the controversies over Drs Arnold and Somerville, it is hardly surprising that unfriendly and mischievously exaggerated comments appeared in the press. One such was the claim that

> The smothered fires of this establishment are now bursting into public notoriety, beyond the means of concealment . . . the fierce contention in the medical school has grown to such a pitch as to render it expedient to revoke the charter, in order to reorganize the body politic.

And an 'FRS' from Bloomsbury, wrote to *The Times* that

> During nearly two years' existence of this abortive monument of the good faith of Mr Spring Rice, and of the good temper of

Mr Warburton, his ally and joint partner in the patronage, the meetings of the pseudo senate have been one perpetual scene of wrangle and personal vituperation, and consequently no advance whatever made in promoting the professed purposes of the institution.[25]

CHAPTER 10

Examinations and Faultlines

Once some progress was being made on shaping syllabuses for examinations it was not long before the question of who should do the examining came to the fore. The resolution of that question, and subsequent troubles, were the outcome of the original failure to make any clear distinction between the Senate as a governing body and the Senate as a board of examiners. There is no doubt that several members of the Senate joined under the firm, and correct, impression, that they were expected to act as examiners. On the other side there were several who either did not understand or did not take seriously the possibility that they might be called upon to examine and who, when the issue came to the fore, felt that it was a mistake to mix the two functions of governing and examining. The first group expected to be paid for their service as examiners; the second group thought it a grave mistake for senators to accept payment, especially when the Senate as a body proposed the rates of pay to the Treasury. The basic confusion caused by this structural fault in the system was to lead, eventually, to an embarrassing public row.

As it turned out, there was no obvious shortage of people in or near London who were qualified and keen to be examiners. But at first there were some doubts. At the beginning of 1838, Airy wrote to the Vice-Chancellor of the need for:

> an immense number of examiners, and where shall we find them? The examination hall at Oxford is in the midst of seven hundred idle fellows of colleges, and the thing is practicable there: but how to find seven persons equally competent and equally unemployed in London I do not know.

And three months later Airy was assuming that it would be necessary to hire examiners from Oxbridge, 'for the present at least if not for the future.' In fact, a few examiners were to be fellows of Oxford or Cambridge colleges, but this was never a problem for the Senate. More significant was the response to another of Airy's question –

'Has the question as to the amount of their stipend been mooted at all?'[1]

It is clear from correspondence that, early in 1838, there was substantial ignorance, or at least substantial lack of recollection, of the terms on which senators had been appointed. At the same time there were those who believed – to a considerable degree quite correctly, as was to become clear – that the Senate was entirely free to decide who, and to recommend on what terms, examiners should be employed. The serious internal debate began in March, when Jerrard 'contemplated the appointment of permanent examiners at large salaries.' Burlington demurred, thinking that such a move would be 'very prejudicial to the University.' But Jerrard was able to convince both Burlington and Lubbock that his basic expectation of employment as an examiner was not unreasonable.

The situation with which the Senate was faced, and which had to be accepted in 1838 – though with much reluctance expressed by some members – was laid out clearly by Burlington three years afterwards in a defensive letter to the new Tory Chancellor of the Exchequer, Henry Goulburn:

> most unquestionably, as the charter stands, it is clearly contemplated that the members of the Senate should themselves be examiners; and most persons will, I think, be of opinion that it was intended not merely that they should be occasionally appointed, but that other examiners should be appointed only in case the requisite number was not found among the members of the Senate. In confirmation of this opinion I may refer to the letters written by Lord Melbourne . . . to the different members . . . inviting them to form part of the contemplated University, in which they are requested to become members of the Board of Examiners. Some of them were also informed that it would be necessary to resign certain situations which they held, as being inconsistent with their new position of examiners in the London University. One gentleman [Jerrard], in consequence, resigned the office of Principal of Bristol College, another [Billing] a lecturership at one of the hospitals.[2]

In the Spring of 1838, however, there was no such certainty about the role of members of the Senate. Lubbock wanted to appoint examiners from outside the Senate and to pay them 'from £100 to £150' annually. Jerrard and those who followed him argued that senators could be examiners and should be paid £300 per annum. Without settling the question of who should examine, the Senate compromised on a maximum fee of £200 for the matriculation and BA examiners at its meeting on 17 March 1838.[3] It was not until May of 1839 that a maximum of £250 was agreed for medical examiners. Initially, the Treasury accepted these figures.

From the beginning of the consideration of the appointment and remuneration of examiners, Henry Warburton was clearly unhappy about the prospect of a self-perpetuating, closed circle of senatorial nominees, and of the establishment of a system of narrow patronage. Nor was he any happier about the size of the salaries proposed, and in particular thought the medical examinerships were too highly paid. He began a continuous and consistent campaign at the end of March 1838 by giving notice, in the Senate, that at the next meeting of the Faculty of Arts he would move that no examiner should serve more than four years consecutively. On 4 April that motion was carried by a vote of 9 to 8: the close division led to the law officers being asked to clarify the Senate's authority in respect of the appointment of examiners. Their opinion was quite unequivocal:

> the Chancellor, Vice-Chancellor, and Fellows may select whatever subjects of Examination they may think fit, and may appoint whatever Examiners they may approve, without submitting what they are doing to the Secretary of State; and they may choose the Examiners annually, or otherwise, at their discretion. . . . The Senate cannot pass any valid By-law restricting the class out of whom the Examiners are to be chosen. . . . The Examiners may be chosen, partly from Members of the Senate and partly from Strangers, or wholly from the Senate or wholly from Strangers.[4]

When this opinion was made known, the motion restricting the reappointment of an examiner to four consecutive years, was rescinded. Annual election was to become the normal practice.

Late in July, the Faculty of Medicine decided that, for the medical degree, up to fifteen examiners would be needed, and that at least a majority of them should be selected from medical members of the Senate. This spurred Warburton to move that, as

> all individuals, whether Fellows of this University or not Fellows, are equally eligible as Examiners, it is not expedient, and would be unjust, to proceed to appoint Examiners, without previously

making it known within the precincts of the Universities of the United Kingdom, that on some day to be signified in such notice, the Senate intends to proceed to the appointment of Examiners.

But Warburton was not to win this round. At meetings in August his motion was amended, and the procedures for choosing examiners laid down, after considerable argument, by less than a dozen fellows, almost all from the medical faculty. Those who carried the day were Arnott, Bacot, Clark, Hammick, Kiernan and Ridout, all medics; and they were joined by Jerrard. Opposition came consistently only from Warburton himself and Billing, though Faraday and Austin gave them some limited support on different occasions. The Vice-Chancellor was in the chair, and cast no vote, but at an earlier stage he had been troubled, as he continued to be, by the idea of senators being examiners, and had cast his vote in favour of restricting the tenure of any examiner to four consecutive years.[5]

The solution accepted was in the form of an amendment to Warburton's motion, introduced by Dr Arnott, which stated that

the objects of the University will be best secured by first choosing from among the Members of the Senate such Members as are willing and competent to undertake the duties of Examiners; and if a sufficient number be not so found, by selecting others after direct application to persons known to the Senate to be worthy.

The Registrar was instructed to find out which senators were willing to be examiners, if elected. By 22 August he had received only four positive replies, one of which was conditional, and twenty-two negative ones. There is no record of later responses to this first approach from the remaining fellows. Warburton then argued that, because there were so very few fellows willing to serve, and as it was desirable to select 'the most competent persons,' no appointment should be made until the Senate had an opportunity of knowing 'what other persons are candidates.' But this challenge was rejected by the same team of six medical men and Jerrard as had imposed their will in the earlier divisions, and who went on to approve an internal voting procedure for the selection of fellows as examiners.

The first three examiners of the new University of London to be elected, therefore, were three senators – Thomas Brande in Chemistry, J.H. Jerrard and Connop Thirlwall in Classics. Thus was a precedent set, and subsequently followed, that senators who wished to be examiners never failed to be elected. And despite the initial lack of interest, Brande, Jerrard and Thirlwall were only the first of twelve senators who, as we have seen in Chapter 6, acted as examiners for spells of very varied lengths. All twelve were original members of the Senate, and those of them who wished were enabled to go on holding paid office as examiners until they decided to retire, or until they died. But after 1840, in large part as a result of a controversy still to be described, the practice of election to examinerships was not extended to new senators.

The early decisions about the salaries to be offered were focused on a perceived need for examiners who would have full responsibilities for reasonably heavy workloads. But less heavy responsibilities were recognized, as well as sub-divisions of subject matter, and lower levels of remuneration were introduced from time to time. No distinction was made between the remuneration of senatorial and non-senatorial examiners. And despite the rather odd phrasing of the resolution which provided that the selection of non-senatorial examiners would be made 'after direct application to persons known to the Senate to be worthy,' there was, effectively, open advertisement, and no lack of worthy candidates. With rare exceptions, however, once a non-senatorial examiner was appointed, he was normally assured of practically automatic reappointment. That this was expected from the outset may be illustrated by Rothman's attempt to interest Charles Babbage in becoming an examiner, as early as 13 August 1838: Rothman explained that there would be annual election, but went on, 'I do not think in practice [the examiners] will be changed every year.'[6]

For both senatorial and non-senatorial examiners, therefore, the whole system had potential tendencies towards cosy privilege. Those tendencies were to be challenged and eventually somewhat weakened by internal and external controversies about money and the future constitution of the University. But in the next few months there were signs that attitudes of compromise were developing over the matter of payment. Hodgkin pressed on Lubbock the idea of 'a modest uniform fee . . . plus a sum dependent on days or hours actually worked,' and felt that 'The members of the Senate composing the committee of examination might not unreasonably think themselves entitled to some compensation, but I think that for the present at least they would do well to forgo it.'[7] But on another issue, within weeks, Hodgkin's Quaker toleration deserted him.

The full corps of twenty-two examiners was assembled in the latter half of 1838 and the first half of 1839, and the eleven places not filled by fellows attracted between them some ninety candidates. The procedure of choice seemed to have worked smoothly, and the only evidence of serious perturbation over an individual came as the result of the election of a fellow, John Bacot, to an examinership in surgery. This so outraged Hodgkin that he considered resignation from the Senate in protest, and pressed on the Vice-Chancellor and Warburton, among others, the desirability of persuading Bacot to withdraw. Hodgkin argued that

> For our examiners in Surgery we ought unquestionably to have only pure surgeons – men who if not hospital surgeons are at least clearly eligible to that office and such as the College of Surgeons would recognise as teacher and examiner in surgery. If this be not the case our B.M. and M.D. can neither of them have the value of a diploma from the College of Surgeons and we shall lose in the number as well as character of our graduates. I can have no personal objection to John Bacot whom I have never met but on friendly terms and who is I doubt not a well educated medical man, but being a general practitioner unknown as a teacher of surgery or as a consulting surgeon there is nothing connected with his name to sanction his appointment either at home or abroad. Had he been elected an examiner on Materia Medica or Pharmacy his long and honorable connection with the Apothecaries' Company would so far alter the case as to leave on my mind no other objection than that I have already made to members of the Senate generally.[8]

Sir James Clark also expressed disquiet at Bacot's appointment, but neither Lubbock nor Warburton felt able to pursue Hodgkin's plea, and Warburton responded, pointedly, that 'as disapproving of the rule under which Mr Bacot had been elected, I was not sorry that a practical proof of the inexpediency of the rule had been afforded, by it having occasioned the Senate to make an improper appointment.'[9] Hodgkin did not resign: Bacot remained an examiner in Surgery until 1845. But the episode underlined the deep concern felt within the Senate about the closed selection of fellows as examiners, and foreshadowed the public row which came in 1840.

Examiners' pay was not the only matter of remuneration which was raised during the negotiation of the examination syllabuses. When the Somerville affair was at its height, the medical fellows simply stopped working at the complex problems involved in shaping a new medical curriculum and, after Somerville had gone, it proved difficult to regain the momentum which had been lost. But the politicking over Somerville was felt particularly by the Chairman of the Medical Faculty, Peter Mark Roget who, like all his colleagues, was a busy professional man giving his services to the University for no financial reward. He complained to Lubbock at the beginning of July: 'You have not the slightest idea of the serious inconvenience to which all this encroachment on my time is putting me at the present moment.'[10] But Lubbock was almost certainly aware of this problem, for the Chancellor had written only days previously to warn Spring Rice:

> I have never heard any of them [fellows] use any expression which leads me to think that they suppose they have any claim to remuneration, but I have lately heard some of them remark that it occupies so much of their time, seriously to interfere with their professional emoluments. I cannot help feeling some apprehensions that it will be impossible permanently to obtain the gratuitous assistance of such persons as the interests of the University require.[11]

Burlington's concern was proved valid. The pressure to complete the scheme of medical examinations was considerable and, even with Somerville removed, progress with the committee work was so slow that the Faculty of Medicine, realizing the need for and the burden of leadership, proposed in November 1838 that a Dean should be appointed and paid a salary of £500 per annum. Roget, the most obvious candidate for such a place, was clearly a man of rather short temper, prone to offering to resign if crossed. He was deeply suspicious and disapproving of Warburton, partly on account of the latter's earlier moves to reduce the salary paid to the Registrar. Roget first told Lubbock that he would be disinclined to take the proposed Deanship without a salary and, on 4 December – perhaps with the intention of forcing the issue – he submitted his resignation as Chairman of the Faculty.[12]

The Medical Faculty's proposals were not to be debated by the Senate until 12 December, but Lubbock, now acting on his own, Burlington being abroad, at once wrote to Russell, explaining the situation, stressing Roget's high qualifications for being Chairman of the Faculty, and expressing his fears if new support was refused: 'Some of the Medical Faculty who have attended constantly are losing patience and if any new difficulty starts up I much fear that Dr Roget and several of our most valuable members will cease to give us any assistance whatever.'[13] But within a couple of days the proposal for a salaried Dean was simply ruled out of court, informally at that stage, by Russell and Spring Rice.[14] Lubbock appears to have kept this hard news to himself, however, at least until after the matter was debated by the Senate.

On 12 December, Arnott moved that a Dean of Medicine be appointed with a salary of £500. Warburton raised a technical issue as to whether there was a Faculty of Medicine or only a Committee, and called for the discussion to be delayed until the medics had produced their examination scheme. This was defeated, but Locock, accepting Warburton's technical point, proposed that the proposals be referred back to the Medical Committee, which should be empowered to consider the salary of a Dean. The first part of this amendment was accepted and the second held over. As in the voting on the appointment of examiners, the fellows present were overwhelmingly medical.

Lubbock reported, gloomily, to Airy that Warburton's 'verbal quibble' had successfully prevented discussion of the salary issue, but felt that the proposal was dead. The Government's refusal to contemplate a salaried Dean must have been made known soon afterwards for, at the next meeting, on 15 December, the second half of Locock's motion was withdrawn, and no more was heard of the Deanship. The ministers had apparently called Roget's bluff successfully: Roget would not go back as chairman, but he did not leave the Senate. Lubbock's legitimate worry about the medical curriculum was that 'unless some one acts as chairman who is a *man of business* and understands how matters of this kind are to be conducted the Committee may attend forever without coming to any conclusion.'[15] He was relieved, however, when Sir James Clark took over as Chairman of the Medical Faculty, and produced the new scheme of examination for its first reading to the Senate on 13 March 1839.

The minutes for the last months of 1838 and for the year 1839 show that the Senate was busily occupied with the detail of completing the examination regulations, with overseeing the first examinations, and with handling the applications of medical schools and teachers to be recognized as providers of instruction to students preparing to take the University's degrees. The system was, at last, working. The wounding rows of the past two years were over, though there was plenty of argument, especially within the medical camp, over the disciplinary demands of the various specialisms and, as we have just seen, some disquiet over the election of examiners. But for the first time the minutes give a sense that here was a devoted body of men, hard at work in relative harmony, without being continuously involved in awkward and potentially disruptive disputes. When the Chancellor returned to England in mid-June 1839, after an absence of eleven months, he recorded in his diary that the University 'has been going on very well . . . and I think for the present its chief difficulties are over.'[16]

If there were very few major eruptions of anger or dismay, however, there was an undercurrent of anxiety and discontent. The experience of 1837 and 1838 had revealed to several fellows what they saw as grave weaknesses, constitutional and political, in the condition of the University, and at the same time the troubles with Arnold and Somerville had disturbed Lord John Russell and Spring Rice. The political climate in which the University had begun life was also much changed in 1839, when for a few days in May the continuance of the Whig Government in office was interrupted by the Bedchamber Crisis, and the Senate faced the possibility of having to deal with a Tory administration. Though that immediate possibility quickly receded, the Senate was left with reduced confidence in the idea of long continued, basic ministerial sympathy with their enterprise. Moreover, in August/September, Spring Rice left the Government, though he was raised to the peerage as Lord Monteagle and was appointed Comptroller-General, while Russell moved from the Home to the Colonial Office: his successor, Lord Normanby, was a newcomer to the University's affairs.

The resentment felt by many fellows that the ministers, in drawing up the revised Charter, had ignored the Senate and had consulted only the highly politically motivated Warburton, was strengthened throughout 1838 by the experience of the Somerville episode. And that episode, which involved a virtual stoppage of the work of the Medical Faculty, led to the subsequent claim of overwork, the resignation of Roget as Chairman, and the failed attempt to secure a salaried Dean of Medicine. The deteriorating situation, as it developed, made the case for considering some further change in the constitutional arrangements apparently acceptable to Russell and Spring Rice, though the latter was particularly anxious 'to avoid any adverse question from being mooted in or out of Parliament.' In early December 1838, the Home Secretary, in turning down any idea of paying a salary to a Dean, nonetheless advised Lubbock that 'the Senate should appoint a committee of members to suggest alterations for a new Charter.'[17]

Within a week of this, and in part at least coincidentally, there reached the Vice-Chancellor the first written analysis – or, at least, the first which has survived – of the weaknesses of the existing set-up. It came from the Astronomer Royal, George Airy, who had been relatively detached from the Somerville affair and was rarely able, or willing, to attend meetings. Airy had put the essence of what follows in a private letter to Spring Rice in July 1838, when he asked whether he should resign his place on the Senate because he was so frequently unable to attend, but also because he found that 'there is an extensive impression that some organic change may perhaps be made' in the University's constitution.[18] Spring Rice persuaded him to stay on but, by December, in the light of his continuing concern, Airy expressed his worries to Lubbock. As always, the Astronomer Royal declaimed in trenchant fashion:

> I believe it will be found absolutely necessary to attach a stipend to some or all of the offices of Members of the Senate; and that a change in the constitution of the Senate, referring in some degree to its stipendiary character, will eventually be found necessary.
>
> The Senate at present may be considered as mainly constituted of two classes of persons. The first comprises dignitaries and official persons, who are favourable to the general plan of the University, and whose time, it would seem, might fairly be claimed by the government which patronises the University (though no such claim, so far as I know, has been distinctly made). The second consists of individuals unconnected with office, who have been led to join the University by their conscious desire to see an institution of its peculiar principles firmly established.
>
> With regard to the first of these classes, I can say from my own experience, and the assertion will be confirmed by the working of other committees and boards as well as of one man, that it is quite impossible that official persons can aid materially in the general conduct of the affairs of the University. If the business of the University could be put in such a form that the decisions on leading points could be referred to a few meetings of which ample notice was given, the official persons might be able to make themselves acquainted with those points and to attend at such meeting with good effect. But at most their attendance introduces irregularity in to the general mode of proceedings and is in my opinion injurious rather than beneficial. Considering that the propriety of making pecuniary payments to such persons will always be disputed, and perhaps fairly so; and considering that without some advantage gained to the person there will always be an unwillingness to undertake the

labour of a Senator, with all the confusion that it occasions in offices already overburdened with business; I think it is doubtful whether such persons should not better be excluded.

As to the private persons constituting the second class, however desirous they may be of giving their assistance to the University, the absence of a feeling of responsibility (which will surely die away when the office produces no advantage to themselves), the addition of considerable labour to that of their respective professions, and the great inconvenience caused in all private arrangements, will make it difficult for them to act zealously and steadily in the concerns of the University. And, even while attending frequently at its meetings, the fluctuations occasioned by their not attending *uniformly* will be extremely inconvenient. I need not to recall to any member of the Senate that, at consecutive meetings, different members have attended, and resolutions most opposite in spirit have been passed.

I see no remedy for this but attaching a stipend to the office in general (which, as in some other instances, might depend upon attendance at meetings) and an extraordinary stipend to the most important offices. And on the ground of justice from the public to the individuals, I do not see that this can be disputed.[19]

Before this is dismissed as an overly professional, bureaucratic and drastic view, it has to be put in the context of an operation which had been uneven, to put it mildly, and was now at its most intense, with meetings two or even three times a week, quite unlike the 'normal' expectation of the duties of an unpaid board, and bearing little resemblance to how the pattern of senatorial activity would develop within a few years.

Lubbock may have written about Airy's ideas to Burlington, in Italy, along with his worries over the slow progress with the medical curriculum, and his concern about new possibilities which were appearing of some co-operation with the College of Surgeons (and, of which, more later). Burlington, obviously out of touch, replied that he was reluctant to approach Russell without having more communication with the Senate, but agreeing that if the College of Surgeons were 'ready to join', a new Charter would need to take account of it.[20] Lubbock was left to his own devices for another six months, until Burlington's return in June 1839.

It would appear that, insofar as the ministers were willing to contemplate a changed Charter, they concentrated on the notion of strengthening the working membership of the Senate rather than devising new constitutional machinery. Those on the Senate who wanted more independence, on the other hand, would have agreed with Sir James Clark, who had pressed the need for a new Charter on Lubbock at the end of 1838:

> Only think what might be the fate of our University if a change of Government were to take place – Not only its character but its utility might be entirely destroyed. Let us get a new Charter, and the Senate have a voice in the appointment of new members and we are safe. Nothing else will save us.[21]

But only new names, not new measures, seem to have been taken seriously. Russell put forward Macaulay as a possibility, and wanted suggestions from Lubbock for new medical members. Airy and Clark, however, were particularly anxious about the dangers of medical dominance. Airy tried to persuade the astronomer, Sir John Herschell, to accept Russell's invitation to join the Senate, arguing that

> The great danger to be faced is that the University should become exclusively medical, not only to the invalidation of degrees in other faculties but also to the partial suppression of the examination of medical students in general subjects. The authority of your name and the occasional expression of your opinion would do more to prevent this than the constant fighting of half a dozen smaller men.[22]

But Herschell could not be tempted. Meanwhile, Warburton must have shared the anxieties of Airy and Clark, for he promised Lubbock that he would try to prevent the appointment of two medics who had probably been suggested by Russell.[23]

Nothing had happened, perhaps mainly because of the political crisis of May 1839, by the eve of Burlington's return. At that point in time the second surviving, thoughtful survey of the University's experience and problems, and some forthright recommendations, were produced, in a strong letter to Lubbock, by Sir James Clark:

> The Medical Faculty of the University may want *strength*, but, comprehending very nearly one half of the whole Senate, certainly does not require *number*, and I do trust Lord John Russell will not think of adding a single additional member who will not add to the character of the Institution. I feel assured you will agree with me, that no new member should be appointed to the Senate who is not *known* as a man of high character and of *reputation* in the profession

to which he belongs. In the medical faculty, you know, it is especially necessary that this principle should be rigidly acted on. The late proceedings in the Senate afford sufficient proof of the necessity that its members should be men of enlarged views. By our election of Examiners from among ourselves I fear we have imflicted an injury on the Institution, and have greatly disappointed the expectations of the profession and the Public.

I would entreat you, as you value the success of the University, to press this matter upon Lord John Russell; as his Lordship is too just, and has the interests of his own Institution too much at heart, to do voluntarily that which could not fail to injure it.

The faults which were committed in the original formation of the University have been, as you well know, most detrimental to it, and will long continue to retard its progress and diminish its utility. It is a duty therefore which we owe to Lord John Russell, to the University, and to ourselves to point out to his Lordship how similar errors may be avoided. The appointment in future of ordinary men to the Senate would be to repeat one of the radical errors in its original formation. Every such man who is put upon the Senate weakens its character, and, by adding to its number, impedes its operations. Another and a still more grave error would be to permit political influence to interfere with the appoinment of members. The character of the individual should be the only passport to the senate, and the good of the Institution the only motive for his appointment.

Pray excuse this long communication, but I do feel strongly on the subject, and so I know do many of our colleagues. We have been three years anxiously labouring to give effect to the University, and this under difficulties which nearly led to the resignation of some of our best members, and produced a lukewarmness in others almost equally injurious. Under any circumstances, I think you will agree with me, that the moment when the University is coming into operation, and when every step that is taken requires the utmost consideration, is not a time to introduce new members into the senate. Any addition to the Senate should be better made after we get our new Charter, a matter which I hope will not be deferred after the return of our Chancellor.[24]

Burlington discussed the University's situation with Russell at the end of June 1839, and recorded in his diary, very ambiguously, what appears to have been a mildly encouraging conversation. It would seem that Lord John was no longer thinking of adding any medical fellows, though he still had in mind one or two other people who, in Burlington's phrase, 'might be added with benefit to the University.' More clearly, when the Chancellor raised the spectre of 'the helpless state of the University in the event of a change of Ministry,' Russell was 'not inclined to think there is much danger that the Conservatives would alter our body in any great degree.' There is no mention of any discussion of possible constitutional amendment and, in mid-July, when Burlington met Maltby, the Bishop of Durham, who inveighed against 'parts of the present Charter,' the Chancellor wrote in his diary, 'I do not think it would be advisable to have any change at present.'[25]

Given this rather complacent attitude, it is not surprising that there seems to have been no immediate urgency in the progress towards further constitutional discussion. The long summer vacation, the more immediate concerns of examinations and the absence of any new controversies, all made for a more leisurely pace in University business. But, despite a lack of much written evidence, it is clear that some quiet probing of the possibilities of making what were regarded as desirable changes must have gone on during the winter months of 1839–40.

In February 1840, for instance, on the question of introducing Certificates of Proficiency for non-graduates, Rothman wrote to the Registrar of Cambridge for some relevant information, and remarked in explanation that 'arrangements are now pending between the Government and the University of London in framing which both parties are anxious to avoid doing anything which might give umbrage to the ancient universities, or appear to encroach on their priviliges.'[26] And on that particular question, Burlington discussed the desirability of change with the new Home Secretary, Lord Normanby, and found the minister had no objection. Another channel of communication was through Empson to Phillipps, at the Home Office; Rothman wrote to Empson in March:

> I have just seen Mr Phillipps, who is quite satisfied and ready to prepare the new Charter if you will send up the Memorandum having inserted in it a clause, which shall specially provide against the University having the power to grant Degrees or Certificates of Proficiency in Divinity.[27]

It is clear from subsequent events, however, that the rankling question of the method of appointment of senators, and the vexed matter of senators as examiners, were certainly to the fore. And there are a few indications that the old, very basic argument about opening the University's examinations to all comers, rather than only to those who were enrolled in particular institutions, had reappeared high on the agenda. On the latter, the Chancellor recorded, privately, his own commitment to openness: 'I myself see very little use in any restriction on candidates for degrees and think all should be permitted to offer themselves for examination.'[28]

Burlington, with the help of Lubbock and Empson, and doubtless with other important fellows, had obviously been pursuing with the Home Office the possibility of having some constitutional changes made without having to go through the intricacies of obtaining a new Charter. There is no hint of any such attempt in the Senate minutes, though there is little doubt that interested fellows would have been aware of it. In any event, by March, Burlington found, to his chagrin, that 'the propositions we had made to Government,' and 'the alterations we suggested,' could only be effected by a new Charter.

Despite his disappointment, the Chancellor claimed, soon after apparently reporting the situation to them, that

> The Senate were pretty unanimous in wishing for certain alterations in the event of a new Charter; on one point great difference of opinion prevailed – the exclusion of future members of the Senate from becoming Examiners. Something is to be said on each side, but I think the reasons for exclusion prevail.[29]

On 20 March, 1840, Normanby told Burlington that he was ready to receive any suggestions, and five days later the Senate – after more sharp disagreement about senatorial examiners – agreed to form themselves into a Committee of the Whole to consider alterations to the Charter.[30]

The device of moving into Committee of the Whole no doubt had some procedural advantages so far as internal debate was concerned, but it would be wrong to think that it made any change of participants in the discussion. Indeed, it is as well, at the risk of labouring the point, to spell out again that the handful of men engaged was small and that in the most controversial contexts the balance was almost always tilted in favour of a core comprising half a dozen medical fellows and J.H. Jerrard. When Burlington wrote of 'a large party . . . for retaining the same Examiners and for always giving preference to the members of the Senate,' he really meant a sometimes slightly shifting majority which usually included Bacot, Hammick, Kiernan, Roget and Jerrard, all of whom had been elected examiners.[31] The Committee of the Whole met eight times in the six weeks from 30 March. Attendance was very comparable to that at the formal meetings of the Senate: the medical men who turned up to five or more meetings of the committee were Arnott, Billing, Clark, Hammick, Hodgkin, Kiernan and Roget; the others were the Vice-Chancellor, Jerrard, Senior and Warburton.

However much Burlington and Lubbock may have conducted diplomatic relations with the ministers to prepare the way, within the Committee it was Warburton who was the driving force. And though that combative and abrasive politician lost some points on the most important, long-term questions, his colleagues were usually willing to follow his lead. Warburton's concern was to bring about specific changes within the existing framework, rather than to design a new constitution for the University, and a drastically reshaped relationship with Government. This was a view doubtless shared with the great majority of his colleagues, who may well have calculated that, given the apparent weakening of the Whigs' grasp on power, this was no time to expect sympathy in Westminster for a root-and-branch reform. The one comprehensive plan for such a reform, reflecting some of the kinds of wider anxieties voiced earlier by Airy and Clark, was presented by Hodgkin, but it was turned down at the second meeting.[32] Hodgkin's scheme can be more meaningfully discussed in another chapter.

Nonetheless, the committee, led by Warburton, made some radical demands. They agreed on the need to break away from government appointment of the Senate, and voted in favour of creating an electoral body composed of graduates of three years' standing, together with present and previous senators. This body was to be effective as soon as there were three hundred graduates and, until then, if the Secretary of State intended to appoint a new fellow, he was to give one month's notice to the Senate of the name of the individual to be appointed. The committee would not accept Senior's wish to extend the membership beyond thirty-six, exclusive of the Chancellor and Vice-Chancellor, but they did agree that one-sixth of the members should retire annually, three by rotation and three 'in consequence of their having given the smallest amount of attendance during the last year.' The electoral body would then fill the vacancies, and 'not more than two persons belonging professionally to the same Faculty shall be elected annually Members of the Senate.' Thus the committee envisaged that by about 1850 the University would be governed by a Senate elected, in effect, by a convocation.

Governmental involvement was carefully respected in the other major proposal, which nonetheless called for a complete reversal of policy.

There was a large majority in favour of admitting candidates to examinations for the degrees in Arts and Laws, 'wheresoever such candidates may have received their education, under such regulations as the University shall determine, subject to the approval of one of Her Majesty's principal Secretaries of State.' Certificates of Proficiency should be awarded at the Senate's discretion, which reflected the desire to be free of the restriction of such certificates to graduates. And, as had been hinted as desirable by the Home Office, the University should have power 'to grant any Degrees that are granted by other Universities, with the exception of Degrees in Theology.'

Only on the question of examinerships was there serious disagreement within the committee, but even here a basic compromise had been made before Warburton's proposal was put forward. The clear evidence that, at the outset, at least some members of the Senate had been recruited as examiners, and had been required to give up professional, remunerated positions as a result, made it impossible to deny the claim of those fellows who wished to examine to be paid for their labours. Warburton therefore moved, simply, 'That with the exception of the members of the present Senate no member of the Senate shall be eligible to an Examinership.' This was carried by six votes to four. Those in favour were the Vice-Chancellor, Clark, Hodgkin, Senior, Warburton and Billing (despite his having had to give up a lecturership). Of those six, Billing and Senior were examiners. Opposed were four examiners – Bacot, Jerrard, Kiernan and Roget. Jerrard held the extreme view that all senators should be examiners.

At the final meeting of the committee, Warburton tried to modify further the tenure of all examiners by providing that no person could be elected an examiner for more than five years consecutively. Again, he was to see the words, 'with the exception of the present members of the Senate,' added to his clause by Lubbock, the Bishop of Chichester, Arnott, Hammick and Kiernan. In the ultimate vote, Warburton, the practical politician, supported the amended clause, while Jerrard, rigid in his belief in the virtue of senatorial examinerships, opposed it.

That final meeting of the Committee of the Whole was held on 13 May 1840. In the existing circumstances, the committee's proposals comprised some significant and progressive notions about wider recruitment of examinees, and about long-term academic independence, together with some sensible compromises about the vexed matter of the senatorial examiners. But by the time the last resolution had been debated, the prospects for quiet acceptance of the scheme had already been shattered. Five days earlier, the estimate of the money needed to support the University in the forthcoming financial year had come before the Committee of Supply in the House of Commons. What had been said on that occasion caused a delay in constitutional reform which was to last for almost a decade.

CHAPTER 11

Towards Stalemate

Late in 1840, in the still early stages of an argument involving the Government, the House of Commons and the University, the Earl of Burlington wrote to the Home Secretary, Lord Normanby:

> I imagine that when the Charter was first granted the Government supposed the fees on Degrees would pay all the expenses; whether this may ultimately be the case it is impossible at present to foresee, but I think it is quite clear that for many years to come, it will be quite impossible for the University to go on without the aid of an annual vote from Parliament, though of course as the number of candidates for Degrees increases a smaller grant will be required.[1]

It was a proposition easy enough to accept a century and a half later. But the extent of financial backing has never been settled without argument. Such argument began in the years 1840–2 when, even though the principle of state support was not drastically challenged, the University had to undergo severe parliamentary criticism and some financial deprivation as a result of its policies hitherto. And in this first encounter, as the Chancellor was not averse to claiming at least privately, the Whig Government, which had created, funded and controlled the University, did not defend it wholeheartedly against parliamentary attack.[2]

The cost of running the University had been minimal before the financial year which began in April 1839. In that and each of the two subsequent years the total expenditure was, respectively, £4,563, £5,061 and £5,288: fees paid in those years were £405, £783 and £988, so that the percentage of expenditure met by fees rose from 9.8 per cent to 15.4 per cent, to 18.6 per cent. The estimate of money needed from public funds in 1839–40 had been passed through 'on the nod', but a year later, on 8 May 1840, the request for some £5,400 came before the Committee of Supply, and a new kind of trouble for the University began.[3]

A strong believer in conspiracy theory might well suggest that the embarrassment caused to the University by this first debate on its financial need was plotted by Henry Warburton. The challenge to the estimate was made by fellow radicals – William Smith O'Brien, Joseph Hume and Thomas Wakley – and Warburton himself joined in with a contribution which was to cause anger and despair among some of his colleagues on the Senate. And though there is no supporting evidence that this was more than a routine debate which Warburton had attended as the only direct representative of the Senate, it is not unlikely that he may have briefed a group of colleagues, including Hume, whom he knew were zealots for public accountability and for whom the questioning of estimates was simply part of the regular watch which they kept up in all the sessions of the Committee of Supply.

The objections were concentrated on the size of the salaries offered to examiners and on the self-appointment of those members of the Senate who wished to be examiners. The restriction of entry to the University's examinations to those educated only in a few schools and institutions approved by the Home Secretary, was also raised. But Wakley launched into a much wider, and wilder, criticism of the whole venture and produced a story of irregularity in one instance which Rothman, weeks later, protested to the ministers was completely false.[4] It was in part in response to Wakley's attack that Warburton spoke, protectively of the basic mission of the University, but without hiding his own opinion:

Although a member of the senate of this university, I do not feel disposed to defend all the items. In the senate as in this House, I am frequently in a minority; and I may think the sums voted for the examinerships, in some particular instances, too large. I think that such is the case with respect to the medical examiners.

Warburton went on to argue that £250 a year was too much for a medical examiner, and 'that £100 a year would really be considered an ample allowance.' He had no doubt that the whole problem arose 'from the professors having nominated themselves.' For the Conservatives, Henry Goulburn added his concern. Faced with this degree of hostility, the Chancellor of the Exchequer, Sir F.T. Baring, withdrew the vote and promised to make further inquiries, but refused to agree to produce the proceedings of the Senate.

Five days after this the Senate met for its final session as a Committee of the Whole, to hammer out the agreed version of their proposals for changes to the Charter. The minutes give no hint as to how much the members present knew the details of what had transpired in Committee of Supply. Ten days further along, on 23 May, the Senate met to discuss the proposals made by the Committee of the

Whole. Attendance was much the same as at the Committee on 13 May, save that Roget was absent and that Airy, Empson and Walker were present. When the Committee's report was introduced, Hodgkin made what was, at first, a successful attempt to amend the clause relating to the composition of the electoral body which was to take over the function of appointing senators. After complex debate and several votes, the clause was designed to read:

> As soon as those who have taken the Degrees of MA, LLD, and MD shall amount in number to 100, it will be expedient to constitute the said Graduates and all such future Graduates together with all other Graduates, of not less than five years standing, together with the persons who then, or henceforth, shall, or shall have been, Members of the Senate, the Electoral Body of this University.

But when this more conservative motion was put as a fully amended version of the first clause, it was defeated by six votes to four. And when Senior tried to leave the size of the Senate open by proposing to omit the figure 36 in the clause governing the size of the body, his motion was defeated by six to five.

That discussion effectively ended the formal consideration by the Senate of the proposed desirable changes to the Charter. Those changes were referred to in subsequent negotiations, and the proposal for a convocation, in particular, was to be quoted many times before the principle was conceded in 1849, and only implemented in 1858. But no further resolution on the package was ever passed. What was accepted in practice, however, was that no senator, other than those originally appointed, was ever elected to be an examiner. All the possibilities for significant constitutional change were, in fact, stifled, in no small part because of the shadow cast by the challenge to the estimate in 1840. But looming behind the specific problems was the hard reality that, after Russell and Spring Rice were moved from the departments directly responsible for its operation, the University had no enthusiastic ministerial backing. After the summer of 1839, and for many years to come, ministers in the governments of Melbourne and of Peel, kept it at arm's length.

We have seen that an attempt to have the Senate minutes laid before the House of Commons had been refused by ministers as early as June 1838. But the Chancellor of the Exchequer's agreement, on 8 May 1840, to ask the University to provide 'the names of the parties employed in offices, the offices or posts in which they were so employed . . . and the parties examining the students,' was not the next occasion on which details of the University had been demanded by Parliament. On 26 August 1839, in the House of Lords, Brougham had moved for the Charter, rules and details of the degrees of the University to be laid on the table. What motive he had for doing so is unclear: certainly the speech which he made in presenting his request, while devoted to the need for some compromise between Anglicans and Dissenters in the general context of education, made no mention of the University of London at all.[5] And that such demands for information were not met quickly can be seen from the fact that the data was not laid on the table until 28 January 1840, and was not ordered to be printed until 17 February.

There was much more urgency in the wake of the first debate on the estimates in the Commons. Informal communications between the University and the Treasury began by the middle of the month, while Hume and Goulburn, unwilling to accept Baring's offer, successfully moved for a comprehensive set of documents on 19 and 26 May respectively. The University, for its part, assured both Baring and Normanby that they had no objection to producing the Senate minutes. Some of the documents were laid on the table by 10 June, but it was not until August that all that had been demanded was ordered to be printed. Thereafter, a document of 319 pages was available to anyone who wished to consult it, and included almost every official record of the University's life hitherto.

Long before that document could have been absorbed, however, the estimate for 1841–2 had been brought back for reconsideration and had been approved.[6] But the whole episode, though not to be reopened in Parliament, deterred the Whigs from further action on the Charter, and carried over its negative influence into the new Conservative regime which began in September 1841.

By the beginning of June 1840, verbal reports of what had been said in the House of Commons on 8 May had reached members of the Senate, and at least two of them were incensed by what they regarded as Warburton's disloyalty and duplicity. Roget took the lead in demanding that Lubbock press on the Home Secretary 'the justice of our proceedings,' and to deny 'the imputation thrown upon us by Messrs Wakley, Warburton, & Co., of fraud, humbug, venality, etc.'[7] Not satisfied, apparently, with Lubbock's attitude, Roget and Jerrard went together, later in the month, to see first Robert Gordon, the

Financial Secretary to the Treasury, and then Normanby at the Home Office. Roget reported to Lubbock that Gordon

> confirmed our worst fears; telling us that nothing could be more injurious to the University than Warburton's speeches . . . and he seemed to despair of the result of the next debate from the part that Warburton was likely to take in it.

Normanby seemed 'fully sensible' that 'we had been vilified,' and 'wished that we would exert ourselves in making similar representations to as many members [of Parliament] as we could.'[8]

The depth of Roget's hostility to Warburton is apparent. He refers to the Senate minutes to show that Warburton was present when the medical examiners' fees were approved, and claims (though Roget himself had not been at the meeting) that he had 'made not the slightest objection to them.' But in the House, Roget asserted, Warburton had 'artfully' led

> his auditors to believe that he had divided the Senate on that question, and had been left in a minority. He had also the impudence to assert that these high salaries arose out of the circumstances that they had nominated themselves.
>
> Save us from such *friends*!

The provision of relevant material by the University, and the lobbying by at least some of the Senate, ensured that when the estimate came back to the Committee of Supply at the end of July, the short debate was better informed and the ministers, Baring and Gordon, more willing to defend the proposal. The existence of Spring Rice's original letters, asking senators to be examiners, was admitted. The University as an institution was approved by Hume, and accepted by Goulburn. But the specific criticisms made earlier were repeated, if more concisely and accurately, and Sir Robert Peel insisted that 'There cannot be so absurd a provision as that the Senate shall, out of its own body, find the examiners and that those shall fix their own salaries!' When Warburton pointed out that the Treasury had to approve the salaries, Peel turned his wrath on the Government. But the resolution was agreed, after Baring had assured the committee that the Home Secretary would investigate further the appointment and remuneration of examiners. Warburton unrepentantly stuck to his original points:

> It is quite true that the examiners appoint themselves, and I believe a better choice would have been made if that had not been the case. Lord Monteagle's reason for introducing such a provision

in the charter was, that it was necessary, in the first instance, for the purpose of starting the institution; but he never intended that such a power should be permanent. I have always objected to that mode of appointment; and, when applied to, I declined to become an examiner, although I consented to become a member of the Senate. I trust that the charter will be so altered as to provide a different mode of appointment, and that a provision will be introduced for the purpose of throwing open the University to candidates wherever they may have been educated.[9]

With the University safely funded for the year, and with summer at its height, nothing transpired during the next two months.

Before taking up the multi-sided story again, it is as well to recall that Lady Burlington died on 27 April 1840. Her illness and death removed Burlington from most of the consideration of the possible changes in the Charter, and from all but rare contact with his colleagues during the summer crisis over money. Sir James Clark confided to Lubbock that 'his Lordship will be unfit for anything in the way of business for many months, I fear,' and certainly the Chancellor was reluctant to come to London.[10] It is unlikely that his presence would have made very much difference to what happened in the middle of 1840, though his absence certainly threw more responsibility onto Lubbock. But, as his grief was modified by time, Burlington turned back to University affairs and, when the new Conservative Government came to power in the late summer of 1841, his high, aristocratic status ensured him relatively easy access to its suspicious members – an access which would have been far less easy for Lubbock, acting alone. Even so, both Chancellor and Vice-Chancellor found little for their comfort in 1841 and 1842.

In the two years from the late summer of 1840, the University of London's desirable future shape, functions and financing were subjected to rather fragmented consideration, twice over. First, during the last twelve months of Lord Melbourne's administration, and then, almost beginning afresh, during the first year of Sir Robert Peel's Government, when the University had to deal mainly with Sir James Graham at the Home Office and Henry Goulburn at the Treasury. The outcome might be described as the *status quo* with proportionately less money, and with the loss, at the end of the period, of the first Vice-Chancellor, perhaps in part at least as a result of disillusionment. Three interrelated themes dominated these considerations of the future: the resolution of the row over examiners and their salaries; the attempt to achieve agreement with the Colleges of Physicians and Surgeons; and the search for a more satisfactory constitution. Only the first of these produced a partial solution; everything else was deadlocked.

Given the Treasury ministers' pledge to the House of Commons, it is understandable that the University would have felt sure that the Treasury and the Home Office would take the initiative in starting their investigation into the appointment and remuneration of examiners. But nothing had happened by the beginning of October 1840 and, when Lubbock had to write to Normanby about the recognition of some medical schools, he scribbled, as a diplomatic afterthought, 'Have you ever written to Lord Burlington as to an inquiry into London University as promised in the House of Commons?' The reaction reveals the closeness of ministerial family connections, and raises the question as to whether, had Lady Burlington lived, matters would have moved more quickly and effectively. It also indicates that Lubbock, as Vice-Chancellor, did not feel able, himself, to act independently of the Chancellor.

Normanby minuted:

> I will write to Burlington about this enquiry. I had delayed until I could learn whether it would be agreeable to him . . . to be consulted on such matters and in the press of business last week when I saw Morpeth [Burlington's brother-in-law] I forgot to speak to him about it.[11]

And when Burlington was asked, he admitted his inattentiveness to University affairs: he was 'not aware till I received your letter that an inquiry into the state of its finances was in contemplation.' But he went on to assure Normanby of full co-operation, made the sensible observation that 'the points to be enquired into can be so very few and of so simple a nature that all the information that can be obtained will be immediately procured from the Registrar,' and recommended the Home Secretary to consult Lubbock.[12]

It took some days for the Treasury and Home Office to decide what exactly was wanted. The business was delegated to Robert Gordon at the Treasury and to Fox Maule, Normanby's parliamentary secretary, at the Home Office.[13] Gordon had to explain that he had promised

'a searching enquiry . . . under the direction of the Home Office into the system of appointing Examiners – their numbers, efficiency and pay, and whether it were advisable to accumulate different duties in the same person. For grievances generally I refer you to the debates. . . . What I ask is that the enquiry should be *speedy* as well as searching.[14]

This produced a flurry of activity, including a meeting of the Senate which confirmed Burlington's willingness to help, and much correspondence ensuring that all involved were fully briefed. The demands of the departments were so insistent that by the end of November Burlington and Lubbock were becoming irritated, and the Chancellor agreed that

it is a great pity they do not leave us alone. In my opinion the Government having sanctioned the salaries of our Examiners and all our Regulations, ought to have been prepared without asking for any further information, to defend the Vote in Parliament.[15]

Within the Home Office, however, Fox Maule had produced, before the end of November, a concise memorandum which shows the official concerns and assumptions at that time. It is interesting that he gave prior place to the controversy over whether degree candidates should be restricted to persons who had attended colleges approved by the Secretary of State. His first point implies that either the original plan would have allowed any 'school' or college to put forward candidates for examination, or would at least have given the University freedom to recommend institutions which would prepare candidates for Arts and Laws degrees, in the same way as it was given the duty of recommending the approval of medical schools. There is, however, no evidence to support either possible implication, though there was clearly a difference of view about the college requirement between Spring Rice and Warburton.

Fox Maule wrote:

As far as I can see from the Debates the whole objection turned on these points.
1. The original intention in founding the University was not carried out and Schools were only partially admitted at the option of the Minister of the Crown.
2. The Examiners were too highly paid for all they had to do.
3. The Examiners were appointed by the Senate from their own body and fixed their own salaries.

4. That two or more examinations were concentrated in one and the same individual.

To the first point answer has been given that a change may take place in the Charter which shall remedy this defect.

To 2, 3 & 4 Inquiry was promised and it will be desirable to obtain an immediate return

> 1st of the number of Examiners, the period devoted by them to examination – the numbers whom they examine and the salaries they receive.
> 2. The numbers of Examiners who hold more than one examination.
> 3. The number of Examiners who are Members of the Senate and the number not belonging to the Senate.

When this return is obtained, it would be well to consider the two principles of complaint:

> 1. The exclusion of Schools from the benefits of the University.
> 2. The propriety of Examiners being Members of the Senate.[16]

This crisp summary doubtless helped to initiate and accelerate the flow of information needed to the Home Office. But two-and-a-half months later it is clear that there was little sense of urgency. On 10 February 1841, the Treasury sent the University's estimate for 1841–2 to the Home Office and asked, rather sharply, what steps had been taken to make the promised inquiry.[17] Meanwhile, Burlington had become acutely aware that time was running out for the Whig administration. They were unlikely to last long, he told Lubbock, and it was important to know if they really had any ideas about altering the Charter. At least he hoped, though somewhat sceptically, that the present inquiry would 'bring the subject under their notice, and probably induce them to place on a better foundation the question of members of the Senate acting as Examiners.'[18]

There is no sign that Burlington or Lubbock tried to exercise any further personal pressure on ministers, though they and others may well have done so. But credit for the next move probably should rest with the Treasury, whose denizens seem to have lost patience with the Home Office. At the end of May, Robert Gordon wrote formally to Fox Maule, and after referring pointedly to the two previous requests, in November 1840 and February 1841, went on:

If an enquiry has not yet been made . . . their Lordships would suggest that it may be entrusted to Lord Monteagle who is highly qualified to conduct the Enquiry in such a manner as to be satisfactory to the Government and to Parliament, and who is willing to undertake this Service.[19]

On the following morning, Normanby invited Monteagle to consider the regulations for examiners:[20] but Monteagle was to interpret the request as an opportunity to cover a much wider area. He did not report until late July. Before discussing what happened thereafter, it is as well to go back to mid-1840 and review the progress of negotiations with the Royal Colleges of Physicians and of Surgeons.

Four years had elapsed since Russell and Spring Rice failed to persuade the Royal College of Physicians to accept that the medical graduates of the new University of London should have the same privilege as the graduates of Oxford and Cambridge, which was to be licensed to practise without further examination. Nor, once the first Charter was promulgated, had the ministers followed up their threat that legislation would be introduced to ensure that the privilege was extended. But there were those among the medical members of the Senate who had an ambitious vision of the impact which the University should have on the turbulent and fragmented medical fraternity. Clark saw the new University 'as the means, not only of improving but almost revolutionizing medical education.' Empson recorded, when the Senate first came together, that 'Our Doctors expect that we shall have, sooner or later, the examination of the *whole Medical Profession.*'[21] And Henry Warburton was to continue for many years to be a leading figure in the general agitation for medical reform.

While argument over the organization of medical education was an integral part of that tortuous movement towards some rationalization of the structure and supervision of the profession, which reached a major milestone with the establishment of the General Medical Council in 1858, the part which the University of London was able, or was allowed, to play in that movement was very limited. Even so, the long, messy struggle of the 1840s and 1850s, the detail of which cannot be treated fully here, was a background of negotiation and conflict which caused the University much anxiety and disappointment.[22] As an institution, London's immediate objective, eventually achieved only in 1854, was to gain the same privilege for its graduates as was guaranteed to graduates of the ancient universities.

The main theme of those set on reforming the whole medical establishment was the need to bring about some more comprehensive and satisfactory oversight than was provided by the three professional bodies – the Royal Colleges of Physicians and Surgeons, and the Society of Apothecaries. A big part of the long-drawn-out struggle was to reduce and harmonize their powers of controlling entry to professional practice. In that struggle, those bodies were determined to safeguard their independent identities, but were prepared to go some distance – not too far – to co-operate with each other and with an institution like the University of London, in order to retain their separate status and influence. The University does not seem to have been involved in any direct negotiation with the Society of Apothecaries, but approaches were made to the Senate by both colleges, beginning with that of the surgeons.

Whether by accident or design, a Dr Thomas Smith, of Leeds, asked the Registrar, early in June 1840, whether 'the Degree of M.B. or M.D. confers on its possessor a right to practise in England and Wales, or must the candidate obtain in addition the licence from the College of Physicians in London.' This enabled the Senate to have the legal limitation of the University's medical degrees clarified. Counsel advised that the law officers' view should be sought, and the latters' opinion was given a month later. It was unequivocal: 'no right to practise as a Physician or Apothecary in England is conferred by the degree of Doctor or Bachelor of Medicine from the University of London.'[23]

Before this opinion was received, however, Burlington had been visited by Sir Anthony Carlisle, who had become President of the Royal College of Surgeons, for a second time, in 1839. It was the first piece of official business which the Chancellor faced since his bereavement, and he recorded briefly that he did not feel Carlisle's suggestions could be agreed to, as they tended 'to lower the University.'[24] He referred his visitor to the Bishop of Durham and to Lubbock.

Sir Anthony Carlisle was in his 72nd year, which he was fated not to survive: he died on 2 November 1840. One biographical fragment described him as 'handsome and good humoured, but very vain and crotchety.' Another revealed that in his later years complaints 'were brought against him in proof of neglect and incapacity,' and characterized him as being guilty of 'self complacency and egotism.'[25] It is impossible to judge whether his removal from the scene was significant in the context of relations between the College and the University.

Probably not very much, judging from the rather incoherent letters which he sent to Lubbock in July 1840. The Vice-Chancellor had given him a batch of documents, which presumably contained the details of the new medical curriculum and some examples of the examination papers set during the first year's operation.

Carlisle's reactions are worth quoting at some length, because they reveal the anxiety and scepticism which prevailed among the supporters of the *status quo*.

The author or authors of the [University's] scheme seem to me to have aimed at creating a higher educated class in the medical profession than could be expected from the established mode of remunerating the *general* practitioners, under the passing wants of a vast population. To create a higher and superiorly instructed body of medical men for the service of the Rich, and a lower grade for the Poor would indeed prove a rank injustice. Under the existing division of the profession into Physicians, Surgeons, and Apothecaries they often minister to the necessities of every class of society with some harmony and satisfaction - but I apprehend that a jumble of the Profession into one commonalty would degrade the whole, and expose the less honorable to a sordid scramble; a state not easily suppressed under present Regulations. The degraded state of medical men on the Continent of Europe shows the mischievous effects of low remuneration and of being placed in a low caste.

I still retain strong conviction that the medical profession of England may under the instrumentality of the London University become steadily improved, but not so if the rights of one class are to be sacrificed to another. A broad system of unequivocal equity can only assure any good to the public from changes bearing consequences unknown. These are however important topics, which I am not prepared to discuss, but I will venture to say that the last programme of medical questions are not applicable to 20 out of 500 candidates who appear before the London College of Surgeons, and we feel ourselves bound to consider the probable future income of those persons while we measure their degrees of education. We have no alternative but that of leaving the public to the uncontrolled mercy of unexamined Practitioners and the acceptance of moderately, but *practically* instructed men.

Individually, I see no difficulty in your University granting medical honors above the average of our obligations; of your constituting Normal Instructors – and of an amicable co-operation for England *only* - to put down unauthorised Practitioners, and to apportion medical officers adapted to every condition of men. I will go further, and say that a favourable occasion is now presented for bringing about those desirable ends, without clamour or injustice.[26]

But more letters, of a couple of weeks later, reveal that informal discussion of defensive tactics was seriously advanced between influential members of the two Royal Colleges. A set of 'Suggestions upon the Medical Department of the new London University,' was sent to Lubbock with a letter in which Carlisle and his unnamed colleagues ventured

> to assume that the medical business of the London University would be more successfully conducted if placed in amicable alliance with the London Colleges of Physicians and of Surgeons *in London* and that under such united auspices the Apothecaries and Chemists of England might be better ordered.[27]

The first paragraph of the 'Suggestions' stated, bluntly, that the University could not grant licences to practise to its graduates 'without disturbing the chartered privileges' of the Colleges and the Society, and without disturbing 'the established system of educating Physicians.' It then went on:

> In order that the new London University should be honorably and beneficially occupied it may without damage or offence to the present Medical Establishments become importantly useful by undertaking to appoint and control those Teachers of Medical Knowledge, who are not attached to Universities or Colleges which unite elementary Instruction with granting Diplomas or Licences to practise.
>
> And . . . whereas at the present time both the London College of Surgeons, and the London Society of Apothecaries, are kept in continued turmoil with their Members and others about the appointment of professional Teachers, and further it may be justly assumed that the power to select such Teachers should not be vested in the same Persons who have to sit in judgement upon the merits of candidates for legal authority to practise,

> It is proposed

> To constitute especial Boards in the new University of London, to take charge of the professional instruction of the candidates for examination for the Diplomas or Licences of the Royal College of

Surgeons in London and of the Society of Apothecaries in London by conducting probationary examinations in elementary education viz. in Anatomy, Chemistry, Natural Knowledge and Physicks, and by granting to duly qualified candidates, certificates or testimonials as graduates in those professional studies which are required by the Royal College of Surgeons and Society of Apothecaries shewing proofs of competence to go before the Judicial tribunals of the Licensing College or Corporation in London to obtain authority to practise medicine or surgery.

It further appears to come within the province of the new London University to give effect to some of the . . . officers of the London, King's College and London University College, by receiving from them Testimonials of Scholastic Education, as well as probationary degrees in elementary medical studies.

In his covering letter to Lubbock, Carlisle made it clear that he and his colleagues would not move further 'until we have established an united Medical and Surgical Committee, when their wishes shall be conveyed to you before they are laid before Lord Burlington.' This implied at least a natural delay due to the beginning of the summer break and the end of the Parliamentary session. Before either of these things happened, however, the 'turmoil' in the medical world, which had been noted in the 'Suggestions', must have been intensified by the introduction into the House of Commons, by Wakley and Warburton, on 11 August, of a Bill for the Registration of Medical Practitioners and the Establishment of a College of Medicine.[28]

The Wakley/Warburton Bill, the first of many on the same theme during the years before 1858, came to nothing. And in the autumn of 1840 there was no more correspondence with the University about Carlisle's initiative. Its author's death – and a presumed prior illness – is the most likely explanation. Nonetheless, the 'united Medical and Surgical Committee', of which he had written to Lubbock, did get under way. The College of Physicians took the lead, but its historian admits that the Surgeons had made the first move at the end of September, though no credit seems to have been given to Carlisle. The Physicians established a conference committee in November, and under various titles it continued to organize liaison between the three medical corporations during the negotiations of the next decade and a half.[29]

The new committee conferred 'with the Deputation from the College of Surgeons and the Society of Apothecaries' and, on 22 December

1840, produced a set of resolutions directed to the many petitions which had been made to Parliament about the whole state of the medical profession. A copy was sent to the Vice-Chancellor in mid-January 1841 by Dr Francis Hawkins, the Secretary to the Royal College of Physicians. The report suggested

> That it is desirable that uniform medical qualifications should be demanded of all Candidates for the Degree of M.D. in England, Ireland, and Scotland, and that the degree of M.D. so obtained in either country should henceforth confer a right to practise in all, provided the Graduate shall have enrolled himself in the College of Physicians of the country where he resides.
>
> That the University of London having required for the Degree of M.D. a high standard of education, which is to a great extent in accordance with the views of the College of Physicians, the College will be ready to admit into the order of Licentiates the Doctors in Medicine of that University, provided that they shall respectively have attained the age of twenty-six years, and that the Censors shall have assisted at their Medical Examinations.[30]

This proposal was treated at first in the University with considerable reserve. Lubbock referred it, initially, to Sir James Clark, who pointed out that the draft contained

> not the resolutions of the College – merely of a *Committee* of the College, and there is only one resolution with which we have anything to do, and that resolution according to our Charter we cannot entertain; at least so it appears to me.[31]

It took a few letters, and the intervention of Sir Henry Halford, the President of the Physicians, to clear the way for the printing of the proposals in the Senate minutes, despite the likelihood of publicity, and to establish that the College was indeed prepared to ask, formally, for the University's reaction to the committee's report.

The exchanges were very civilized, and Hawkins went out of his way to express approval of the University and to explain the delicacy of the committee's situation:

> I am not aware that any objections whatsoever have been raised in the College of Physicians to the scheme of examination adopted by the University of London. The truth is that the sincere expressions of our Report must not be weighed too critically as they were drawn up cautiously and sometimes perhaps a little vaguely by a small number

of persons who had to feel their way with comparatively a very large number by whom, however, the Report was most cordially received and its principle fully sanctioned and adopted.[32]

Despite the civilities, the nub of the problem posed by the College's proposal, for the University, was pinpointed immediately by Lubbock.

> Does the word *'assisted'* in the paragraph in which the University of London is mentioned mean *being present*, or does it mean that the *Censors* shall propose written questions in addition to those of our Examiners in the printed papers and *viva voce* questions in the *viva voce* examinations, both or either?
>
> In the former case I apprehend no difficulty would arise: but if the Censors are to take part in the examination, this becomes a very delicate question.[33]

To this, Hawkins replied:

> I feel sure it was intended that the Censors should take a share in the practical part, at least, of the Examinations of Candidates for Medical Degrees, in order that they may be able to give the sanction of the College of Physicians to those who graduate in Medicine, and enable them to practise without a second examination before the College, which the law at present directs.[34]

There is, unfortunately, no unequivocal evidence of who proposed and negotiated the compromise which was struck at the Senate on 3 February 1841. But a letter sent to Lubbock late in January by George Burrows, a senior fellow of the Royal College of Physicians and a lecturer at St Bartholomew's Hospital, contains a clear-headed restatement of the whole problem and presses for the solution which proved acceptable, no doubt after much hard-headed assessment of the self-interest of both institutions.[35] In any event, there was no division in the Senate on the resolution

> That the Censors of the College of Physicians be invited to attend at the *viva voce* examinations in Medicine of this University, and that upon application of any candidate desirous of the Licence of the College his written answers to the printed papers shall be forwarded to the College so that the Censors may be satisfied of the proficiency of the Graduates for medical practice.

In the same spirit, Rothman sent Hawkins all the questions put to candidates for the medical degrees during the past year, with the hope that 'this communication will not prove unacceptable; in which case it will be repeated annually.'[36]

Halford was probably well pleased, but the chronicler of the College admits that its official response was 'not handsomely' done; the Physicians conceded only that the Senate's resolution would, 'in a great measure fulfil the object which it is [the College's] duty to maintain, namely, to secure the proficiency of the Graduates for Medical Practice.' But Halford foresaw no problems, and the College set up a committee, on 13 February, to settle the details with the University.[37]

The Royal College of Physicians' rather grudging acceptance can be seen, retrospectively, as the herald of a false dawn. Those led by Halford into accepting a possible compromise were, perhaps, conscious that they would almost certainly be overruled, in the longer run, by the doubts and suspicions of the majority of the profession. And it is quite conceivable that the College clung to the hope that a change of Government would give them relief from the pressure which had forced them to offer an agreement. If that was their belief, it proved to have been fully justified. We shall follow the fate of the Senate's invitation in due course.

The difficulties under which even the moderate medical reformers laboured should not be underestimated. The basis of widespread opposition to organizational change within the profession was well presented in an article in the *Quarterly Review* of December 1840, which was later attributed, by one of the medical journals, to 'the pen of Sir Benjamin Brodie.'[38] Reasoned objections to any replacement of the three old corporations by a single new one, rather than reform and improvement of the former, were discussed at length, and the fledgling University of London was subjected to a patronizing scepticism no doubt typical of attitudes held by many, if not a majority, of contemporary practitioners of medicine. In 'the medical department of the metropolitan university,' wrote the author,

> the faults of its predecessors seem to have been rather exaggerated than otherwise . . . it is responsible only to itself; and it will be remarkable if, eventually, it does not look to its own interests more than to those of the community. The degree of bachelor of medicine is said to be intended for the class of general practitioners. Those who wish to obtain this distinction are allowed to matriculate and begin their profession while they are yet boys, at the age of sixteen years, and to present themselves for the last examination so as to be

esteemed practitioners as soon as they have passed their twenty-first birthday. Fourteen different kinds of lectures are included in the curriculum, being five more than those which are required by the College of Surgeons and Society of Apothecaries: while the attendance on hospital practice, which we believe to be of more importance than all the lectures put together, is actually less. The whole system, as it appears to us, is unnecessarily complicated. Yet we must acknowledge that it affords evidence of good intentions on the part of those who framed it. They seem to have been really anxious to place the medical profession on as high ground as possible: but they have not had that experience in hospitals and schools, nor that intercourse with students, which they should have had, to enable them to understand the true principles of medical education. . . . We conclude that it was the failure of the metropolitan university which led Mr Warburton, at the close of the last session of Parliament, to lay on the table of the House of Commons his Bill 'for the Registration of Medical Practitioners.'[39]

The Earl of Burlington recalled this article, ruefully, fifteen months later, when the new Conservative administration was showing little sympathy to the University, as being 'altogether extremely hostile'.[40] What Warburton and the medical senators thought of the *Quarterly's* characterization of them, is perhaps best left to the imagination. Among established medical leaders, the Professor of Surgery at Edinburgh, Sir Charles Bell, probably spoke for many opponents of change in claiming that 'the University of London, with its offspring, University College and King's College, . . . has confused all things, and that confusion will be worse confounded by the enactment of the bills now before Parliament.'[41]

By the spring of 1841 at least some journalists had found time to master the mass of the University's minutes and papers which had been published in response to Hume's demand in the House of Commons. There is a hint that Jerrard and Roget, perhaps the senators most passionately concerned about the appropriate level of examiners' salaries, and the most apprehensive about further trouble when the estimates for 1841–2 came before the Commons, may have persuaded the *Morning Chronicle* to take up their cause. On 21 April that paper carried a well-informed and accurate defence of the 1835–6 arrangements, and was entirely supportive of the presence within the Senate of examiners and laymen, as likely to give a better balance than having a governing body separate from a board of examiners subordinate to it. It is possible that the article was written, or certainly inspired, by Jerrard and Roget.[42]

Though the article was not followed by any debate in the *Chronicle*, it may well have helped the University by its concise explanation of the examiners' position, and by introducing more rationality into the criticism of the institution's situation. Its appearance was timely, in that it coincided with a letter sent by Lord Monteagle to the Vice-Chancellor, who must have been gratified by its generally encouraging tone. Monteagle implied that he was unwilling to concern himself only with the salaries question, wanted to explore all the problem areas, including relations with the medical colleges, and even raised the possibility of making passage of the University's examinations a pre-condition for the enrolment of barristers. Burlington was pleased, and during May he and Lubbock had long discussions with Monteagle.[43]

But as May gave way to June, and June to July, the Chancellor and Vice-Chancellor began to lose hope. The Government had been defeated in the House of Commons in June, and a general election followed. By 21 July, Burlington, already aware of the significant loss of seats by the Whigs, wrote gloomily in his Diary:

> We had some conversation on the problem [of] the effect of a change of government. I fear Lord Monteagle has entirely neglected the report he was to make to Lord Normanby. At all events it is now too late for a new Charter as the Government will be out immediately, but we hope to obtain a supplementary one giving us some additional powers.

While his fears were entirely justified, Burlington was a little hard on Monteagle, whose report was delivered to the Home Secretary only two days afterwards. It was a wide-ranging document, whose constitutional suggestions will be discussed in the following chapter. Its immediate impact, however, was practically nil.[44]

Burlington had been pressing the desirability of early action to have put into effect the changes proposed by the Senate in April and May 1840. For him, Monteagle's recommendations, with most of which he agreed, were far reaching - they would need 'full consideration and would not be acceptable to all members of Senate'. He advised Normanby, at the end of July, in the knowledge that the Home Secretary would be out of office very soon, that

The University is undoubtedly, as at present constituted, very much at the mercy of any Government, but I should not think it very probable the new Government will take any hostile measures towards it. Altogether if I may venture to give my opinion, I think if the Government could be prevailed upon to give us the supplementary Charter to which I called your attention some days ago, and which does appear to me of great importance, it would under present circumstances be a more prudent course than to adopt the extensive alterations recommended by Lord Monteagle.[45]

The Chancellor cannot have had much faith in the possibility of any move by the expiring Government, however, and cannot have been surpised to hear from Normanby that 'in present circumstances' – which meant in the few weeks, at most, before Parliament would meet and the resignation of Melbourne would be forced – they could only do 'minor things'. Burlington doubted if they would do anything, and his disillusion was deepened when, just before the Government resigned, he learned that the retiring Home Secretary had expected the University to 'prepare its own supplementary charter and submit it.' In a rare expression of disgust, Burlington told Lubbock that 'Normanby has done nothing and it is now too late.'[46]

The University was left to face a new administration with its Charter unchanged and its financial provision still a matter of potential controversy. The only advantage of the political upheaval of the last months was that, because of it, the estimate for 1841–2 went through the Commons unchallenged. A less sympathetic Government would ensure that the request for the next year would be pruned before it reached Parliament.

CHAPTER 12

Official Indifference:
Internal Assessment

Sir Robert Peel's Government showed no basic hostility to the University of London, but were not disposed to enthuse about it or to promote any particular extension of its activities, or to change its constitution. Sir James Graham, Home Secretary throughout the Conservatives' tenure of office from 1841 to 1846, tried very hard, though unsuccessfully, to carry fundamental reform of the medical profession, but in those efforts he showed no sympathy for the University's hope that their medical graduates would be automatically licensed to practise. Henry Goulburn, who became Chancellor of the Exchequer, devoted part of his first months in office to enforcing some reduction of the University's expenditure, but thereafter seemingly lost interest. By the time Peel resigned office after the repeal of the Corn Laws, the University of London's affairs had long been of no obvious political concern.

In the autumn of 1841, though, the issue of what should be done about the examiners' appointment and pay was made an immediate priority by the ministers, and particularly by Goulburn. The Treasury asked for an estimate for 1842–3 'as soon as possible' after mid-October, and the University responded on 13 November, using the same salaries for examiners as in the two previous years. Goulburn's reaction was a long rehearsal of the criticisms made in the Committee of Supply in 1840, ending with a request for some

> reconsideration; for it appears to me . . . more for the advantage of the Institution that they should voluntarily conform to the wish expressed by the House of Commons, than impose on any department of the Government the disagreeable but necessary duty of acting in a matter of pecuniary concern in opposition to their wishes and opinion.[1]

But this smooth threat was not one to which Burlington and Lubbock were ready to accede. The Vice-Chancellor merely acknowledged Goulburn's letter and promised that the request would be laid before the Senate on 8 December. Burlington had earlier confided to Lubbock that the Government 'will want reductions where practicable,' but did not think that they had formed a clear view of how it should be done. When Goulburn's formal letter reached him, Burlington told Lubbock that he was unwilling to compromise: he felt strongly that the Chancellor of the Exchequer's letter

> does not contain a fair statement of the circumstances. The cause of the disagreeable position in which we are now placed, seems to me to be that the late Government did not defend our scale of salaries when it was attacked in the House of Commons; after having sanctioned it they became responsible for it and ought to have defended it. As however they were lukewarm in our cause, I am not surprised that the present Government think there is a good opportunity for them to make some saving. I am strongly inclined to agree with you, that we should leave the subject entirely in their hands, and let them either with enquiry or without it fix what scale of expenditure they deem expedient.[2]

Lubbock's own thoughts on the situation were confided to Airy a few days later, in a letter which throws an interesting light on attitudes within the Senate, and on Lubbock's own vision of a completely self-contained institution:

> My impression is that Warburton is the only member of the Senate who thinks the salaries should be reduced. My opinion is that *we* ought not to originate any alteration until the University is on a firmer footing with a large body of graduates from whom examiners can be taken, and I think if we appoint members of our own body Examiners to which I see great objection we are the last persons that ought to be called upon to have anything to do with fixing the salaries.[3]

Warburton had lobbied Graham at the end of September,[4] but there seem to have been no meetings between the Home Secretary and the Chancellor and Vice-Chancellor until early in December, when Burlington requested a meeting after receiving Goulburn's threatening letter. In fixing an appointment, Graham also laid out his view of the situation:

> In the last Parliament the opinion of the House of Commons appeared to be strong, that the demand of the London University on the Public Purse was larger than necessity required. If I mistake not, Members of the Senate are Examiners receiving salaries: by multiplying Examinations the salaries also are increased, and the Senate not

only selects the Examiners from their own Body, but fixes the remuneration thus requested by a few of its members.

This system was considered objectionable: and it was hoped that the governing authorities of the University would have applied the remedies. I know that Mr Warburton considered the existing practice inexpedient, and was anxious that it should be corrected by the Senate. If this be not possible, the Government, which propose the Estimate, adopts it, and is responsible.

We are sincerely anxious not to take any step, which may be inconsistent with the respect due to the learned Body, over which Your Lordship presides: and I shall gladly avail myself of the opportunity, which you are so obliging as to give me, of endeavouring to adjust this matter in the way which shall be just and satisfactory.[5]

Graham saw Burlington and Lubbock on 7 December, on the eve of the Senate's meeting. The University officers came away apparently comforted. Graham had 'received us in a friendly spirit, and appeared to be considerably shaken in the opinion he had previously entertained.'[6] Nonetheless, they faced a long and difficult session. Attendance at the Senate meeting was larger than usual, fourteen members being present, but no doubt because of its length, the numbers dwindled, and the crucial voting was restricted to a group of nine, which included all the regulars. The minutes, supplemented by a note about the proceedings sent by the Chancellor to Goulburn, demonstrate the extent to which, on the issue of the examiners' salaries, it was practically a case of Warburton *versus* the rest.[7]

When Goulburn's request was faced, Warburton set the ball rolling with what may have been either a partly humorous, or a pointedly vicious personal attack on Jerrard, by moving that the salaries of the Classical examiners be reduced from £200 to £150. This was defeated by five votes to two, and it was then agreed unanimously that all the examiners should be asked to make a return of the time which they had devoted to their duties during the year. But the main debate followed Lubbock's motion:

That the Senate are not prepared to recommend any reduction in the Estimate, and fear that a diminution in the inducements which they have it in their power to offer to Candidates for the office of Examiners, might be attended with injury to the

Institution; they wish, however, to leave the matter entirely in the hands of the Government, feeling confident that they will give the subject mature consideration, with the desire to render the University as efficient as possible for the purposes for which it was founded.

A motion to delay, until the return requested of examiners had been received, was lost by six to three, its supporters being Airy, Ridout and Warburton. Airy, true to the dislike of what he considered unjustified remuneration which he had demonstrated with respect to the Registrar's salary, tried to secure the deletion of the phrase concerning the fear of not being able to entice candidates to be examiners, but he was joined by only one unnamed colleague, quite possibly Warburton, and the original motion was then put. Warburton alone opposed it, against the votes of the Vice-Chancellor, Beaufort, Billing, Hammick, Hodgkin, Jerrard and Roget.

The next day, Burlington entered in his diary his belief that the Government 'will deal fairly with us,' and described how, after the Senate meeting, he 'was occupied till late . . . in drawing up a statement of the grounds upon which it appears to me our expenditure must necessarily be high for some time.' This persuasive and thorough document was despatched forthwith to the Chancellor of the Exchequer.[8] We have no hint of whether Burlington felt aggrieved by Goulburn's response, or whether he had calculated on losing and had merely been hopeful of keeping the damage to a reasonable figure. The minister delivered his decision in measured and politely regretful style:

I do not conceal from your Lordship that the situation in which this proceeding of the Senate has placed me is one from which, not more for my own sake than for that of the University, I should have been most happy to have been relieved. It would have been far more agreeable to me to have acted in concert with its governing body: to have supported their attempts to reconcile the interests of the institution with the generally expressed desire of reduced expenditure, and not to be compelled to propose reductions, which they decline to recommend or sanction. In the difficulty in which I am placed I have had recourse to the opinion of eminent men conversant with the subjects of examination, and animated by the most friendly feeling to the University. I am happy to say that the view which I am disposed to take of the extent of practicable reduction, under the head of salaries, meets with their concurrence.

In submitting the estimate to the House of Commons, I shall, therefore, propose a sum of £3370 in lieu of the £4170 which is now allotted to the salaries of examiners and others; and I must leave it to the Senate to distribute that sum among the several candidates in the manner which may appear to them best calculated to promote the welfare of the institution.[9]

However miniscule these figures may seem to those used to the enormous expenditure involved in late twentieth-century university provision, one can imagine the depth of the reaction today, were it to be proposed by Government that academic salaries be reduced by almost 20 per cent! But the almost complete indifference with which the reduction was received outside the University; the fact that the only obvious casualty suffered by the University was the resignation of one senatorial examiner; and the continuance in office of all the other examiners, mostly for many years ahead; must suggest that the Radical, Henry Warburton, and Sir Robert Peel's ministers, were shrewd judges of what the informed public considered to be the appropriate material reward for a London University examinership at the beginning of the 1840s. Graham wrote a graceful note to Burlington, insisting that the reductions would not be injurious: but he gave a justification of them which, perhaps unconsciously, points to the influence of Warburton:

> The sums paid by the College of Surgeons to Examiners at the Head of their own Body have been denounced as a proof of abuse naturally flowing from a System of Self-Election. I do not think that this Precedent is an Example to be followed.[10]

The Senate settled the new order at two meetings in February 1842 in which the atmosphere cannot have been particularly pleasant. Peter Mark Roget, the angriest examiner, tried to have an equal percentage reduction adopted across the board. But this was not acceptable to the others, and the proceedings were extended to take account of the Registrar's earnings as well as the examiners' fees. Rothman had expressed an interest at an earlier stage in having more time to devote to his own studies in astronomy, and in the new situation it was arranged, after some bickering from Warburton, that henceforward he would have several weeks free each year, and would lose £100 of his salary.[11] But it was the medical examiners who took the biggest cuts, while smaller reductions were imposed on Classics, Mathematics and

Philosophy. The final formula was proposed by Kiernan. Roget resigned his examinership, but remained on the Senate. The rest was silence, though very probably an injured silence in several quarters. Warburton, however, must have been pleased.

If the bulk of the Senate could feel some satisfaction at having forced the Government to take direct responsibility for cutting the salaries of examiners, they could not but be aware, at the same time, of having suffered a degree of humiliation. And in the following months they were to be made more aware of their vulnerability. Sir James Graham was becoming deeply involved in medical reform, and the University was hoping that they might benefit from any legislation which might be introduced. But when it was reported that no Bill was likely in 1842, Burlington confessed to Lubbock that 'from what has recently occurred . . . we must not look for much support from the Government.' By the end of May he was confirmed in his pessimism, and wrote in his diary that 'The Government show an unfriendly spirit towards us, and I doubt the future success of the Institution.'[12]

We have seen that the censors of the Royal College of Physicians had been invited to attend the *viva voce* examinations of the University in the autumn of 1841. There is evidence that some such attendance did take place, but neither the minutes of the College's committees, nor the University's archives, contain any reference to it and, indeed, there are no censors' reports on the whole subject in 1841 and 1842 in the College's surviving records. In effect, even the slight progress which had been made to bring the College and the University closer came to nothing. When, in August 1842, Rothman sent out an invitation to the censors to repeat their attendance of the previous year, the reply read:

> The Report of the late Censors [on the 1841 examinations] . . . represents that it is impossible for the Censors of the College of Physicians to be present at examinations so numerous and extensive until more definite arrangements be made between the two bodies.[13]

Six years later, Wakley's *Lancet* suggested to his readers the probable cause of the College's disengagement: 'It is said . . . that the date of the retirement of the College from the University was coeval with the advent of a conservative ministry, and the diminution of the parliamentary vote to the University.'[14]

But long before the medical examinations in 1842 were due, it became clear that the University was being largely ignored in the consideration of future medical educational arrangements by the Government and the College of Physicians, whose new President, Sir Benjamin Brodie, was a close adviser to Sir James Graham.[15] Informed by Lubbock that the Government was intending to bring in a medical reform 'very unfavourable' to the University, Burlington called on Graham, afterwards recording that the Minister 'was very civil, but did not disguise that the measure would probably interfere materially with us. It will in fact I believe entirely suspersede our functions as far as medical degrees are concerned.'[16] The strength of his reaction may have disturbed the minister, however, for a week later Brodie tried to mend fences, telling Lubbock that:

> Sir James Graham has requested [me] to assure you that nothing is further from his wishes than to injure in any way the Metropolitan University. He does not feel that he can with propriety [award] to that institution any new privileges such as are not conceded to the old English Universities; but his proposed Bill will take from it no privileges which it already possesses: and my *private* opinion is that it will not be difficult for you to make some arrangement with the College of Physicians, which will enable the graduates of the Metropolitan University to obtain the licence to hold medical appointments on easy terms.[17]

When the Senate met on 15 June, Burlington reported his concern about the Government's plans to a thinly attended meeting. Apart from himself and Lubbock, only five medical men were present – Bacot, Billing, Clark, Hammick and Kiernan – and none was inclined 'to take any measures on the subject.' Clark may well have felt particularly ambivalent: he had only recently delivered a lecture in which he called for the establishment of a single board in England which would examine and license all medical practitioners and have the power to grant degrees. He had gone on to argue that the University of London could readily 'supply such a board,' but only if its presently 'extremely defective' constitution was amended. It is not surprising, therefore, that later in June, when the Chancellor and Vice-Chancellor discussed the situation with Clark, they came to no 'very decided opinion,' and left Burlington to conclude that 'nothing can be done.'[18]

Graham's major legislative plans for medical reform were not to be presented to Parliament until 1844 and 1845. And, despite drastic revision, his proposals were ultimately withdrawn, in the face of the apparent impossibility of finding formulae which would accommodate the demands of all the parties concerned. The worst that the University of London had feared did not come about, therefore, but to use the language of the late twentieth century, the University of London, in the medical context, in the early autumn of 1842, was back at square one.

It is possible that the threats and disappointments over the medical outlook, together with the forced reduction of the examiners' and Registrar's salaries, may have been partly responsible for Lubbock's decision to resign the Vice-Chancellorship. He confirmed this on 1 June 1842, on the same day as he warned Burlington of the Government's medical plans. They could have been the last straw, for he had in fact approached Burlington in May.

> During the time I have had the honor of occupying the post of Vice-Chancellor I have from delicacy abstained from giving the opinion that it is extremely unreasonable on the part of the government to expect any individual to discharge the duties of that situation *or* those of Treasurer without remuneration. At present having signified to your Lordship my wish to retire it does not seem to me that it is improper for me to give this opinion in favor of my successor, and although I leave it to your Lordship to make any use of this letter, if you think otherwise I should be glad to be guided in that respect by your Lordship's better judgement and not make any remark to the Senate on the matter.
>
> It seems to me that the V.C. is in a very different position from any other member of the Senate, *he* must be on the spot always, *he* must always attend every meeting of the Senate and although the meetings are not so numerous as they were at first, still it is extremely inconvenient to be tied to London and to have engagements from which there is no escape. To this must be added applications for subscriptions to Hospitals, etc., which press upon the V.C. and which as the institution increases he will find it uncomfortable to meet with a negative.
>
> All this I submit to your Lordship and if you take a different view nothing need be said about it.[19]

To this Burlington was entirely sympathetic. He had previously made the same points to Lord John Russell and was quite sure nothing would be done to improve matters by the present Government. Lubbock took the hint and no more was said: the new Vice-Chancellor, John Shaw

Lefevre, was Joint Permanent Secretary to the Board of Trade, but there is no suggestion that the fact that he already enjoyed an official salary played any part in his appointment.[20]

In July 1842, and again in September 1844, the Home Office enquired about vacancies in the Senate. In 1843 the Senate petitioned the House of Commons, praying that London LL Ds should be permitted to practise in the proposed new Court of Arches; and in 1845 they sent a memorial to Graham about the need to give London medical graduates privileges equal to those enjoyed by the graduates of the ancient universities. This latter move was in response to the Home Secretary's medical bills, which had ignored the University. As it turned out, the proposed legislation for the ecclesiastical courts and for medical reform were eventually withdrawn.[21] With one exception, these were the only communications which passed between Senate, Parliament and Government which had any bearing on the University's constitution during the last four years of the Conservative administration, and no action followed any of them. Nor was there any apparent response, private or official, to the one exception – which seems to have been the only other possible indication of political interest in the structure of the University during Graham's term of office.

Among the papers of Nassau Senior is a rough draft of a letter to Graham, undated but by virtue of some of its references almost certainly written in 1843–4. It consists of 'some remarks on the present constitution and powers of the University of London and on the alterations which I venture to think advisable,' and is being submitted to the Home Secretary, 'In pursuance of your kind permission.'[22] There is no final version, and no trace of it in Graham's archives or in the Home Office papers. Whatever its origins or reception – assuming it was ever sent - it is the fifth extant document calling for change in the constitution of the University of London, to be put alongside the contributions of Airy, Clark, Hodgkin and Monteagle.[23] It is worth looking at all five.

Despite some inevitable differences of emphasis among five diagnoses and sets of proposals, there is a remarkable degree of concensus as to what was wrong with the University's fundamental arrangements. As the report of a senior politician and ex-minister, Monteagle's opinions would probably have carried most weight in government circles, and his three-thousand words of rather rococo prose combine a strong defence of the institution, and much praise of its members, with attitudes on the whole shared with the other commentators. There is plenty of evidence to show that Burlington, Lubbock and Warburton were in general sympathy with what all of them said. Indeed, it can be claimed, with due caution, that at the very least a sizeable group of the most devoted and influential fellows would have supported the opinions expressed by these colleagues and by Monteagle: in a more limited context, they had already shown their support in their deliberations as a Committee of the Whole, in 1840.

All the reviews put the confusions about the appointment and remuneration of examiners in a proper perspective, and agreed that the sensible forward move was to stop appointing new senatorial examiners but to leave the original appointees to examine so long as they wanted to and so long as the Senate wished to employ them in that capacity. Far more important was the concern to widen the opportunities for students to take the examinations of the University. Even Monteagle came round fully to the view that the Senate should be given the same powers to recommend schools, colleges and other institutions as appropriate sources of non-medical candidates as it already enjoyed with respect to medical schools and teachers as educators of medical students. Monteagle went further in suggesting that

> it would be unjust and inexpedient wholly to exclude from matriculation and from degrees, persons whose education has been private and domestic . . . on special and individual application such persons should be placed on a level with other students.

Monteagle also pushed again his particular enthusiasm for 'the admission of Students of the Inns of Court for examinations in Law and Jurisprudence.' In this, and in his advocacy of extending the granting of certificates of proficiency in a whole range of subjects to candidates who were not graduates, he had a strong ally in Senior. The enthusiasm of the non-medical men for these changes in admissions policy was driven by their keenness to promote educational advance: it was the equivalent, in a larger context, of the medical people's demand that London have the same privilege of licensing doctors as was enjoyed by Oxford and Cambridge. Monteagle argued that 'the enlargement of the circle from whence students are received cannot but exercise an important and beneficial influence on the general system of Education,' while Senior claimed that the availability of certificates of proficiency to non-graduates would be 'a greater stimulus . . . to the education of the middle and upper classes than the English Government has ever before been able to afford.'

1 Lord John Russell
  Home Secretary 1835–9
  Prime Minister 1846–52

2 Thomas Spring Rice
  1st Baron Monteagle
  Chancellor of the Exchequer 1835–9
  Fellow 1850–66

3 Henry Warburton MP
  Fellow 1836–58

4 William Cavendish
  2nd Earl of Burlington
  Chancellor 1836–56
  Fellow 1856–91

5 Sir John William Lubbock Bt
 Vice-Chancellor 1836–42
 Fellow 1842–65

6 Sir John George Shaw Lefevre
 Fellow 1836–79
 Vice-Chancellor 1842–62

7 George Biddell Airy
 Fellow 1836–47

8 John Sims
 Fellow 1836–8

9 Neil Arnott
  Fellow 1836–74

10 Archibald Billing
   Fellow 1836–81
   Examiner in Medicine 1839–61

11 Sir James Clark Bt
   Fellow 1836–65

12 Thomas Hodgkin
   Fellow 1836–66

13 Sir James Graham Bt
   Home Secretary 1841–6
   Fellow 1850–61

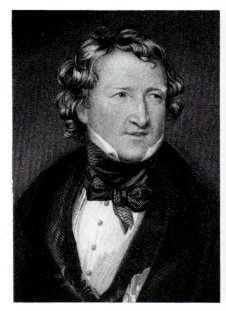

14 Thomas Wakley
   Editor of *The Lancet*

15 Peter Mark Roget
   Fellow 1836–69
   Examiner in Physiology and
   Comparative Anatomy 1839–41

16 Nassau William Senior
   Fellow 1836–64
   Examiner in Political Economy
   1840–61, and in Law 1849–61

17 Sir George Grey Bt
Home Secretary 1846–52, 1855–8

18 Spencer Horatio Walpole
Home Secretary 1852, 1858–9

19 George Leveson-Gower
2nd Earl Granville
Chancellor 1856–91

20 George Grote
Fellow 1850–62
Vice-Chancellor 1862–71

21 Michael Faraday
   Fellow 1836–63

22 John Stevens Henslow
   Fellow 1836–61
   Examiner in Botany and Natural
   History 1838–61

23 William Thomas Brande
   Fellow 1836–61
   Examiner in Chemistry 1838–9:
   1845–58

24 William Withey Gull
   Fellow 1856–89

Some Leading Members of the Graduates' Committee 1848–58

25 Charles James Foster
   Fellow and Chairman of Convocation
   1858–63

26 John Storrar
   Fellow 1858–85
   Chairman of Convocation 1864–85

27 Robert Barnes
   Sometime Secretary of the Graduates'
   Committee

28 Frederick John Wood
   Fellow 1856–92
   Chairman of Convocation 1885–92

Some Non-Senatorial Examiners

29 Henry Alford
  Logic and Moral Philosophy 1842–57

30 Thomas Graham
  Chemistry 1845–55

31 Jonathan Pereira
  Materia Medica and Pharmacy
  1840–52

32 Alexander Tweedie
  Medicine 1839: 1841–62

So far as the basic constitutional structure was concerned, there was virtual unanimity on the present weakness. As Clark put it, succinctly,

> The number of Fellows, thirty-five [sic], is too numerous for an executive body, and not sufficient to admit of the formation of an effective executive council. Accordingly, the working of the University has been very difficult, and its decisions often most unsatisfactory to a large proportion of its members; and this chiefly from the want of that deliberate consideration and calm discussion, which a more limited and responsible body necessarily exercises.[24]

And the solution was seen by all the reformers in similar terms: Monteagle put it simply – 'I think that the University should in future consist of two bodies, a Council or Executive body, and a Senate.'

The Council was to comprise the Chancellor and Vice-Chancellor together with seven or eight members (Senior and Monteagle), or 'comparatively few' (Hodgkin). Senior suggested that the whole Council should be appointed by the Secretary of State. Monteagle wanted the Chancellor to be appointed by the Crown and to hold office for life, with the Vice-Chancellor named, annually, by the Chancellor from among members of Council or Senate, and with other members selected by the Secretary of State from a slate of candidates put forward by the Senate. Hodgkin would have entrusted the election of the Vice-Chancellor and members to the Senate. All agreed that the Council should be a genuinely effective executive body, with Senior and Hodgkin hinting that some payment of its members would be appropriate. And while the Council should be powerful, the Senate should have the right to initiate, amend or reject legislation. As Hodgkin put it:

> By the formation of an Executive Council the more arduous duties of the Senate, which cannot be laid on any unpaid individuals for a long continuance, will thus be placed in hands of a comparatively few, who will find that there is more honour and less to dread in the undertaking than if it were less personal and defined and more lasting. The business still left in the hands of the whole Senate will be a means of securing the confidence of the public, and tend to keep the Senate together as a body and to satisfy the Members individually that they have not received an empty and unmeaning title.

While the word 'senate' is used throughout the reviews, the body being described by it may better be thought of as 'convocation.' Senior seemed only to have in mind some continuance of the original Senate, but most of the others clearly accepted the idea of a body of graduates, though variously defined. Monteagle envisaged a time, clearly not far ahead,

> when a succession of students have received the honor of a University degree, who have thereby acquired and who should be encouraged to retain those associations of affection and respect felt by enlarged and liberal minds for the seats of learning where they have studied. As the numbers of graduates increases, these graduates will furnish the best elements for the future government of the University, and for the promotion and extension of its influence and the performance of its duties. In order to keep up the connection between the University and its graduates, the latter should be entrusted with powers . . . and called on to perform duties. The experience of the ancient Universities furnishes analogies which may here be most usefully applied.

That, apart from the tacit acceptance of the *status quo* in the matter of the appointment of senatorial examiners, some of these suggested changes never took place, and others only occurred many years later, cannot be blamed wholly on the immediate indifference of a Conservative Government, for the inertia of Senate and Government extended well into the following regime. The arguments of those whose opinions have been summarized were made known and recorded on paper: but while that group certainly included several of the continuously active members of the Senate, there were, as Burlington appreciated, many other fellows who were very capable of turning out to be potential opposers of change.

No rounded, written statement of all-round opposition to these ideas seems to have survived, if indeed any such existed, other than the article in the *Morning Chronicle* of April 1841. But there were some serious doubts even among the reforming element over particular features of the constitution. Airy, for example, impatient as he was with the fickleness of the Senate as a decision-making body, was pertinently sceptical about the cohesion of the London graduates who, unlike the Oxbridge men, were merely examinees brought from a variety of places, and as a total group had no experience of living and studying together; they would thus be without the experience which would produce a powerful loyalty to the University. Jerrard, one of the probable authors or sponsors of the article in the *Morning Chronicle*, was earlier recorded as being convinced that the Senate should be a body composed of none but examiners: it is highly unlikely that he would have supported a division into an essentially lay council, a group of mostly non-senatorial examiners, and a 'convocation.'[25]

But the most probable cause of inaction in the constitutional context was not any determined opposition, either in Government or in the Senate. What is more likely was the operation of what is often said to be a national characteristic – a reluctance to make formal changes to an organization if that organization is working with apparently reasonable effectiveness. Once Parliament had satisfied itself that the University of London was no longer being extravagant and that its internal appointments were not scandalous, there was little or no political interest, let alone enthusiasm, for interfering with arrangements which were allowing steady, if not exciting, progress to be made with the essential task for which the University had been set up. And from the government side of the House, insofar as that task was the provision of a channel of opportunity for Dissenters, it would not attract Conservative sympathy.

One can imagine that, in the mid-1840s, the few ministers and those few senior advisers who may have been well informed about the University of London might have answered a plea for a change in the Charter with the following argument. In practice, the call for a small executive council which should concentrate its energies and attention on running the University, is already being met: and as for giving new powers to a group of graduates, save for the opinions of a tiny handful of thoughtful men ambitious for their institution, where is the evidence of any significant pressure to bring such arrangements into force?

CHAPTER 13

A New Round of Controversy

It is improbable that the dispute over salaries and the unfruitful negotiations about a revised constitution had any significant effect on the number of candidates for the new University's examinations and degrees. The number must have been kept down by the policy of admitting to examination only candidates who had been educated in approved institutions. There is no way of estimating the extent of any such frustrated demand, though it would almost certainly have been greater in the non-medical than in the medical context. At the same time, many potential medical students could have been deterred by the failure of the University to have its degrees accepted as licences to practise. And the Senate may have discouraged a more rapid growth of applicants by their unwillingness to lower the standards of the examinations which they had established at the outset. The academic reputation of the University was enhanced by this, but the number of examinees who gained its qualifications grew only slowly.

Table 2 shows the small numbers generally over the whole period of this study, the modest increase in arts graduates, only patchy growth of medical successes, and a derisory output of those with law degrees. At the same time, the pass rate was high – close to 90 per cent. Candidates were predominantly London based, with UCL producing about 40 per cent of the graduates. By 1858, the Home Office had accepted some 37 colleges across the country, in addition to all the Universities of the United Kingdom, and the Universities of Sydney and Toronto, whose students could become candidates for degrees in Arts or Law. Almost all the colleges were Nonconformist, Roman Catholic, or non-denominational. Meanwhile, the University had successfully recommended the affiliation of over 70 medical schools.

Table 3 shows that because of the lack of any substantial increase in activity, the Treasury's annual grant never exceeded £4,000 after 1842, and the University was never allowed to carry over more than £2,000 from one year to another. But receipts from fees, together with very small sums from the sale of publications, etc., did rise noticeably to over £1,600 by the early 1850s, constituting about a third of total annual

Table 2 Number of candidates for matriculation and degrees,
and number of passes

	Matric		BA		MA		LLB		LLD		1st MB		2nd MB		MD	
	C	P	C	P	C	P	C	P	C	P	C	P	C	P	C	P
1838	23	22														
1839	31	30	17	17			3	3			25	16	10	9	2	2
1840	77	69	32	30	4	3	3	2			49	38	20	19	1	1
1841	89	64	40	35	1	1	10	9			80	50	21	18	7	7
1842	82	66	33	20	4	3	2	2			38	25	23	19	5	5
1843	96	80	29	28	1	0	1	1	2	1	41	21	22	21	4	4
1844	95	79	33	30	3	3	1	1	1	0	35	26	22	20	14	14
1845	113	104	40	37	1	1	2	2			33	25	17	16	10	10
1846	110	99	32	30	2	2	2	2			31	26	14	13	13	11
1847	161	151	44	36	3	3	2	2			33	24	21	20	9	9
1848	171	161	47	41	4	4	4	4	2	2	41	27	24	20	12	11
1849	181	167	63	53	7	7	2	2	1	1	32	25	17	13	9	8
1850	206	190	70	58	10	10	3	3	1	1	31	23	18	12	16	13
1851	241	214	67	49	2	2	5	5			34	27	21	19	9	8
1852	244	206	62	49	8	6	7	7	1	1	27	21	14	13	11	10
1853	218	201	81	64	10	8	6	6			30	23	17	10	8	8
1854	241	199	93	73	8	8	6	6			30	28	17	12	5	5
1855	209	172	75	63	3	3	5	5			36	30	18	14	12	12
1856	255	209	71	58	10	10	12	11	1	1	45	26	12	9	5	5
1857	266	224	75	66	5	5	6	6	1	1	43	35	31	30	12	12

income.

These figures of examinees and money underline two decades of quiet academic consolidation which, however valuable in itself and full of significance for the long-term future of higher education, could not by any stretch of the imagination be described as dynamic. In the early 1840s, the level of expectation must have fallen. It would not be surprising, therefore, if unspectacular progress, added to the rather bruising rebuff to all pleas for constitutional change, the humiliating reduction of salaries forced by Parliament and Government, and the non-recognition of medical degrees as licences to practise, should have induced in the Senate some general lowering of morale. In turn, this could have encouraged a tendency to avoid trouble, and no enthusiasm for new initiatives. And while the internal and external political arguments of 1840 to 1842 were largely irrelevant to the actual immediate work of the University, they concealed the fact that much of the excitement and satisfaction of creating a new system must have been greatly diluted for several members of the Senate, especially those who

Table 3   Income and Expenditure
£s

	Income				Expenditure
	Treasury	*Fees*	*Other*	*Total*	
1837–8	1000			1000	522
1838–9	2000	44	1	2045	2498
1839–40	4700	405	2	5107	4563
1840–1	4000	783	36	4819	5061
1841–2	4442	988		5430	5288
1842–3	4000	652		4652	4681
1843–4	4000	725		4725	4578
1844–5	4000	868	100	4968	4751
1845–6	4000	911		4911	4953
1846–7	4000	843	60	4903	4782
1847–8	4000	1022	41	5063	4659
1848–9	4000	1297	27	5324	4604
1849–50	2000	1412	54	3466	3539
1850–1	3000	1585	105	4690	4652
1851–2	3000	1453	217	4670	4856
1852–3	3000	1514	185	4699	4961
1853–4	3000	1601	118	4719	4804
1854–5	4000	1653		5653	5388
1855–6	3000	1513	60	4573	4842
1856–7	3000	1638	57	4695	5341

Source: Taken from a Return made by the Registrar in response to a request by Joseph Hume, MP, in February, 1854 (UL/RO 1/2/16), and from Senate minutes, 1854–8. The figures have been rounded to the nearest pound. The 'Other' income came from the sale of publications and of waste paper, etc.

were not directly involved as examiners, once syllabuses were agreed, matriculations began and the first degrees were awarded. All this was reflected in the pattern of attendance by fellows which was examined in broad terms in Chapter 6.

From the day when John Shaw Lefevre was elected Vice-Chancellor in June 1842 until March 1850, which saw the appearance of the first new fellows to be appointed since 1837, there were only 74 meetings of the Senate – a settling down to the traditional nine monthly meetings during each academic session. Of those 74 meetings, only ten attracted an attendance of more than 12 senators. Nine men were present at more than half the meetings, and six others turned up to a third of the sessions. Eleven other names will be found scattered across the minutes, but between them those entries represented an average appearance by each man less than twice a year – and several came nowhere near that figure. The Chancellor came to only one in three meetings. The major part of the burden was taken by the Vice-Chancellor, Jerrard, Warburton, and six medics – in order of their attendances: Kiernan, Billing, Hammick, Bacot, Hodgkin and Ridout. Jerrard and four of the medics were examiners. The 'second string' comprised, in addition to the Chancellor, two more medical men, Arnott and Clark, together with Senior, Faraday and Brande. Senior and Brande were examiners.

It is a simple fact, therefore, that it was examiners and the medical faculty who held the institution together. In 1847 the Earl of Burlington did not hide his concern that the situation was 'unsatisfactory':

> the whole management of the University at present rests in fact with a few members of the Senate, who being also Examiners consider themselves under an obligation to attend, and indeed if it were not so, the requisite number required by the Charter would rarely be obtained.[1]

The Government's unwillingness hitherto to take seriously the argument that the University needed a formally separate executive body, about ten or a dozen strong, which Senior, Hodgkin and Monteagle had all prescribed, might well have been based on the fact that the Senate was already providing just such a body. And, in practice, Jerrard's claim that the governing body should all be examiners was close to the reality, despite all the contumely which had been heaped on the Senate for confusing the two functions. And so far had the whole notion of constitutional reform slipped out of consideration by 1847 that Burlington, in the letter quoted above, recollected that

> in the year 1841 just before the resignation of Lord Melbourne's Government, the subject was brought under the consideration of the Home Secretary, and at various meetings of the Senate it was discussed what alterations were desirable in the Charter. If I am not mistaken the principal proposal was to give ultimately to the Graduates of the University in some mode or other a considerable share in the management of its affairs. The whole subject however at that time dropped to the ground in consequence of the change of government, and the matter has never since been taken up.

It is fair to suggest that the experience of having to preside over the Senate during the rather spiritless interlude from 1841 onwards, together with the sadness of his private life, had weakened Burlington's response to drift in the University's affairs, even though he was aware of the consequences of that drift. As he confessed to Airy in the late summer of 1847,

> I am myself strongly of opinion that the constitution of the University requires amendment, but as it secures the great object of enabling dissenters from the Church of England to obtain degrees I have always felt that minor objections may be submitted to for a time.[2]

But from the middle of 1846 onwards several of the 'minor objections' could no longer be ignored.

That a new era of controversy in the Senate set in after the middle of the 1840s can be attributed to several factors. First, Sir Robert Peel resigned as Prime Minister on 29 June 1846, to be replaced by Lord John Russell, whose Whig administration was to survive for more than six years of the new era of relative political instability which set in with the Tory split over the repeal of the Corn Laws. The change of Government, and the assumption of supreme authority by the man who had been the most powerful advocate of the University's creation, must have given fresh heart to those senators who hoped for expansion of the University's role and a more flexible and sympathetic response to its problems from Westminster and Whitehall.

The second factor was the University's continuing insistence that Government and the established institutions of the medical and legal professions should give London graduates the same privileges as were enjoyed by the graduates of Oxford and Cambridge. Third – and very closely related to the second factor, though its main outward manifestations were not to appear until 1848 – was an agitation by the London graduates for the place in the University's governing machinery which had been held out as a possibility in 1840 but had been ignored subsequently.

Behind, and in addition to, these manifestations of the hopes for and the desire that, in one way or another, the status and scope of the University of London would be enhanced, was the growing pressure of the Dissenting churches for a removal of the special privileges of the adherents of the Anglican community. In 1843 the Rev Edward Miall had started to publish the *Nonconformist*, which was to be a major journal of dissenting opinion. In the following year Miall and others had founded the Anti-State Church Association, whose long-term aims included the abolition of church rates and the eventual disestablishment of the Anglican Church. The association set up a Dissenters' parliamentary committee to liaise with sympathetic MPs in 1847: and after the general election of 1852 there were no less than 38 Dissenters in the House of Commons, representing the hitherto unsuspected numerical strength of Dissent revealed by the census of 1851.

This blossoming of non-Anglican power has been attributed to 'that alliance of the left wing in Dissenting politics with radicalism in secular politics . . . which was to be increasingly influential.'[3] From the mid-1850s onwards, after the Anti-State Church Association had changed its name to The Society for the Liberation of Religion from State Patronage and Control (the Liberation Society), it was

> extremely successful in making the Liberal Party feel the weight of Nonconformist views on questions of religious equality, and its small but cumulative victories on minor questions, gained through unrelenting but unsensational electoral and Parliamentary pressure, made it the epitome of rational agitation.[4]

The very existence of the University of London was already a matter for pride and satisfaction among Dissenters. The new activism of Dissent was certainly sympathetic and helpful to the claims of the University for further enhancement of its position, and must have increased substantially an awareness of its potentialities and achievements. But in the years after 1846, and particularly in the early 1850s, it is not surprising that, in the context of higher education, a major objective of the non-Anglican interest was to force the Universities of Oxford and Cambridge to allow Dissenters to be admitted to their degrees. However, the Dissenting pressure was peculiarly prominent in the struggle which set in for the involvement of graduates in the governance of the University of London, largely through the personal involvement of Charles James Foster, who was simultaneously the most tenacious of the graduate leaders and an important Dissenting activist.

Of Foster and his colleagues we shall hear much more. But it is surely significant that the incident which caused the most immediate upsurge of senatorial concern, in 1846, was the attempt by the Senate's most articulate Anglican, J.H. Jerrard, to raise again, only two weeks before Peel's fall from power, the introduction of compulsory examinations in Scriptural studies.

Jerrard's tactics in 1846 might have been different if he had known of

Peel's imminent resignation. Not that Peel had shown any personal sympathy for Jerrard: only as recently as July 1845 he had brushed off a plea for ecclesiastical preferment.[5] But, despite his earlier devotion to Whiggish causes, Jerrard may have come to believe that the introduction of compulsory scriptural examinations would be given support by a Conservative administration, and he must have planned his campaign many months before Peel's crucial parliamentary defeat. Be that as it may, Jerrard's original convictions, thwarted in 1838 by Arnold's intransigence, were strengthened by the wide interest excited by the publication of Arnold's biography and letters in 1844, and by the failure of 93 per cent of the University's candidates for degrees to choose to take the examinations in scriptural subjects. Jerrard convinced himself that the time was ripe to call on his colleagues in the Senate to reverse their decision of eight years previously, and to make scriptural examinations, henceforward, a compulsory part of the BA syllabus. He lodged a Notice of Motion to that effect, which was to be discussed at a meeting on 15 July 1846 – just two weeks after the fall of Sir Robert Peel's government.

Fourteen senators turned out on 15 July – by far the largest attendance during a session at which six to eight was normal – and the debate was not pleasant. Burlington identified the main antagonists. 'Dr Jerrard brought [the motion] in and he is not judicious. Warburton opposed in a most violent and ill-conditioned way.'[6] Senior wanted approval for the existing system to continue. Eventually Warburton's suggestion that the whole matter be adjourned until the following March was accepted, along with a directive that Jerrard's proposition should be sent to all the colleges who were affiliated to the University. This gave both sides time to prepare, refine and press their cases in a wider sphere.

Though there is no surviving correspondence in the University or departmental archives between institutions or persons on the subject during the following seven months, the outcome of the approach to the teaching bodies is made clear in a document drawn up for the meeting of Senate on 10 March 1847. Of 26 colleges consulted, eleven, defined as either Anglican, Baptist or Independent, supported Jerrard's proposal; seven Catholic colleges, UCL and Manchester New College, were opposed; and a mixture of six Catholic, Presbyterian and Independent places did not answer. Immediately after the meeting, Warburton sent a copy of this list, together with his own comments, as a confidential memorandum to the Prime Minister, Lord John Russell.

There had been sixteen senators present on 10 March, and Warburton's account of what happened, though quietly triumphant, seems likely to have been fair:

> On counting the Members present, and their probable votes, Dr Jerrard, on the pretence that in consequence of the opposition given to his motion by a number of the Colleges, he intended so to amend it as to render it palatable to the Catholic Colleges, abstained from making any Motion on the subject at all. An entry in the Minutes was made, that he had made no Motion; of which Notice was directed to be given to all the Colleges connected with the University.

Warburton added his own forecast of how fifteen of the sixteen senators would have voted, had they been forced to do so. He believed that only the Bishop of Norwich, Airy and possibly Ridout would have joined Jerrard. He listed the Chancellor and Vice-Chancellor, Amos, Arnott, Bacot, Billing, Empson, Henslow, Hodgkin and Kiernan as likely to have voted with him, against the motion. The minutes show that Senior was the sixteenth member present, but either he took a firmly neutral position, or Warburton simply forgot to indicate his supposed preference.[7]

Jerrard may not have been judicious, but he was determined and persistent. Defeated by the Senate over University examinations, he turned instead to the colleges which provided the candidates for the BA. Less than three months after the *débâcle* of 10 March, he put forward the suggestion that the Senate should require all candidates for the BA to hold a certificate of having passed an examination in scriptural history. He did not ask that the Senate should immediately vote on that proposal, but called for it to be referred to all the affiliated colleges. He took his ally, George Airy, into his confidence, and expressed to him very bluntly both his tactics and his opinion of his fellow senators:

> I have no intention of referring the *voluntary* part of the plan to the affiliated Colleges. They have *all* acquiesced in the *principle* of Voluntary Scriptural Examinations, and to consult them as to the *details* would lead, in this case, to interminable delay and confusion. Before *this* part of the measure is discussed I trust there will be an infusion of New Members into the Senate. So many of the present body were appointed under Mr Warburton's influence, and so few of the Medical Members (who form an overwhelming majority of our *actual* Legislature) have had the benefit of an English University Education, that I have always looked upon them as a most unfavourable and provoking tribunal to refer the question to.[8]

This was to be Jerrard's final move on scriptural examinations: it failed, not on its merits but, rather sadly, as the result of a procedural misunderstanding which led to a wholly unexpected confrontation between Airy and Warburton, followed by the former's resignation. The unpleasantness generated cannot but have shaken the whole establishment, and may have been a contributory factor in the events which led to the Supplementary Charter of 1849.

On 16 June, when Jerrard introduced his proposal and asked that the opinion of the colleges on giving certificates be obtained, there were again sixteen senators present, though the composition of the group was slightly different from that in attendance on 10 March. Some concern was voiced as to whether the requirement of certificates was legal, and Bacot suggested that the advice of the law officers should be sought. Jerrard and his seconder, Airy, were quite prepared to accept this. The Chancellor, following procedure in both Houses of Parliament, therefore put the first, enabling question – that the original motion be amended. Airy and Jerrard voted in favour, as did Bacot, Beaufort, the Bishop of Norwich and Ridout. But these six were opposed by a group of equal size comprising Amos, Arnott, Billing, Empson, Kiernan and Warburton. The issue was settled by Burlington's casting vote in favour of putting the amendment.

The question was then put on Bacot's amendment, which provided for reference to the law officers. But on this occasion the Chancellor did not need to vote: those who had carried the first division otherwise remained unchanged, but the opponents were reinforced by Hammick and Roget, and the amendment was lost by eight votes to six. To Airy and Jerrard, as, no doubt, to many laymen, this simply meant that the question of asking for a legal opinion was out of the way, and the Senate could proceed to discuss and vote on the substantive motion. But to this Warburton made objection, arguing that under parliamentary rules, the whole proceeding had been negatived by the defeat of the amendment. Burlington, the only other parliamentarian present, who was under some pressure of time, upheld the objection, and the meeting was closed, leaving Jerrard and Airy angry and bewildered.

If Jerrard was a persistent man, Airy was a pugnacious one. He at once began a detailed, technical and barbed correspondence on the theory of amendment with Warburton, after which he was still convinced that he and Jerrard had been unfairly used. He objected to the draft minutes of the meeting and wanted the following statement included in the final version:

Mr Airy stated to the Chancellor that his vote on the general question of Dr Jerrard's motion was given on the supposition that, in the event of rejection of the specific Amendment, the question would be put on the original Motion.

Airy's request reached a troubled Burlington at Holker Hall, to which he had repaired for the summer. Burlington would not be at the next meeting of the Senate, but he told the Astronomer Royal that he had directed Rothman to read Airy's letter to the Senate, and went on:

I have also added that in my opinion your wishes ought to be complied with. It is my intention to request the Senate to come to some definitive resolution as to how motions and amendments to motions are to be put in future. The course I have hitherto followed is that adopted by both Houses of Parliament, but I fully admit that it does occasionally lead to inconvenience and deprives members of the Senate of the power of expressing their opinions precisely according to their own views. My own wish is simply to put questions in future in such a manner as may most readily give all members an opportunity of giving expression to their opinions.

It may be that, on a less contentious issue, some gracious compromise might have been achieved which would have re-established harmony on the procedural front and allowed a further debate and vote on the basic issue. And it would seem, from a long perspective, that the chances of Dr Jerrard ever succeeding in enforcing scriptural examinations either at college or university level were very far from strong. But the hard reality was that the opposition to Jerrard's idea was as unflinching as his own devotion to it, and that the personalities on each side were abrasive. On 28 July, when the Chancellor, the Vice-Chancellor, Airy and Warburton were all absent, and when attendance was down to seven (Jerrard and six medical senators), there was some bitter argument about the accuracy of the unconfirmed minutes of the meeting of 16 June, but only Jerrard voted against approving them; and when he moved that Airy's letter and statement should be inserted in the minutes, he could not find a seconder. The letter was 'laid on the Table.'

This was the last straw for Airy. He 'determined never to sit with Warburton again,' and later described the procedural manoeuvre which had prevented any discussion of Jerrard's motion in June 1847 as 'a very mean subterfuge . . . of Messrs Warburton and Co.' At the beginning of August he submitted his resignation to Burlington, who passed it on to the Home Secretary, Sir George Grey, at the end of the month. Nearly two years later, and again apparently with Jerrard's encouragement, Airy reopened with Burlington and Shaw Lefevre the possibility of rejoining the Senate, but only so long as some amends were made by the University for the insults which he felt he had suffered in 1847. Correspondence on the subject ran for some weeks in May and June 1849, without much progress being made, and thereafter petered out. Airy never served on the Senate again. But, as we shall see, in 1847 he had pressed for some constitutional reform along with several other senators, and his fiery departure may well have helped to raise the temperature of debate about the University higher than it had been for many years.[9]

The attractiveness of the law degrees of the new University was apparently very limited – an average of less than four candidates per year for Bachelors degrees and only eight candidates for the doctorate in the first sixteen years. But the University had a little more success in law than in medicine in getting the privileges available to Oxbridge graduates extended to their London counterparts. The admission and enrolment requirements for attorneys and solicitors of persons having degrees from Oxford, Cambridge or Dublin, whereby the duration of articles was reduced from five to three years, was extended to London graduates by an Act of the first year of Victoria's reign.[10] In 1843, London and Durham graduates at the Middle Temple were given the same privileges as Oxbridge men with respect to calls to the Bar and, by 1845, the period of studentship for the Irish Bar at King's Inn, Dublin, had been reduced by five terms for London graduates. But no similar gestures had been made at Gray's or Lincoln's Inns, or at the Inner Temple, and admission as students to the Inns usually involved, for those who were not Oxbridge men, the payment of a deposit of £100.[11]

As we have seen, in 1843 the Senate had petitioned the House of Commons to include, in a bill then before the House designed to reform the ecclesiatical courts, that doctors of Law of London should be permitted to practise as advocates in the proposed Court of Arches; but the bill was withdrawn.[12]

The medical road was even harder. Nothing had been conceded by the medical corporations, and only minor concessions to London graduates were made in wholly government-controlled services such as the army, navy and poor law administration – which reflected the influence of M'Grigor within the War Office and Admiralty, and of Shaw Lefevre, who had been a Poor Law commissioner from 1834 to 1841.[13] In April 1845, as already noted, the Senate, reacting against being entirely ignored in Sir James Graham's various medical bills, approved and forwarded to ministers a closely-argued statement in support of the University's claims.[14] And even though Graham had to abandon his attempted legislation almost a year before he went out of office in 1846, the University's medical men were left to fight their battle with the professional establishment. In this, they were somewhat hindered because they did not all share the same views across the wide context of medical reform. Of the active medical fellows, Billing, Clark and Hodgkin were imaginative, reforming spirits, for example; but Bacot and Ridout were both senior members of the Apothecaries Company. That loyalties must have been divided is not surprising, and at a later stage Ridout was criticized for having put his signature to a scheme of reform drawn up by the two Royal Colleges and the Apothecaries Company, without even mentioning the existence of the plan to the Senate.[15]

The fact was that the Peel Government was not particularly interested in, and certainly not actively supportive of, the University's aspirations for its graduates in law and medicine. It was suggested earlier that the withdrawal of the Royal College of Physicians in 1842 from the arrangement whereby their censors attended the University's examinations, in order to ease the licensing of graduates to practise, was in all probability a reflection of the College's confidence that the University had lost governmental support with the defeat of the Whigs.[16] It is understandable that, conscious of a lack of political sympathy, and painfully aware that they were still a new, small, relatively powerless and not always internally harmonious participant in controversial, long-drawn-out arguments, the Senate was unwilling to take any strong initiative during the Conservative administration. The various attempts made in Parliament to introduce measures of general medical reform were watched carefully by the fellows, but the normal outcome of any faculty or senatorial discussion was a decision to keep official silence.[17] The petition on ecclesiastical law in 1843 and the medical memorial of 1845 stand alone.

But with a new Government taking office in the summer of 1846 and strengthened, though only slightly, by the general election of a year later, fresh initiatives were to make the University much more aggressive in its search for attention, recognition and constitutional change. The reforming pressure came to be dominated by the demand from graduates for a share in the governance of the University; but that demand was intricately connected to the concurrent campaigns by London graduates in medicine and law for the same rights within their professsions as were enjoyed by the graduates of Oxford and Cambridge – and, in the medical context, that was part of the continuing controversy over the registration of practitioners and the status of the existing medical corporations.

A proper account of the graduates' crusade must include some rehearsal of arguments and developments prior to their major challenge, which began in 1848 and was to continue for a decade. But the case for constitutional reform of the University was not solely related to professional equality and graduate participation. Quite separate moves within the Senate, which dated from at least early 1847, led to a Supplementary Charter being issued in 1849, which scarcely touched the larger issues by then agitating the University and, though much less acutely, the Home Office. It is as well, therefore, to mention, briefly, the re-emergence of concern for issues which had been raised but also buried in 1840 to 1842.

It may be that when Dr Jerrard introduced his intention to move for the introduction of compulsory examinations in biblical studies, he not only raised the temperature in the Senate, but also turned the thoughts of members back to the apparent problems of the structure of the University which had been analysed previously but left untouched. Certainly his main ally, George Airy, bewailed the fact, in his autobiography, that, after Jerrard's move in 1846, 'there was no peace.'[18] And, in March 1847, many weeks before the unfortunate disputes which led to his resignation, Airy had opened with Burlington the desirability of constitutional reform. What he suggested was, in his own word, 'crude'. It mirrored a good deal of the attitudes which he had expressed in 1838, and of what Monteagle and Hodgkin had said in 1840–1. But it is still interesting to read what this shrewd, observant and prickly, though rarely attendant, fellow was thinking early in 1847:

I may mention that two considerations, to which many others are reducible, have long since presented themselves to me. The first is, that our present foundation is too narrow, and our privileges too small, and that in consequence we do not occupy a sufficient place in the eye of the public. The second is, that we are not sufficiently in contact with the officers of the various Colleges. In both these respects I think our position is worse than that of the Universities of Cambridge and Oxford.

The idea which occurs to me . . . is the following. Suppose the Senate to consist of two bodies – a larger body and a smaller body, whose powers and order of business might be defined. Suppose the smaller body to consist of persons appointed by name (as at present) and also of the Principals of the Colleges or of some of the Colleges (to be named in the Charter) not more than one from any College. And suppose the larger body to consist of Professors of the Colleges and of Graduates (under some limitation of numbers, degrees and the like.)

Several details of working must of course be arranged: as for instance that the meetings of the larger body take place on certain appointed days, that the meetings of the smaller body take place on certain days for certain business of importance and on any other days: that a vote of the larger body may always be negatived by a vote of the smaller body, but that a vote of the smaller body repeated in two sessions cannot then be negatived by a vote of the larger body. That actual privileges be attached to our degrees.[19]

Two-and-a-half months later, and still before the final row in the Senate about the scriptural examinations, Burlington had gone to talk with the Home Secretary, Sir George Grey, to report that 'Some of the members [of the University] are rather dissatisfied with its stationary condition.' He had also had 'a long discussion on the subject . . . with Mr Ridout,' but felt that Ridout's 'views are . . . not easily carried out.'[20] Unfortunately, Ridout's ideas on that occasion went unrecorded though, as will be seen, he was later to espouse a generally cautious and conservative approach to constitutional changes.

One matter, arising out of the practical experience of attracting candidates, also produced a case for constitutional change, far less basic than that for restructuring the Senate, but nonetheless important for the effective working of the University. Rothman found that he had to tell students of the ancient universities who wanted to take London qualifications that they could not be candidates for London degrees because Oxford, Cambridge and Trinity College, Dublin, were not affiliated colleges. He brought this to the notice of Nassau Senior, seemingly because he felt that Senior might have some special influence in government circles and be able to persuade authority of the need to change the rules.[21]

But by the end of 1847, while there was no lack of realization on the part of senior members of the University that all was not well with its structure and powers, there was no obvious sign of recognition that a totally new force for change, which had been growing sporadically from very small beginnings over the previous seven years, was about to appear on the scene and to influence all future consideration of constitutional reform.

CHAPTER 14

The Beginnings of Graduate Participation

George Airy had surely not been unreasonable in doubting Monteagle's somewhat romantic conviction that affection, loyalty and ambition for the University would well up from its graduates. Most of those graduates had done their degree studies in colleges widely scattered across the country, not all of which offered residential academic experience, and had only come together for short spells in the examination halls in London. But Airy's reasonable doubt did not take sufficient account of four other factors. One, the most significant, was the existence of an institution which was offering to students a close-knit living and learning experience, only half a mile from Somerset House, and which was providing the examiners with 40 per cent of their candidates. University College London enjoyed in its own right the loyalty of its alumni, many of whom had also been pupils at University College School; but a considerable body of that alumni were to extend a similar loyalty to the University which awarded them their degrees.

The second factor was that London, as the great centre for medical and legal employment, inevitably became the workplace of many graduates of the University. Their everyday professional contacts and common concerns, and a growing consciousness of the comparative disadvantages which they suffered after graduation, ensured that a sizeable group of them became devoted to the achievement of an enhanced status for the University. And as a large proportion of the graduates working in London were UCL men, their collegiate, their university and their professional loyalties and concerns overlapped. The same could be said of the very much smaller number of King's men among the graduates, and the professional interest brought into the camp graduates who had done their training, wholly or partly, in the hospital medical schools of the capital. But it was UCL graduates who tended to dominate the campaigns for recognition, and to a degree this proved, on occasion, to be something of a disadvantage to the cause.

The core of London graduates who identified themselves strongly with the University, and who were to spearhead the drive for the establishment of convocation and the rationalizing of professional privileges, was, therefore, London based. But to their direct and often personal commitment must be added, as a third factor in the development of a sense of community among London graduates, the connection with the affiliated colleges across the country. It would be absurd to overstate the case, and particularly to claim that the personal loyalty of provincial graduates was as evident as the official co-operation and support of the institutions in which they were taught. But it is increasingly noticeable in the correspondence and in the references to conversations and verbal statements, as the years pass, how the governing bodies of colleges accepted and asserted, with pride, their affiliation with the University. In the late 1840s and early 1850s, this sense of belonging was often converted into outspoken advocacy on the University's behalf.

And this brings in the fourth, closely-related factor. Most of the non-medical institutions affiliated with the University were strongly Nonconformist or Roman Catholic. Though there was no likelihood of the two sets of colleges sharing doctrinal beliefs, their governors, their staffs and their students must have had faith in the very existence of the University of London as a guarantee of their still precarious acceptance by the English Establishment, and have supported its religious neutrality as a safeguard against any sign of militancy on the part of aggressive Anglicans. Again, it is impossible to quantify the extent of loyalty which graduates may have carried with them because the University accepted their religious affiliations without question. But the view that London had been established primarily to accommodate the legitimate demands of Dissenters for a place in the constitutional, professional and political sun, was expressed so often during the late 1840s and early 1850s that it must to no small degree have reflected among many of its graduates a pride in their connection and a readiness to press for a fuller development of the University's status.

UCL had been operating for a decade before providing many of the first candidates for the examinations of the University of London. The College, by virtue of its very conception and impact on the society of its times, was something of an intellectual and political powerhouse of the non-Anglican middle and professional classes. It is entirely feasible, therefore, that among its students and graduates were many who were inspired by the aims of its founders to carve a new channel of entry into the English Establishment for those hitherto excluded, particularly on religious grounds. And in this context, probably more by accident than by design, UCL made a move which enhanced the political effectiveness and the opportunities of some of its brightest graduates.

In 1842–3, a scheme of fellowships was introduced which provided for the admission of selected students, who had graduated with honours, 'to the privileges of Proprietors for Life'. That status enabled the new fellows to take part in meetings of the College and to be eligible for election to its council. A number of shares to allow the awards to be made were contributed by senior members of council, including Warburton, Sir Isaac Goldsmid and David Solomons. The first three elections were made in 1843, and thereafter from three to six fellows were added each year.[1] Thus was created a small body of intellectually superior young men who were given the opportunity to become well acquainted with the inner workings of the administration of the College, and well informed about the politics of the University. It is not surprising that a considerable proportion of the group of graduates who led the campaign for convocation were holders of the new UCL fellowships.

It is understandable that the graduates of UCL, a private institution, and of the new University of London, in fact a government agency, would see that one of the clearest routes to full incorporation of both College and University into national life was to achieve for them, separately or together, the status of the ancient universities. And the governance of Oxford and Cambridge was in the last resort entrusted to their graduates, who also enjoyed the privilege of returning to Parliament their own members.

Thus the ultimate aim of the politically conscious London graduates, whether from UCL or elsewhere, was the creation of convocation as the governing body of the University and as a parliamentary constituency. Charles James Foster, one of their leaders, put the traditional case for direct representation of universities in a book published just after the middle of the century: it rested

> mainly on the provision which they have made for supplying the country with a large number of young men, whose education may be supposed to be above the ordinary standard, and in many cases, of the highest character. Such provision consists of the great facilities they offered for study; of the prizes and emoluments they hold out for its encouragement; and of the securities on which they insist for insuring its successfull prosecution.[2]

Why should not London graduates be enabled to send a member to the

House of Commons, asked Foster, just as did the graduates of Oxford, Cambridge and Dublin?

We have seen that, in 1840, the Senate considered with some apparent sympathy, moves towards the involvement of graduates in the government of the University. The matter was dropped after the change of administration in the following year. When the subject was raised again, it was by the graduates themselves, who were to find the Senate very defensive of its existing status and power. But during the years from 1840 to 1848, it is difficult to disentangle the concern of the graduates for an eventual full-scale transfer of power to convocation, from more limited and specific aims relating to the need for relief from particular grievances. There is a strong case for arguing that it was anger at the existing barriers to some medical and legal privileges which brought into being an effective and persistent, and ultimately largely successful, lobbying organization. In any such movement, personal ambition and ideological vision, short-term private relief and longer-term communal advantage, are all pursued and not unusually confused. But some of the leading graduates, who were involved in the issues for many years, always had their eyes on the wider constitutional issues and, once the movement was firmly launched, fundamental constitutional demands – wisely in terms of political strategy – were given pride of place over narrower professional objectives.

The first evidence we have of any stirrings among the graduates is contained in the records of Lincoln's Inn. Only weeks before the Whigs went out of office, in the summer of 1841, the benchers of the Inn were petitioned by three UCL men to extend the special privileges of Oxbridge graduates to their London counterparts. The benchers were asked

> to consider the propriety of permitting persons who have been matriculated students during two years in the University of London to become Members of your honourable Society without making the customary deposit of £100 and of admitting persons who have taken the degree of MA or BL in that University to be called to the Bar after having kept terms during three years and to make such regulations touching these matters as may to your honourable Bench seem fit.[3]

The petition was the work of three of the earliest London graduates - Charles James Foster, Frederick John Wood and Jacob Waley. Foster and Wood were major leaders of the movement: they were to become the first and third Chairmen of Convocation respectively, and both were to be members of the Senate of the University. Waley does not seem to have taken any early, major role in the constitutional struggle, but he became a fellow of UCL in 1843, a member of the Graduates Committee in 1851 and, like Foster, he became a professor at UCL. Foster was appointed Professor of Jurisprudence in 1849, and Waley was made Professor of Political Economy in 1854.

Wood pleaded with Lord Brougham to attend the meeting of benchers of Lincoln's Inn at which the petition would be considered. He was careful to flatter the great man, and insisted that he and his colleagues 'were influenced by no selfish motives, but simply by a desire to promote that civil and religious liberty, of which your Lordship has so long been the distinguished advocate and firm friend.'[4] Doubtless Brougham would have accepted the flattery, smiled at the disclaimer, appreciated the tactics and agreed with the objective.

The petition was turned down, but in all probability the petitioners lobbied persistently and the point they had raised was taken up by senior members of the Inn two years later. In June 1843, only a month after the Senate had petitioned Parliament about the ecclesiastical courts, the Council of Lincoln's Inn agreed to refer to a committee a motion of Matthew Davenport Hill, one of the remarkable Hill family, whose most famous member was his brother Rowland. Matthew Davenport Hill, a powerful advocate of reform of the criminal law, had moved that

> Advocates admitted to the Bar of Scotland, and Members and Masters of Arts of the Universities of London and Durham, be respectively admitted to the same privileges as are enjoyed at this Inn by Members and Masters of Arts of the Universities of Oxford, Cambridge and Dublin.[5]

Hill's motion was referred to a small committee of which he was a member and which enquired over the following seventeen months into the rules of the other Inns of Court and also learned, through Rothman, of the exact degree requirements, and the status of the affiliated colleges, of the University of London. But, as we have seen, the Middle Temple did not wait for the completion of Hill's enquiry, and agreed to treat the graduates of London and Durham on the same terms as those of Oxford, Cambridge and Dublin in November 1843, so far as calls to the Bar were concerned. But the Middle Temple still required a £100 deposit on admission as a student, save from those who had 'kept two years' terms' at Oxford, Cambridge or Dublin.

Despite the lead given by the Middle Temple, it was not until November 1844 that the Council of Lincoln's Inn agreed to confer with the other Inns and, after some delay, a joint meeting of four delegations, numbering altogether about twenty benchers, decided, on 7 February 1845, that they would meet again two weeks later to consider the proposal 'That at none of the Inns of Court any distinction shall be made in the admission of Gentlemen as Students, keeping terms, or calls to the Bar, founded on their place of education.' But there was no consensus. The minutes of the follow-up meeting record simply that Lincoln's Inn and the Middle Temple were in favour, the Inner Temple dissented, and Gray's Inn was 'inclining but doubtful'. A common path seemed, for the present, to be blocked.[6]

This defeat may have been one of the reasons why those particularly concerned with the training of lawyers turned to a more direct and exclusive involvement of the Inns of Court. In July 1845, Brougham proposed to his colleagues at Lincoln's Inn the setting up of a lectureship and the provision of exhibitions for students, to be open to those from all Inns. This idea must have been communicated at least to the Middle Temple, where it was taken up strongly by Richard Bethell, the future Lord Westbury. A pattern of joint discussion between the four Inns followed, in much the same fashion as it had in the previous context, but this time with more success. By the middle of 1846 a committee on legal education was in being and, by the beginning of 1847, preliminary arrangements had been approved and recommendations for lecturerships and a professorship were being put forward.[7]

But the notion of easing the way for graduates of universities other than Oxford and Cambridge was not abandoned. At the end of January 1846, Sir George Rose persuaded the Inner Temple to set up a committee to consider, with the other Inns, the rules of admission and calls to the Bar. Perhaps it was of some significance that the distinguished historian Henry Hallam, a bencher of the Inn, who was to become a fellow of the University of London four years later, was added to the committee.[8] And, at almost the same time, the Attorney General - Frederick Thesiger, the future Baron Chelmsford – wrote to the Treasurer of Gray's Inn, calling his attention to a forthcoming motion of William Dougal Christie, the liberal MP for Weymouth, for the production of a return from all the Inns of Court, 'specifying any distinctions made between Graduates of the Universities of Oxford and

Cambridge and others.' Christie was eager to know whether the motion would be opposed, and the Attorney General thought that the Treasurer 'may wish to consult Benchers,' on the subject. As it happened, the motion was successful, and the return was published in March 1846.[9]

It is highly probable that this internal soul-searching in the Inns of Court was a factor in the move by Thomas Wyse, MP, to call for the establishment of a Commons select committee 'to inquire into the present state of Legal Education in Ireland, and the means for its further Improvement and Extension.' His motion was accepted on 8 April 1946, but on 5 May was extended to include England. The committee's membership included Wyse, who became its chairman, and Christie: they sat from May to August and reported two months after the fall of the Conservative Government. Evidence was taken from several men directly connected with the University of London – Amos and Empson, who were fellows, and Thomas Graves, who had been Examiner in Laws since 1840. In addition, the comittee heard from Brougham and Bethell. The evidence, and the committee's report, comprised a serious and disturbing review of the shallow realities of the current provision of legal education, and some prescription for the future. But, while the new efforts of the Inns of Court to establish their own training schemes were supported strongly, and a big expansion of university concern for teaching law was advocated, the report did not touch specifically on the problem of abolishing distinctions at the Inns of Court between graduates of Oxford, Cambridge and Dublin, and those of other universities, including London.[10]

The publication of the report of the select committee, coinciding as it did with the return of the Whigs to power, must have given a boost to the hopes of the reforming barristers. And perhaps as a partial result of the changed political climate, the Committee on Legal Education of the four Inns of Court, while continuing to give priority to their own scheme for providing training, returned to the request made first in 1841 by the three London graduates, which had been conceded by the Middle Temple in 1843, and dropped by the other Inns early in 1845. Christie's return must have helped to force the issue, but the initiative for this new move may have come from the Inner Temple's committee set up in January 1846. The proposed widening of the enquiry seems to have been formally accepted at a meeting of the Committee on Legal Education at the Inner Temple on 10 March 1847. Among recommendations about the appointment of lecturers, it was resolved 'That each Inn appoint a Committee of three members, to consider and report upon the adoption of a uniform system for the admission of Students and calls to the Bar.'[11]

At this promising sign of a renewed approach to meeting the aspirations of graduates of universities other than those of Oxford, Cambridge and Dublin, who wished to become barristers, we may pause, and turn to the experience of the medical men.

There is no record of any formal attempt by medical graduates, comparable to the petition of Foster, Waley and Wood to Lincoln's Inn, to appeal against the inequity caused by the ability of the Oxbridge doctors to practise without further examination until 1845. But it is unlikely that there were no earlier mutterings of discontent, or no gatherings of kindred, disaffected spirits among the London men. And it can well be imagined that, at least within the community of University College, the medicos were well aware of the lawyers' concerns, and that there were exchanges of views, not merely about the medical and legal grievances, but about the general desirability and prospects of graduate participation in the University. Speculation about early medical graduate militancy might centre on John Storrar, who was to be the initial and controversial leader of formal graduate organization in 1848, and was to become – also controversially – the second Chairman of Convocation and a long-serving member of Senate.

Details of Storrar's early career are exiguous. He had been a student at UCL until 1832, when he was twenty-one, but during the previous four years had also 'gained practical knowledge' in some undefined capacity at St George's and St James' Dispensary. For ten years from 1832 he was secretary to Dr James Somerville, work which ended only on Somerville's dismissal from the Inspectorship of Anatomy at the Home Office in 1842. During those years his duties left him 'occasional leisure to prosecute professional studies,' and he pursued those studies to such good effect as to enable him to graduate MB and MD from the University of London in 1839: he was one of the first two men to be awarded the MD. In 1844 he was for some months physician to the St Pancras Dispensary, but resigned, apparently because he wanted to 'avail himself of the superior opportunities afforded by the [University College] Hospital.' At the latter institution he took temporary charge of outpatients in the summer of 1846, and applied – unsuccessfully – for an assistant physicianship in December of that year. He seems to have worked only sporadically in private practice.[12]

Storrar's previous experience suggests that, as a result of being so close to Dr Somerville, he might well have regarded the majority of the Senate's medical members with some distrust and disfavour, and he certainly was no friend to the Royal College of Physicians. It is very probable that he was known to Warburton, and very likely that he would have aligned himself with Warburton's attitudes. Even so, however active Storrar may have been in promoting graduate interest, his name does not appear on any relevant surviving document until the end of 1845.

That the medical graduates were as much incensed as the Senate by the exclusion of the University from the Graham proposals is clear from a letter of the usually extraordinarily discreet Rothman to F.R. Manson of King's, in March 1845. After giving a private view of the proposed legislation, Rothman went on:

> This University will use all the influence it may possess to obtain the best conditons for its graduates. But should the Graduates feel themselves injured by any clause of the Medical Reform Bill, it would, I think, be very advantageous for them to memorialize the Home Office or address a petition to Parliament on the subject.[13]

Six weeks later, on 25 April, whether in a connected or a separate move, and whether or not graduates were involved, a petition was drawn up by 'Students of University College London,' with 180 signatures. It was presented to the House of Commons by Thomas Wakley. In protesting against the Bill for Regulating the Profession of Physic and Surgery, it deplored, *inter alia*, the absence from Graham's proposed Council of Health of any representative of the University of London, which was 'now rapidly rising in the estimation of the medical profession and the public, from the nature of its examinations and the number of its graduates.'

The petition was not printed in official records, but it was reproduced in the *Lancet*, though no names were attached.[14] This is the first clear evidence we have of what was to be a significant element of support throughout the subsequent years. Henceforward, Wakley and the *Lancet* were outspoken in their backing for the graduates, with a natural emphasis on the interests of the medical fraternity.

Only a few days before the students' petition was presented to Parliament, W. Tyler Smith, a graduate who had been trained at the Bristol Medical School, applied to the Registrar for permission to use a room for a meeting. Rothman refused on the grounds that he had no authority to give such permission; but assured Tyler Smith that he would 'happily put a memorial to Senate.'[15] While no reason for such a desired meeting was recorded, there can be little doubt, given the date, Rothman's response, a similar episode and Tyler Smith's continued involvement in a later year, that this was another precursor of more organized pressure.

No doubt continued efforts were made during the following months to recruit and bring together graduates across the board, but the immediate pressure to withstand the Government's medical proposals was relieved by Graham's virtual abandonment of his Bill at the end of July. The graduates' sense of deprivation had been sufficiently aroused, however, to make it certain that the recruitment efforts were successful, and good political judgement prevailed in widening the issues from narrowly medical and legal grievances to those more generally constitutional.

A 'preliminary Meeting of Graduates in Laws Medicine and Arts of the University of London,' was held, probably in November 1845. Unfortunately the record of it is undated, and there is no sign of where it was held, or who was present. At that meeting it was resolved that a 'London University Union' should be established, designed

> to combine the Senate and Graduates of the University into one body; to impart to them a more corporate spirit, with a view of promoting the interests of the University and establishing and maintaining a friendly feeling and intercourse amongst all its Members.

This resolution was sent to Rothman, together with a renewed request for 'rooms in the University in which occasional meetings of the Members may be held.' He was also asked to receive a deputation. The Registrar must have complied with the request, and met the deputation which, if it comprised the signatories to the resolution, was composed of one lawyer, John Quain, from UCL, and three medical graduates – Joseph Hullett Browne of Guy's Hospital, George Johnson of King's and John Storrar of UCL. Rothman then referred the business to the Senate, which discussed it on 10 December.[16]

It is impossible to know how much this graduate initiative was given close attention by more than the seven fellows who were present on 10 December 1845. Nor is is possible to know how and whether those seven reacted to it as a serious, constitutional proposal. From his previous constitutional suggestions, from his later attitude and from the fact that he moved the resolution approved and recorded – there was no report of the debate – it is likely that Thomas Hodgkin was in broad sympathy with the graduates. But, if so, he may have had to accept that there was so little wish, round the table, to encourage further discussion of the idea of a 'Union', that the least discouraging decision was to record 'That the Senate regrets that the want of accommodation prevents them from complying with the request of the Petitioners.' The other fellows present were the Vice-Chancellor, Bacot, Hammick, Jerrard, Kiernan and Senior.

This rebuff did not produce any formal protest by the graduates, nor any early renewal of the request. It may be that the absence of the immediate threat of new medical legislation, and the apparent lukewarmness of the Senate, weakened any attempt by leaders to make any new effort. In any event, nothing seems to have been attempted in the first half of 1846. When the Conservative Government fell, at the end of July, and Lord John Russell became Prime Minister, the change must have promoted an atmosphere of expectation that action favourable to the London graduates would follow in good time, and that patience was therefore in order. It seems entirely likely that any tendency there may have been to extend that patience indefinitely was scotched by the reappearance as major innovators on the legislative scene of the two veteran Radical politicians and medical reformers, Thomas Wakley and Henry Warburton.

Less than six weeks after Russell assumed office, Wakley and Warburton introduced a Bill for the Registration of Medical Practitioners which, however, was given only brief consideration and in effect shelved, before the end of August. But it had served its purpose of re-energizing those who were determined to find some formula for the supervision of the medical profession which would either be acceptable to all concerned or be imposed by Parliament. During the following autumn and winter, while consideration of the major problems doubtless preoccupied the minds of the reformers and defenders of the medical establishment, there must have been some significant discussion about the future place of the University of London, involving Warburton, Wakley and at least some of the emerging group of graduates, particularly those in medicine, who wanted constitutional reform.

On 6 March 1847, a long leading article in the *Lancet* was devoted to a very well-informed critique of the existing state of the University of London, and to a strong call for the introduction of graduate participation in its future governance. Two extracts give the flavour of the argument:

In the theory and practice of the University of London there are three bodies – the university; the colleges who discipline and transmit certified students; and lastly, the graduates who have passed the examinations: but all three are in a state of separation from each other. Neither the colleges nor the graduates have any real, tangible existence within the University, nor any share whatever in its government. A strict *union* and correspondence has been the principle recognised at Cambridge and Oxford: in London, the principle which prevails is that of *isolation*.

The slightest hint that [the Senate] intended at any time, however distant, to apply to the Crown for a charter which should make its graduates an integral part of the University, would give a great stimulus to education, and more particularly to medical education – a stimulus which would be felt among our most ambitious students, in all our schools, and among all the University graduates. It would raise up a faithful band of defenders in any emergency that might occur. It would tend to draw benefactions and endowments toward the infant institution, which might soon spare her the humility of going to the State as beggar year by year, for the paltry sum doled out with the miscellaneous estimates. It would soon give her strength enough to remove from her present location as a lodger in Somerset House, with a side-bell, up two pair of stairs, and a council chamber in a second-floor back! But these things can hardly be accomplished, unless some scope for the affection and reverence of her children – some natural tie between parent and offspring, be permitted.

If the rhetoric is Wakley's, the background and the argument is surely Warburton's. As a controversial, nationally recognized authority on medical politics, and a prominent member of the Council of UCL, as well as of the Senate of the University, Warburton needed no additional expert advisers among the ranks of top medical and educational figures. And he may indeed have had the sympathy and support of a few senatorial colleagues like Hodgkin. But it is very likely that he had also been open to and influenced by the support of those graduates, particularly of UCL, who had been raising the issue of convocation, however unsuccessfully, over the past few years.

In the article quoted above there are listed fifteen London graduates who were at the time teaching in the various London medical schools: at least seven of them were to be among the leading members of the graduate organization which was set up in 1848. One of them, Edward Ballard, who taught at UCL, contributed a letter of approval and gratitude three weeks later.[17] And of the other medical men already mentioned as petitioners to the Senate – Manson, Hullett Browne, Tyler Smith (also one of the teachers) and John Storrar – all were to be heavily involved in future negotiations. Indeed, from the spring of 1847, though there was still no formal organization of graduates, it is reasonable to suppose that, at least on the medical side, there was a group, in which Storrar would have been a leader, which was waiting, prepared, as it were, for a call to action. They were to wait a little less than a year.

Wakley's editorial decision to raise the issue of the University was part of his and Warburton's overall strategy. The next, early move was to bring in another bill, this one for the Registration of Medical Practitioners and for Amending the Law relating to the Practice of Medicine. The bill was introduced on 22 April 1847, and included a clause which would have removed practically all influence over qualifications and licensing from the established medical corporations. This caused a huge reaction, with petitions from all over the country pouring into Parliament. A second reading debate was repeatedly deferred, and in the middle of May the Home Secretary, Sir George Grey, supported a motion by Wakley to set up a select committee on medical registration, so long as the bill was not proceeded with until after the committee had reported.[18] The bill was referred to the committee early in June, and was withdrawn from the legislative process some three weeks later. Evidence was taken by the committee and reported to the House of Commons on 16 July. But the dissolution of Parliament followed almost immediately.

Henry Warburton did not stand at the subsequent general election, but Wakley was returned. On 30 November the select committee was reappointed, though with a considerably changed membership, only Wakley and five others, out of fifteen, having served in the previous session. The committee was also retitled to indicate that it was concerned with medical registration and medical law amendment, and took evidence until July 1848. As with the 1847 committee, only the evidence was reported: that evidence, taken along with what had been given to the preceding Committee, provides a mine of information about the attitudes and the obstacles to change, most of which were not to be unravelled for another ten years.[19] But it was the reaction of the medical corporations to the proposals included in Wakley's bill, and their main submission to the select committee early in 1848, which at last brought into being an organization of the London graduates which would become, ten years ahead, Convocation of the University.

In February 1848 the Colleges of Physicians and Surgeons, the Apothecaries Company and the recently created National Institute of Medicine, Surgery and Midwifery – an organization claiming to represent 'General Practitioners', headed by the elderly Richard Rainey Pennington, one of the original non-attending senators of the University – published their collective response to the challenge posed by Wakley's bill. It took the form of a statement of *Principles for a General Measure of Medical Reform*[20] which made no concessions to meet the major grievance of the University of London. That grievance was that London's examinations were more demanding than those of the traditional medical corporations, and that it was totally unjust that their graduates should have to submit to re-examination before being licensed to practise, especially when graduates of Oxford and Cambridge were exempted from such additional examinations.

One immediate consequence of the publication of the Principles was the calling together of aggrieved London graduates and the establishment of a joint committee of medical and non-medical members. The two groups thereafter tended to operate separately, but kept together in a loose but effective coalition. Storrar became the first chairman of the combined committee,[21] and when that committee was divided into medical and non-medical segments, he remained chairman of the medical branch. The first secretary was Robert Barnes, later to become the founder of the Obstetrical Society and the British Gynaecological Society. He was to be lauded as having 'first place as initiator of the movement,' along with Storrar, C.J. Foster, F.J. Wood, T.S. Osler, G. Jessel amd J.R. Quain.[22] Indeed, the most influential group of leaders remained in office throughout the next decade, and from time to time came under fire from those who regarded them as a closed clique. In the later part of the period there were major internal disagreements, but such quarrels were unforeseen in the surge of shared indignation and reforming spirit in 1848.

It is impossible to produce an exact chronology of the establishment of the graduates' organization, or to allocate responsibility with precision. There were men prominent in these early days other than those listed already, and it is highly probable that the first gathering was of 'half a dozen' medical men, called together in his home by Frederick R. Manson, of King's.[23] That meeting may well have been the result of what we might call, today, a 'consciousness-raising' letter in the *Lancet* of 4 March 1848 from William E. Humble, MD, to fellow London medical graduates. Humble attacked the medical establishment full-bloodedly, and issued a call to arms:

> The different corporations have too plainly shown that their only object is individual aggrandizement. Let not, therefore, the graduates of London suppose that their rights will be respected unless they vigorously insist upon proper respect being shown them. It appears to me to be now urgently required that the graduates in medicine of London should combine and act with deliberation and firmness; that they should communicate seriously with the chancellor and fellows on the one hand, and with the government on the other; that they should impress on the senate the necessity for active co-operation on the part of the heads of the university, and on the government of the country the high character of their degrees, and of the qualification of which those degrees are the representatives; that they should watch carefully every movement on the part of their pretended friends and professed opponents, and be ready to act combinedly and firmly against every aggression.

Humble went on to invite all London graduates to send him their names, by 15 March, so that 'a provisional committee may be forthwith formed.' And he ended with a splendid piece of purple prose, somewhat reminiscent of the style of another and more famous manifesto of 1848!

> Doctors, remember that by law you hold a rank in society inferior only to knights, and those above knights; your rank is at stake at the present time. Graduates of London, your university is assailed, and every blow struck at your university will be felt by you individually.

Shortly after 15 March, a letter was sent to the Senate, raising again the request for a room in which the graduates could meet, and asking for a deputation to be received. This was signed by six medicos – Manson, Snow, Humble, Tyler Smith, Robert Barnes and Alfred J. Tapson, and by one lawyer, Philip Edward Barnes.[24] At their meeting on 22 March the Senate agreed to meet a deputation on 5 April, and on that occasion they also had before them the Principles of the medical corporations. There were eleven graduates in the deputation, but we do not know exactly who was there in addition to Storrar and Foster. The Senate then devoted a special meeting, a week afterwards, to consideration of the graduates' requests, but merely repeated the formula they had used two years before – that they could not provide a room, but were willing to receive and consider any communications from the graduates. There is no record of the discussion, and no vote was taken: those present, in addition to the Chancellor, were Bacot, Billing, Brande, Hodgkin, Jerrard, Kiernan, Ridout, Walker and Warburton. Burlington recorded, almost as an aside, that 'The meeting was held to consider a request of the graduates who wished to hold a meeting in our rooms. This was refused in courteous terms.'[25]

The active group of graduates, who had by then come to regard themselves as a 'provisional committee of management,' were moved by this polite but discouraging response, and by the urging of Wakley in the leader columns of the *Lancet*, to call a general meeting at the Freemasons' Tavern for 8 June, to legitimize the establishment of a more formal organization. 'Upwards of a hundred' graduates attended, including several from outside London; the chair was taken by William Allen Miller, Professor of Chemistry at King's College; resolutions were passed, and twenty-four graduates, twelve from the medical and twelve from the arts and law faculties, were elected as committee members.[26] In the next two months two more were added to each group, and four provincial, 'corresponding' members were appointed from Bristol, Huddersfield, Liverpool and Southampton.

Of the non-medical men on this committee, at least seven were lawyers, two were clergymen, two were masters at University College School, and one was an architect. Seven were fellows of UCL, and all but two of the others had come through UCL, the remainder being from King's. On the medical side UCL was less in evidence, with only five members: but this was still the largest group, for King's provided three and the rest were the products of various London teaching hospitals, with one trained in the Bristol Medical School. Of the whole committee, therefore, nearly two-thirds had strong links with UCL, and almost half taught in teaching hospital, university or school: one might argue that the movement for graduate participation in university governance concealed within itself a bid for the recognition of professional academia.

In the first half of 1848 the nature of the University of London as a political system had changed radically. But, in the Senate, the change had not registered fully. The Senate and the graduates were soon to discover the complexity of their new relationship, and to find themselves further embroiled with each other and with Government and Parliament, in constitutional and medical controversy.

CHAPTER 15

The Supplementary Charter

The changed tempo and atmosphere of the arguments about the University of London at the mid-point of the nineteenth century have to be seen against the changing political, economic and intellectual conditions in society generally. The Home Office was inevitably preoccupied, in 1848, with containing the Chartist movement, which reflected, if weakly, the revolutionary uprisings in Europe; and with the continuing miseries of Ireland. The confusion of political allegiances which followed the repeal of the Corn Laws, the emergence of the Peelites, and then the sudden death of Peel himself, made government in these years an uncertain business, dependent on shifting and irregular parliamentary support. The growth of population, the progress of industrialization and the blossoming of technology and prosperity, symbolized by the Great Exhibition of 1851, encouraged those who wanted education and training to be more scientifically inclined, and must have benefitted the cause of those calling for more rigorous preparation for medical work and more effective supervision of medical practice. And the tide of reform, the attack on privilege and religious exclusiveness, was now reaching to the gates of Oxford and Cambridge, both of which were to be subjected to searching enquiry into their governance, by Royal Commissions set up in 1850, and by resulting legislation which was passed in the mid-1850s. But in those years the Crimean War inevitably diverted much energy and attention from purely domestic matters.

During this restless period, a corresponding change affected the public position of the University of London, largely because of its growth and its achievements, even though both may appear to have been modest. The numbers of students and graduates seem tiny to modern readers, but they constituted by the late 1840s a sizeable group within the limited professional population of the time. In the context of medicine especially, but also in arts and law, nothing is more striking than the change in the tone and content of public utterances concerning the University, from scepticism and scorn in the late 1830s and early 1840s, to considerable respect at mid-century for the high standard of its degrees and for the comprehensive, scientifically-oriented content of

its medical curriculum. The arguments and struggles over the future of
the University were conducted, as it were, in the shadow of its enhanced
academic prestige.

It will be remembered that Burlington had talked with Lord John
Russell, on 30 June 1847, about the affairs of the University. The next
surviving indication of what had happened in government circles subsequently is dated almost exactly twelve months later. The Chancellor
recorded, on 21 June 1848, that he had 'lately' seen the Home Secretary,
Sir George Grey, and had gained the impression that 'a few changes
will be made and new members added.'[1] It became clear from a letter
of Grey to Russell that the Prime Minister had 'suggested alterations in
the Charter . . . in order to extend the power of granting degrees.' At least
by the beginning of July 1848, the Home Office, after discussions with
Burlington and Shaw Lefevre, was able to report to Russell that there
was a draft of the proposals ready, and that Burlington had proposed
several new members of the Senate – the Bishop of Manchester,
Macaulay, Wyse, Sir John Herschell and Dr Herries, 'all of whom if
they would consent would be valuable additions.'[2]

The clear implication of this line of development was quite unrelated
to the impending concerns of the London graduates. It followed from
the unease expressed earlier by Burlington about the smallness of the
closed circle of men who, effectively, constituted the Senate; from the
discovery that Oxbridge graduates who wanted to take London degrees
were unqualified to do so under existing regulations; and from a desire,
whose implementation would be controversial, to allow the University
to examine candidates, whether or not they were graduates, in single,
specialized subjects, and award to those who passed certificates of
proficiency.

These limited proposals for change, entirely legitimate in themselves
so far as the future of the University was concerned, were to be pushed
through relatively unaltered, though of the five possible senators
mentioned by Grey, only Macaulay was among the eventual list of
new members. But during the final negotiation and authorization of
the Supplementary Charter, the new demands of the graduates for basic
constitutional amendment, and the concern of both the Senate and the
graduates to have the same professional privileges in law and medicine
as were enjoyed by the Oxbridge men, were to make the provisions of
the new Charter seem of relatively minor consequence. Moreover, the
first regulations issued under the powers contained in the Supplementary

Charter were to be strongly challenged by the increasingly militant London graduates.

The desire to equalize the privileges of the legal and medical graduates of Oxbridge and London was fully shared by the Senate and the London graduates, and by UCL. We shall follow the problem on the legal side to its ultimate solution in the next chapter, and merely mention here that the case for the London law graduates was raised in the Council of UCL in May, and pressed on the Senate of the University by the Council early in June 1848.[3] At almost the same time, the Senate received an invitation to nominate representatives to give evidence before the Select Committee on Medical Registration, and nominated Billing and Hodgkin. The newly founded Graduates' Committee also gave evidence to the Select Committee; their witnesses were Robert Barnes and John Storrar. This double representation of the University was not co-ordinated, but each couple presented a strong and compatible case against the proposals of the medical corporations and pressed the qualifications of the London graduates for the same recognition as was given automatically to their Oxbridge counterparts.[4]

But while co-operation and understanding were very evident in these legal and medical contexts, on the constitutional issue the Senate and the graduates were to run into difficulties and misapprehensions. As we have seen, the first, formal meeting of the graduates was held on 8 June 1848, with nearly a hundred present. They passed resolutions which were presented to them by their interim committee, and which expressed respectful hope of close co-operation with the Senate:

> while the Graduates recognize their competency to act as an independent body, they nevertheless earnestly desire that their proceedings should be as far as possible in harmony with the views of the Senate; being fully persuaded that the Senate can only have for its aim the attainment of objects in which the Graduates have a common interest.

> the Graduates are fully sensible of the benefit the University has received under the government of the Senate as hitherto constituted; but strongly feel the great advantages that would result from occasional and stated communication between the Senate and the Graduates, until the Graduates shall form the constituent body.

The sting was in the tail, and the graduates' aspirations were almost immediately reported and supported strongly by the *Lancet*, in its issue of 17 June:

> The senate itself appears to rule the University, but it is dependent upon an annual parliamentary grant, and the Secretary of State can, at any time, swamp the senate by the introduction of new fellows into the body, who may have no interest in, or knowledge of, the University. This awkward position of the senate, between the Chancellor of the Exchequer on the one hand, and the Secretary of State on the other, is one from which the senate must be happy to escape. The graduates themselves are the only body from whom they can derive true strength, and we trust the proceeding of both graduates and senate will be cordial and energetic, having mutual trust and confidence in each other, and acting with a single purpose for the advancement of the University.

And on the medical scene, the journal proclaimed that,

> As the body most emphatically in the van of medical education, the University of London ought to have been represented by its senate and its graduates at the conferences which took place between the other London bodies. As this did not occur, the only mode of remedying the mistake is, that both the senate and graduates should be heard upon their respective positions, and the proposed measures of legislation before the Parliamentary Committee.

The graduates' leaders, who might well have been somewhat euphoric at their early good fortune, followed up with a request that Senate should receive a deputation and, on 28 June 1848, eight of them – of whom we can identify seven (two lawyers, Charles James Foster and George Jessel; a schoolmaster, William Arthur Case; and four medicos - Robert Barnes, Edward Ballard, George Johnson and John Storrar) - attended a meeting, were asked to put their wishes in writing, and did so before departing. Their firmness must have caused some raising of the senatorial eyebrows: even the normally equable and patient Chancellor commented in his diary, 'We had an interview with a deputation of our Graduates whose views are rather aspiring and who wish to rule the University.'[5]

But the graduates' persistence produced results. They had reminded the Senate of the resolutions of the Committee of the Whole in 1840 which, had they been formally approved, would have come into effect by the end of 1848, when there would be 300 graduates of three years' standing. The Senate, while claiming, correctly, that those resolutions had never been passed, nonetheless were 'fully alive to the extent and serious purpose of the present movement,' and 'consented to represent the wishes of the Graduates to the Secretary of State.' Within a month, a deputation of graduates was received by Sir George Grey. On that occasion, on 28 July, they were led by Storrar, who had with him the joint secretaries of the new committee – Barnes and Foster – together with William Allen Miller, William Tyler Smith, John Richard Quain and George Jessel.

The essence of the discussion between Sir George Grey and the deputation was reported in a comprehensive review of the work of the graduates committee hitherto, entitled *An Address to the Graduates of the University of London*, dated 16 August 1848.[6] The deputation had told the Secretary of State

> that by the present Constitution of the University the Senate was a body completely isolated from the Graduates and without any author-ized channel of communication with them, and consisted principally of members of other Universities, who could not be supposed to feel that peculiar and exclusive interest in the University of London which must be necessarily felt by its Graduates: that at present (and the consciousness of this had created great uneasiness) the Graduates had no share or influence whatever in the management of its affairs, but as soon as they received their degrees, (perhaps by the post or a messenger,) they had nothing more to do with the University: and that their desire was to be made a part of the Corporate Body of the University, (being in fact the parties principally interested in its welfare,) with privileges similar to those enjoyed by the Graduates of Oxford, Cambridge, and Durham, (in accordance, as it is understood, with a promise to that effect from Government at the foundation of the University,) and subject to such modifications as the peculiar nature and objects of this University might render proper.

The graduates then went on to tell Grey of their intention to submit a proposed scheme which they hoped would be acceptable to the Senate, and to themselves, and would 'meet with the approval' of the minister. Grey responded cordially and carefully:

> he could not answer definitely without consulting the Senate; but that the desire of the Graduates was very natural and proper; and if the Deputation would oblige him with a written statement of their views, it should have his best consideration. Allusion being made to

a rumour that it was in contemplation to fill up some of the vacancies in the Senate, Sir George Grey spontaneously assured the deputation, that if that measure were resolved upon, it should in no way prejudice the Graduates, or their ulterior object of obtaining a new Charter.

The leaders of the graduates accepted that they could not expect an early reply from the Home Secretary, but set out their preliminary, alternative notions – either a convocation as at the ancient universities, with defined powers; or Warburton's idea of 1840, vesting 'the entire administration in the Senate, who should become in process of time the Representatives of the Graduates'; or some combination of the two.

Thus, by the end of August 1848, all parties were aware of the graduates' aspirations, and were also aware that some changes to the University's Charter were being contemplated at the highest levels. But as the months went by, it is clear that, whether by accident or design, the possible changes to the Charter were being planned in the context only of the previous ideas of the Senate and the Government, and that consideration of the graduates' main concerns suffered from a combination of bureaucratic confusion and the emergence of opposition within the Senate itself.

Foster and Barnes waited until early December 1848 before they reminded Grey that they were hoping for a response to the requests made in the course of the meeting with the graduates' deputation in the previous July, and stressing their concern to be incorporated into the University. The latter point was ignored, accidentally or deliberately, by Grey, who simply instructed his officials to tell the graduates that he was in touch with Burlington about additions to the Senate. The resulting letter from Horatio Waddington, the Permanent Secretary, was received with consternation, and Foster replied, with some understandable impatience, that the graduates were seeking incorporation, not additions to the Senate. Grey then ordered an emollient response, telling Waddington to 'say that any plan for carrying into effect [the graduates'] wishes which they may transmit to me shall be fully considered.' In turn, by mid-January 1849, this produced a promise from Barnes and Foster that such a plan would be transmitted 'with the least possible delay.'[7]

But it was not until 3 April 1849 that the graduates were able to come up with their *Proposed Basis of a New Charter for the University of London*. There are no papers extant which would enlighten us about the internal discussions of the graduates' leaders. But it is unlikely

that there were any serious disagreements, and at a meeting on 27
February, the existing committee had been given extensive powers
to conduct the negotiation of the establishment of Convocation. A
number of resolutions were passed unanimously, the constitutionally
most significant of which declared

> That the graduates in future shall form part of the corporate body of
> the University; that the government of the University shall consist of
> a Chancellor, a Senate and a Convocation, the last to be composed
> of all graduates of a certain standing; that eventually the Senate shall
> be elected by Convocation; that all alterations in the fundamental law
> of the University shall require the assent of Convocation; and that,
> while the general executive management of the University shall be
> confided to the Senate, it shall be subject in certain cases to the veto
> of Convocation.

This was received by the Senate at the end of February, without
comment, in part at least because it was accepted that a more detailed
proposal would be forthcoming later.[8]

The delay, which was not unusually long in such affairs, may well
have been caused by the pressure to deal with two closely related
developments. The first was the threat posed by the prospect of a new
Medical Registration Bill, to be introduced by the Lord Advocate, which
was based on the Principles of the medical corporations, and failed to
meet any of the University of London's concerns. The second was the
completion of a search by the graduates for unequivocal confirmation
of the original pledge by Melbourne's government in 1835, that London
would have the same privileges, save in respect of ecclesiastical matters,
as were enjoyed by Oxford and Cambridge. In addition to these two
causes, however, it is necessary to take into account parallel activity
within University College.

Throughout this period, Henry Warburton, no longer in the House of
Commons, kept up a high profile at both the University and at UCL.
He was frequently in the chair at UCL Council meetings, and was in
attendance at all but one of the sessions of the University Senate during
1848–9. It is easy to believe that he must have been available to the
graduates' leaders for advice, and it is clear that he used his close
contacts with Lord John Russell to good effect.

On the medical front, the first move in 1849 was made by the
graduates. In January they established a medical sub-committee, whose
members were Storrar, Barnes and Foster, together with Edward

Ballard, Stephen J. Goodfellow, John Richard Quain and William Tyler Smith. They then urged action on the Senate, and the Senate readily complied, with the appointment, on Billing's motion, of a committee to communicate with the graduates and to prepare a memorial to present to Government on the Medical Bill. The Vice-Chancellor and Warburton were joined by five medical senators – Billing, Clark, Hodgkin, Kiernan and Ridout.[9] Two days later, Warburton gave notice to the UCL Council of his intention to move for a committee to be appointed to draw up a memorial about the proposed medical legislation to be presented to Sir George Grey. Such a committee, with Warburton as a member, was set up on 3 March.[10]

But it was the outcome of the research into the events of 1835 which was to produce the most dramatic effect, almost immediately in the matter of the medical qualifications, and over time for the overall constitutional debate. And it is clear that it was Thomas Hodgkin who pointed the graduates in the relevant direction. He told a member of the Graduates Committee that 'a distinct promise was received from some member of the [Melbourne] government' about extending the privileges of the other universities to London, and that he believed the 'Document' containing the promise was in the files of University College. On the strength of this, Foster asked Atkinson, the secretary of UCL, late in December 1848, whether he could confirm Hodgkin's belief, because 'We are about making a further representation to Sir George Grey and I could not miss a fact of this importance if it can be relied on.' Foster had been a fellow of UCL since 1845, and was very soon to become Professor of Jurisprudence there: his local standing doubtless gave Atkinson authority to co-operate, but the secretary may have been reassured by Foster's comment in a later letter that 'There are besides myself ten Fellows on the [Graduates] Committee.'[11]

Atkinson produced the evidence – Spring Rice's letter to John Romilly in November 1835 – quite quickly, but it is probable that he recommended Foster to ensure that Lord Monteagle had no qualms about the graduates making use of his correspondence. He need not have been worried on that score, however, for Monteagle considered 'the letters and memoranda of 1835 to be entirely at the disposal of the Council of University College who are at liberty to use those documents in any way they think fit.'[12] This confirmation, which was received early in March, must have strengthened the confidence of the graduates in the constitutional proposals which they put before Sir George Grey and presented to the Senate at the beginning of April 1849.

Those proposals took the form of a draft Charter, according to which

the University was to consist of a Chancellor, Vice-Chancellor, Fellows and all graduates and matriculated undergraduates. Its affairs were to be administered by a Senate and Convocation, sitting separately; the members of the present Senate were to be members for life but a proportion of future Senators were to retire annually and all vacancies in the Senate were to be filled annually by Convocation. Convocation was to elect all future Chancellors. The Senate and Convocation were to make regulations for their own proceedings and certain powers were to be reserved for the Senate although some of these, e.g., the recognition of institutions from which candidates could be admitted, and the appointment of examiners, were to be subject to the approval of Convocation. Convocation was to have 'power to address the Senate upon all matters.'[13]

By April 1849, however confused or merely discreet may have been recent relations between the Home Office, the Senate and the Graduates Committee, the publicity given to the graduates' demands for constitutional reform had not gone unnoticed by senators, who were already aware of the less contentious provisions of the projected Supplementary Charter. A group of the more conservative senators put together a memorial to the Home Secretary. The signatories were the three Bishops – Durham, Norwich and St Davids (Thirlwall) – Bacot, Beaufort, Jerrard, Locock, M'Grigor, Roget and Senior: their memorial was sent to Sir George Grey by the Bishop of Norwich, together with a separate note from Ridout.[14]

The initial complaint of this group was the shrinkage in the number of senators over the years, and the fact that of the twenty-five whom they regarded as active, eleven were medical men. This meant that there were

only fourteen left to represent the two other faculties, and that of those who more peculiarly belong to the Faculty of Arts, the majority are so much occupied with their other duties as rarely to have it in their power to be present at meetings. . . . The Department of Arts is most inadequately represented and . . . we are decidedly of the opinion, considerable injury has resulted to the University in that Department.

While the concern of these eleven gentlemen is to their credit, many of them were among those they described as rarely having the power to attend. Before 4 April 1849, Thirlwall had come on four occasions only, and had been seen at no Senate meeting between May 1839 and February 1847. His fellow bishops had been more attentive in earlier years, but during the 1840s had rarely been to more than a couple of meetings, on average, each year. Beaufort and M'Grigor fell into much the same category. Locock had turned up only twice since 1842. Bacot, Ridout, Roget and Senior were serious, moderate attenders, but only Jerrard was a member of the inner core who had kept the Senate operating. One might suspect, indeed, that Jerrard had been a moving spirit behind this expression of concern, though there is no proof: Ridout, as we have seen, had expressed worries of his own to Burlington as long ago as 1847.

The more compelling anxieties of this group of senators were concentrated on the graduate pressure for a new Charter. They felt that 'much calm and patient thought' would be needed of a strengthened Senate, 'to enable it to recommend, with full authority, such alterations . . . as it may consider advisable and . . . to resist such proposed changes as it may deem unreasonable.' And the special focus of their apprehension was UCL:

> if the agitation for a new Charter on the part of the Graduates be . . . subjected, *in time*, to the effectual control of the Senate, it will not be unproductive of good; but if not, we are convinced that, as regards the *general* interests of the University, its consequences will be deeply injurious: more especially since we observe that a large majority of those who take the lead in it belong to *one* Institution and since we perceive that, notwithstanding a show of liberality (which may deceive the Graduates themselves), the practical tendency of the changes which they propose is to destroy the comprehensive character of the University and, ultimately, to place its entire management in the hands of Graduates belonging to University College.

John Ridout's contribution spelt out his objections more specifically:

> while he entertains a hope that some individuals may be selected from the Graduates of the University, fully qualified, and in every way fitted, to become Fellows and members of the Senate, would deprecate in very strong terms the selection being made by the Graduates themselves as in his opinion, the choice, if made by an election on the part of the graduates at this time, and most probably

for a few years yet to come, would be productive of much and very serious mischief.

Ridout's position as a senior member of the Apothecaries Company could well explain his apparent antipathy to the existing leadership of the graduates, which was uncompromisingly unhappy with the position which the medical establishment was taking in the context of any reform of the oversight of the medical profession.

But Ridout also underlined the more general concern of his colleagues about a London-based Convocation:

> an election . . . in the way which has been proposed by the graduates, would necessarily consign the power of choice to those who are resident in or near London, and to the alumni of colleges within its immediate neighbourhood; a proceeding which would inevitably give rise to jealousy between Colleges situated in and out of London; – to contention between the several Faculties – and to religious animosity between parties who entertain different religious faith and colleges which inculcate different systems of doctrine: and contention alike injurious to the character and usefulness of the University and the interests of the public who are involved in its well-being.

The Bishop of Norwich, in sending these views to Grey, remarked that the state of the University is 'certainly at present very unsatisfactory,' and hoped that the minister's 'kind intervention may apply a remedy not only to the existing but to anticipated future evils.'

But Grey by now seemed determined to keep the issue of the contents of the proposed Supplementary Charter, and the additional membership of the Senate, quite separate from the wider constitutional demands of the graduates, and not to commit himself about the latter. He scribbled directions for an acknowledgment, ordered copies of the correspondence to be sent to Burlington, and contented himself with telling the Bishop of Norwich that 'I hope such additions will very shortly be made to the Senate as will meet the views and wishes of the fellows and members of the Senate who have addressed this memorial to me.'[15]

The graduates' scheme had come to the surface almost contemporaneously with an advanced version of the much more limited Home Office proposals for a Supplementary Charter. The latter was drafted, originally, by parliamentary counsel as early as September 1848, after the notion of achieving the same end by the legally simpler device of a Queen's Letter had been overruled. The draft was based on a plan by Senior and on Burlington's interpretation of the University's most immediate needs. Whether Senior's plan was related to the one which he had originally drafted for Sir James Graham, some years earlier, cannot be known, given the lack of documentary evidence. Counsel's draft was sent privately to Burlington early in 1849 by Grey, and seemed to the Chancellor to meet 'the objects it was desired to embrace,' though he wanted to have the opinion of 'some other members of Senate.'[16]

The draft was concerned only with removing obstacles to graduates of other universities taking London degrees, and with a widened provision of examinations for certificates of proficiency. There were no names of any additional senators. The Senate, at the same meeting – 4 April – when they received the graduates' plan for a new constitution, referred the proposed Supplementary Charter to a Committee of the Whole, which considered it first on 25 April and reported on 2 May. On that day the Senate agreed that it would be desirable to add the University of St Andrews to the list of universities whose students should be enabled, if they wished, to take London degrees, and that 'it will be expedient to carry the proposed new Charter into effect without delay whether any change be made in the future constitution of the Senate or not.' Grey was so informed by the Vice-Chancellor. Very quickly, parliamentary counsel was ordered to revise the draft to take account of the Senate's proposed amendments. Subsequently the law officers of the Crown were consulted, the Supplementary Charter was eventually approved by them early in June, signed by the Queen on 7 July and laid on the table of the Senate on 18 July.[17]

Well before then, however, the promising harmony between Senate and graduates had been disrupted.

Warburton may have been shown by Burlington the memorial of the eleven senators unhappy about the graduates' proposals. Or its contents may have became known to him through other channels. In any event, he was not slow to react. On 19 May, at UCL, the draft memorial to Sir George Grey about the proposed medical legislation was approved and it was agreed that a deputation, including Warburton, should seek an appointment with the Home Secretary. Four days later, at the University Senate, Warburton presented and saw approved a report and draft memorial from the committee concerned to counter the proposed medical legislation. At both meetings the 1835 promise of equality with Oxford and Cambridge was made clear. On 24 May he led the UCL deputation to Sir George Grey, and the very next day took the same deputation to see Lord John Russell. No doubt Warburton had used his influence with the Prime Minister to obtain such an audience, and he did not worry about the fact that the deputation had no authority from the UCL Council to approach Russell. The Council approved the move retrospectively.

It is very improbable that Warburton would have needed any reminder of the promises which Spring Rice had made in 1835. But it is unlikely that Foster's request to Atkinson, on Hodgkin's nudge, and Atkinson's production of the relevant documents, would not have been made known to him. In any event, to Sir George Grey, in the context of the forth-coming medical legislation, Warburton and his colleagues produced the 1835 documents and argued that University College had withdrawn its demand for a Charter as a university on the understanding, clearly expressed by Spring Rice, that the graduates of the new University of London would have the same privileges as were enjoyed by those of Oxford and Cambridge. When Grey replied 'that any such declaration must be considered as depending on the contingencies of Parliament consenting to place the Graduates of the University of London on such an equality,' Warburton played his master card. He 'thought that the present Government on whom the mantle of the Government of 1835 had fallen, were morally bound to use all their influence to give effect, if possible, to the declaration referred to.' The report of the meeting in the UCL Council minutes concludes, tersely but with a hint of triumph, that 'Sir George Grey admitted that the present Government were morally bound to do it.' Either on that occasion or soon after, Grey made it clear that he would consider no further legislative proposals for medical reform which did not address the matter of equal privileges for London and Oxbridge.

With the Prime Minister, Warburton moved to the wider consti-tutional questions. First, he addressed the matter of increasing the membership of the Senate, referred to the memorial of the eleven apprehensive senators, and to a rumour that the Bishop of Manchester, James Stephens of the Colonial Office, Airy, and 'a present member of the House of Commons,' would be appointed fellows. He then concentrated on the repeated efforts which had been made to hoist compulsory examinations in scriptural studies on to the University, and argued that the majorities by which such efforts had been defeated were small. He also raised the strong desire of the graduates for a share in the governance of the University. Both because places should be reserved for graduate representation, and because he feared that those persons so far named as possible new senators would support 'Dr Arnold's views,' and would endanger the narrow majority now in favour of the *status quo* on scriptural examinations, Warburton pleaded that the number of new fellows to be added in the near future 'should be very limited.' He also remarked, rather pointedly, that Sir James Graham, when Home Secretary, had consulted Burlington and himself as to the desirability of new senators. The Prime Minister is recorded as saying only that he had not changed the views he held about scriptural examinations in 1837, and that he would discuss the whole situation with Sir George Grey.[18]

Warburton was no doubt among the University's deputation which also saw Grey about the Medical Bill sometime between 23 May and 20 June, though no exact date is recorded. But the Senate minutes for 20 June state that the Lord Advocate was present at the meeting with the delegation, and heard Sir George Grey's verdict. The more junior minister, and the medical establishment, must have been not a little discomfited, for it meant the abandonment of the legislation on which he and they had been counting. Doubtless, Sir George's admission of a moral obligation to find a way of equalizing the privileges of Oxford, Cambridge and London was welcomed by the Senate insofar as it applied to the status of legal and medical graduates. But it was not regarded, apparently, at least by some fellows, as necessarily relevant to the demands of the graduates for a new Charter.

Despite the weightiness of all these developments, only thirteen Senators turned out for the meeting on 20 June 1849, at which the graduates' written proposals were debated: only four of them belonged to the group of eleven who had memorialized Sir George Grey - the Bishop of Norwich, Jerrard, Ridout and Senior. There is no detailed record of the debate, and no record of any vote having been taken. The detailed suggestions were turned down, but the principle of participation was conceded. The Senate resolved that while they felt that 'the graduates should hereafter be admitted to a share in the government of the University, cannot recommend to the Secretary of State the adoption of a charter founded on the propositions submitted to him by the committee of graduates.'

Warburton, who may have had his own doubts as to the wisdom of the graduates' specific proposals, or who may simply have seen that there was no majority in favour of them, then put forward a compromise motion:

That, for the purpose of enabling the graduates of the University of London to express formally their collective opinion on matters concerning the University, it is expedient to sanction meetings of the graduates of the University in Convocation assembled. That the Convocation of graduates ought to meet at a stated period once in every year, and sit *de die in diem* until they shall have completed their business, or shall be prorogued by the Secretary of State. That the Convocation may meet for special business at any time, at a month's notice, if authorised by the Secretary of State.

But any consideration of this was postponed, as it turned out, indefinitely.

Within a few weeks of this meeting, with the Supplementary Charter approved and referred to a committee to recommend how it should be applied, the graduates were left in a very unsatisfactory no-man's land. They were aware that both the Home Secretary and the Senate were sympathetic to the basic idea of there being, at some future date, some participation by graduates in the running of the University. At the same time, they found that the Home Secretary would not discuss the matter with them until they were able to send him further representation in writing of their views. In turn, the graduates tried to persuade the Senate to receive a deputation to discuss with them what further steps could be taken. But the Senate would only agree to hearing views, not discussing them, and this the graduates would not accept.[19] The stage was set for future developments which would have about them the spirit of a war of attrition.

CHAPTER 16

An Unripeness of Time

For some fifteen months after the graduates had set up their organization, the tide had flowed with them. Despite some delays and misunderstandings, the new Graduates Committee had been recognized and heard, as a legitimate body, by the Senate and by the Home Secretary. A civilized three-way relationship had been established, and by the middle of 1849 the Senate had accepted, in principle, the desirability of graduate participation in the governance of the University, while the Home Secretary had reacted sympathetically to the idea.

But the Senate's formal agreement in principle was linked with their opinion that the time was not yet ripe for that principle to be translated into any effective scheme of graduate participation. It was to be a year before the Senate made another significant pronouncement, and that was merely to explain their belief that they had neither the authority nor the responsibility to take an initiative to have the constitution of the University changed in order to accommodate the graduates. Thereafter it was a further three years before real progress was made, and five more years after that before the existence of convocation was guaranteed in a new Charter. Some account of the long, tortuous process will be given later. But some suggestions as to what factors caused the years of argument and delay may be appropriate at this point.

No small part of any explanation must relate to the surfacing, or resurfacing, of issues other than the single question of graduate participation, and to the impact of those issues not only on the Senate, but also on the graduates. While differing attitudes within the Senate on such matters as medical reform, scriptural examinations, certificates of proficiency and the requirement of examinees to have attended approved institutions, etc., had become well understood, the graduates were to discover, often to the consternation of their leaders, that they, too, were not necessarily of one view about such matters. As the concerns of the graduates widened to include some aspects of educational policy, it became clear that a simple scenario, Senate *versus* Graduates Committee, while existing in certain contexts and at certain times, did not extend to the whole relationship. For instance, the unsettled state of the medical profession split both the Senate and the graduates into those who were defensive of the existing powers of the medical corporations and those who saw those corporations as antipathetic to the future status of the University. As we shall see, the major irritant of the distinction between Oxford and Cambridge medical graduates and those of London and other universities would not be removed until 1854.

There is very little reliable evidence on which to base an analysis of internal Senate divisions. The reluctance, expressed in 1849, of those apprehensive of the influence of UCL and of the likelihood of sectarian and geographical conflict, must have forced a tactical retreat by those fellows who may have been willing to make some immediately effective concessions to the graduates: Warburton's compromise motion was allowed to wither on the vine. Indeed, it is clear that even those fellows most sympathetic to graduate representation in the Senate were by no means happy about the extent of the powers which the Graduates Committee envisaged for Convocation. Only a few weeks before the 1858 Charter came into effect, the radical George Grote, who joined the Senate in 1850 and would become the University's third Vice-Chancellor, confessed to Lord Granville, who had been Chancellor since the end of 1856:

> What I have always feared, and still do fear, is the establishment of Convocation as a body of *opposition* against the Senate. The *anti-graduate* feeling, which you justly notice as existing in the Senate, was stronger formerly than it is now. It was under this feeling that the Senate opposed as much as they could of passive resistance against the admission of the Graduates. I always deprecated this as much as I could; foreseeing that it would only have the effect of provoking hostility on the part of the Graduates – and that moreover they would be quite sure to obtain their admission, whether the Senate liked it or not. . . . That the Graduates should have the *whole control* of the University would doubtless be inexpedient . . . but I fear that it is not beyond the range of possibility.[1]

To some degree the opposition to graduate membership may also have been due to personal antagonism towards some of the graduates' current leaders, and to a distaste for the notion of having some of them as colleagues. This could have been the case with Charles James Foster, whose double role as political activist for both the graduates and the Liberation Society, to be spelt out in the following chapter, may well have antagonized some senators – and some ministers. John Storrar could be awkward, persistently argumentative, and 'somewhat brusque in manner' – qualities likely to cause friction in a long-drawn-out altercation. He was an able campaigner who felt neither fear of nor undue respect for the established order, and would have brought a sharp edge to his advocacy.[2] In short, it it very possible that there was, over the years of argument, some plain speaking which left lasting resentments. But there is little written evidence, save for a few abusive, anonymous letters in the *Lancet*.

In March 1850, the small group of fellows who had been, for many years, the working Senate, were joined by seven new colleagues drawn from the highest reaches of politics, money and scholarship. The most interesting of the new appointments was that of Sir James Graham, despite that statesman's tenure of the Home Office during the previous Conservative administration, and his apparent lack of sympathy for the University's medical aspirations in 1844–5. It is hard to believe that Lord John Russell was not involved in the two relevant moves. On 27 February 1850, the Council of UCL elected Graham to be one of their colleagues; and on 21 March, he was appointed a fellow of the University of London. Graham, who had left the Whig cabinet in 1834 over the question of Irish church revenues, was now one of the leading Peelites, and therefore a crucial figure in all the political calculations of the middle years of the century. How much his sudden acceptance of this degree of involvement in London academia was a reflection of high level political wooing, rather than a result of any reassertion of personal enthusiasm for a Whiggish experiment in the cause of liberal higher education, is not likely to be assessable from surviving records.

Next came George Grote, banker and reformist politician, whose famous *History of Greece* was just appearing, to great critical acclaim. A much richer man was Lord Overstone, a financier of major influence, and a brother-in-law of the Vice-Chancellor, John Shaw Lefevre. Grote, like Graham, was currently a member of the Council of UCL, and Overstone (as Samuel Jones Loyd) had served on it from 1841 to 1845. To Graham, Grote and Overstone was added Lord Monteagle, who thus joined the Senate he had originally recruited. And the last three newcomers were Thomas Babington Macaulay, whose *History of England* had just been published; Arthur Hallam, an older but equally influential historian; and Sir George Cornewall Lewis, a rising politician and literary man. Of these seven new fellows, three had already been

Cabinet ministers, and one – Lewis – would become Chancellor of the Exchequer in 1855. Grote had been an important Radical MP for nine years. Overstone was a major City figure whose expertise was used by Government. Hallam had no direct, elective political experience, but he had been a Commissioner of Taxes in early life.

These appointments reflected a deliberate intention by Lord John Russell, prompted by Warburton, to add to the University some worldly heavyweights. As in 1839, an unsuccessful attempt was made to recruit Sir John Herschell, to whom Warburton admitted that

> Those who have been requested to advise the Government on this occasion have proceeded on the plan, of recommending none but men of acknowledged eminence, and of moderation in their views. And of limiting the addition to a small number of persons, lest a bad example should be set to a future Government.[3]

The newcomers must have given the Senate more political prestige, but may also have increased the self-consciousness – and perhaps the self-importance – of the body as a Crown-appointed, government agency. In turn, this could have encouraged the application of the *gravitas* of very senior people, with its tendency to play down the notion of any popular, representative element, to take a cautious view of power and responsibility, and to be resentful of interference. Undoubtedly, over time, one of the main sticking points was the Senate's unwillingness to concede any chance that a Convocation should either dominate or manage the University. Certainly, after the appointment of the new fellows, there was revealed, on the constitutional issue of graduate participation, a reluctance to proceed at more than a slow pace.

Inevitably, attendances of the new men varied, but Monteagle, Overstone and Grote were quite frequently present. Graham, too, was attentive at first, but found it difficult to attend after becoming First Lord of the Admiralty at the end of 1852. Lewis was rarely at meetings, and if Russell had thought that the appointment of the two famous historians, Macaulay and Hallam, would improve attention to the arts, he must have been sorely disappointed, for they rarely appeared. And, in passing, it might be suggested that the character of Senate proceedings may well have changed markedly with the sudden death of Jerrard, from apoplexy, early in 1853. Thereafter, while Shaw Lefevre and Senior could be said to have given law some regular representation, George Grote must have been practically as single-handed a spokesman for the arts as Jerrard had been.

Opposition; doubts; the scrupulousness of new, powerful members within the Senate; soul searching by the graduates; fundamental disagreements about reform of the medical profession; and caution at the Home Office, do not add up to a full explanation of the long years of negotiation before Convocation, with severely modified powers and functions, was conceded. An overarching problem was that parliamentary support for governments was brittle, and the governments themselves were, as a result, weak and short-lived. There were general elections in 1847, 1852 and 1857, but none produced anything like a comfortable one party majority. There were five ministries in office between 1846 and 1858 - including two distinctly minority Tory administrations under Lord Derby, and the coalition Ministry of Lord Aberdeen for much of the Crimean War. There were four Prime Ministers – Russell, Derby, Aberdeen and Palmerston, and three Home Secretaries – Grey, Palmerston and Spencer Walpole.

A small institution like the University of London, drawing on the state's purse for only £4000 a year, was easily swept aside by greater interests and events in Westminster and Whitehall. On the whole, Russell and Derby, Grey and Walpole were friendly and genuinely interested in trying to persuade the various parties to come to some workable agreement; Palmerston was less interested but very capable of an occasional firm decision; Aberdeen seems to have been little involved. Each change meant that the new incumbents of office had to be either briefed or rebriefed. Catching their attention at all must have been difficult. In the circumstances, it was probably very beneficial to the University that Horatio Waddington remained in post as the permanent head of the Home Office throughout the period, and was willing, to judge from his marginal comments, to give the negotiations a discreet push now and then.

As for Parliament, while quite a number of MPs were supportive of the University and of graduate participation in its governance, their contributions were normally confined to discreet lobbying or interventions in debates on specific points. As we shall see, there were a few significant parliamentary episodes concerning the University, some of them being interesting pointers for the longer term, but in neither House was there any serious debate on the University's general situation or its immediate future. The annual vote of money was never challenged. The bitterness of religious animosity surfaced occasionally, though producing debating points rather than any expression of deep antipathy. There was a tendency to refer, aggressively or defensively, to 'the Dissenters' University,' and one may quote as a fairly mild example of feeling the occasion, in 1852, when the salaries of certain Oxford and Cambridge professors were questioned. Mr Chisholm Anstey proclaimed that the University of London was 'an institution which opens its doors to every class and every creed; it is not sectarian,' to which the redoubtable defender of the Anglican interest, Sir Robert Inglis, retorted 'No, the University of London is not sectarian, but it is worse than sectarian, because it is nothingarian.'[4]

In effect, Parliament showed only moderate concern and took almost no direct initiative in the context of the University during this run-up to the emergence of a new Charter in 1858. The long delay in reaching a constitutional settlement was primarily due to the internal politics of the University, of UCL and of the general body of graduates; to the doubt and hostility of several of the fellows, which lay behind a masterly inertia on the part of the Senate; and to the frequent changes of ministers, which ensured that the bureaucratic ground had to be covered several times. In the face of this active and passive obstruction, a less tenacious pressure group than the Graduates Committee proved itself to be might well have fallen, exhausted, by the wayside.

One positive step forward, which could be welcomed by all parties in the University, was the agreement reached by the four Inns of Court to adopt uniform rules for graduates of all British universities to govern admission of students and calls to the Bar. This was achieved by the group of reforming benchers, under the chairmanship of Richard Bethell, who formed the Committee on Legal Education. After the Committee made the matter part of its brief in 1847, negotiation continued for four years, but whatever informal and unrecorded lobbying may have gone on, the formal involvement of the London academic community would appear to have been quite limited.

In April 1848, Edwin Wilkins Field, a reforming solicitor who was Auditor of UCL and would become a member of Council in the following year, wrote calling the College's attention to the continuing exclusion of London law graduates from the privileges enjoyed by their Oxbridge contemporaries, claiming he had 'good reason to think' that an approach through the University of London would 'easily get the distinction removed.' With Brougham in the Chair, the Council called for a report to be prepared, Warburton to be briefed, and representations made.[5] The UCL resolution reached the University Senate in June 1848, when a committee was set up 'to communicate with the Inns of Court.' Its members were the Vice-Chancellor, Amos, Arnott, Jerrard, Senior and Warburton. Alas, the archives of the Inns of Court and of the University yield little data on any subsequent consultation. As late as October 1850, Rothman was asking Gray's Inn whether London graduates were 'enjoying any advantages either as to the amount of deposit required, or the duration of the term of Studentship.' Two months after that the Senate minutes recorded that a memorial from UCL on the subject was referred to a committee of the Faculty of Law. A final version of the memorial would appear to have been sent to the Master of the Rolls by Warburton, not later than June of 1851: it contained a brief review of the outstanding differences in each of the Inns in their treatment of London graduates.[6]

There must have been considerable quiet lobbying of the Committee on Legal Education by members of UCL and London University, along with representatives of the Scottish universities and Durham University, who were all seeking similar reforms. Within the Committee were John Romilly, by then Solicitor General; and Henry Hallam, who had been a bencher of the Inner Temple since 1841. Outside the Committee it is unlikely that Lord Brougham, a prime mover in its formation, would have failed to add his weight to the reform; and Shaw Lefevre, who had recently become Clerk Assistant and *de facto* Clerk of the Parliaments, would have had ample opportunities to make the University's claims known to sympathetic benchers. Among the law graduates of London, John Richard Quain, Frederick John Wood and Charles James Foster were articulate and persistent advocates, whom it is hard to believe would not have raised their voices in favour.

Whatever credit may be owed to these men, the sub-committee on the subject of uniformity of practice as to admission of students, etc., headed, interestingly enough, by Sir Edward Ryan, who would later become a fellow and Vice-Chancellor of London University, recommended uniformity of treatment in November 1851. The final report of the Committee on Legal Education was signed in the following February, shortly before Lord Derby replaced Lord John Russell in Downing Street: the new rules came into effect in Trinity Term, 1852.

In retrospect, in the constitutional context, it can be seen that the graduates had asked for too much, too soon; and the Senate had reacted too strongly. After the stand-off, in the late summer of 1849, the graduates tried to continue negotiations, on the basis that their first demands were simply an opening gambit, and that they were prepared to try to find an acceptable compromise. But they asked, not unreasonably, that they should have the chance to discuss with the Senate what the University was really thinking, before they came forward with new proposals. To this, however, the Senate responded negatively. In turn, this drove the graduates to appeal to the Home Secretary and to collect as much support as possible for their basic demand for a part in the University's governance. The Senate's recalcitrance took the form of denying that they could do anything unless asked for an opinion, or given a directive, by the Government. Thus the graduates had to try to persuade the Home Secretary to ask or push the Senate to address the graduates' claims. This cat and mouse game was to be played until just before the the fall of Russell's administration early in 1852.

During this two year interlude, relations between the Senate and the graduates deteriorated. The graduates became embroiled in controversies over the implementation of the new Supplementary Charter, and lost some sympathy, temporarily, among the more radically inclined politicians and educationalists. At the same time, to no small degree because of the graduates' campaigning, the colleges across the country affiliated with the University of London were drawn into the constitutional and educational arguments. The future of the University began to be regarded more of national than of merely metropolitan concern, and the interests of it and its associated colleges were seen as increasingly aligned with the more persistent demands of the non-Anglican communities for full inclusion in all educational and social privileges.

Aside from the pressure which the graduates kept up in pursuit of their main constitutional aims, they brought a welcome urgency to the idea of publicizing the University and increasing its sense of internal cohesion. It was largely due to them that academic dress was introduced and that the first Presentation Day was held, in 1849; and the reportage of their meetings must have brought the very existence of the institution to the notice of many who had not hitherto been much aware of its presence. They also threw their weight behind the University's efforts to find a more suitable home than Somerset House.

But their first intrusion into matters of educational policy thrust them into real conflict with the Senate. They took exception to the regulations, passed by the Senate and approved by the Home Secretary, to govern the entry to London examinations of graduates of other universities. And they attacked the policy, enshrined in the Supplementary Charter, whereby the University could examine candidates, in single subjects, who were not necessarily graduates, and award them certificates of proficiency. The first of these controversies revealed the passionate concern of the graduates to protect the high standard of the London degrees: this struggle they won. The second argument reflected important splits between institutional, conservative and elitist notions of the University, on the one hand, and ideas of radical individualism and widening opportunity, on the other hand: that argument, fiercely fought, was won – at a later stage – by the Senate.

The course of these disagreements is most vividly told in the pages of the *Lancet*, which give a succinct description of the first intention of the Supplementary Charter:

> This Charter, by giving to the other English, the Scotch, and Dublin universities, a connexion with the University of London, (which they might previously have had by application to the Senate, but which they were not disposed to seek,) enables some few dissenters educated at those institutions, but prevented by religious scruples from obtaining their degrees, to present themselves for examination at the University of London.

Both Senate and graduates would readily have agreed with the editor of the *Lancet*, that, in principle, 'This arrangement appears as unobjectionable as it is judicious and useful.' But the trouble arose from the Senate's regulations to govern the scheme, which provided for a very liberal treatment of those candidates who wished to take advantage of it:

> the candidates for the degree of B.A. shall only be examined by their examiners on those subjects in which they have not been examined in their own Universities. If they have not been examined in any of the subjects, they must then be examined in all; if they have been examined in all, they must still be examined in some one subject, by the examiners of the University of London.[7]

To the graduates, this was a dilution of demand on candidates which they could not accept. Their spokesman was Robert Barnes, MD:

> every graduate who has the interest of the university and the reputation of his degree at heart, will strenuously oppose the admission of any candidate who is not subjected to the same ordeal which he has himself undergone. Surely he has a right to expect this. Upon what does the credit and influence of the University of London repose? By what means has its fame been built up in a few short years in the face of prejudice and of ridicule? Nothing else but the known extent and

severity of its examinations. We have no snug fellowships, no rich endowments, no fat benefices, little social influence, and above all, no representative government, or other academic authority, which render an Oxford or a Cambridge degree so valuable an acquisition. The London University graduate has nothing but his degree. The only value of that degree lies in the fact, that it cannot be obtained without a stringent examination. Surely a determination to maintain that examination in all its integrity ought not to be stigmatized as illiberal? It is difficult to conceive on what just ground exemption from any part of the examination can be claimed for one candidate in preference to another. A proper regard for the character of our university will also suggest to us that it is unbecoming to its dignity, if not a dereliction of its duty, to substitute the examinations of other bodies, however venerable or respectable, for those which it ought itself to conduct.[8]

The Senate had promulgated its regulations on 27 February 1850, but immediately thereafter both the Graduates Committee and the Council of UCL (clearly responding to graduate pressure) made their strong objections known to the Home Office. Moreover, in a rather significant move, very probably initiated through graduate action, several of the affiliated colleges also petitioned the Home Office to the same effect. Protests came in from early March well into May. This outburst of indignation was referred to the Senate by the Home Office on 19 March, with a request for their observations.[9] In the Senate the task of producing a draft reply was entrusted to the small committee which had handled the initial framing of the controversial regulations - Chancellor, Vice-Chancellor, Billing, Senior and Warburton. Those fellows, except for the Chancellor, must have agonized a great deal over the matter, for the result was a report which ran to 22 pages and an appendix, reproduced in the minutes of the Senate's meeting on 19 June.

There are no papers extant, and the committee was apparently unanimously agreed in recommending the abandonment of the Senate's position. The argument put forward for so doing, however, was narrowly legal and technical, rather than an acceptance of the emotional appeal of the graduates. Exclusion from examination was dropped, but graduates of Oxford, Cambridge, Dublin and Durham were exempted from London's matriculation requirements.

The Senate resolved, on 21 August 1850, that the the Vice-Chancellor should write to the Home Secretary and ask for his agreement to the retraction of the regulations. Sir George Grey's approval was delayed until December.[10] By this time the Senate, no doubt uncomfortably aware from past experience that all its records could be demanded by either House of Parliament and published, had become obviously reticent about how much of their discussions should be recorded in the minutes. There is no sign of argument or voting on the issue on the floor of the Senate. The graduates could claim, therefore, that they had won, hands down.

It was another story, though, on the question of certificates of proficiency. Even Robert Barnes, in his letter already quoted, admits that there was 'more room for difference of opinion.' He went on to present, in a nutshell, the case of the objectors:

> It is felt to be incompatible with the functions of a university to grant certificates of proficiency in any particular art or science, and which must have the character of a diploma, apart from any evidence of a liberal education. It is not too much to ask, that, before a candidate shall be examined for a certificate or degree in engineering, he shall undergo the preliminary examination in classics, mathematics, and general education, to which the graduates in law, arts, and medicine, have to submit.

On this matter the Senate stood their original ground, refusing to argue the case on its basic merits, but taking the view that no plans to introduce any certificate examinations had yet been put forward, so that discussion would be premature. There seems to have been no open disapproval of that position, or at least no stomach to appeal against it, and the matter was dropped, to be taken up fiercely another day.

In a longer perspective, perhaps the most significant reaction to the objections made by the graduates to the regulations was published in Wakley's *Lancet*. That journal felt the objections were 'neither judicious nor well founded,' as much or more because it saw them to be tactically mistaken, as because of their substance. It is worth quoting this criticism at length, because it illustrates the impatience of a Radical strategist with the impulsiveness of political inexperience, on the one hand, and a fundamental disagreement, from the Radical standpoint, with the self-protectiveness of a new group of privileged people, on the other hand.

> It is paltry cavilling to say, that the proposed regulations, when taken in connexion with the regulations for the degree of B.A. in the older Universities, will permit men, on easier terms, or of inferior education, to enter the University of London. However anxious the

Senate may be to remove the disabilities, in a religious point of view, of such candidates, they have evinced too profound an interest in the welfare of the University, and too much tact in its management, to sacrifice its welfare to their own feeling. The graduates might take a lesson from their seniors in this respect . . . .We must tell the graduates that they ought to use more discretion in their proceedings. We regard with confidence and with hope the rising interests of their institution, as a great medical, as well as institution of general science, and we protest against those interests being damaged by the quibbles of lawyers, the sophistries of scholars, or what is perhaps not less injurious in the present instance, by a puerile selfishness, which leads men to forget that it is the graduate, and not the degree, which will be judged by the public and the profession. Let this be borne in mind, and there will be less objection to another sphere of usefulness proposed by this Charter for the University of London. That is, granting, independently of degrees, certificates of knowledge on certain subjects, mere statements of fact – for example, in natural history, to those seeking appointments in this department of science; to civil engineers; to masters of vessels in hydrography, and navigation, etc. Scientific knowledge might thus be greatly advanced, whilst the bearers of these certificates would throughout the world be found the friends and the heralds of the University of London. Forsooth, these certificates must not be given, lest they may be confounded with, and diminish the value of, degrees. Ridiculous! Why, by the same argument all associated objects must lose their distinctions. The private soldier must be mistaken for the field officer; the deacon for the bishop, the printer's devil for the editor, or the matriculated student for the full-blown LL.D. We cannot see in such a regulation, a justification for assailing the University with such epithets as a 'Governing Board,' or 'a Licensing Office,' nor in reviving the old slander of one of its greatest enemies, when he called it 'a graduating machine.' The graduates may be assured that those who possess the feelings of the individual just referred to desire no higher connection with the Senate. In exultation may such men cry, ' A house divided against itself cannot stand,' whilst those who have the welfare of the University at heart exclaim. Be wise, keep your grievances, if you have any, at home – be patient, discuss them with the Senate and do not, by rushing after Government interference, which you will not get, weaken its influence as well as your own.[11]

The *Lancet's* leaders were often explosive, and not necessarily indicative of long-term switches of attitude or support. The graduates were to continue to find Wakley's journal one of their strongest allies: their success over the Supplementary Charter was accepted without comment, and it was not long before new leader columns appeared, pushing the consitutional case for Convocation. But perhaps the 'candid friend' approach in mid-1850 helped in the longer term to persuade the Graduates Committee to reduce their demands and thereby enhance the prospect of a compromise settlement.

Not at once, however. After their victory in having the offensive regulations withdrawn, the graduates used the winter months of 1850–1 to prepare the next offensive on the constitutional front. This took the form of a Declaration signed by 'no less than 361 . . . of the 470 graduates mentioned in the calendar for 1849,' as well as by 38 members of the Graduates Committee.[12] This document, together with a long 'Statement of Reasons inducing the Graduates of the University of London to desire Changes in the Constitution of the University,' reached the Senate on 10 February 1851. The arguments were almost all well worn, though a hint of readiness to find some moderate solution can be read into the final sentence of the Declaration, which called for the immediate admission of graduates into the corporate body, 'with such share in [the University's] government as may be deemed proper.'

The Senate were in no hurry to respond. They discussed the documents on 19 March, but the minutes give no clue to the nature of the discussion. It was not until 2 April that a committee was set up to draft an answer to the graduates. Its membership was an interesting commentary on the involvement of new members – the Vice-Chancellor and Warburton were joined by Macaulay and Overstone. Alas, the records of their meetings have not survived. But one item probably in their basic advice to the Senate is contained in a letter which Warburton addressed to Overstone three years later, when the essential problem was still being faced. Warburton then wrote:

> Having to adminster not corporate funds, but Public monies for Public objects, we can not properly be parties, without the entire approbation of the Government, to give other parties a control over those Monies. We must desire Lord Palmerston to refer the matter to the Government, and say that before taking the important step of petitioning the Crown for a New Charter, there must be complete understanding between the Senate and the Government upon what principle the future constitution of the University is to be based.[13]

Whether this was the main, or only one of several reasons, the Senate resolved, on 21 May 1851, that:

> It seems . . . that the question raised by [the] Declaration is not
> one which the Senate can with propriety discuss. The members
> of the Senate have, under the present Charters, been selected
> by the Crown. They act under the superintendence of the Sec-
> retary of State. It is, in their opinion, not for them, but for
> the authority which appointed them, to determine whether the
> fundamental constitution of the University does or does not require
> alteration.

It has to be admitted that, in a strictly technical sense, the recently
rejuvenated Senate were correct. And it was certainly open to Government to decide whether they wanted to ask the Senate's opinion on the
desirability of any such changes. Not surprisingly, however, this attitude
of distancing themselves from the problem did not endear the Senate to
those pressing the graduates' cause.

Even before there was any exchange of official letters as a result of
the Senate's declaration, the *Lancet*, after some judicious admonition of
both parties, pressed its advice on the graduates. Its editorial of 7 June,
warned that:

> the Senate may learn the danger of alienating the sympathy and
> the support of those who have a natural claim upon, and natural
> affection for, their Alma Mater . . . the graduates may learn the
> no less useful lesson, that a just demand, pursued with energy,
> with resoluteness, with moderation, yet without compromise, must
> ultimately prevail. It is worthy, however, of important consideration,
> whether, considering the position which the Senate has assumed,
> the graduates ought not forthwith and continuously henceforward
> to bring all their energies and exertions to bear upon the judge-
> ment and feelings of the Secretary of State, with whom vir-
> tually is invested that power which alone can furnish a legal
> compliance with the just and reasonable demands of the gradu-
> ates.

Three weeks afterwards, the graduates took this advice. Their secretary, William Fowler, a lawyer, sent to the Home Secretary a copy of
their Declaration with a reasoned letter expressing the willingness of the
graduates to try to find a formula for their inclusion in the governance
of the University, which would be acceptable to the Senate.Sir George

Grey sent it on to the Chancellor, apparently without comment. On 4 July, Burlington replied to Grey:

> I do not understand that you wish me to lay the Honorary Secretary's letter before the Senate. If you desire it, a meeting shall be called to consider the subject, but it has been already so repeatedly discussed by the Senate, that I am convinced they can but re-affirm the resolution they have already come to.[14]

But hardly was the ink dry on Burlington's missive than Wakley, who had, as it were, got his second wind, launched in the *Lancet*, on 5 and 19 July, two withering attacks on the Senate's refusal to offer any opinion on the matter of graduate participation. First came a comparison of the Senate's position in 1840, when they 'had acted as independent men, invested with general discretionary powers to promote to the best of their judgement the high objects of the university,' with the Senate of 1851, among whom were 'four individuals who had held prominent positions in the present or former administrations.' The 1851 senators

> now avow themselves to be the mere exponents of the wishes of the Secretary of State. They now discover that 'this question of the constitution of the university) is not one which they can with propriety discuss.' . . . This, then, is the condition of the university. The graduates have no status whatever; the Senate formally acknowledges that it has no independent authority. It merely executes certain routine duties under the superintendence of the Secretary of State.

This was followed by a challenge, aimed particuarly at Monteagle, Graham, Macaulay and Hallam:

> We will ask [the Senators] if an office of servile dependence upon a minister – an office in the execution of which they are required to carry out to the letter the restricted duties of a mere Examining Board, without heed for, or liberty to promote, the final object of the Institution at the head of which they are ostensibly placed, – is an office befitting them to hold? Can it be that men whose names are illustrious in the ranks of the advocates of freedom, are prepared to repudiate the principle of representation? Have they who have so patiently traced the history and dwelt upon the advantages of constitutional institutions, so little faith that they dare not recommend the extension of the system in an instance where they possess the power to give effect to their opinions. Some of them are members

of the older universities. Will they be guilty of the inconsistency, of the injustice, of denying to the graduates of the University of London, the privileges they themselves enjoy?

And there is much more, in the same vein. The most interesting aspect of this diatribe, however, is the explanation which the *Lancet's* editor found for the present *impasse*. He threatens to show that 'EVEN NOW, the principle of religious freedom which the University was founded to protect, is in the most imminent jeopardy,' and claims that London, alone among the English universities, 'feels the oppressive, the deadening, the intolerable incubus of the fatal spirit of centralization.' And he goes on:

> If we ask why, but one reason appears. There is one feature by which the cosmopolitan University is broadly distinguished from the rest. *She is not orthodox* like her sisters; she has dared to vindicate the independence of Learning from Theology; she has recognised the disciple of Science, whether Roman Catholic or Protestant; she embraces the citizens of every region of the British Empire, and does not question whether they be Hindoos or Mussulmen, Jews or Brahmins. Is this indeed, the ground of exclusion? It will hardly be avowed. Yet where is there another?

Finally, there is an appeal to 'the minister' – Lord John Russell – but which could surely be interpreted as including both the Prime Minister and Sir George Grey:

> To remove the imputation which will otherwise stain the fame of the minister of civil and religious freedom, let him hasten to make amends; let him no longer expose himself to the reproach that he is insincere in his advocacy of equal rights for all, irrespective of creeds; let it no longer be said the the promised removal of religious restriction from the acquisition of academical honours is a mockery in performance; let the graduates be in the University of London what they have long been in the ecclesiastical Universities of Oxford, Cambridge, and Dublin.

There is no hard evidence to support Wakley's 'explanation,' but it reflects the intense religious preoccupations and prejudices of the mid-century, and the fact that, though the 'nonconformists gained from every successful attack upon anglican privilege . . . on the whole, their attitude towards the church was unfriendly and often bitter.'[15] Certainly, as already noted, the non-Anglican affiliated colleges were beginning to make themselves heard in favour of the graduates' case: and we have seen the scornful reference of a prominent Churchman to the 'nothingarianism' of London. But there is an absence of any detailed reportage of Senate discussions, and a lack of any public signs of sustained objections to the 'cosmopolitan' nature of the University. Perhaps the most that can be said is that the Senate's apparent determination to force the Government to take any initiative in the matter of graduate participation, gave rise, not unreasonably, to such suspicions as were entertained in the *Lancet*. It would be particularly fascinating to know exactly where and what influence, if any, Warburton was exerting on Wakley, his old ally – perhaps Warburton himself had been persuaded by his new Senate colleagues to let circumstances force a decision on ministers. But it will be remembered that in the crucial meetings with Grey and Russell in 1849, Warburton had made use of the threat to the University from Church interests which the *Lancet* repeated in 1851.

Neither Wakley's rhetoric nor Burlington's scepticism seem to have registered at the Home Office. A complete silence descended, and it was not until mid-December 1851 that Fowler tried again, with an extremely polite approach to Sir George Grey, asking for his 'early attention to the matters referred to' in Fowler's letter of 28 June. Grey, perhaps a little conscience stricken, scribbled to his staff: 'Send a copy of this letter and of that of 28 June to the Senate of the University requesting them to favour me with their opinion upon the application from the Committee of Graduates.'[16] It was a turning point, but came in the last days of the shaky administration of Lord John Russell.

Grey's request was despatched by Waddington on 2 January 1852. It was laid before the Senate on 18 February, when it was agreed that a special meeting should be held to discuss its contents. But only two days later, on 20 February, Lord Palmerston achieved his famous 'tit-for-tat with John Russell,' avenging his exclusion from the Government a year earlier, by joining with the protectionist Tories in a successful vote in favour of a national militia. Russell resigned. It was to be under Lord Derby's first, short-lived, Conservative administration that some real progress would be made towards finding a solution to the constitutional problems of the University of London.

CHAPTER 17

A Parliamentary Constituency?

In retrospect, some of the graduates felt that it was not until 1856 that 'the most important step . . . in the course of the ten years struggle' was taken, when two members of the Graduates Committee were nominated to hold seats in the Senate.[1] And even so, it was a further two years before Convocation came into being in accordance with the provisions of a new Charter. But the campaign to achieve graduate representation reached its peak during the Derby and Aberdeen governments, from February 1852 until February 1855. After that, it was left to Sir George Grey and Lord Palmerston to override a last arid legal obstacle and for the graduates and the Senate to survive and settle, by the thinnest of margins, a final, major controversy over admissions policy. During this extended period, a central figure in the whole of the constitutional argument, the parliamentary lobbying, the raising of outside pressure and the negotiation of a settlement, was Charles James Foster, Professor of Jurisprudence at University College.

Foster was born in Cambridge in 1817 and, as a Baptist 'experienced many of the inconveniences to which Nonconformists were subjected.'[2] He was a student at UCL, and one of the earliest London graduates, taking his BA, MA and LL B in the early 1840s, and being elected to a College fellowship in 1845. His doctorate followed in 1849, the year in which he was appointed to the Professorship of Jurisprudence at UCL. His main professional ambition was to practise successfully at the Equity Bar, but in the early 1850s he felt that a reputation for occasional deafness, which he believed to be undeserved, was making that ambition unachievable.[3]

While Foster did have a law practice, his political activities must have taken a great deal of his time. His contributions to political and religious developments in the 1850s and early 1860s have been discussed hitherto much more in the context of his work for the Liberation Society than they have been related to his leading role in the affairs of the London graduates.[4] In 1858 he gave up his chair at UCL on becoming the first Chairman of Convocation and a member of the Senate. In 1863 he resigned from Convocation and from the

Liberation Society, and emigrated to New Zealand, where he practised
and taught in Christchurch and lived until his death at Sumner in 1896.

As neither the bulk of the papers of the Graduates' Committee, nor
the pre-1850 minutes of the Anti-State Church Association have been
found, it is impossible to make definite assertions about the extent of
Foster's earlier involvement in the Dissenters' organization. That he
was one of the first lobbyists for equal treatment of London graduates
at Lincoln's Inn, as early as 1840, and that he was effectively secretary
or joint-secretary of the graduates for most of the years from 1848 until
1858, is clear enough. What is uncertain is how much, if at all, he was
prominent in the work of the Anti-State Church Association before it
became the Liberation Society in 1853. But as he was proposed as
one of three secretaries for the annual conference of the Association
in October 1853, and was appointed to a paid chairmanship of the
Liberation Society's parliamentary committee in January 1854, when
his committedness to the cause was much quoted, it would be reasonable
to assume that he had devoted a good deal of his time and energy to the
Dissenters' campaigns prior to 1853.[5]

We have already quoted from Foster's book, *The University of London: A Parliamentary Constituency*, which was published in 1851. The
claim made in it was not left for long, remote, academic consideration,
but was forced to the forefront of the graduates' campaign at the
beginning of 1852,and has its small place in history as part of the
confused, partisan fumblings to take further the fundamental changes
made in the representation of the people by the Reform Act of 1832. An
exact chronology is hard to establish, but whatever previous discussions
had taken place, the Graduates Committee wrote on 17 February 1852
to the Prime Minister, Lord John Russell, seeking his support for the
acceptance of the London graduates as a parliamentary constituency.
It was claimed two months later, well after Russell's resignation, that
'The noble lord is understood to have expressed himself in very explicit
terms, both in and out of office, as to the desirableness of giving the
franchise to the University of London.'[6] However, before pursuing the
progress of this new claim for graduate recognition, it is as well to
record what had been happening, perhaps to no small degree on Foster's
initiative, in UCL and in other colleges affiliated to the University of
London.

During the long delay in the latter part of 1851, before Sir George
Grey was reminded of the graduates' request to reopen the whole

constitutional enquiry with the Senate, the Graduates Committee had circularized the affiliated colleges, asking their support for representation in the University's governance and for the establishment of a parliamentary seat. As a large proportion of the colleges were of non-Anglican persuasion, and as Foster was probably already much involved in the Anti-State Church Association, he would have been admirably placed to encourage persuasive and sympathetic liaison with them. We do have evidence that in the long vacation of 1852 he visited 'the principal towns of Lancashire and Yorkshire where he succeeded in enlisting the sympathies of the leading liberals in those cities in favour of the Reconstitution and Parliamentary Enfranchisement of the University.'[7]

The response of some twenty colleges was an impressive endorsement of the demands of the graduates. Only one institution was hostile. Many of the memorials were sent to the Home Office, and among the first to arrive there, at the end of January 1852, was one from the Trustees of Manchester New College, apparently sent to Sir George Grey by James Heywood, MP for North Lancashire, and Thomas Thornely, MP for Wolverhampton.[8] Others came in steadily from February to April. All of them came to the notice of the Senate, but some were also brought to the notice of the Council of UCL by Foster and Frederick John Wood, now an elected member of it. As might be expected, UCL took a strong line. At the annual general meeting of the College on 25 February, a motion drafted by the Graduates Committee, of which notice had been given almost a month before, was proposed by John Richard Quain: 'That this meeting is of opinion that the time has arrived for re-constituting the University of London, on the basis of the admission of the Graduates to a recognised position in the Corporate Body.' No less a person than Sir James Graham was in the chair when the motion was approved, and the resolution was sent to the Home Office on 2 March.[9]

On the following day, the Senate met, as had been arranged, in order to consider Sir George Grey's request for their opinion on the graduates' proposals. But Sir George Grey had gone, and there were before the Senate not only his letter, but the further letter of the Graduates Committee to Lord John Russell, raising the issue of parliamentary representation of the University, and the recent UCL resolution. Graham was present, and the depth of feeling at UCL, together with a knowledge of the support for the graduates being expressed by many affiliated colleges, must have made the senators acutely aware of the delicacy of their position. But whatever may have been said, the only action approved was that the

Vice-Chancellor should ask the new Home Secretary, Spencer Walpole, whether he wished to have their opinion on the matters referred to them by Sir George Grey.

When the Vice-Chancellor's letter reached the Home Office, Waddington minuted on it, 'I should think it would be extremely desirable,' to have the Senate's views, and his new chief approved his writing to the Senate, asking for 'their opinion on the application of the Committee of Graduates with any observations which they think might be useful for determining the propriety of granting or declining it.'[10] Faced with this, on 17 March, the fifteen fellows present found it impossible to accept any clear way ahead. The only motion recorded was put forward by Nassau Senior, who proposed 'That the Senate is of opinion that a change in the constitution of the University is advisable.' Discussion of it was adjourned. Senior's motion might be interpreted as a gesture favourable to the graduates cause, but a later, private observation of his suggests that his motives were unsympathetic and devious.

Meanwhile, on 10 March, William Shaen, as Secretary of the Graduates' Committee, sent to Walpole a copy of their printed *Statement – The University of London and its Graduates*, and requested him to meet a deputation made up of two medical men, Storrar and Gull, and four lawyers, Foster, Quain, Wood and Shaen himself. They wanted to include some discussion of the question of a parliamentary constituency.[11] There is no sign that any such meeting occurred but, on 15 March – only two days before Senior's motion in the Senate – Joseph Hume moved in the Commons for papers relating to the organisation of the University.[12] According to the *Eclectic Review*, a journal well-disposed to the graduates' cause, 'Overtures of an amicable nature subsequently came from a leading member of the Senate to a member of the committee of graduates. These negotiations led to the reception by the senate of a deputation from the graduates' committee.'[13] A delegation did meet the Senate on 24 March; perhaps, given the parliamentary interest, the 'negotiations' were quietly urged on the Senate by Walpole as a response to and a substitute for the graduates' plea for a meeting with him. In any event, the group which met the Senate was slightly different from that named in the letter to the Home Secretary. Quain dropped out and George Jessel and Timothy Smith Osler, both lawyers, were added.

It was at that meeting, on 24 March 1852, that the graduates put forward, in essence, proposals the bulk of which were eventually incorporated in the University's Charter. Having heard their verbal presentation, the Senate asked them to put the scheme in writing, with any additional observations they might wish to make. Such a statement was before the Senate on 31 March. Its salient points have been thus summarized:

(1) A new Charter should be obtained, admitting all graduates into the corporate body of the University and giving them the right of meeting in Convocation;

(2) Convocation should be a deliberative body, with the right to record its opinion on any subject, but no power of veto except on the surrender of an existing or the acceptance of a new Charter;

(3) Convocation should have the power of submitting to the Crown a list of persons, not necessarily graduates, from whom 'a certain proportion' of all future Senators should be selected;

(4) Convocation should have the right to regulate its own proceedings;

(5) the Senate should communicate all its proceedings to the officers of Convocation and should be entitled to require the opinion of Convocation upon any matter.[14]

How much, if any, of the reduction of demand represented by this list from the original claims of the graduates was due to acceptance of advice from senators and others sympathetic to the idea of Convocation can only be a matter for speculation. So, too, is any full and accurate asessment of the positions taken by individual senators when, at the meeting on 31 March, discussion of Senior's motion was resumed. Warburton moved an amendment to send the plans of the graduates to all the non-medical affiliated colleges, in order to have their responses; but this motion was lost – no vote is recorded, so there is a possibility that Warburton could not find a seconder. Then Senior withdrew his original motion and replaced it with another:

That the letter of Mr Secretary Walpole, and all documents connected therewith, be referred to a Select Committee . . . to report . . . whether the change suggested by the Committee of Graduates, either in whole or in part, or any other modification of the existing constitution of the University, can be recommended as useful and not endangering the fundamental principles on which the University of London is established.

This was accepted, again without any recorded vote, but nominations to the select committee were postponed to the next meeting.

From these four March meetings the Chancellor was absent; in fact he had attended only one meeting in each of the years 1850 and 1851, and would appear only twice in 1852. The Vice-Chancellor missed the meeting on 31 March. It is perhaps significant that there was a solid attendance thoughout by five fellows who had considerable public reputations and much contact with the political world – Graham, Grote, Hallam, Senior and Warburton. Three medical men were present at each session - Billing, Hammick and Kiernan. Arnott, Brande and Jerrard each missed one meeting; Bacot, Clark, Faraday and Roget came twice, Hodgkin and Monteagle once. If there were those for whom the prospect of any change was anathema, the worldly wise were probably numerous enough and wise enough to avoid a confrontation and to negotiate some further contemplation of what must have been recognized by all as a moderate proposal.

Though there is no correspondence to support the claim, it is surely likely that some intensive discussion ensued as to who would be the appropriate fellows to form the new committee. In the event, on 21 April, the composition of it showed the extent to which the matter was being entrusted to the politicians and the lawyers. In addition to the Chancellor and Vice-Chancellor, the members were Arnott - the solitary medical man – Graham, Grote, Lewis (who made his very first appearance at the Senate on the day of his appointment to the committee), Monteagle and Senior. The most notable absentee was Warburton, perhaps because his position was so clearly known and understood. That the proceedings of the committee were to be kept private is underlined by the defeat of Grote's motion that they should have the power to communicate with the Graduates Committee. This last decision was taken badly by the graduates, who saw it as

> one of the most unfortunate steps ever taken by the Senate. It came just at a time when by a more gracious course they might have acquired great popularity, and removed from the discussion everything having the semblance of dissension.[15]

Whether, in fact, the participation of the graduates in the debates of the committee would have prevented dissension must remain an open question. Such evidence as we have does not encourage a positive answer to it. The minutes of the select committee of 1852 are not among the records which have survived. But a single letter – from Nassau Senior to Overstone, five months after the committee reported

– gives, briefly and vividly, a vision of much contention within it. Senior wrote:

> I send you our report, in two stages – the first, and the last but one – Rothman will send you the final one. You will see that between the first draft and the fourth there is a great difference – I found that the Committee would not support me in refusing any convocation whatever – and I doubted whether the Public would do so. So I introduced a convocation as little mischievous as I could. The first draft should not be shewn – or indeed preserved.[16]

An agreed report was presented to the Senate on 16 June, though, clearly, strongly-held minority opinions had been sacrificed to the strategic advantage of apparent unanimity. For, before and during the committee's brief existence, the graduates and their allies kept up a level of pressure which may well have convinced their strongest sympathizers within the committee that a solution satisfactory to the graduates was a foregone conclusion, even if not one which would be reached immediately. At the same time, Senior's conviction that his total opposition would not be acceptable implies, nonetheless, that he had enough influence and support within the committee to enforce only a diluted version of the graduates' demands.

The *Eclectic Review*'s support for a convocation dated back to 1851, and was expressed in thoughtful and careful articles reviewing relevant publications.[17] The *Lancet* was more presistent and more outspoken in its pleas on behalf of the graduates' case. But it also urged the graduates to be demanding while at the same time showing themselves to be worthy of becoming 'the immediate recipients of a great public trust . . . which they will be expected to exercise in the promotion of free education.'[18] On the notion of parliamentary representation of the University, the editor was as enthusiastic as on the matter of graduate participation in running it, and despite his earlier strictures on some of its senators, asked: 'Who would not welcome an electoral body dignified by their learning, secure against corruption, who might restore to the national councils a MACAULAY or a GROTE?'[19]

The *Lancet* had a particularly acute sense of timing, and several of its leaders appeared at such appropriate moments as to raise reasonable suspicions that the editor's contacts with members of the Senate and of the Graduates Committee were very close. But it may have been mere chance that the leader of Saturday, 8 May, preceded by only two days a memorable meeting, arranged by Foster 'at a few hours notice . . . for a deputation of graduates to be received by Lord Derby.'[20] The Prime Minister's agreement to see Foster and his colleagues must reflect the political seriousness of any prospective extension of the franchise, and the Conservatives' anxiety over declarations by Russell and Graham in favour of conferring, in the latter's words, 'the representative power . . . on parties possessing intelligence and science to an eminent degree who do not now return representatives.'[21]

Derby and Disraeli both went on record on 10 May in favour of giving the graduates of the University of London a seat in the House of Commons, which was a considerable boost for the Graduates Committee, who henceforward could declare that the leaders of both the main parties were sympathetic to the idea. But the most significant immediate result of their support was to increase the pressure on the Senate to face the problem that such parliamentary representation was out of the question unless the graduates were to become legally part of the University. Disraeli's speech in the Commons, only hours after the deputation had met Derby, included a stark exposition of the difficulty. He was speaking to the proposal of Thomas Barkett Lennard, Liberal MP for Malden, that two seats should be apportioned to the University of London.

> My colleagues and myself have considered not only the case of the learned societies, and not only the case of the Scotch Universities, but also the claim of the London University; but I am bound to say, with every disposition to recommend such a measure . . . we do not find, in the present state of the London University, the conditions which are necessary for making a concession under the circumstances of such a nature as this. The constitution of that university is, at present, too immature, its development too imperfect, for urging any well founded claim of the nature now in question. . . . I think it right, however, to add, that in considering the claim of this institution, Her Majesty's Government have felt that the principle upon which it is urged is a principle entitled to respect and approbation; that there is nothing fantastic or unfitting in the claim; but that it is in perfect unison with principles which are already acted upon in this House, in the case of Oxford, of Cambridge and of Dublin.[22]

The Senate select committee's report began by setting out simply the unique nature of the constitution of the University of London, comparing it with that of other universities, and admitting that the comparison made their task particularly hard.

We feel considerable difficulty in proposing any change in a constitution which appears to work well. And the peculiarity of that constitution increases this difficulty, by depriving us of the aid of experience.

The examples of the older Universities are inapplicable. They are Institutions principally for the purpose, not of examination, but of education. During a long period, ending only in the present century, there were no examinations by University authority in Oxford.

The older English Universities are bodies of great wealth and extensive patronage, comprehending many persons of different classes entitled to share in their revenues, enjoying their social and literary advantages, and resident under their jurisdiction. Constitutions giving to some of these classes a part in the government of a Corporation which presides over their moral, and social, and intellectual, and indeed over their pecuniary, interets, seem natural and almost necessary.

The claim of the Graduates of the University of London to participate in its government does not rest on these grounds.

Those who do not intend to proceed to a second degree – and this is the case with respect to a very large majority – though they may take, and we have no doubt do take, a grateful interest in the welfare of the University, – are not directly affected by its proceedings. It has done for them all that it professes to do, – prescribed their period and subjects of study, examined them, and rewarded them with its Degrees and Honours.

Those who intend to take a further degree are directly interested in it only as respects the selection of subjects of examination and the selection of Examiners, for that further degree.

We may add, that the bulk of the Graduates are allowed a very small share in the management of the older Universities, deeply as they may be affected by it. The Convocation itself is permitted to exercise the powers which it possesses only under narrow restrictions. It considers only the matters submitted to it by the governing authority, cannot discuss them except in Latin, and cannot propose an amendment. It can simply accept or reject.

But having thus laid out, very reasonably, these facts and opinions, the report does not go on to examine the arguments put forward by the graduates in the light of any fundamental principle, or to challenge the basis of their claim. Instead, it addresses only the specific alterations to the existing constitution submitted by the Graduates Committee, and in effect produces an alternative scheme of representation which they must have intended from the outset would be recognized as a basis for negotiation.

The committee accepted without demur the desirability of including the graduates in the body corporate of the University: 'we see no objection, and so far as it would facilitate the grant of the Parliamentary franchise and a representation in the House of Commons to the Graduates, we give it our cordial approbation.' And with the basic proposal for a Convocation as a self-governing body, free to discuss any subject and record its opinions, but without power to interfere with or annul any acts of the Senate, save when a new Charter was under consideration, the committee (*pace* Senior!) was content.

> We believe that [the Graduates] are animated by a genuine interest in the continued success of the University, and by the desire of the personal dignity which is associated with the performance of active and honourable functions in its service. These are sentiments which, far from reproving or discountenancing, we desire to encourage, and to which we shall be glad to afford a means of tranquil and effective manifestation.

But with the size and composition of the graduates' version of convocation, the committee, yielding to Senior, was unhappy. They argued that while the 'necessary standing of the members' was 'not absolutely defined,' it appeared that what was intended was membership open to all graduates of three years' standing. They felt that this would imply an increase of more than eighty every year, producing soon a 'very numerous' Convocation.

> It appears to us that a large body meeting at pleasure with no legislative or administarive functions, whose whole powers and whose whole duties would be to discuss and to adopt resolutions, would not be likely to act beneficially on the government of the University.

Instead, the committee suggested that Convocation should consist of:

> all the Masters of Arts, of all who have been, are or shall be Univer-

sity Scholars, and of the senior half of the Doctors in Medicine, and the 50 senior Graduates in Law.

This would afford immediately a body of about 160 persons, annually, and quickly, increasing, which would include the most distinguished of the Graduates, and from which no one capable of taking the degree of Master of Arts would be excluded.

The report also rejected the idea that Convocation should have the power to submit the names of persons, not necessarily graduates, to the Crown, to fill a proportion of places on the Senate, on two grounds. First, they believed, drawing on colonial experience, that 'nominated and elected functionaries have not been found to work well together.' Secondly, they argued that the University was mainly supported by the State, and that 'The Minister is therefore responsible for the proper application of the money, and is in duty bound to select the fittest persons to form the governing body.' However, the committee believed

that the Senate would derive advantage from the presence of Graduates who have had the experience of the University examinations and who are intimately acquainted with the feelings of their own body. We believe also that the prospect of a seat in the Senate, to be obtained by honourable exertion, would be a useful stimulus both to our Graduates and to our Undergraduates.

And they went on to recommend 'the propriety of the Crown from time to time selecting Graduates to fill vacancies in the Senate, and of adding to the Senate three Graduates forthwith.'

These points, taken together with one or two specific procedural suggestions, completed a report which, its authors claimed,

would connect the Graduates permanently with the University, would constitute them an integral part of the Corporate body with some functions, honourable, though not extensive; would enable them twice in every year to express all their opinions and all their wishes on every subject connected with its management; would render their concurrence in every modification of its Charter necessary; would enable their opinion to be taken as to every other matter which the Senate would think it right to submit to them; and probably would be a further step towards their obtaining a parliamentary franchise.

The Senate received the report on 16 June 1852, and deferred consideration of it until 'a day to be fixed by the Chancellor after the next meeting of Parliament.' Any chance of a quick decision on the recommendations of the committee were dashed by the dissolution of Parliament and the subsequent general election, held in July. The new Parliament did not assemble until November; within a month Derby's Government had fallen, and there then began Lord Aberdeen's coalition Ministry, including Lord Palmerston's tenure of the Home Office. The Senate had met on 1 December 1852; long before that time, the report of the select committee had been the cause of much further controversy.

CHAPTER 18

The Tomlinson Factor

The *Lancet* printed a very fair summary of the report of the Committee, ten days after it was presented to the Senate. The editor, after having been congratulatory about the 'liberal spirit' of the enquiry, had no doubt that the Senate would 'be prepared to entertain with equal liberality the suggestions that will assuredly be offered them, with a view to the improvement of the scheme of their Committee, and the perfection of the constitution of the Metropolitan University.'[1] Almost simultaneously, a confident Foster told Brougham that 'Our case for incorporation into the University itself, and for the Parliamentary Franchise is now so far advanced that the Graduates will probably feel justified in soliciting your Lordship's attention to the matter soon after Parliament meets.'[2]

These optimistic comments, however, did not herald any relaxation of the pressure on the Senate. The committee's proposals for the composition of Convocation were quickly regarded as unacceptable by the Graduates Committee and their supporters. Foster's tour of the northern cities during the summer of 1852, in which he pleaded for the help of Liberal MPs, was no doubt closely related to a successful campaign to arouse the indignation of the affiliated colleges: over the next few months letters from many of the colleges, written almost to a formula, gave a general blessing to the scheme recommended by the Senate committee, but demanded a wider composition for Convocation. And information about the University's relevant attitudes and actions throughout the constitutional debate was made public when, as a result of Joseph Hume's address of 15 March, the Commons authorized the printing of a substantial collection of Senate minutes and correspondence on 30 June.[3]

The Graduates Committee recorded, many months later, that they had been 'advised by many gentlemen whose opinions they respected, to accept' what the Senate committee had put forward. But those who felt that the 'permanent exclusion from Convocation of the Bachelors, as a body,' was unacceptable, carried the day. The Committee felt that, 'independently of other objections,' this matter itself compelled their 'strenuous opposition.'[4] Their formal response to the Senate was contained in a letter of 10 November 1852, and their case was supported, with an interesting slant from the viewpoint of medical reformers, by a diplomatically worded but hard-hitting leader in the *Lancet* three days later.

The *Lancet*, analysing the proposed membership of Convocation, took grave exception to the

> utter absence of any intelligible principle of selection. What can be conceived more arbitrary or more inconsistent than to take a different measure for each Faculty! *All* the Masters of Arts; *half* the Doctors of Medicine; the *fifty senior Graduates* in Law!

The leader insisted that each faculty had 'an independent right to a place in Convocation,' and while admitting that anyone who took an MA would be eligible for membership, asserted that

> To shut out half the Doctors of Medicine from entering on their own claim as such, and to tell them they may get in by a bye-way, by taking the M.A. degree, will be interpreted as a degradation to the Faculty of Medicine.

But the leader then widened the issue, very significantly for future development, by linking it with the whole question of the necessary enrolment of examinees in affiliated colleges.

> The Senate . . . have enabled a certain section of the Graduates in Medicine to graduate in Arts, and so to gain a seat in Convocation, which they deny to others. This is only one of the anomalous and unequal operations of the existing laws, and one which has already created a feeling that certain institutions are unduly favoured by the University authorities. We submit to them that the most effectual remedy would be to open the doors of the examination-rooms much more freely; to place more confidence in the efficacy of their examinations, as a proof of fitness for the degrees they confer; and to be less punctilious, or at any rate more equal, in the exaction of formal certificates.

While the Senate committee had endorsed the desirability of a parliamentary franchise for the University, the extent to which that possibility was by now receiving public attention must have added to the sense within the Senate that the demand for some decisive constitutional change, whether welcome or not, could hardly be denied. On 30 November, the day before the Senate was due to meet to discuss the committee's report, the movement in favour of enfranchising the London graduates was enhanced in status by being adopted, enthusiastically, as the responsibility of a committee chaired by James Heywood, MP, 'of the friends of the University of London,' made up of MPs, peers, other public figures, representatives of affiliated colleges and graduates.[5] This was almost certainly, in large part, the achievement of Charles James Foster's patient and persistent lobbying, and the support he drew from the leaders of the Anti-State Church Association and from the governing bodies of those affiliated colleges which catered primarily for Dissenters.

It is as well, at this point, to mention another aspect of Foster's efforts through which, by constructive collaboration with the University and with UCL, he must have garnered goodwill for the Graduates Committee. This was his careful monitoring of legislation going through Parliament in order to ensure that, through the help of friendly MPs and peers, amendments to protect or to promote the interests of the University were pressed – a technique which he took further on behalf of the Liberation Society later in the decade. So far as the University was concerned, these efforts resulted in amendments to the Militia Bill of 1852, and to the Charitable Trusts Bills of 1852 and 1853, ensuring that privileges proposed to be conferred on the older universities were extended to London. Among Foster's most helpful parliamentary collaborators was Thomas Thornely, a retired Liverpool merchant, who sat for Wolverhampton and was chairman of the Committee on Public Petitions.[6]

Burlington presided at the Senate on 1 December 1852, when the various responses to the committee's report from the Graduates Committee and the affiliated colleges were on the table. Shaw Lefevre was absent, but there were sixteen present, including almost all those who had been consistently involved in the year's previous discussions. There is no indication of basic reactions to the criticisms which had been levelled at the proposed membership of Convocation, but the fact that the Senate suffered uncertainties and misgivings may fairly be assumed from the nature of the only decision taken – which was that the minutes of the select committee's proceedings and 'all documents connected therewith,' should be laid on the table, and that the draft of a letter to the Home Secretary based on the report, should be referred to a Committee of the Whole Senate.

From December 1852 until April of 1853 there is scanty evidence on paper. The minutes of the Senate's Committee of the Whole have disappeared, but fortunately two successive versions of their draft letter to Walpole have survived; the minutes of the Senate meetings carry no mention of what was going on in connection with the proposed constitutional changes; there are no manuscripts surviving from the Graduates Committee, and even the *Lancet* had no gossip with which to regale its readers. At the end of December 1852, Lord Aberdeen replaced Lord Derby, and Lord Palmerston took over the Home Office from Spencer Walpole, but the Home Office files are barren in this context.

The only reported activity concerned the possibility of extending the parliamentary franchise to the London graduates, which was almost certainly viewed by the political world as being of more general, partisan and constitutional interest than it was seen, other than by the University community, as a matter vital to that institution's concerns. Nonetheless, it involved the leading graduates, some senators, and many university and college teachers, and must have kept up the temperature of whatever private arguments over the Convocation issue were under way.

The enfranchisement committee which had been set up on 30 November 1852 was chaired by James Heywood, MP; William Shaen was secretary, and Foster and T. Snow Beck, a medical member of the Graduates Committee, were joint honorary secretaries. In mid-March 1853, Heywood led a large deputation to Downing Street to see Aberdeen and Russell, but the latter had left town. Heywood introduced the deputation, but 'The case of the University was then explained in an able memorial read by Dr. Foster.' Among supporting speakers were Drs Billing and Roget. Aberdeen responded:

> I have no hesitation in acknowledging the very strong claims you have urged for the favourable consideration of the object you have in view; and I readily admit that the constituency afforded by the University of London is such a one as it would be most agreeable to the government to organise. You will not, perhaps, expect me to give a final answer to-day, but . . . I do, in the most sincere and warmest manner possible, assure you that the matter will be taken under the most serious consideration of the government. I do not say this as mere words of course, but I beg you to believe that such will positively be the case.[7]

Not surprisingly, with this third Prime Ministerial endorsement so strongly expressed, the deputation withdrew, in 'evident gratification.' Governmental support for enfranchisement, however, as Derby and

Disraeli had emphasized, was of no avail unless the University's graduates were incorporated in its governing body, which brings us back to the discussions of the select committee's proposals. And it is interesting, in passing, to note that whereas the Senate had asked Walpole, on taking over from Grey, whether he wanted the Senate's opinion requested by his predecessor, the procedure was not followed when Palmerston replaced Walpole. Perhaps, by then, there was an acceptance that some constitutional change was inevitable, irrespective of who presided over the Home Office.

Exactly how the Committee of the Whole proceeded is open to question, but its discussions came to be dominated by a legal opinion given by the University's counsel, Thomas Tomlinson. Tomlinson was one of the University's occasional examiners in law, and was an old friend and collaborator of Nassau Senior.[8] His first involvement in the constitutional debate came in May 1852, some two or three weeks before the select committee's report was finished, when he was asked, urgently, for his opinion on whether the unanimous or majority consent of the Senate would be required to any new Charter issued by the Crown, and whether the consent of affiliated colleges would also be needed.[9]

To this enquiry – perhaps pressed by the reluctant Senior – Tomlinson responded, in a straightforward opinion apparently generally accepted, that the existing Charter could not be revoked by prerogative act of the Crown; that a new Charter would have to be accepted or rejected in its entirety by the Senate; that a majority of those present at a Senate meeting, so long as they constituted a quorum, would be competent, but that a majority of the entire body of the Senate would be safer; and that there would be no need for the consent of affiliated colleges.[10]

But the constitutionally significant Tomlinson opinion was given on the referral of a case by the Committee of the Whole, seemingly in late February or early March 1853. Despite their importance, neither the case nor the opinion are to be found, either in the University's archives or in the Public Records. There are, however, two drafts of what the Committee of the Whole thought the Senate should report to Palmerston. They are similar in their content, save for changes made in an attempt to take some account of the problems raised by Tomlinson, whenever his opinion became available. One draft is dated 24 February 1853, and states that the Committee of the Whole were agreed upon their resolutions, the most fundamental of which was their willingness to recommend the incorporation of the graduates in the

University. This draft does not mention Tomlinson, but recommends incorporation, 'subject to the opinion of the law officers of the Crown upon the legal effects of such a change in the Charter.' The second, and probably though not necessarily, the later one, though it is undated, is headed, 'The following Draft, with a Case, has been submitted to Mr Tomlinson for his opinion as to the legal effects thereof.'[11] The text was exactly similar to the final draft approved by Senate, save for changes which were obviously inserted to specify the impact of Tomlinson's opinion.[12]

Whatever the order of events, and whenever the opinion which caused all the trouble was submitted by Tomlinson, it seems clear that a sizeable majority, if not all, of the Senate's regularly attending members, had by the beginning of 1853 come to accept that the graduates should be incorporated; and that the objections made by the Graduates Committee and the affiliated colleges to a limited membership of Convocation should be met. But the Tomlinson opinion, whenever it was given, cast a pall over the whole prospect of significant change.

Though we do not have the text of the opinion to quote from, we have a statement by a later reviewer of the case which explains that the legal difficulties which Tomlinson envisaged were

> founded mainly on two points:– 1st. That the Graduates, being the majority of the Corporate Body, cannot by any restrictive clauses be legally prevented from surrendering the University Charter, although the Senate should not consent to such surrender; and 2ndly. That collectively, or individually, they will practically have powers of intereference with the actions of the Senate, by means of legal proceedings, or otherwise, more extensive than are proposed to be vested in Convocation, and capable of being exercised otherwise than through that body.[13]

Horatio Waddington translated this, for his master, as meaning that admitting graduates into the corporate body of the University would create a situation 'fraught with danger,' (Tomlinson's words) because 'real power might eventually get into their hands by their out-voting the Senate.' Indeed, Tomlinson went so far as to recommend that, rather than establishing Convocation, it would be preferable to include 'all matriculated Members without recognizing the Graduates as a distinct body . . . thereby prevent[ing] the latter from attempting to acquire distinct powers.'[14]

But despite this advice the Senate, in their formal reply to the Home

Office – sent to Lord Palmerston on April 21 1853 – expressed their willingness (subject to a solution being found to Tomlinson's objections) to see all graduates eligible for Convocation if they had

> A standing of Five Years for Bachelors of Arts, and of Three Years for Bachelors of Medicine; of Five Years for Bachelors of Laws who have not graduated as Bachelors of Arts in this University; or the Degree of Doctor of Laws, Doctor of Medicine, or Master of Arts.

As for method of appointment, they stood by the select committee's position, but dropped the specific notion of adding three graduates to the Senate. They echoed the committee's general hope 'that the expediency of selecting Graduates in common with other duly qualified persons to act as Members of the Senate, will be favourably considered by the Secretary of State.' At the same time the Senate declared that they were prepared to recommend that the consent of Convocation should be necessary 'to give validity to the surrender or acceptance of a Charter.'

It would seem likely that the crucial Senate meeting to finalize the contents of the letter which the Chancellor sent to Lord Palmerston was held on 6 April, when an unusually large attendance of 22 was recorded. In fact the letter was only formally blessed two meetings later, on 20 April, when attendance was down to 13, and it was printed in the minutes of that session. It is probable that at the earlier, larger meeting, the Senate had to face the desire of a significant majority to agree the offer worked out in the Committee of the Whole, but also to acknowledge the existence of Tomlinson's legal view that there was real danger in incorporating the graduates.

With no recorded debate, and no divisions, one must assume that all present felt it best to declare their willingness to find an accommodation with the graduates, but to hedge it with the legal problem posed by Tomlinson. The result was a somewhat odd formulation, and two crucial extracts are necessary in order to make subsequent controversy more easily understood:

> The Senate were prepared to recommend 'that the Graduates be admitted into the Corporate Body of the University, as a titular honour; but that no power of interfering with the measures of the Senate be granted to the Graduates so admitted into the Corporate Body, except such as are hereafter granted to them when acting in Convocation.' and the Senate are prevented from making such recommendation only by the Opinion of Mr Tomlinson, which

raises various doubts of a legal character as to the safety of such
a course. . . .

Had the Senate ventured to recommend admission of the Graduates
into the Corporation, they would also have recommended that the
consent of Convocation should be necessary to give validity to the
surrender or acceptance of a Charter. But as, in consequence of Mr
Tomlinson's opinion that such an admission would be fraught with
danger, they do not venture to make the former recommendation,
they think that the latter would be inoperative, and therefore refrain
from making it.

In all probability, there were many fellows who thought the legal
obstacle was bound to be overcome, while any remaining, outright
opponents of the creation of Convocation may have been confident that
Tomlinson's Opinion made such creation impossible. Thus there was
probable unanimity in forwarding the apparently vulnerable scheme to
Palmerston, explaining that they (or at least a majority of them) would
have liked to have recommended incorporation but were prevented from
doing so:

The Senate transmit . . . herewith the Case referred to Mr Tomlinson,
and his Opinion thereon. They trust that the Law Officers of the
Crown may be instructed to consider how far the danger apprehended
by Mr Tomlinson can be guarded against by adequate provisions in a
new Charter.

The response of the graduates and their allies to the Senate's suggestions
and doubts was immediate and aggressive. They must have had instant
access to the text of Burlington's letter to Palmerston, and within days
had requested from Rothman copies of the case submitted to Tomlinson
and his opinion on it.[15] That request was quite quickly refused,
whereupon the graduates sent the correspondence directly to the Home
Secretary, pressing him to do for them what the Senate was unwilling to
do. They also asked Palmerston not to take any action on the Senate's
recommendations until he could consider the results of the annual general meeting of the graduates, which was due to be held on 3 May.[16]
    It is as well to mention that this stage in the constitutional negotiations
coincided not only with the graduates' annual meeting, but also with the
beginning of an important devlopment in their long struggle to gain the
same priviliges in respect of medical practice as was enjoyed by graduates of Oxbridge. That development will be treated in the following

chapter. But the juxtaposition of these three strands in the relations between the Senate, the Home Office and the graduates meant that, in May 1853, the graduates had a very full agenda. At their AGM, which was held on a day when the weather was poor and attendance therefore restricted, the members present played their hand coolly and judiciously.

On the question of appointments to the Senate, the graduates gave ground, graciously and cleverly:

> although the Graduates cannot but think that a voice in the nomination of the Senate should on principle, and might with advantage, be entrusted to them – especially remembering that the affairs of Oxford and Cambridge are entrusted to their own Graduates exclusively – yet, if upon further advice the Senate should adhere to the views expressed in their letter to the Secretary of State, this meeting authorise their Committee not to press that portion of their claim as part of the present arrangements.

But on the Tomlinson problem, the Graduates Committee were diplomatically firm. They told their members that,

> As at present advised,they are aware of no legal difficulties, but such as are incident to every corporate body in the kingdom, and against which the Senate will be still, as now, protected by the Parliamentary resonsibility of the Secretary of State. And they cannot without the most clear evidence that your incorporation in to the University will endanger its well-being, recommend you to abandon this part of your claim . . . Your Committee cordially ackowledge the evident desire of the Senate to place you as nearly in the position of a constituent part of the University as your non-admission admits of; but assuming that the scheme of the Senate can be made practically to work, or is secure of permanence, you will still, as now, be dependent for your influence on moral considerations only, and will be impeded in its exercise by restrictions from which you are now free. Moreover, the main objection of Lord Derby to investing you with the elective franchise will be left not only unremoved, but perpetuated.[17]

The resolutions of the AGM were sent to Palmerston on 9 May, and the next day Robert Barnes, MD, wrote to the editor of the *Lancet*, enclosing the full text of Burlington's letter to Palmerston, and requesting its insertion in the journal, 'in order to make the report of the Graduates' Committee and the resolutions passed by the graduates at their general meeting, which was printed in the last *Lancet*, intelligible.'

Wakley duly obliged, and towards the end of May added a supportive and typically scornful leading article, accusing the Senate of giving vent 'to mysterious apprehensions – a vague dread, an ominous foreboding of something terrible to the future destinies of the University, should they yield to their own earnest desire to admit the graduates into the corporate body.'[18]

Meanwhile, the hand of Foster can be sensed in the manipulation of the affiliated colleges: from late May until mid-July, at least twenty-five colleges, led by UCL, requested copies of Tomlinson's case and opinion – requests very efficiently made available to the Senate and to the Home Secretary.[19]

Palmerston pushed the Tomlinson case and opinion to the law officers on 27 May.[20] A week before, he had told the graduates that he did not feel 'justified in furnishing copies of this case and opinion without the permission of the Senate,' but by the end of the month he had apparently asked Burlington how the Senate was intending to respond to the agitation, though his letter has not survived. The Senate gave way to the pressure to the extent of releasing copies of the case which they had put to Tomlinson, in mid-June, but the Chancellor reported to Palmerston that they objected to the idea of 'rendering public the professional opinions of the Counsel whom they consult.'[21]

By the end of June, therefore, all channels seemed to be closed except legal ones, and the graduates had recourse to their own counsel, the young Irish barrister James Shaw Willes, who was soon to be raised to the Bench. His opinion was not made available until the autumn. The law officers had completed their work by 31 August, however, and were the first to offer a way around Tomlinson's view. The Solicitor General was Richard Bethell, who had been prominent in the reforms at the Inns of Court which brought about equal treatment for all graduates. He and the Attorney General, A.E. Cockburn, reported that:

We concur with Mr Tomlinson in the opinion he has expressed as to the consequences of an unqualified admission of the graduates as Corporators, but we are of opinion that if it be deemed right to preserve to the Senate any special exclusive powers, such reservation may be effected by provisions to be inserted for that purpose in any new Charter; at the same time we must observe that it would be repugnant to the nature of a corporation to vest the whole authority in the Senate, leaving to the graduates the name only but none of the ordinary functions of corporators.[22]

Palmerston sent the law officers' opinion to Burlington on 14 September, without comment. There had been no response by the time that Willes' opinion was made freely available to all parties. That opinion was dated 23 August, and was quickly submitted to the Senate, but after several weeks' delay, the graduates were told by Rothman in November that

> as the Senate originally considered this matter by desire of the Secretary of State, and have reported their opinion to him, they can hardly with propriety reconsider the matter, except by the desire of the same authority. Nor is it clear what it is the Senate is asked to reconsider. The only difficulties suggested are of a purely legal character, and it is clear that *they* cannot be decided *here*.[23]

On receiving this, Foster wasted no time and at once wrote directly to Palmerston, enclosing the opinion of Willes and copies of correspondence with Rothman. He asked the Home Secretary to refer all this material to the Senate,

> in order that the [Graduates'] Committee may become informed by your Lordship's kindness, whether the Senate still entertain objections to the incorporation of the Graduates into the University and whether their objections are of a character such as to be susceptible of removal.[24]

Willes was outspokenly dismissive of the dangers seen by Tomlinson. Such dangers, he remarked, 'have been survived by Oxford and Cambridge,' and he pointed out that 'it would require the concurrence of the Crown to give effect to the apprehended contumacity of the Graduates.' He regarded the dangers as 'practically . . . so remote, that they ought not to weigh a feather in determining the really important questions under consideration.'[25]

It is certain that Palmerston had his mind on far more pressing problems than those facing the University of London, but it is just possible that he was becoming impatiently aware of being made the only channel of communication between the contending parties. He minuted to Waddington: 'What is the Specific Question to be reconsidered?' to which the Secretary replied: 'Whether the Graduates can be admitted with the Body Corporate under such restrictions as will obviate the dangers which are apprehended by the Counsel.' To this, Palmerston responded: 'Let me have memo stating shortly the arguments both ways.'[26]

It may be that Horatio Waddington, who had watched the tortuous development of the argument about convocation from the beginning of the graduates' campaign, now saw his chance to push for a settlement. He wrote a formal memorandum for Palmerston, which simply rehearsed the opinions of Tomlinson, the law officers and Willes. But on the back of it he scribbled a message to his minister of a more unbuttoned nature.

> I am afraid this Memo will not throw much light upon the subject. The truth is, I believe, that the Senate do not wish to have the Graduates introduced into the Corporate Body as Members, and have therefore caught at a legal crotchet suggested by their Counsel, which ought to go for very little – there may be more substantial objections, for anything that I know. But it seems to me that if it is desirable to admit the Graduates upon general grounds, there would be no great difficulty in framing the new Charter so as to avoid the dangers pointed out by Mr Tomlinson.

Palmerston noted, rather ambiguously, on 4 December, 'Let this be done,' and Waddington drafted a letter which, enclosing Willes' opinion, was sent to Burlington with the suggestion

> that it may be desirable that [the Senate] should reconsider the question of the admission of the Graduates, with the assistance of the legal opinions of the Law Officers of the Crown, Mr Tomlinson and Mr Willes from which, when taken together, it appears to Lord Palmerston not impossible that a satisfactory solution of the difficulties which have presented themselves may be derived.[27]

In mid-December 1853 Palmerston offered his resignation as a result of disagreement over further franchise reform, and did not withdraw the offer until 24 December. He was, to put it mildly, unenthusiastic about any sizeable extension of the right to vote, but it is unlikely that his distaste would have embraced the modest proposals to add one or two seats in the House of Commons for representatives of the graduates of London and the Scottish universities, had that question been an isolated measure. Within their greater schemes, however, such a proposal was being considered seriously, in November and December 1853, by Aberdeen and Russell, and the Prime Minister told Russell that in 'granting the franchise to the London University it was held to be essential that the graduates should form part of the governing body.' Russell and Graham must have been of the opinion that such incorporation was a foregone conclusion, because in the Reform Bill which they introduced in the Commons in mid-February 1854 it was provided that 'In all future Parliaments the University of London shall return one member to serve in Parliament,' and that those graduates entitled to vote would be the same as those who had been accepted by the Senate for membership of Convocation in the latest of their recommendations.

The reformers were divided, however, about the Scottish universities. Russell, pressed by the Duke of Argyll, wanted to include them, but Aberdeen felt they would be 'a poor constituency since [their graduates] had no continuing connection with their universities.' Argyll declared 'that he could not show his face north of the Tweed if representation was given to London but not to the Scottish Universities.' His resentment foreshadowed his opposition, only a few months later, to the extension of medical privileges to London graduates. In any event, the struggles over representation were overtaken by the outbreak of the Crimean War, late in February. The bill of Russell and Graham was withdrawn: the enfranchisement of the graduates of the University of London was not to be achieved until 1869.[28]

The Senate addressed themselves to Palmerston's concerns about graduate incorporation at the beginning of February 1854. A few days before the Senate met, Warburton reminded Overstone that neither of Palmerston's letters, sent in the previous September and November, calling attention to the legal opinions at issue, had been answered. Warburton may have assessed the internal situation of the Senate and decided that there was little hope of agreement. He had a draft ready for discussion, and his letter to Overstone, part of which has been quoted earlier, but can stand repetition in this context, contained phrases which were incorporated in the document which was sent to Palmerston after the meeting of 8 February. Warburton wrote:

consideration of the two [letters from Palmerston] makes me think that there is only one course open to the Senate; and that is to request that the whole matter be referred to Her Majesty's Government.

Having to administer not corporate funds, but Public monies for Public objects, we can not properly be parties, without the entire approbation of the Government, to give other parties a control over those Monies. We must desire Lord Palmerston to refer the matter to the Government, and say that before taking the important step of petitioning the Crown for a New Charter, there must be complete understanding between the Senate and Government upon what principle the future Constitution of the University is to be based.[29]

The minutes of the meeting on 8 February include the long reply which was to be sent to the Home Secretary, preceded by the bleak statement that 'After a discussion in which various Amendments were proposed, of which some were carried, the draft' was adopted. The Vice-Chancellor was in the chair, and the other ten present were Billing, Faraday, Grote, Hammick, Hodgkin, Kiernan, Lewis, Overstone, Roget and Warburton.

Only one specific legal point was raised. The Senate stated that in the case they had submitted to Tomlinson they expressed willingness

> to assent to the Admission of the Graduates into the Corporate Body, if its effect would be merely to alter the name of the Corporate Body, but not to give the Graduates, either collectively or individually, any power of interfering with the acts of the Senate. But it appears to be the opinion of the Law Officers of the Crown, that to admit the Graduates into the Corporate Body, but to restrict their powers in the way the Senate were prepared to recommend, would be to give to the University a Constitution repugnant to the nature of a Corporation.

But having raised this point, the rest of the letter represents a comprehensive abandonment of hope that the Senate could make any further progress, and an appeal to the Government to settle the University's destiny.

> As the questions which have been recently raised respecting the University do not concern merely its ordinary administration, but extend to its entire reconstitution, and to the greater or less participation of some class or other of New Corporators in the management of its affairs, the Senate trust Your Lordship will agree with them in thinking that it is expedient to refer the whole matter now pending to the consideration of Her Majesty's Government, in order that the Senate, in any further consultations thereupon, may have the advantage of the deliberate opinion of the Government what should be the future Constitution of this University.
>
> Her Majesty's Government may think it advisable, either that the University should remain on its present footing, or that, with the consent of the existing Corporation, the Constitution should be

amended. Should Her Majesty's Government incline to the latter alternative, the Senate would think it essential, before they took the important and decisive step of petitioning the Crown for a new Charter of Incorporation, that there should be a clear understanding between the Senate on the one hand and Her Majesty's Government on the other, what are the principles on which the future Constitution of the University should be based.

In what manner this mutual explanation should be given and received, the Senate must leave to the discretion of Your Lordship. Whatever suggestions, if any, Her Majesty's Government may think proper to make, will receive from the Senate their most respectful and attentive consideration.

This letter was sent on 10 February 1854; it was received on the following day, but seems to have been lost, almost immediately, within the Home Office; a copy would not reach the then Home Secretary – Sir George Grey, Palmerston's successor in that post – until the middle of 1855. When Shaen wrote to the Home Office on 15 March 1854 pressing for a settlement to be imposed and sending printed comments issued by the Graduates Committee, Palmerston asked how the matter stood, and was apparently informed by his officials that no reply to his letters of September and November 1853 had been received from Burlington. Palmerston then asked that Burlington be reminded, and a letter went off to the Chancellor on 28 March.[30] There is nothing to show if the Chancellor expressed justifiable indignation. More than a year later he simply recorded the loss of the letter, without comment.[31] In 1854, the files of all parties are blank on the constitutional issue for months thereafter, save for one rather odd episode.

On 22 July, Henry Fitzroy, parliamentary under-secretary at the Home Office, wrote to Rothman asking for a full set of minutes and papers, concerning the University's constitutional affairs since 1852, in continuation of the return made in that year in response to the request by Joseph Hume. The new demand was to meet an order of the House of Commons of 20 July. A month later, Rothman despatched a bundle of papers to Fitzroy, 'agreeably to the desire of Lord Palmerston expressed in your letter of 22nd ultimo.' But he also enclosed a private letter, explaining to Fitzroy that the bundle included the case which the Senate had sent to Tomlinson in May 1852 and Tomlinson's opinion on it. Rothman assured Fitzroy that there was nothing in that case and opinion which the Senate would object to being made public, but felt that 'there is some reason to apprehend that such a publication might be drawn into an objectionable precedent, and quoted as inconsistent with the refusal of the Senate to communicate the other opinion of Mr Tomlinson,' which had proved so controversial.

Fitzroy handed the matter over to his chief, asking 'Is the Opinion referred to . . . to be added to the return to the House of Commons.' It was not until 16 December that Palmerston minuted, '*not* to be laid before Parliament.' The outcome was rather strange. Not only did the opinion not appear, but nor did any document, and there is no entry in the Journal of the House of Commons, or in Hansard, referring to an order of 20 July, even though references to it are to be found in the Home Office documents and in the Senate's minutes. It can only be assumed that without the Tomlinson opinion there was so little of significance that Palmerston's veto forced a dropping of the whole exercise and a deletion of any record of the order.[32]

In the middle months of 1854, medical issues dominated the University's relations with Parliament and Government; constitutional debate was effectively put aside until 1855. But before turning to the medical story, it is as well to quote Waddington's undated memorandum, scribbled on the back of the letter which the Vice-Chancellor sent to Palmerston on 10 February, and from which the long extracts quoted above are taken:

> It seems clear from this that the existing Corporation (consisting of Chancellor, Vice-Chancellor and Fellows) will make no specific proposal themselves – perhaps Sir James Graham (who is a member of the Senate) may have given his attention to the subject; the difficulty is to admit the Graduates (now a very numerous body) without too much diminishing the power of the Senate.[33]

CHAPTER 19

Medical Equality

As we saw in Chapter 15, Sir George Grey decided, when he was Home Secretary in 1849, to withdraw a medical bill which had been introduced that session by the Lord Advocate. His decision was taken on various grounds, but his intimation that no future bill would be supported by the Government unless it placed 'the London Medical Graduates upon the same footing with those of the other universities,' no doubt helped to discourage any early attempt by the medical corporations to seek further legislative change.[1] It was not until 1853 and 1854 that new proposals were put forward, and it was in part as a response to them that the London graduates succeeded in their sponsorship of a bill which gave them virtual equality with the graduates of Oxford and Cambridge. Their bill reached the Statute Book in August 1854,[2] but it had to survive some weeks of complex and rather hair-raising parliamentary manoeuvres before scraping through all its stages.

In a wider context than the immediate and limited concerns of the London graduates, the essential nature of the problem of establishing medical equality was described succinctly by the Duke of Argyll. It was, he said, 'a subject of much controversy in the medical profession, namely, whether the licence for general practice should be given by the old licensing bodies, or whether the University degrees should carry with them the right to private practice.'[3] But that definition extended the matter to universities other than London, whereas the London graduates (and the Senate) saw their narrower demand as justified, primarily, by the promises given by Government in 1835 and honoured by Grey in 1849. As the graduates' consistent champion, Wakley's *Lancet*, put it:

It is clear that the fulfilment of this promise is not a medical question. The question is, whether faith shall or shall not be kept with those classes who are excluded from participating in the benefits conferred by Oxford and Cambridge. That this plighted faith ought to be kept is a principle that has been again and again asserted by Parliament. By a series of enactments, the several privileges pertaining to the degrees in Arts and Laws granted by Oxford and Cambridge have been formally given to the corresponding degrees of the University of London. The time has come when it is considered necessary to extend the similar rights to the degrees in medicine. Upon what principle can this claim - the last instalment of the debt contracted – be resisted? Why should the Faculty of Medicine alone be slighted?[4]

During 1853 the Provincial Medical and Surgical Association, the forerunner of the British Medical Association, and the College of Physicians both tried to attract Palmerston's support for new legislation. The Association's draft bill, largely the work of Sir Charles Hastings, the founder of the Association, was quickly condemned by the Senate and by UCL as failing to recognize the University of London. The UCL Council made good use of two of their prominent ministerial members, Graham, in the Cabinet as First Lord of the Admiralty, and Edward Strutt (later Lord Belper), who was Chancellor of the Duchy of Lancaster until June 1854. The Council authorized a deputation to the Home Secretary which included two leading graduates – Frederick John Wood (by now a member of the Council) and John Storrar. The Senate also asked, formally, that a deputation be received to oppose a proposed new Charter for the College of Physicians, and Rothman wrote privately to Waddington 'expressing the hope that Lord Palmerston will not introduce any bill on the subject . . . before he has heard the observations of the Senate.' Whatever weight these objections carried, Lord Palmerston, doubtless reflecting on the futility of previous attempts to achieve any agreed solutions, told the House of Commons early in June that 'the present condition of the medical profession required considerable regulation and amendment: it was, in fact, a labyrinth and a chaos.' By the beginning of August, Strutt could tell the UCL Council that the Home Secretary had abandoned the projects of both the Association and the College.[5]

Before the summer recess of 1853 began, Wood told the UCL Council that the London graduates were themselves preparing a bill to give them the same rights of practice as were enjoyed by Oxbridge men.[6] That bill was not introduced into the House of Commons until 9 May, 1854, three months after a trio of Liberal MPs – John Brady, a doctor who sat for Leitrim, Thomas Phinn and Danby Seymour, respectively Members for Bath and Poole – had introduced a Bill for the Registration of Medical Practitioners – a Bill quickly abandoned in favour of a second version which enjoyed the support of a fourth

Liberal Member, Montague Chambers, representing Greenwich. Both versions ignored the University of London.

In the middle of March the Senate directed their lawyers to 'renew the Caveats against the granting of any Charter or Letters Patent to the Royal College of Physicians,' and, late in April, medical members of the Senate were invited to attend a conference called by the Physicians to discuss the bill proposed by the Provincial Medical and Surgical Asociation. Whatever discussions took place apparently made no impact on the content of the bill, which was given a second reading, on the day immediately before the London graduates' bill was introduced. The Registration Bill, however, received so much criticism that its committee stage was deferred for six months, thereby effectively killing it. Its demise ensured that the debates on the London graduates' bill were reflective of the wranglings over the failings and loss of the more extensive measure which had been shelved.[7]

The graduates' bill was before Parliament from May until August. It is time to look at its uneasy progress.

We have no records of the Graduates Committee, and the Senate's papers are singularly uncommunicative about the passage of this legislation. The Hansard record provides the bulk of the story. It is hard to believe that the Senate could have been anything but pleased with the outcome, but there is evidence of only one piece of formal encouragement being offered by them. Individuals, however, certainly made important contributions. The Chancellor at one stage made a special journey, at the request of the Graduates Committee, in order to be present at a crucial vote,[8] and Lord Monteagle, appropriately enough in view of his efforts nearly twenty years earlier, guided the bill through the Lords and played a significant role.

The one formal Senate intervention occurred in mid June, on the motion of Thomas Hodgkin, two weeks after the first major opposition had been voiced in the House of Commons. The Vice-Chancellor was asked to write in favour of the bill to the Home Secretary. Such a letter, strong and comprehensive enough, but without any mention of the fact that the bill was sponsored by the graduates, was addressed to Palmerston, and Monteagle agreed to present it to him.[9]

Apart from the fundamental demand for equality with Oxbridge which it represented, there was a very specific and immediate practical need to be met by the bill. Recent legislation on vaccination and lunacy had, inadvertently, made London medical graduates liable to misdemeanour charges if they signed certificates drawn up under the new Acts. Some indemnity provision was required urgently.[10]

The bill, as originally drafted, was brief and straightforward. It provided that London graduates 'be entitled to practice Physic, including surgery, in the same manner as Graduates of the Universities of Oxford and Cambridge,' and indemnified London graduates against charges brought under the Lunacy and Vaccination Acts. Its sponsors were two established friends of the graduates, James Bell and Thomas Thornely, and it came up for second reading on 24 May, then being committed to the whole House, without debate. It was when it reached committee on 29 May that opposition to it was voiced.

In all the bickering which followed, it is fair to say that no animus was expressed against the University of London – indeed much that was said was complimentary. The Colleges of Physicians and Surgeons were simply opposed to any reduction of their monopoly. Both objected, and Palmerston was lobbied heavily by their presidents. Only the Surgeons won a concession, however. Despite a strong argument in the Vice-Chancellor's letter, Palmerston claimed that his initial opposition to the bill would be removed by the acceptance of

a change in the wording . . . which would have the effect of merely carrying out the understanding that he conceived had been come to between the supporters and opposers of the Bill . . . the purpose of which would be to exclude the surgical practice and confine the privilege to be given to the London University to medical practice, in the same manner as practically the degrees of Oxford and Cambridge were confined.

As a result, the words 'including Surgery,' were struck out of the original text.[11] Clearly, it was felt that this was not, for either the University or the graduates, a matter for which the acceptance of the bill should be jeopardized.

There were those, of whom Spencer Walpole was perhaps the most senior and best informed, who objected to the bill not because of its specific content, but because they feared that its acceptance would detract from and make more difficult the introduction and passage of comprehensive legislation to reform the whole of the medical profession. The discontent with the failure of the Registration Bill no doubt intensified this feeling, and it is interesting that an attempt to bring in another bill on medical reform – by two more Liberal MPs, E.H.J. Crawfurd, sitting for Ayr, and Lord Dudley Stuart, eighth son of the Marquis of Bute, who was Member for Marylebone – was defeated on 7 July, only five days before the London bill was debated seriously in committee, by 70 votes to 9.[12]

The most threatening opposition, however, came from other universities, who felt excluded from the extension of privilege which the bill offered to London. Durham at first received a sympathetic hearing, and an amendment was agreed during the committee session on 12 July which gave the Oxbridge privileges to both London and Durham. But in the Lords, Brougham objected strongly, claiming that 'Durham included no hospital practice in its requirements' and was 'totally unfitted for the teaching of medicine.'[13] At committee stage in the Lords, Durham was struck out. A far more dangerous challenge came from Scotland and Ireland.

The backstage negotiations which must have gone on during the gap of six weeks between the second reading of the bill, on 24 May, and its being debated in committee on 12 July are maddeningly undocumented. But that some fierce bargaining went on may be assumed, even allowing for the pressures of parliamentary time, from the fact that committee consideration was deferred on no less than four occasions, and not until 24 June was the second version, with the inclusion of surgery dropped, recommitted. Even so, almost three more weeks elapsed before there was serious debate.

By 12 July it must have been clear that Palmerston was not willing to give way to the argument of the Scottish universities and Dublin that the London bill should be delayed in order that a more general measure could be framed to take account of their wishes. Its opponents, however, were well prepared to do battle. In the Commons the first attack, on 12 July, came from E.P. Bouverie, MP for Kilmarnock, and Charles Cowan, Member for Edinburgh – both Liberals – who forced a division on going into committee, but lost it by 90 to 26. In the following debate, after Palmerston had argued against holding up the bill, a second division, on a motion that the chairman should report progress, was defeated by 109 to 50. The bill survived another motion, by William Michell, MP for Bodmin: he and John Brady were the only medical men in the House. Michell's motion provided that the London graduates should be enabled to practise not only anywhere in England outside the area seven miles around London, which was the privilege enjoyed by Oxbridge graduates, but also in the London area, thus destroying the College of Physicians' monopoly there. This was objected to on the same grounds as had been applied to Scotland and

Ireland – that it would open up too much debate about wider matters of medical reform – and was defeated by 147 to 5.[14]

The Celtic members, however, were not to be easily repulsed, despite the relatively heavy defeats they had suffered. On the following day, Lieutenant Colonel Francis Plunkett Dunne, described as 'a very liberal conservative,' who sat for Portarlington; and Colonel James Hunter Blair, Conservative MP for Ayrshire, joined with Charles Cowan to introduce a Medical Graduates (Ireland and Scotland) Bill, identical in form and wording to the London Graduates Bill, save for the difference that the entitlement to practise Physic, in the same manner as Oxford and Cambridge graduates, should be enjoyed by the graduates of the universities of Ireland and Scotland. The new bill was given a second reading without debate on 18 July, but four days later its third reading debate was adjourned by a vote of 82–43, and not resumed until early August.[15]

The London bill received its third reading, without debate, on 20 July, and was passed to the Lords. It now entered its most crucial stage, and that doubt of its success was felt quite strongly can be inferred from a letter which Rothman sent to an Irish enquirer at this time. 'I believe,' he wrote, 'that the Bill is not likely to pass; at all events not this session.'[16]

In the Lords, Monteagle took charge of the bill, thus representing a welcome combination of senatorial and graduate effort. When the second reading took place on 25 July, he was aware of petitions against the bill by the Royal Colleges of Physicians and Surgeons of Edinburgh, the Faculty and Physicians of Glasgow, and the President of King's and Queen's College of Physicians in Ireland. In addition, much to his chagrin, he had to listen to strong objections from the Lord Privy Seal the Duke of Argyll, a champion of the Scottish universities, already Chancellor of St Andrews's and soon to be Rector of Glasgow. Argyll was backed by Lord Campbell, and also, rather equivocally, by Brougham who, despite his objections to the inclusion of Durham, was generally sympathetic to Argyll's views. However, there was no division, and the second reading was agreed.

Monteagle, recognizing that the Bill was under serious threat, was much upset, and turned for help to Lord John Russell, who had recently become Lord President of the Council. His appeal may well have been particularly important, and it is worth quoting at some length. He began by rehearsing the essential background and by insisting on the limited nature of the bill's objectives. He then went on:

The Bill was introduced and was submitted to the Home Office. Palmerston suggested an amendment subject to which he gave his approval and support to the Bill. In the Committee his amendment was made. *He shortly redeemed his engagement.* He spoke strongly for the bill. There were three divisions. In *all* three *you and he* together with *every member of the Government present* and many of the opposition voted in each of those three divisions. So did Goulburn, representing *Cambridge*, and George A. Hamilton and Napier a member for *Trinity College Cambridge* [*sic* Hamilton and Napier, both Conservatives, represented Dublin University]. The last division taken was 147 to 5.

The bill is now in the Lords and was read a second time yesterday evening. But to my great surprise and regret this bill which was actually settled with the Home Office and supported by the Government, is opposed by the Privy Seal acting apparently on behalf of the Government. It is true the Duke of Argyll was not, like all the members of Melbourne's Government, a founder of the University of London and party to the engagement then made, nor perhaps was he aware of what had taken place this year in the Commons and of your vote Palmerston's Molesworth [*sic*], and those of all the subordinate members of the Government including your two *Whips*.

I have written to Lord Aberdeen on the subject, as he was out of town. But to you who recollect the foundation of the University and who as a member of the Cabinet who founded it – and one who voted three times in one night this year in favour of the bill – and one who proposed in the Reform Bill to give our University a Parliamentary Representation, as *President of the Council* too I appeal to you as one interested in securing perfect equality to our graduates as compared with their fellows at Oxford and Cambridge, I appeal fearlessly. Do not let us be thrown over, from an ignorance of all that has passed. It is a jealousy of the Scotch Colleges which is stated. *Our Bill takes no one privilege from them. It leaves them just where we found them.*[17]

This spluttering outburst of indignation may have helped his cause, but not immediately. On 28 July, in committee, Monteagle had to move for a further delay, which was agreed to after more firm objection from Argyll, who claimed that the bill 'prejudiced the great question of medical reform, and did so in order to favour the University of London, to the exclusion and injury of other and older universities.' Lansdowne, in the Cabinet without portfolio, came to Monteagle's aid, but clearly the eventual outcome was doubtfully balanced. It was not until 1 August that the motion to go into committee was debated and, after objections by Argyll, and by no less a personage than Lord Derby, the two being joined by Lords Campbell, Galloway and Wynford, was carried by only 17 votes to 15. Unfortunately, there is no division list extant.[18] The objectors then apparently gave up: there was no further debate, the proposed inclusion of Durham was dropped, and the bill went on to third reading.

Two days afterwards, in the Commons, Palmerston persuaded Colonel Dunne to drop his Medical Graduates (Scotland and Ireland) Bill when its third reading debate was resumed, promising that the Government would make an enquiry into the problem in the following session.[19] On 4 August the Lords gave the London bill its third reading, without debate, and on 9 August the Commons accepted the Lords' amendments after a single objection from a discontented supporter of Durham. The Royal Assent came on 11 August.

The victory of 1854 removed the last major, formal distinction between London and Oxbridge graduates, save for the absence of degrees in ecclesiastical studies from the London curriculum. In the medical field, it also cleared out of the way a concern which had almost certainly taken precedence, in the minds of many of the London people, over considerations of the future position of the University in the wider organization of the medical profession. The debate over that complex subject now intensified, and the period from 1855 to 1858 saw a succession of conflicting legislative proposals whose detailed experience would require a specialist analysis of some length.[20] The Senate, and doubtless the Graduates' Committee, kept sharp eyes on relevant developments, but those developments, leading to the solution represented by the Medical Act of 1858, which set up the General Medical Council, do not seem to have caused any internal University argument. All the universities were mainly concerned to protect their independence of the medical corporations and the eligibility of their graduates to practise. The biggest relevant controversy within London University was to erupt after the establishment of both Convocation and the General Medical Council, and centred on the Senate's nomination of Dr Storrar as the University's representative on the Council, without prior consultation of Convocation. But that is a story told elsewhere.[21]

CHAPTER 20

The Insistence of Sir George Grey

When the leaders of the graduates reported to their members on the year 1854, they admitted that during the later part of the parliamentary session they had 'deemed it advisable to direct their efforts mainly to secure the passing of the University of London Medical Graduates Bill.' And while this understandable preoccupation took the pressure off the constitutional arguments about the Tomlinson opinion, subsequent events in the autumn of 1854 and the early days of 1855 ensured that little or no progress was made, even after the medical problem had been surmounted. For this was the period when the discontents of the Crimean War ensured that little ministerial time was available for anything else, and when the internal politics of the Government led to the fall of Aberdeen and the succession of Palmerston as Prime Minister, in February 1855. As the Graduates' Committee admitted, 'the incompleteness of the arrangements of the ministry, and the general aspect of public affairs, rendered it impossible to act upon the Government with any useful result, either by private representation or parliamentary pressure.'[1]

It was not until late in March 1855 that the graduates approached the Home Office and asked that the new Secretary of State receive a deputation to discuss the apparent *impasse* which had been reached a full twelve months earlier. Sir George Grey was then told that there had been no response from the University; he gave instructions that the Chancellor should be contacted, and that a deputation would be received after he had the University's response.[2] No doubt to considerable official embarrassment, Burlington wrote to Grey a month afterwards, enclosing a copy of the Vice-Chancellor's long letter of 10 February 1854, together with the restrained comment that 'It appears from a private note from Mr Waddington to the Registrar dated 3 April 1854, that the letter of the Senate . . . had been received at the Home Office on 11 February preceding.'[3]

Both Grey and Waddington were no strangers to the constitutional affairs of the University of London, but both found it hard to give their full, immediate attention to them. Grey asked Waddington for 'his opinion on the course which ought to be taken in this matter,' and thought it would be as well if Waddington conferred 'with Mr Lefevre upon it.'[4] The Vice-Chancellor, now Clerk of the Parliaments and a very busy, senior public servant, was much involved with Grey through his membership of the Church Estates Commission and other enquiries, and was held in high regard by the Home Secretary.[5] Waddington sent him papers relating to University business at the beginning of June, but admitted to Grey that he had not had time to consider 'this troublesome question so as to become sufficiently master of it to discuss it usefully with Lefevre.' Burlington assured Grey, towards the end of May, that the Senate would be happy to appoint a deputation if he wished to meet them: but there was no response.[6] Grey, meanwhile, had found a new informant.

Sir William Clay, 1st Bt, was a merchant and shipowner of 'advanced radical views', who sat for Tower Hamlets from 1832 until 1857. There is no evidence of his having any close connection with the University of London or with the Graduates Committee, and no obvious explanation why Grey turned to him, as he apparently did, for some inside information and advice. But there was certainly familiarity and shared experience between the two men: both were 1832 entrants to Parliament, and both had been junior ministers in the later years of Melbourne's administration. Clay was to be a major force in the attempts to abolish Church rates, and later evidence suggests that he came well within Foster's network.[7]

On 1 June 1855, from his home in Hertford Street, Mayfair, Clay sent Grey a batch of documents which he claimed would 'put you fully in possession of the existing state of the question of the re-consideration of the Charter of the London University.' He went on to give a summary and recommendations well worth reproducing:

> you will see first that the Senate are not unwilling to concede the amendment of the constitution of the University, and that the differences of opinion as to the nature of that amendment between themselves and the Graduates are but slight – but – secondly that the initiative in originating any change should be taken – they think - not by them but by the Government – substantially, that is to say - *formally* I apprehend it would be considered right that the Senate should petition the Crown – a step which they would no doubt be ready to take.
>
> It rests therefore with the Government to decide whether they will recommend to the Crown to grant the reform wished – and so patiently waited for by the Graduates. I am inclined to hope that

the Government will think it advisable to do so. In that case the best course perhaps would be (the first formal steps – namely the petition for alteration from the Senate, and the assent of the Crown, having been taken) that the Senate should discuss with a deputation from the graduates the various details which it would be necessary to consider in carrying out the principles on which they are agreed. I have reason to believe there would be no indisposition to such a proceeding on the part of the Senate – and it would relieve the Government from much trouble and difficulty.

The one point of the new Charter on which the Government would be especially called on to pronounce an opinion would be – the power of Convocation to submit to the Crown a list of persons from whom a certain portion of the future Senators should be selected – such persons however not to be necessarily graduates. There are reasons I think with which I need not trouble you – which will indeed no doubt occur to you – why this point should be conceded.[8]

The cryptic remark at the end of this letter presumably refers to the possibility of some political unpleasantness if no concession was made. Clay's views must have been communicated to Shaw Lefevre, who also must have talked with Grey before writing to him, on 16 June. The Vice-Chancellor stressed that Grey would have to make an independent judgement on the two major issues – how to solve the Tomlinson problem, and 'whether . . . a definite portion of [the Senate] should be chosen by the Crown out of a limited list selected by the Graduates.' On the Tomlinson opinion, Shaw Lefevre wished that he could join in a conference himself with Tomlinson and Willes, but felt it would not be appropriate, and he suggested that Waddington might see the two lawyers.

On the issue of representation of graduates on the Senate, Shaw Lefevre, characteristically, took a carefully balanced view. He felt that graduates as senators would be regarded as guardians of graduate interests, and this would 'in a considerable degree impede the efficient working of the Senate, who ought to look to the general interests of the public.' He admitted that the graduates were not asking to elect senators, only to present a list to the Crown from which the Crown would select. Nonetheless,

any members of the Senate thus chosen . . . would approach more nearly the character of representatives or delegates of the Graduates than if appointed by the unrestricted choice of the Crown – but the difference does not appear to me to be very great – or worthy of much contention. This, however, is only my individual opinion and I believe that the Senate think the difference of great importance.

A clear hint of the tensions now manifest is given in Shaw Lefevre's dismissal of Clay's notion that there should be a meeting of the Senate with the graduates. 'I do not think,' he told Grey, 'that at present (if ever) it would be expedient to have a discussion.'[9]

Subsequent consideration is poorly documented, but it would seem certain that the crucial decisions were made in the summer of 1855 by Grey, in conjunction with George Cornewall Lewis, by now Chancellor of the Exchequer. Though Lewis had rarely appeared at Senate, and had not attended since June 1854, he was clearly in a stronger position than Grey to understand the nuances of the situation. One has to assume that there were also some preliminary discussions with the lawyers, and there was definitely contact with Shaw Lefevre, who concurred 'in the propriety' of the draft which Lewis drew up towards the end of July, and proposed that Grey should send to the University. By mid-August 1855, Grey was instructing Waddington to prepare a letter to the Chancellor, suggesting 'for the consideration of the Senate the arrangement proposed.'[10]

Grey tackled the two outstanding problems head-on:

> as to the legal difficulty adverted to in the opinion given by Mr Tomlinson, I am prepared to advise the Crown that in the event of a new Charter being issued to the University a clause be inserted in it making the consent of the majority of the Senate necessary to the surrender of the Charter, provided that upon an examination of the law, it should appear that a clause of this nature can be made effective for its object.

> the new Charter should provide that every alternate vacancy in the Senate shall henceforth be filled up by the Crown with a graduate of the University of London, until the number of graduates in the Senate shall amount to one quarter of the whole amount, and further propose that every such graduate appointed by the Crown shall be selected from a list of five graduates to be chosen by the graduates at large.[11]

The Senate did not have this proposal before them until 7 November: if there was discussion of it, there is no record, and no action was taken. Grey's letter found its way into the leader columns of the *Lancet* on 6

January 1856, accompanied by expressions of editorial enthusiasm, and some heavy sarcasm about the Senate's fear

> lest the Graduates, being entrusted with the power of meeting in convocation, should be seized with a paroxysm of suicidal insanity, and, acting like a maniac who found a knife in his way, should, by surrendering the Charter . . . involve the Senate, themselves, and the University in perdition.

More to the immediate point, the editor hoped that the year would not close without a new Charter having been issued. It was a vain hope.

In mid-January, Foster wrote to the Home Secretary, in an attempt to hasten the production of a new Charter, asking permission for the Graduates Committee to submit to him a draft Charter based on his letter to the Chancellor of 18 August 1855. Waddington responded to the effect that it was the Senate's job to prepare a new Charter, and that the Graduates should 'place themselves in communication with the Senate.' Accordingly, Foster wrote to Rothman, enclosing the correspondence with Grey and pressing for 'the speedy settlement of this long-protracted affair.'[12]

The Senate met on 20 February and had this exchange of correspondence before them. The minutes of the meeting record no other action in that context. In their Annual Report for 1856, however, the Graduates Committee claim that, on that occasion, a motion was made to take the correspondence into consideration at an early date; that the motion was not seconded, and that the Committee's approach had not been acknowledged.[13] It is possible, though a little unlikely, that this omission from the record, if not a fiction, was the result of the sickness of the Registrar, Rothman, who was in the last few weeks of his life: he died on 28 March. But he was still signing letters up to 11 March and would, long before then, have compiled the minutes of a meeting held three weeks earlier. He may well have been under considerable strain, however, because of simultaneous pressure to deal with queries as to how the University should respond to new medical bills.

There is, in fact, nothing to confirm or deny whether the silence of the Senate on the subject of a new Charter after August 1855, and even more notably after 20 February 1856, was due, simply, to the firm insistence of all or a majority of those attending that the Government should be left to make the first move. Nor is there any hard evidence of informal consultation with the Home Office. Indeed, the internal attitudes of the Senate to constitutional matters during 1855–6 cannot be assessed with sufficient precision to make the exercise worthwhile. Meetings, throughout, continued to be attended by the same group of about a dozen men: only the choice of a new Registrar brought a bigger turn-out. But the likelihood that there was, in fact, some deep division of opinion running through that group because of the existence of particularly bitter opposition to the graduates' demands, might be inferred from Burlington's pessimistic entry in his diary for 20 February. 'A communication [was received] from the Graduates about a proposed new Charter,' he wrote, 'but nothing was done respecting it. I foresee difficulties and trouble from this affair.'

It must be assumed, therefore, that either Grey lost patience and decided, entirely on his own initiative, to present the Senate with a *fait accompli*; or that he did so after talking privately with people like Burlington, Shaw Lefevre, Warburton and, even more probably, with his Cabinet colleague George Cornewall Lewis. On 6 May a somewhat terse note was sent by Grey to Burlington:

> Referring to the letter which I addressed to Your Lordship on 18 August, 1855, on the subject of granting a new Charter to the University of London, I have the honour to inform Your Lordship that I have given directions for the Draft of a Charter to be prepared, in order that it may be submitted for the consideration of the Senate of the University.[14]

Whether or not he knew about it, Grey had chosen Presentation Day to send his letter. In the evening the graduates held their annual dinner: the Vice-Chancellor had found time to send Foster news of Grey's move, and the chairman, Robert Barnes, was able to announce, to the delight of his audience, that the Home Secretary was contemplating the preparation of 'a Draft Charter embodying those measures of reform in the constitution of the University for which the graduates had so long contended.'[15]

Any major celebration was premature. Whether there was any subsequent informal consultation involving the Senate or the Graduates Committee, there is no relevant recorded discussion or action between the arrival of Grey's letter on 6 May 1856 and the receipt by the Senate of a draft Charter from the Treasury solicitor in December of that year. The draft was at once referred to Tomlinson for his advice.[16] But by then it had become obvious that Grey had decided to grasp this academic nettle quite firmly. Not only was there a draft Charter by the end of 1856, but there were substantial changes of personnel. And there had been signs of at least one quite new challenge to come.

Nothing demonstrates the strength of the graduates' yearning for recognition better than the efforts they made to try to ensure that the new Registrar would be one of themselves. Over time they and their allies had pointed out that no attempt had been made to recruit to the Senate, or to the body of examiners, graduates of the University. As always, the *Lancet* was outspoken on the matter. The issue of 12 April 1856 attacked on two of these fronts. On the appointment of a new examiner in Chemistry, they remarked that

> This is an admirable appointment. It will give general satisfaction. The time, however, has arrived when it has become necessary to notice the remarkable fact – one calculated to excite very wide inquiries - that hitherto, although graduates of the University of London are filling with the utmost distinction the highest educational posts in the kingdom, not one has yet been deemed worthy by the Senate of the office of Examiner. Assuredly, when graduates can be found of equal merit with other candidates, it is but just that the circumstance should have weight in the minds of the electors.

And in a short notice of Rothman's death the paper pointed out that the Registrarship was a post 'of honour and responsibility. It is, for both these reasons, an office which we strongly feel ought to be filled by a graduate of the University.'

In the matter of the Registrarship the Senate moved quickly. They set up a committee – Chancellor, Vice-Chancellor, Kiernan and Warburton - on 2 April, to consider the election of a successor to Rothman. The committee recommended the same conditions for the job as had been in force, and the Senate decided on 16 April that the post should be advertised. The advertisement produced 36 candidates, and the election took place on 21 May, when there was by far the largest turn-out of fellows for more than three years – indeed, the second largest attendance since 1839! This is an interesting aspect of the priorities which a number of senators apparently applied to their duties. And as in the case of Rothman's election, there was no shortage of lobbying.

The Graduates Committee sent a memorial to the Senate on 30 April, pressing the desirability of appointing a London graduate. By 3 May the rumour mill had been working furiously, and the *Lancet* declared that the Senate was less concerned with 'what is best for the University of London, what is just to the graduates,' than with 'what particular phase of *Cambridge* politics shall prevail.' After emphasizing the claims of three London graduates – Dr Edward Smith, Mr Todhunter and Mr Hutton – the editor claimed that they and graduates throughout the country were doing

> more now than either the Senate or the Examiners in extending the influence and raising the fame of the University. But they are only permitted to work outside. Oxford and Cambridge and Scotch graduates rule the University of London. And this is the reason why the University . . . has so long struggled on, fettered by an anomalous constitution; this is the reason why a radical reform has become doubly imperative.

And a week later the same journal fired its last shot in the campaign, with a long, reasoned article which ended with some playing down of the post of Registrar:

> It is a good, practical, business-like man, of good education and position, which is called for by the duties of a Registrar, and not a man so deeply read on one subject only that he is eminently fitted for another post – viz., that of Examiner in the University. Such men abound amongst the graduates, and we are assured that the Senate will hold out the hand of friendship to the graduates, and gracefully concede that which appears to be so justly their due. Senators, of whom the Earl of Burlington, Mr Macaulay, and Professor Faraday, may be mentioned in illustration, can afford to set aside all party ties, and can deeply feel for their own graduates.

It is impossible to know to whom the *Lancet* was referring: there were several Cambridge men among the candidates, and one of the leading contenders had been a student at Trinity and a fellow of Sidney Sussex, but had certainly not worked in Cambridge since 1838. But the last criticism, that academic specialization was not a necessary quality for a Registrar, may well indicate that the *Lancet* was aware of the developing realities of the forthcoming election. For the two candidates who emerged to contest a final vote on 21 May, after a series of ballots had eliminated other possibilities, were both examiners.

The slightly more senior was the Rev James William Lucas Heaviside (1808–97), a Cambridge graduate and fellow who had been teaching mathematics at Haileybury since 1838, had been Registrar there since 1850 and had been a London University examiner since 1843. He corresponded with Brougham about the job, and implied that he had the probable support of the Chancellor and Vice-Chancellor, Beaufort, the Bishop of Durham, Graham, Monteagle and Warburton. Nearer the election Heaviside learned that Durham would vote for his main opponent, but thought that Hallam's favourite candidate, a Dr Latham, had no chance. Heaviside felt that Hallam might be persuaded by Brougham to support him in the subsequent ballots.[17]

But on election day, although Burlington announced that Heaviside would receive his vote, the mathematician failed at the last hurdle, and was overtaken, on a ten to nine vote, by the West-Countryman, William Benjamin Carpenter. It was only a partial victory for the graduates and the *Lancet*, inasmuch as Carpenter, though not a London graduate, had been a medical student, first at Bristol, then at UCL from 1833 to 1835, and afterwards at Edinburgh.[18] He had been a freelance writer on physiology, biology and comparative anatomy before holding the Fullerian Chair of Physiology at the Royal Institution in 1845, when he was elected to the Royal Society. He became a London Examiner in Physiology and Comparative Anatomy in 1847; edited the *British and Foreign Medical Review*; and held the Chair of Medical Jurisprudence at UCL in 1849. He has been described as 'one of the most eminent physiologists in Britain during the mid-century.'[19]

There is no division list, but all nineteen who were present must have voted. We know that Burlington and Warburton voted for Heaviside. Neither Monteagle nor Beaufort, on whom Heaviside had counted, were at the meeting. Nor was the Bishop of Durham, who was expected to vote for Carpenter.[20] Though many combinations were possible, perhaps the most likely explanation of the result is simply that there were two chemists, Brande and Faraday, and nine medical men present - Arnott, Bacot, Billing, Clark, Hammick, Hodgkin, Kiernan, Locock and Roget; and that professional loyalty triumphed, though one of the eleven must have voted for Heaviside. The opposition to Carpenter, if this division of opinion is correct, would have been a rather strange mixture, including the Chancellor and Vice-Chancellor, Graham, Macaulay, Overstone, Thirlwall (Bishop of St Davids), Walker and Warburton. Thirlwall had not attended a meeting since 1849.

Whether or not Carpenter's election was seen as a victory for the medical faculty, it was certainly a strong comment on the strength and prestige of the London medical establishment. Carpenter was to prove himself a more aggressive administrator than his predecessor, and would hold the position for 23 years.

It will be recalled that Grey had driven through the Supplementary Charter negotiations of 1849, and had organized the addition of powerful political figures as new members of the Senate. In 1856 he moved again to make new appointments, in part to meet the pressure from the graduates, and in part to continue to add to the political strength of the University. But on this occasion his initiative coincided with the decision of the Earl of Burlington to resign the Chancellorship. By the end of 1856, Grey had found a new Chancellor and six new senators.

The Home Secretary had clearly accepted the view of the graduates that they should be represented in the Senate, and was persuaded to appoint two of them, irrespective of the delay in meeting claims about Convocation and a new Charter. In a letter to Burlington of 30 July, he asked for the Chancellor's opinion on the suitability of two leading graduates as members of the Senate. This approach was the outcome of protracted negotiations initiated and conducted on the graduates' side by Foster, who insisted that he himself would not accept nomination, and who was prevented by the Home Office from consulting anyone else. Foster did claim, subsequently, that the two new graduate senators were his appointees, which was almost certainly the case. At the same time he implied that the new draft Charter had been drawn up by the Graduates Committee; as we shall see, this was, at best, only a half truth.[21]

Grey put to Burlington the names of Frederick John Wood and John Storrar. The Chancellor replied:

> I am not aware that any objection can be raised to their fitness – at the same time I think it right to add that I should not myself have thought it right to recommend Dr Storrar for a seat in the Senate, on account of the strong part he has taken in the proceedings of the Committee of Graduates, and the probability that his appointment will on that account be unacceptable to several members of the Senate. Either Dr Gull or Dr Miller are also I believe quite unobjectionable. Lefevre, I understand thinks Quain a superior man to Wood.[22]

Burlington's doubts about Storrar, because of his 'strong part' in negotiation, underline the assessment of the latter's personality given earlier, and foreshadow later controversies which accompanied Storrar's tenure of a place on the Senate and on the General Medical Council during the early years of Convocation.[23] It is very likely, however, that it was his particular unpopularity among many senior members of the medical profession and his hostility to the College of Physicians which raised the Chancellor's doubts as to his acceptablility in 1856.[24]

Burlington's and Shaw Lefevre's opinions were enough to make Grey drop both Storrar and Wood, who had only been proposed because 'theirs were the first names in the two classes in the list sent to me.' This suggests that the lists may have been sent to Grey by Foster, who would have put forward the two chairmen of the arts and medical sides of the Graduates Committee. Grey told Burlington that he would substitute John Richard Quain for Wood and choose 'one of the Doctors you mention.'[25] Subsequent approaches, of which there is no record, must have restored Wood to favour. In December, Wood and William Withey Gull were nominated.

Lord Palmerston received what might be regarded as a very normal letter of resignation from Burlington. The Chancellor had served in the office for twenty years, and he foresaw a new era for the University with the forthcoming Charter. He was not much in London, but he would like to go on as a fellow. The letter, like his service as Chancellor, was civilized and reasonable: it was acknowledged gracefully but not contested by Palmerston and Grey.[26] However, the retiring Chancellor, in his own quiet but admirably independent fashion, did not wait to be asked what he thought about one possible source of a successor.

> It would of course be improper for me to offer any suggestion as to the appointment of my successor and I have merely to observe that if Lord Palmerston should as is not improbable think of appointing the new Chancellor from among the existing members of the Senate it would be difficult to find a person possessing all qualifications for the office.[27]

Grey was only too ready to discuss other possibilities with Burlington. He had thought of Lord Wrottesley and of 'the new Peer Strutt' (Lord Belper), and he added:

> I have omitted Lefevre as one whose long connection with the University and high attainments would probably place him before the last of the names I have mentioned. If *rank* is not requisite I know no one better qualified. But you will be able to form a better judgement than I can.[28]

By the beginning of September, Burlington had given the matter more thought, and was more sympathetic than formerly to some of his colleagues. He told Grey that

> The members of the Senate who either from their position or the

part they have taken in the affairs of the University seem to me the only ones out of whom the choice for the Office of Chancellor can be made are the following – Lord Monteagle, Lord Overstone, Sir James Graham, The Chancellor of the Exchequer [Cornewall Lewis], Macaulay, Lefevre, Grote, Warburton.

Your colleague [i.e. Cornewall Lewis] and Macaulay have so seldom attended the meetings of the Senate that I put them aside at once. Grote and Warburton are both very useful members of the Senate but there would be grave objections to the appointment of either.

As I think it of importance to the University that the Chancellor should either be a person of rank or hold a very distinguished position in public estimation I should prefer the appointment either of Lord Overstone or of Sir James Graham to that of Lefevre. I should doubt the consent of the latter [i.e. Graham] to accept the office, and there is one objection to him though perhaps not a very strong one that he is closely connected with University College. On the whole Lord Overstone's appointment seems to me the best. Since he became a member of the Senate he has been a very regular attendant at the meetings and has taken great interest in its proceedings.[29]

Thereafter there is very little evidence of the progress of the search, but none of the people listed either by Burlington or Grey turned out to be acceptable, or to be willing to become Chancellor. The desirability of rank, however, seems to have been a dominant factor. By the end of November, Palmerton and Grey were pressing Brougham, and Shaw Lefevre joined in the exercise. They sang a song very different from that with which Burlington had been serenaded twenty years previously:

There is little which Your Lordship would call trouble attaching to the Chancellorship of the University of London. At the present moment there is a great opportunity of increasing its utility and of making it one of the most important institutions in the country. The Senate seldom meet more than once a month and in general the business is of a formal character. We shall, very shortly, however, have to consider the provisions of a new Charter, which the Government are about to propose to us, and this will require some attention but it is a subject with which you are so familiar that, as I said before, you will not think it a trouble.[30]

But the ageing Brougham – he was now 78 – was not to be drawn. Nor, apparently, were Russell or the Duke of Somerset. Finally, with some reluctance, Earl Granville, the Lord President of the Council, accepted the post, remarking ruefully that 'John Lefevre was the guilty party. He persuaded George Grey that I should be the best.'[31] The *Lancet* gave the newcomer a rather grudging welcome:

> Granting that Chancellors must be selected from the Peerage, and granting that the Minister must select, no one will question the fitness of Lord Granville. The misfortune is that howsoever worthy to fill that position, and howsoever zealously and efficiently he may discharge his duties, the Chancellor thus selected will always be regarded less as the representative of the great metropolitan university than as the nominee of the Crown.

And having earlier voiced sorrow that Burlington had resigned before the new Charter was in place, the editor could not resist some barbed regret:

> How appropriate as an inauguration of the Reformed University; how conducive to its usefulness; how honourable to the new Chancellor; and how grateful to the Graduates, if the first function of Convocation had been to exercise the power of electing their highest dignitary.[32]

There is no sign that Burlington was consulted about new members of the Senate other than the two graduates, and any correspondence Grey had about them has probably disappeared. Two days before Christmas the appointments of the new Chancellor and six new fellows were announced. Apart from the significant addition of two graduates, the pattern set in 1849 was re-emphasized: no new medical men *per se* - Gull was primarily a graduate representative – and a strong addition of politicians and public servants. And, as in 1849, the political slant was firmly Whig/Liberal, with one partial exception.

When the rejuvenated Senate met on 21 January 1857, its members included three serving Cabinet ministers, Granville, Cornewall Lewis and Matthew Talbot Baines. The last named was MP for Leeds, who was now Chancellor of the Duchy of Lancaster and had previously held office as President of the Poor Law Board. It has to be admitted that, of the three, only Granville was a regular attender. Baines and another newcomer, James Heywood, MP for Wolverhampton and an old supporter of the graduates, must surely have pleased the northern Dissenters.

The third politician was the MP for Kings Lynn, Lord Stanley, eldest son of the Earl of Derby, who had been under-secretary at the Foreign Office during his father's short-lived administration in 1852. The appointment may have been in part a piece of political wooing by Palmerston, who always thought of Stanley as 'more of a liberal than anything else,' and was to offer him the Colonial Secretaryship in 1858, though it was declined. Stanley had shown sympathy to the nonconformists in 1853, when he published a pamphlet in favour of exempting them from the payment of Church rates, and his subsequent career bore out much of Palmerston's claim, for he switched parties in 1880 and served under Gladstone until becoming a Liberal Unionist in 1886. He was to retain his connection with the University of London, and would become its Chancellor for the last two years of his life, in 1891.[33]

The last place went to Sir Edward Ryan, an ex-Chief Justice of Bengal, a Railway Commissioner since 1846, and the recently appointed first Civil Service Commissioner. It is at least conceivable that the Vice-Chancellor, John Shaw Lefevre, might have had a hand in this arrangement, as he was the other Civil Service Commissioner (both were unpaid), and one of his daughters had married Ryan's son. And Ryan, Baines and Stanley were all graduates of Trinity College, Cambridge, thus continuing a strong tradition on the London Senate dating back to 1836.

As might have been expected, the two graduates, Gull and Wood, were keenly attentive, but in this final year before the new Charter took effect, those who came together regularly at Senate were, in the main, either academic doctors or men of affairs. The new men, and doubtless the important changes which took place in 1857–8, did increase attendance to an average of some 14 per meeting, and the medical members were rarely in the majority.

On 10 May 1856, Jessie Meriton White wrote to the Acting Registrar, asking:

> Can a woman become a candidate for a Diploma in Medicine, if on presenting herself for examination she shall produce all the requisite certificates of character, capacity and study from one of the institutions recognised by the London University?[34]

Two weeks later she followed this with another letter to the new Registrar, Carpenter: 'Will you inform the Senate that I am prepared to comply with all the regulations of the University, should its Members decide on admitting me as a candidate for examination.'[35]

This second letter was not put before Senate until 18 June, and no formal action appears to have been taken on it. However, concern – or even consternation – may well have been expressed, and subsequently John Shaw Lefevre wrote to Sir George Grey. After expressing the view that the Charter did not limit the University's examinations to males but that the founders of the University had no extension to females in mind, he told Grey that the Senate would like to have the views of the Government. He then went on:

> It seems to me that it is a question upon which you might reasonably desire the opinion of the Senate, which comprises many medical members of eminence, before you form any opinion of your own, unless indeed you think as some have done that the proposition is palpably absurd or immediately objectionable.
>
> For my own part, I do not think it absurd – for I believe that much good might result from the existence of a certain number of female practitioners well instructed as to the diseases of women and children, but on the other hand I think that there are very grave objections to their pursuing the course of education prescribed for male practitioners.
>
> Their attendance on anatomical lectures in company with male students - their walking the hospitals – could hardly be managed with proper regard to female delicacy and decorum unless there were a sufficient number of females dedicating themselves to the medical profession to form separate classes – and even then their relations with the Demonstrator or Lecturer would be somewhat awkward. I have heard it observed moreover, that the existence of female medical practitioners might lead to a morbid delicacy on the part of women as to consulting medical men in any case.
>
> I have thought it right cursorily to ventilate these points – which may perhaps assist you in the consideration of the subject.[36]

Whether Grey replied at all, let alone in time for his views to be taken into account, there is no record of any discussion in Senate at their meeting on 2 July, which was attended overwhelmingly by medical men. They resolved to ask the opinion of Counsel as to the power of the Senate, under the Charter, to grant Degrees in Medicine, Arts and Laws, to Females; and if so, whether it can refuse to admit them as candidates, presuming that they have complied with all the requirements of the University.

Thomas Tomlinson worked fast, and came up with an opinion whose salient arguments make interesting reading a hundred-and-forty-years later. By the Charter, wrote Tomlinson:

All distinctions of mere class and denomination are abolished, and those of locality modified, but in other respects I can discern no indication of an intention to give the power of conferring Degrees on persons, other than persons of the same description as those on whom University and academical Degrees were habitually conferred i.e. persons of the male sex.

Words applicable to the male sex might include the female, if such an intention could be clearly inferred from the context, or from the Charter, but in the absence of any Evidence of such an intention, the expressions in the regulations must be understood in their ordinary meaning. According to analogy and the Usages of similar Institutions admissibility to such Degrees is limited to the male sex.[37]

There is no sign whether this Opinion aroused argument. On 9 July fourteen senators, including nine members of the Faculty of Medicine, were present: there was no division on the resolution 'That Miss J.M. White be informed that the Senate, acting upon the opinion of its Legal Adviser, does not consider itself empowered to admit Females as candidates for Degrees.' This closed the door. The first attempt to force it open had been made within just twenty years of the launching of the University. But women were not enabled to take degrees until twenty-four years after 1856.

CHAPTER 21

New Perspectives

By the end of 1856, with the appointment of two graduates to the Senate
and the submission of the draft of a new Charter by the Home Secretary,
the long struggle to have Convocation accepted, in principle, had ended.
Between Christmas of 1856 and the final authorizing of the Charter on
9 April 1858, there was no more basic argument over the incorporation
of graduates, the appointment of nominees of the graduates as fellows,
and the power of Convocation to veto changes in the constitution.
There was some not insignificant haggling over the extent and the
procedure of graduate representation and election, and that haggling
will be dealt with shortly. But the outcome was the provision in the
new Charter that every second vacancy in the Senate was to be filled by
a nominee of the graduates until such nominees constituted one fourth
of the Senate. Thereafter, every fourth vacancy would be filled in that
manner. Convocation would elect three nominees for each place on the
Senate, from whom one would be recommended to the Crown by the
Secretary of State. In practice the nominee who had received the most
votes was always chosen.

The long-drawn-out campaign achieved far less power for Convocation than the graduates had wanted, originally. Moreover, the new
Charter was not to provide additional authorization of only those
changes which brought Convocation into being. Other amendments
were introduced, late in the day, and one of them transformed the
final stages of the introduction of the new Charter from a celebration
into a bitter dispute, which split the graduates into warring factions and
reopened some old controversies among the fellows.

It is reasonable to see the whole issue of Convocation as being little
concerned with educational policy and much concerned with the politics
of Dissent; and with the ambition of a new cadre of university educated
men, particularly doctors and lawyers, to break into the established
orders of professional life. Insofar as the somewhat diluted victory
of the graduates represented a welcome intrusion of a degree of
self-government and greater independence into what had become a

closed, and rather stale, Crown appointed corporation, it was well worthwhile. But one can search in vain for much in the way of significant discussion of strictly academic concerns interwoven into the constitutional argument. Whatever was being achieved through the examination system was certainly not enhanced by the politicking which dominated a decade of graduate and senatorial conflict.

But if academic and educational matters had been either absent from or pushed aside in the Senate's affairs by the graduates' struggle for participation in the University's governance, the last battle before the Second Charter was put in place was fought over a major issue of educational policy – whether or not candidates in arts and laws should have to spend two years, prior to sitting degree examinations, at approved institutions.

Although there seems to have been more material produced on paper on this question in 1857 than accompanied the earlier agitation for the establishment of Convocation, the opposing views can be stated quite comprehensively in brief compass. Those who originally enforced, and subsequently defended the continuance of, the necessary affiliation of candidates to approved institutions, believed passionately in the desirability of formal instruction and study, in a collegiate setting, prior to taking a degree. A few extracts from one of the many submissions made on the subject give the essence of that case and a flavour of the bias of what might be thought of as Establishment feeling. Such conservative feeling, so clearly developed among a high proportion of its products, was very unwelcome to those who had always regarded the university as a radical institution, at least mildly subversive of the *status quo*.

The proposed change, whereby no college affiliation would be required for candidates wishing to be examined for degrees in arts and laws, was seen by opponents as 'avowedly intended to transform the University, as regards other than Medical Degrees, into a University of mere examinations.'[1] The core argument in favour of current practice, followed:

> The Degree of B.A. has always been appropriated in England to distinguish the ordinary class of men who have received a general academical education. It is no high honour intended to attest unusual industry, still less to indicate high intellectual pre-eminence. If the examination for this Degree were made so difficult as to exclude all but exceptional men, the whole character of the distinction would be altered, and another name ought to be adopted to show that those

who have attained it are something more than what men in general understand as mere Bachelors of Arts. The body of Bachelors of Arts, however, have characteristics quite as definite as those which distinguish the holders of high University honours, among whom the Masters and Doctors of the University of London must be classed. The existence of the collegiate test (when applied *bona fide*) necessarily produces the result that an overwhelming proportion of Bachelors of Arts are men who have devoted the first years of manhood after leaving school, and before engaging in the narrowing pursuits of life (professional or other), to the exclusive pursuit of general literary and scientific culture in educational institutions adapted to their time of life. The average ages of the candidates in the University of London have in different years varied from twenty-one years to twenty-three years and ten months. Whatever opinions may be entertained as to the relative mental superiority of those so educated, it is undeniable that they form a very marked class. They are emphatically, and as distinguished from all others, the class who have pursued 'a regular and liberal course of education.'

It is equally certain that the stamp of a University Degree is universally accepted in England as denoting that the holder belongs to this class. The Degree derives its value and its meaning from a double test – the Examination test and the College test. It is proposed that in future it shall be no attestation of the holder being an academically educated man, or of anything more than that he has passed two or three not very difficult examinations.

The difference between an examination for Honours, which, in cases of very severe examination, does detect extraordinary proficiency, and the pass examination for the Degree of B.A., must be borne in mind. The perfection to which 'cramming' is carried renders it a most difficult problem to ascertain by one or two examinations alone the possession of that moderate but sound proficiency in a variety of subjects belonging to literature and elementary science, which an ordinarily well-educated man ought to possess. Even if it could be so ascertained, many most important practical distinctions between such a man academically educated, and one equally well informed, but not academically educated, would still remain. Mere application to books, creditable as it may be, produces a class differing essentially from those who have passed several years of early manhood in a regular course of systematic training in seats of learning, which, by bringing together a number of young and fresh minds, afford influences and advantages which nothing else can supply, and which are not less valuable than the mere opportunities of study.

The defence of the proposal to drop affiliation was put, very quietly and succinctly, by Robert Barnes, the secretary to the Graduates Committee, and one of the minority who approved of the suggested change:

> a certificate of study from an affiliated institution was no reliable evidence of learning or of good conduct; . . . a well-devised system of examinations was the only trustworthy qualification for a degree; . . . the exclusion of everyone who could not produce a certificate was unjust and illiberal and contrary to the original aims of the University; and . . . the abolition of the present restriction would enlarge the basis of the University, add to its strength and extend its public usefulness.

But the *Lancet*, always the enemy of the closed system, echoed Barnes' view more colourfully, approving the proposed abandonment, in the new Charter, of

> those restrictions relating to the admission of candidates for degrees which have operated so unjustly, by excluding many worthy men – so injuriously to the interests of the University, by narrowing her foundation, limiting the number of her graduates; and so discouraging to the progress of free education.[2]

To these more ideological emphases on the virtues of open access was added the extremely practical objection, strongly expressed by those who carried the change through the Senate, that the University had no control over the institutions in which candidates were prepared for the examinations, and the fact that certain of those institutions had proved to be very unsatisfactory in that context.[3]

The requirement that candidates should attend an educational institution for two years before attempting the examinations of the University for degrees in arts and laws was insisted on, when the University was established, and consistently supported throughout its first twemty years, by Thomas Spring Rice, later Lord Monteagle.[4] But as we saw earlier, at the outset the radical Warburton wanted examinations open to all comers, and even the middle-of-the-road Burlington could see no especial virtue in affiliation.[5] However, the possibility of any change died with the fall of Melbourne's Government in 1841. By 1857 there were only 37 affiliated institutions, excluding other universities, and six of them had produced no successful candidates. But many of the colleges had obviously come to feel that their own interests would be severely threatened by the loss of the compulsory enrolment demanded by the system.

When the Senate decided to propose a change, there were those who denounced it as an unconsidered and off-the-cuff move to ensure that it would be effected before Convocation was formed and able to object. In truth, the desirability of change had never been forgotten or dropped by its proponents, and the Senate had been memorialized most recently, in favour, in 1854, by the editor of *The Popular Educator*, Robert Wallace, supported by at least two hundred of his readers. Among the most prominent of those readers were Samuel Morley and Matthew Davenport Hill: the latter, who had championed the equal treatment of London graduates by the Inns of Court, was joined by his brothers, who were active in running the most progressive schools of the day at Hazelwood near Birmingham and at Bruce Castle, Tottenham.[6] While the Senate took no action on Wallace's memorials, the idea of dropping collegiate affiliation must have been kept firmly in the forefront of the minds of those members of the Senate who hoped to see notable changes made in the forthcoming new Charter.

The first directions by the Home Office to the Treasury solicitor about the preparation of a draft Charter were given in May 1856.[7] During the following eight months it is clear that the Home Office and the Treasury solicitor were intent on finding an acceptable formulation of a compromise which would suit both the University and the graduates. The Treasury solicitor was directed by the Home Office to draft the new Charter 'in conformity with the terms of the letter of [Sir George Grey to the Chancellor] of the 18 August, 1855,' and was sent all the relevant correspondence and opinions which had been received by the Home Office from the University, the Committee of Graduates, and several of the colleges, and the letter of Sir William Clay to Grey, of 1 June 1855, which has been quoted earlier. The Treasury solicitor had all this by the end of May 1856.[8]

There is clear evidence that the Home Office and the Treasury solicitor took serious account of the ideas of the Graduates Committee. A draft Charter marked 'suggested on behalf of the Graduates,' was sent to Grey by Clay and stamped 'Received 22 July 1856' by the Home Office. Three days afterwards it was sent on to the Treasury solicitor. And late in November, when the first official draft

Charter was practically complete, the Treasury solicitor's office sent a request to Foster for copies of 'the Graduates' plan,' and all relevant correspondence and printed matter, including Willes' opinion, which were needed 'to accompany the instructions sent to the Attorney and Solicitor General.'[9]

There are fewer signs of similar negotiations with the University, but at the end of November the Treasury solicitor wrote to the Vice-Chancellor: 'I send the draft of the proposed new Charter of the London University for your perusal and any remarks you may be kind enough to send me.'[10] Shaw Lefevre must have been reasonably happy, because the draft was sent formally to the University on 12 December, and laid before the Senate five days later, when it was simply referred to counsel for his opinion. At about the same time, a copy of the draft must have been sent to the Graduates Committee, because Foster sent observations on it to Sir George Grey on 19 January, requesting him to lay those observations before the Senate.[11] This was done and, on 21 January 1857, the Senate had before them the draft Charter, Tomlinson's opinion, and the observations of the Graduates Committee.

Unfortunately, while the Public Records include considerable documentation of the later stages of the process, there is no sign of the first draft. The University's archive does not contain either Tomlinson's opinion or the graduates' observations on the draft, and if there was Senate discussion, it was not recorded in the minutes. The Senate merely handed over all the material to a select committee, whose members were the Chancellor (now Lord Granville) and Vice-Chancellor, Clark (the only medical man), Grote, Ryan, Senior, Warburton and Wood. That committee reported back on 4 March, with suggested alterations to the draft Charter: its report, too, has disappeared, but its proposals were made the subject of a special Charter meeting on 18 March.

While the material available is exiguous, there is nothing in any of the surviving documents of 1856 about changing the compulsory affiliation of examinees to colleges, and it is highly unlikely that the suggestion was included in the missing first draft of the Treasury solicitor. The Graduates Committee were later to claim that a Senate committee recommended the change 'Towards the end of the year 1856.'[12] This was almost certainly wrong. No committee had been appointed previously, and none was appointed at the Senate meeting of 17 December, when the draft was first laid on the table.

It is probable that the lost select committee's report contained all the proposed amendments to the draft Charter which were subsequently debated, including the provision to abandon collegiate affiliation. If so, either the report was kept very quiet; or the significance of the proposals were not fully appreciated at once; or there was, from the first revelation of the disaffiliation proposal, so much dissension within the Graduates Committee that their response, and the responses of the affiliated colleges, were unusually slow. The report was made to the Senate on 4 March, but it was not until 5 May that the graduates were called together to consider its implications. By then, the Senate had accepted the desirability of relieving candidates of the need to attend affiliated colleges. Subsequent opposition caused delay, but did not alter that acceptance.

When the Senate opened their special meeting on 18 March, they immediately turned themselves into a Committee of the Whole, and in that state they also held meetings on 25 March and 1 April, and for the first part of a session of the Senate on 4 June. At the first two of these meetings, important changes in the existing constitutional arrangements and in the Home Secretary's suggested legislation were discussed and, in effect, decided. Perhaps because the attention of the Graduates Committee was by then being focused almost solely on the disaffiliation proposal, which did not come up in Committee of the Whole until 1 April, what happened before then went apparently unreported.

The absence of the texts of the select committee's recommendations and the Treasury solicitor's original draft is particularly regrettable, because it reduces to speculation how far Grey had been prepared to go to meet the desires of the graduates. We know that in his letter of 18 August 1855 he directed that the official draft should include provision, (subsequently included in Clause 13), for one quarter of the Senate (interpreted as nine fellows, the Chancellor and Vice-Chancellor being additional to the 36 fellows), to be graduates of the University, and that Convocation should submit five nominees for each vacant place. The select committee proposed amending this so as to drop the requirement that the nominees of Convocation should be graduates of the University, and to reduce the number of nominees from five to three for each vacancy.

But the closely related Clause 14 of the first official draft is likely to have provided that in a situation when the membership of the Senate had dropped below twenty-five, excluding the Chancellor and Vice-Chancellor, twelve or more new fellows should be appointed, of whom one half should be graduates of the University, and that Convocation should provide five nominees for each vacant place in that half. The select committee appears to have proposed amending this by removing the need for the nominees to be graduates of the University, but leaving the numerical provisions unchanged.

In Committee of the Whole, on 18 March, Warburton moved that all the amendments made in Clause 13 by the select committee should be left out, so that the Clause would return to its original form. In that wish, he was joined by Brande, Faraday, Hammick, Kiernan, Monteagle and Overstone. But they were defeated by the twelve others present - the Chancellor and Vice-Chancellor, Arnott, Billing, Clark, Grote, Gull, Heywood, Stanley, Ryan, Walker and Wood. The interesting aspect of that vote is the fact that Warburton was joined only by fellows who were not members of the select committee, while all the other members of the select committee save Senior, who was absent, were opposed to the motion. This in turn raises a nice question of who carried the proposed amendments in the select committee. One can only assume that Warburton must have had allies in the select committee, but that they had changed their minds, for whatever reason – contextual or tactical – by 18 March.

Once Clause 13 had been accepted in the form proposed by the select committee, the Committee of the Whole resolved, apparently without division, that the numerical arrangements of Clause 13 should also apply to the more drastic possibility, envisaged in Clause 14, of having to appoint twelve or more senators at once. Thus the suggestion that Convocation should nominate to half the vacancies was reduced to a quarter, and the number of nominees per place was reduced to three. All these dilutions of the graduates' hopes went unchallenged thereafter. It may be that Grey had been genuinely more radical than the Senate, but it is at least possible that he had included more generous provisions than he really believed to be desirable, because he expected them to be diluted by the Senate.

A week later, on 25 March, the Committee of the Whole turned their attention to the old, vexed question of whether fellows should be examiners. It will be remembered that since the barren constitutional discussions in 1840–1, none but original senators had been appointed as examiners: by 1857 only six fellows were still examining – Billing, Brande, Hammick, Henslow, Kiernan and Senior. On this occasion Warburton saw his old desire fulfilled. The draft Charter provided, in Clause 33, that after three years from its effective date, no senator could be an examiner. Monteagle, rather quixotically, suggested that those fellows who were 'at present' examiners should be excluded from that provision, but his motion was defeated by eleven to three, with only the Vice-Chancellor and Roget supporting him, and with three examiners – Brande, Hammick and Kiernan, abstaining. The practice which had caused such conflict in the early years, came to an end in 1861.

It was on 1 April, however, that the Committee of the Whole came face to face with the proposal to relieve candidates for degree examinations in arts and laws of the obligation to have been enrolled in approved colleges for two years previously. The actual form in which this was proposed to be authorized was what became Clause 36: it provided

> That persons not educated in any of the Institutions connected with the . . . University shall be admitted as Candidates for Matriculation, and for any of the Degrees . . . other than Medical Degrees, on such conditions as the . . . Chancellor, Vice-Chancellor, and Fellows, by regulations in that behalf shall from time to time determine.

But it is probable that the clause did not exist in those terms at that time, for the issue was put in a motion by Monteagle, 'That the original constitution of the University, as regards the affiliated Colleges, be maintained.' The outcome was clear-cut. Monteagle had the support only of Hammick, Roget and Wood. Against them were eighteen senators, including Gull, the second graduate member, thus foreshadowing the division of opinion within the graduate community. The full list of those who wanted the change was: Chancellor and Vice-Chancellor, Arnott, Baines, Billing, Brande, Clark, Graham, Grote, Gull, Heywood, Kiernan, Overstone, Ryan, Senior, Stanley, Walker and Warburton.

The apparent willingness of a clear majority of the working Senate to remove the requirement of college affiliation put the leaders of the graduates into a quandary. After ten years of hard negotiation, they had succeeded in bringing Convocation into sight, and the thought of trying to force the Senate to refuse acceptance of a new Charter incorporating the graduates must have seemed nightmarish. But the bitterness of many of their own people at the prospect of non-collegiate preparation for examinations could not be denied. The protectiveness which graduates showed towards their degrees was demonstrated only weeks before the storm over the new Charter proposal became known, when grave objection was taken to the approval of the Working Men's College as an institution where candidates could qualify to take London degrees. The recently established *University of London Magazine*, in high dudgeon, claimed that 'it was not a college but a mere evening school.'[13] There is little doubt that the majority of graduates felt that the severance of orthodox college connections would cheapen the degree. And many of the arts and law men were incensed that while their successors were to include those without collegiate connections, future medical degrees would still be open only to candidates who attended recognized medical schools.

Foster and Storrar, by now hardened politicians, understanding what they were up against, tried to deflect their colleagues' wrath. At a meeting of graduates on 5 May, they proposed a resolution regretting the Senate's proposals but accepting the new Charter, on the grounds that rejection would delay the incorporation of the graduates in the University. They were not heeded, and a resolution was passed by 84 to 37, stating that the meeting,

> viewing with disapproval and alarm the contemplated renunciation by the Senate of the principle of collegiate education in Arts and Laws, and considering such measure to be a serious blow to regular and systematic education, and calculated to lower the value of the London degree, declines to authorise the committee to accept the charter as proposed by the Senate.[14]

During the rest of May the Graduates Committee went again through the processes of protest. They put together a long statement of 'Facts and Arguments', and collected the signatures of 531 graduates for a memorial to the Senate against the proposal. That memorial, and the first statements of collegiate opposition, from the Principal and Faculty of King's, the professors of UCL, and Regents Park College, were lodged by the time the Senate met on 4 June. But the graduates no longer presented the single front which had carried them through the earlier confrontations. Though there had only been 37 votes favouring the Senate's proposals at the meeting of 5 May, several were cast by prominent leaders of the graduates, including Robert Barnes and John Richard Quain, while many of the medical graduates, being untouched by the proposal, were lukewarm about further opposition to the Senate. The *Lancet*, meanwhile, kept up a virulent hostility to what it regarded as the selfishness of the majority of the graduates.[15] It is not surprising, therefore, that there were signs of possible compromise.

On the official side, the Senate made no move to break the connection established between the University and the 37 colleges already approved as institutions at which candidates could receive instruction for two years before attempting the first degree: they remained listed in the draft Charter. On 4 June, in Committee of the Whole, with Warburton in the chair, a new clause was added after the listing of colleges, providing that

> it shall be lawful for the Chancellor, Vice-Chancellor and Fellows, with the consent of one of our Principal Secretaries of State, to add to the last-mentioned Institutions in connexion with the University of London any other Institutions; and from time to time to alter, vary and amend the list of Institutions in connexion with the said University.

This was approved on the motion of Monteagle, supported by Arnott, Billing, Brande, Burlington, Clark, Faraday, Hammick, Senior and Wood. Only Grote and Ryan opposed.[16]

For their part, the Graduates Committee had included in their memorial the suggestion that

> They would agree to the waiving of the college certificate in some individual and exceptional cases but not as a general rule; they would even agree to non-collegiate candidates being examined and given some form of title so long as it was absolutely distinct from the degree and 'perfectly different from the academic titles which belong only to academically educated persons.'[17]

But among the fellows the tide was running against any major concessions to the graduates. The Committee of the Whole gave place to the Senate, with the Chancellor presiding, and the question was put: 'That the draft Charter as now amended be adopted.' Monteagle may have left the meeting, or have decided to abstain, but with the exception of Wood, all the others (including Grote and Ryan, who had opposed possible extension of the affiliation of colleges), and Warburton, voted in favour. The majority of eleven to one included Gull, the medical graduate fellow.

However, having referred the draft charter to counsel for final settlement, nine of the senators then debated a motion from Grote, who wanted final determination of the approval of the Charter to be delayed for one month in order to give time for comments to be received from the affiliated colleges. There is no account of the debate, and one can only surmise that Grote, who was regarded, with Hodgkin, as a friend of the graduates, felt it desirable to allow the fullest expression of discontent, partly as a therapeutic exercise, while believing that it would not be sufficiently persuasive to change the ultimate acceptance of the new order. Whatever his motives, he carried the day by only one vote, being joined by the Chancellor, Brande, Hammick and Wood, against Billing, Burlington, Senior and Warburton. This prolonged the Senate's consideration of the draft Charter for another six weeks.

The result of the subsequent consultation was the receipt of memorials against the admission of candidates who had not attended approved institutions from eighteen colleges, described in the Senate's own report as 'comprehending the most considerable' of those affiliated. The President of the College of Thurles was in favour of the change; and there was no response from the remaining nineteen. It was not until 15 July that all the quite heavy documentation was put to the Senate. In the interim, Tomlinson had produced suggestions for a few minor, technical alterations to the draft Charter.

If Grote had indeed calculated that the consultation of the colleges would not affect the final issue, he had made a very shrewd judgement. A further compromise proposal was put forward early in July by Foster and 'several gentlemen who concur with me,' suggesting that if Clause 36 could not be deleted, it might be modified by the requirement of a 'progressive system of examinations, adequately to test the qualifications of a Candidate for a Degree, as one who had *bona fide* passed through a regular and liberal course of education.'[18] But this carried no weight – perhaps because, if the *Lancet* is to be believed, by 20 June Foster, along with Barnes, Gull and Storrar, had 'announced their adhesion to the principle of opening the University.'[19]

On 15 July, the Senate addressed themselves first to the technical proposals of their counsel, described as the 'final amendments of the Draft Charter,' and approved them without a division. Then they resolved that they could not see any reason against adopting Clause 36; they appointed Grote and Warburton to prepare a reasoned report for discussion, before sending it, with the amended draft Charter, all the outside objections, and the far fewer approvals, to the Home Secretary. Those present, all of whom apparently concurred in these proceedings, were the Chancellor and Vice-Chancellor, Arnott, Billing, Grote, Gull, Kiernan, Ryan, Senior, Warburton and Wood.

From the Home Office files, it would appear that the decision of 15 July was taken as the formal agreement of the Senate to the amended version of the draft Charter which was to be recommended to the Home

Secretary.[20] The Home Office, therefore, took no account, even if they knew of it, of the remarkable further Senate debate, and vote, on 22 July, on the report of Grote and Warburton, which was to go with the draft Charter to Sir George Grey. That report was a lengthy and robust defence of the Senate's intention to retain and press for Clause 36. It rejected all the arguments put forward by the graduates and the colleges, and the compromises suggested by Foster and his colleagues. It pointed to the 37 per cent of matriculated students who had not been educated in affiliated colleges, and were unable to proceed to degrees unless they abandoned their former teachers and enrolled in approved institutions. And it insisted that those institutions could only cope with a very small proportion of the students in the country as a whole who could be accommodated under the proposed new system.[21]

Given the eleven to one acceptance of the amended version of the Charter on 4 June, and the absence of opposition on 15 July, the proceedings on 22 July underline the difference which variations in the level of attendance were always likely to make to the Senate's decisions. On that occasion the Chancellor was present for part of the meeting, but left before the crucial vote was taken, and Grote took his place in the chair. The Vice-Chancellor did not attend. There is no account of the discussion, but when the motion to adopt the Grote–Warburton report was put, the eight fellows present divided equally, whereupon Grote gave his casting vote in favour. Those who supported him were Billing, Kiernan and Warburton; they were opposed by Monteagle, Arnott, Hodgkin and Wood. Monteagle had been consistently opposed to the proposed change, as had Wood, while Hodgkin had not been present at the earlier crucial meetings. Arnott, however, had been approving of the new Charter on 4 June, and had been present and had not objected to its acceptance on 15 July. No doubt a larger turn-out would have seen the report blessed by a larger majority: and it was a vote on the report to accompany the draft Charter, not a vote on the draft Charter itself. Nonetheless, the close call must have left doubt in some minds, and probably encouraged a continuance of hope on the part of some graduates that they could still delay the Charter's introduction.

Any such hope was unrealistic. Grey received the draft Charter early in August, with all the accompanying documentation, and passed the draft to the law officers for their opinion as to 'its sufficiency in point of law.'[22] And he was impatient for completion of the whole process, for the law officers were pressed for a settlement 'without delay' on 19 October and again on 15 December.[23] Meanwhile the graduates continued to appeal to the Home Office to refuse consent to the Senate's proposals, and to leave the question of the college connection to be decided after Convocation had been set up. They were joined in that appeal by the far more conservative voice of the *London Quarterly Review*.[24]

Sir George Grey was not to be diverted by opposition to Clause 36, but he was delayed, in part by the slowness of the law officers, and also because the Senate, at this late stage, still asked for one or two small changes. One involved adding two new institutions – Queen's University of Ireland, with its affiliated colleges, and the University of Sydney – to the existing list, thus emphasizing the face-saving dual notion, which was, in effect, to continue indefinitely, of students taking degrees from colleges 'connected with' the University, and candidates from elsewhere.

Another change was more important, immediately, in a symbolic rather than a practical sense: it entailed the inclusion of 'science,' as a subject to be examined by the University, along with arts and laws and medicine. The appropriateness of the inclusion was apparent, very soon after the new Charter was introduced, when the Senate inaugurated a B Sc degree. But, again for reasons not at all clear, the new word had to be fought for, and was accepted only on the casting vote of the Chancellor after a division in which Arnott, Brande, Grote, Kiernan and Ryan were in favour, and Billing, Gull, Hammick, Hodgkin and Wood were opposed.[25]

It was not until 20 February 1858 that the final version of the Charter, blessed by the law officers, was received at the University. On that very day Palmerston resigned when censured for the Orsini affair. Lord Derby formed his second administration, and Spencer Walpole returned to the Home Office. The new Charter came before the Senate on 24 February, while the new Government was being put together, and was adopted, without a division, by fourteen senators – the Chancellor and Vice-Chancellor, Arnott, Billing, Clark, Faraday, Grote, Gull, Heywood, Hodgkin, Kiernan, Ryan, Stanley and Walker. A last hope for the overthrow of the new Charter was voiced by the *University of London Magazine* in March, but Spencer Walpole made no attempt to delay the end of a process which no doubt he, like his predecessor, had come to feel had gone on quite long enough.

Early in 1858, Admiral Beaufort died, and the vacant fellowship was filled, certainly on Granville's nomination and on Grey's formal recommendation, by Charles James Foster. Grote, when he heard of this as a possibility, saw it as a shrewd move which would tend to soften the hostility felt by the graduates towards the Senate:

> Assuming (what I do not know) that he [Foster] has troublesome dispositions, he will be a less dangerous enemy within the Senate than without it. . . . I do not feel sure that he will accept it, for if he looks to be elected Chairman of Convocation, he may perhaps prefer not to be in the Senate; but even if he refused it, the offer will still have a good effect.[26]

Foster accepted. He was subsequently elected Chairman of Convocation, and served in that capacity and on the Senate until 1863. He attended his first Senate meeting on 3 March 1858.

The new Charter was signed on 9 April. The Senate formally accepted it on 14 April. Convocation was called for 4 May.

CHAPTER 22

Retrospect

Five months after the University's new Charter was accepted, the General Medical Council came into being. Its arrival on the scene brought to an end a period of bargaining, manoeuvring and bitter conflict which had lasted for seventeen years, since the first comprehensive legislative attempts were made to find a national regulatory framework for the medical profession – and whose origins dated back to well before 1841. The new Council was an inevitable compromise, and did not please the more radical reformers. But it did produce a forum in which the University of London had a place, and it has remained a cornerstone of the regulatory mechanisms within which medicine is practised.

Henry Warburton died, at the age of 73, on 16 September 1858. He would have been among the reformers not a little disappointed at the outcome of the long struggle which produced the GMC; but he was probably not unpleased by the new Charter for the University, which incorporated the graduates and opened access to non-collegiate candidates for degrees - both causes he had long championed. It is, indeed, reasonable to argue that Warburton deserves to be treated as a pivotal figure in the search for regulation of the medical profession, and *the* pivotal figure in the early history of the University of London.

Warburton was well informed about university aspirations by his experience as a member of Council at University College, and thoroughly briefed on the complexities of the medical world through his campaign for the Anatomy Inspectorate and his chairmanship of the 1834 Select Committee on Medical Education. He seized on the idea of the University as only an examining body, to accommodate the thwarted ambitions of Gower Street, on the one hand, and as a device advantageous to the cause of generating better education and a more cohesive and efficient governance of the medical profession, on the other hand. While it is easy to ridicule the new University, with its total lack of teaching functions, such a judgement fails to give credit to what was a clever and workable political and administrative arrangement. While the documentary evidence is not conclusive, it leaves a strong impression that Warburton was especially far-seeing and persuasive in advocating the plan to the ministers, Russell and Spring Rice, who carried it through the Cabinet.

On the Senate, Warburton pressed his medical enthusiasms – not without clashing bitterly, on occasion, with the more conservative doctors - but also gave shrewd support to the cause of Dissent, and revealed a Radical passion for more democratically oriented constitutional practices. He was the major opponent of attempts to enforce compulsory religious examinations, of the confusion inherent in allowing senators to be examiners, and of what he regarded as too generous fees for examiners. And his original scheme for Convocation gave far more power to the graduates than what was eventually conceded in 1858. He was a tough and none too sensitive operator, but he upheld throughout the original intention of the University – to open up higher education to non-Anglicans and to encourage a more scientific medical training. To that he added a drive to offer the examinations to all qualified candidates, irrespective of where they received their instruction. He was the most persistent, attentive and generally successful proponent of the original vision, and zealous in his quest to extend it along radical lines.

The efforts of several others were, of course, admirable, but within narrower limits. Lubbock's achievement was to have driven and held together the hard-working but quarrelsome crew which launched the examination curriculum. Shaw Lefevre fitted the Vice-Chancellorship into a remarkably full life of public service with quiet efficiency and much diplomacy, but scarcely with any fire. Burlington presided with early enthusiasm and always with aristocratic serenity, but over time became a rather remote figure. The small handful of medical men who deserve immense credit for keeping the Senate going, particularly during the mid-1840s, have left little evidence, in that context, save the records of their attendance. Of them, and of the rather larger group who formed what has been called, in an earlier chapter, the outer ring, one can only say that they did their duty, without apparently bringing to it any noticeable *flair*. Perhaps, in the 1850s, that would be unfair to George Grote, who was clearly a formidable influence. But, in truth, *flair* was not a quality likely to have been of as much value, in many years of the Senate's early life, as simple attendance and attention to routine tasks. The intellectual – and, indeed, the political – virtues of many of the faithful attenders were doubtless more apparent in their strictly professional environs than they were in the Senate.

The role of those who, while being 'working' fellows, were in something of a natural minority on the Senate, cannot have been easy. Of all of them, Joseph Henry Jerrard must surely stand out as a courageous, if rather tactless, standard bearer of the Anglican creed and of the humanities. Almost alone, he had to try to resist the hard antipathy of Warburton and the indifference of many others towards his concerns. Nassau Senior, too, obviously found himself torn between his enthusiasm for extending education and his sympathy for the Anglican Establishment. In another context, Bacot and Ridout, as leading apothecaries, were at times very divided in their loyalties. But, on the whole, the medicos and the scientists must have been comforted by the sense that time was on their side, that the world was going in their direction.

Of the senior politicians, Thomas Spring Rice, Baron Monteagle, must be given credit for his genuine good will at the outset, and for his helpful interventions over the question of medical equality in the 1850s. Not a heavyweight minister, he was easily pushed aside by Russell, though he seemed to be able to resist some of Warburton's pressure. But he can be reasonably criticized for failing to see the desirability of distinguishing clearly between senators and examiners - a failure which put the University into a weak position, politically, from the start, and a particularly weak one when the Tories came to power in 1841. Both he and Russell were, perhaps, equally remiss in not following up their declared intention to ensure that the inequalities between London graduates and those of Oxbridge should be removed, if necessary, by legislation – an omission which was not admitted until Warburton shamed Sir George Grey about it in 1849, and was not remedied until 1854. Grey, though he came into the picture only half way through the period, must surely share the political honours with Warburton: as a minister he had an acute sense of when to make a firm commitment and when to drive it home.

The composition of the Senate, and the willingness of its members to serve, was a matter for anxiety throughout, and even after the Charter of 1858 came into effect, continued to worry the University's leaders. In 1858, as earlier, the problem for the future was being seen as essentially a problem of engaging and keeping an able and conscientious body of Fellows. Old divisions and weaknesses had not been banished. When new names were being bandied about, Grote told the Chancellor that

Bishops and Deans are the least suitable of all persons, in my judgement: of medical men, we have already a sufficiently large proportion: moreover anyone answering to the description of a strong medical man is not easy to be found. You may find good physicians, but few who are anything more than physicians: moreover, among those few, it will be scarcely possible to find one who will take a serious and active interest in L.U.

And in the context of the introduction of Convocation, Grote suggested that the graduates could never take the whole control of the University

unless we suppose a total expiration of earnest interest on the part of the *non-Graduate* members of the Senate. I should regret this as a great misfortune: but looking at what the Senate is now, I fear that it is not beyond the range of possibility.[1]

Granville, in turn, was not optimistic. In the summer of 1858 he told Mrs Grote that he had discussed 'several times' with her husband

what would be the best chance of getting for the Senate that sort of assistance even in a very inferior degree, which he has hitherto given. Bad and weak men we do not want, and the good and strong have other fish to fry. Poor Warburton is grown tiresome, and so irritable that it is impossible to do business with him. John Lefevre has all the qualifications excepting decision, for this sort of work. Senior is absorbed by writing down with more or less accuracy, [the sayings] more or less sincere, of persons in every part of the world. Overstone, Graham, Baines, Stanley, C. Lewis and others, will not attend.[2]

Perhaps attendance would have been better if the personnel of the Senate had been chosen without undue regard to political loyalties; but those who set up the University dared not take any risks. Throughout its establishment and its first two decades of operation, the University of London was overwhelmingly a Whig/Radical affair. It helped to meet the aspirations of the Dissenters and the ambitions of reforming medical men. The former was not attractive to the Tories, and the latter posed apparently insoluble problems for any government. The administration of Sir Robert Peel, having slapped the new institution on the wrist for the mess it had made of the appointment and payment of examiners, thereafter simply ignored it, save in the context of medical reform. And Peel's Home Secretary, Sir James Graham, was so responsive to the claims of the Royal Colleges that he could find little place for the University, whose members tended to be anti-medical Establishment. The five years from 1841 to 1846, so remarkable a period of talented national administration in so many spheres, was a slough of despond for Lord Burlington and his men. It is interesting to contemplate what might have been the University's further development had adequately supported Conservative governments run on into the 1850s. As it was, the weak Derby/Disraeli interlude in 1852 was notable for its acceptance of the principle of seeing London University represented in Parliament at some future date. That acceptance was at least a sign that the Conservative leaders were by then acutely aware of the political strength of Dissent, and had come to terms with the existence of a new and respectable academic institution.

But apart from these few manifestations of Tory/Conservative concern, the University was left to be promoted and argued about within Whig/Radical circles. Every appointment to the Senate and every change in the constitution of the University was made by the governments of Melbourne, Russell and Palmerston – though, technically, the 1858 Charter, while it had been prepared and agreed under Palmerston, was actually approved just after Derby came into office. And nearly all the big arguments about the policies and conduct of the University were carried on almost entirely within the interested Whig/Radical groups. Medicine was to some extent an exception, inasmuch as the medical corporations, intent on preserving their spheres of influence, were happy to rely on Peel's Government to ignore the University in the early 1840s. But on the major issue of the collegiate affiliation of examination candidates; on the whole question of Convocation; on the vexed matter of senatorial examiners (which was raised by Radicals and played into the hands of the Tories); and even in the agonizing struggle over biblical studies, the serious differences which existed were fought over amongst Liberals and practically ignored by more conservative elements in the political society of the times.

In the constitutional context, though, it is clear that there was throughout the period reviewed a move to ensure that the Senate was firmly anchored within the power structure of the Whig/Liberal political Establishment. The confusion of senators and examiners at the outset was clumsy and unfortunate, but it did imply the notion that the governing body should comprise mainly academic men with a handful of sympathetic people from the world of political and governmental affairs. As it turned out, the academic contingent did a rather remarkable job, for no material reward, in getting the University under way; and it was a small group of academic senators, mostly medics, who were simultaneously examiners, who held the University together for the years when the Peel Government was in office. But when the Whigs returned to power, they soon effectively rejected the idea of entrusting the running of the University to academics, and particularly to medical professors. No medical man was appointed in 1850 or 1856, and with the exception of George Grote and Arthur Hallam, the new senators (other than three graduates, themselves political activists, not to be regarded, primarily, as academics) were ministers, ex-ministers, an influential MP, a prominent public servant and an immensely rich City figure. If, by 1858, with the public men well entrenched, the day of the graduates had dawned, the likelihood of professorial involvement in the University's governance had clearly declined.

The extension of educational privilege to non-Anglicans, and the reform of the medical profession, were the twin causes which dominated the first years of the University of London. But they were very odd bedfellows. Dissenters, Roman Catholics, Jews and unbelievers were outsiders in the eyes of the social and political *elite*. Many of the most numerous group, the Dissenters, wanted a higher education in order to become or to enhance their status as ministers of religion. At least a third of the colleges affiliated to the University concentrated mainly on the training of clergy for the non-conformist minority: many of them were located in the northern industrial areas of Lancashire and Yorkshire.

At the same time, the apothecaries and surgeons who formed the great bulk of those practising medicine were, similarly, by no means high in the social scale. And as there was no university medical course in England outside Oxford and Cambridge, which produced only a tiny handful of physicians each year, most doctors with university training were either natives of Scotland and Ireland, or had been trained in one of those countries or on the Continent. But those who wanted young men in England to receive a superior medical degree from a new University of London, and in all probability the young men themselves, had no necessary concern with the injustices towards non-Anglicans which would be remedied, to a notable degree, by the establishment of the University. The medical reformers were eager to attract to their examinations men who wanted to be good doctors, whatever their religious affiliations.

From the outset, the University's graduates in law and medicine, whatever their religious denomination, were disadvantaged, within their respective professions, to the extent that they were not graduates of Oxford or Cambridge. It is significant that the first steps towards breaking down this barrier were taken by three non-Anglican London graduate lawyers – F.J. Wood, a Congregationalist; C.J. Foster, a Baptist; and Jacob Waley, a Jew. As men who would not have been able to take Oxbridge degrees, it was natural that they should merge their support for professional equality with their wider concerns about civic and religious emancipation for all non-Anglicans. Foster, who should be bracketed with Warburton as having exercised a substantial influence on the development of the young University, was a major activist for the Dissenting cause. But there is no evidence that the corresponding pioneers of graduate protest on the medical side, including Storrar, Manson and Robert Barnes, who came into the struggle five years later, were markedly non-Anglican, or that they were deeply moved by the search for religious equality: their major concern was to secure equivalent professional treatment to what was available to their Oxbridge counterparts.

In other circumstances, the different clienteles – religious, medical and legal – might well have pursued separate and perhaps conflicting campaigns to achieve their aims: and without some dynamic ministerial interference, or more charismatic leadership than was likely from the Senate, progress towards removal of barriers could have been much slower. It was fortunate, therefore, that the emergent leaders of the medical and non-medical graduate groups found common ground in the basically political demand for a share, by graduates, in the control of the University, and by their aspiration for separate parliamentary representation.

By embracing the wider constitutional perspective, the agitation for Convocation almost certainly did the University a great service, bringing the medical and non-medical faculties closer together, and effectively driving governments, albeit through some tortuous negotiations, to honour the original promise of equality with Oxbridge, and to put powerful political figures on to the Senate, even at the cost of overlooking the professoriate. And it is only just to honour the full-blooded contribution of Wakley's *Lancet*, which consistently brought equal weight – and venom – to bear in favour of professional and religious equality and of the establishment of Convocation.

There is no small amount of irony in the situation which developed in 1857. Here, by then, was an eccentric University, without teaching functions, which, after twenty years of restricted and difficult growth, was ready to celebrate the award of a new Charter which would include a modest sharing of control of its operations with its graduates. The University had been created by the pragmatic decision to sacrifice conventional form and function in order to provide opportunity for higher education to non-Anglicans, and to rationalize and encourage better medical training. It was a radical move, modified by the arrangements whereby only students who were able to find places in approved colleges and medical schools would be eligible to sit the degree examinations of the new University.

But now, when the working Senate, branded by many of its critics as unwilling to concede any shadow of democratic control to its graduates, proposed to take a major radical step forward, by allowing any matriculated non-medical student to attempt degree examinations, irrespective of where he had studied, the bulk of the graduates and most of the affiliated colleges exploded with wrath and accused the Senate of bad faith. Thus did the products of a radical experiment wish to maintain the most socially conservative aspect of that experiment, and to deny to a wider potential clientele the opportunity of taking a degree 'externally'. Perhaps, in the search for and protection of status, 'twas ever thus.

It is to the eternal credit of the Senate and the governments of the day that the proposal to open the examinations to non-collegiate students was put into effect. No doubt, by 1858, the increasing number of colleges affiliated to the University had decreased somewhat the proportion of strictly denominational seminaries, and thus encouraged Anglicans as well as non-Anglicans to offer themselves as candidates for degrees. As the medical schools had not been denominationally restricted, this meant that the University was already attracting a more cosmopolitan mix of candidates for its examinations than had been envisaged, originally. But further progress along that road would have been slow, and opportunities would have been much restricted from parts of the country where colleges had not been established or had not requested affiliation. Though Lord Monteagle was unhappy with the notion of the non-collegiate graduate, one wonders whether, in his final years, he might have come to feel that, by opening its doors wider, Our Minerva, as he had hoped in 1838, was indeed walking 'with less difficulty'.

Examiners
(Fellows in italics)

Arts

Classics, Logic	*Newell Connop Thirlwall*	1839
& Moral	*Joseph Henry Jerrard*	1839–52
Philosophy	Thomas Borrow Burcham	1840–57
	Henry Alford	1842–56
	William Smith	1853–8
	Alexander Bain	1857–8
	Thomas Spencer Baynes	1857–8
Mathematics	George Birch Jerrard	1839–58
	Robert Murphy	1839–42
	James William Lucas Heaviside	1843–58
Chemistry	*William Thomas Brande*	1839
	John Frederick Daniell	1839–44
	Thomas Graham	1845–55
	Robert Dundas Thomson	1856–8
Natural History	*John Stevens Henslow*	1839–58
French	Charles Jean Delille	1839–58
German	Christoph Heinrich	
	Friedrich Bialloblotzky	1839–48
	Adolphus Walbaum	1849–58
Political Economy	*Nassau William Senior*	1840–56
	Jacob Waley	1857–8
Hebrew & Greek	William Drake	1839–58
Texts & Scriptural	Thomas Stone	1839–49
History	Frederick William Gotch	1850–8

Laws

Law &	*William Empson*	1839–40
Jurisprudence	John Thomas Graves	1841–8
	Nassau William Senior	1849–58

In addition, the following served as examiners in special legal subjects, usually for LL B Honours and LL D, but sometimes for LL B examinations when there was a heavy load. *Senior* took additional work in 1842, 1843, 1845 and 1846, and every year from 1850 to 1857. *Empson* and *John Shaw Lefevre* assisted in 1842 and 1843; *Andrew Amos* in 1843 and 1845. Howard Elphinstone helped in 1843, 1845 and 1846; Peter Stafford Carey and David Jardine in 1843. Thomas Tomlinson, the University's counsel, examined in Common Law in 1848, 1850, 1853, and from 1855 to 1857. Sir John Dodgson was engaged to examine in Common Law in 1852; and George Bower examined in Roman Law in 1854.

Medicine

Medicine	*Archibald Billing*	1839–58
	Alexander Tweedie	1839
		1841–58
	Thomas Watson	1840
Surgery	*Sir Stephen Love Hammick, Bt*	1839–58
	John Bacot	1839–45
	Caesar Henry Hawkins	1846–9
	Joseph Hodgson	1850–5
	William Fergusson	1856–8
Anatomy &	*Francis Kiernan*	1839–58
Physiology	Robert Bentley Todd	1839
	William Sharpey	1840–58
Physiology &	*Peter Mark Roget*	1839–41
Comparative	Thomas Rymer Jones	1842–6
Anatomy	William Benjamin Carpenter	1847–56
	Thomas Henry Huxley	1856–8
Midwifery &	*Charles Locock*	1839–40
Diseases of Women	Edward Rigby	1841–58
Chemistry	John Frederick Daniell	1839–44
	William Thomas Brande	1845–58
Botany	*John Stevens Henslow*	1839–58
Materia Medica	Jonathan Pereira	1840–52
& Pharmacy	Owen Rees	1853–8

Five of the six fellows who were examiners in 1858 – *Billing, Hammick, Henslow, Kiernan and Senior* – retained their posts until, under the terms of the 1858 Charter, they were unable to continue. The ban came into effect in April 1861. After that, no member of Senate could examine, and the term of office of examiners was restricted to five years.

APPENDIX II

Institutions, approved by the Secretary of State, whose students, having matriculated, could become candidates for degrees in Arts and Laws of the University of London

1836   University College London
King's College London
1840   St Cuthbert's College, Ushaw, Durham (a)
Stonyhurst College (a)
Manchester New College
Royal Belfast Academical Institution (b)
Bristol College (c)
Old College, Homerton ⎱ These two colleges were merged in
Highbury College ⎰ 1851 to become New College, London
Colleges of St Peter and St Paul, Prior Park, Bath (a) (d)
St Mary's College, Oscott (a)
St Patrick's College, Carlow (a)
St Edmund College, Ware (a)
Spring Hill College, Birmingham
Countess of Huntingdon's College, Cheshunt
Baptist Academical Institution at Stepney (later Stepney College and then The College, Regents Park)
Baptist College, Bristol
Airedale Independent College, Undercliffe, Nr Bradford
Protestant Dissenters' College, Rotherham
College of St Gregory the Great, Downside, Nr Bath (a)
1842   Presbyterian College, Carmarthen
1844   St Kyran's College, Kilkenny (a)

Huddersfield College
Lancashire Independent College
Wesley College, Nr Sheffield
1846   Queen's College, Birmingham
Wesleyan Collegiate Institution at Taunton
1848   Western College, Plymouth
1849   West of England Dissenters' Proprietary School, Taunton
St Patrick's College, Thurles (a)
1850   Universities of the United Kingdom
1851   Owen's College, Manchester
Bedford Grammar Schools
1852   Brecon Independent College
Horton College, Bradford
Hackney Theological Seminary
1856   Queen's Colleges, Belfast and Galway
Trevecca College, Breconshire
Springfield College, Ennis
Bishop Stortford Collegiate School
Working Mens' College, London
1857   Liverpool Institute (also called Queen's College, Liverpool)
Queen's College, Cork

(a) Roman Catholic College
(b) The Royal Belfast Academical Institution was riven by doctrinal disputes. No faculty meetings were held after January 1841 and, though lectures and classes continued until 1849, 'the death throes of the Collegiate Department were already apparent by the end of 1840.' *See* John Jamieson, *History of the Royal Belfast Academical Institution, 1810–1960*, Belfast, 1959, p. 55.
(c) Bristol College closed in December 1841.
(d) The Colleges of St Peter and St Paul, Prior Park, closed in 1856.

Forty-three London degrees were awarded to candidates from colleges which ceased to be affiliated before 1858. No degrees had been awarded to candidates - if there were any – up to 1858, from the following: St Kyran's College, Kilkenny; St Patrick's College, Thurles; Horton College, Bradford; Bishop Stortford Collegiate School; the Working Men's College; and the Liverpool Institute. *See* F.G. Brook, *The University of London 1820–1860, with Special Reference to its Influence on the Development of Higher Education*. PhD Thesis, London, 1958, Appendix III.

Institutions of undoubted university status in the above list were the Universities of the United Kingdom; UCL and King's College, London; and the Queen's Colleges at Belfast, Galway and Cork, which were parts of the University of Ireland set up by Sir Robert Peel in 1845. Apart from them, of the other 37 institutions listed, only 31 produced candidates who successfully took London degrees, and three of those had closed or lost their connection with the University before 1858.

The Universities of Sydney and Toronto were added to the list of affiliated institutions in the Charter of April 1858.

Medical schools whose students, having matriculated, could become candidates for degrees of the University of London

Over eighty medical schools and nearly a score of individual teachers of medical subjects were approved in the first twenty years of the University's existence. But by 1858 all the individual teachers and a dozen schools were no longer listed: no doubt the individuals had retired or died; some of the schools had merged with other institutions, and a few had closed.

Despite this apparently long list of participating institutions and teachers, the 312 medical degrees conferred were awarded to candidates from only 26 or 27 schools(a) – 12 in London, 5 in the English provinces, 2 or 3 in Edinburgh and 7 in Dublin. All those schools had been approved by 1841. And the graduates of the 12 London schools shared 275 degrees, while the graduates from schools in the English provinces, Scotland and Ireland were awarded 19, 4 and 14 degrees respectively. 168 of the 275 degrees awarded to students trained in London medical schools were taken by candidates from UCL and King's.

The following list includes the medical schools affiliated to the University, but does not include the establishments of approved individual teachers. Those schools which trained students who achieved degrees are marked*; those whose affiliation had lapsed by 1858, for whatever reason, are marked+: they include six which had produced London graduates.

The list has been compiled from three sources: Senate minutes; an Appendix to F.G. Brooks's PhD thesis, the details of which are given in the notes to Appendix II; and PP 1845 xxxv, *Return of the Names of the Colleges and Institutions of General Instruction, in connexion with the University of London, and of the County in which they are situated. The same of the Medical Schools in connexion with the University of London.* The records, however, are still in a few cases somewhat ambiguous, and it is possible that, in the first year or two, one or two small schools, not listed here, were approved, but their approval was not included in the minutes of the Senate. No such school, however, produced a successful candidate for a medical degree.

1836   University College London*
        King's College London*

1839   The London Hospital*
        Charing Cross Hospital*
        Middlesex Hospital*
        St Thomas's Hospital*
        St Bartholomew's Hospital*
        Westminster Hospital*
        Guy's Hospital*
        School of Anatomy adjoining St George's Hospital
        Medical School at St George's Hospital*
        Aldersgate School*+
        Hunterian School+
        School of Webb Street, Southwark*+

        Birmingham Royal School of Medicine and Surgery (became the medical department of Queen's College in 1843)*
        Theatre of Anatomy and Medicine, Upper Priory, Birmingham+
        Bristol Medical School*
        Hull and East Riding of Yorkshire School of Medicine and Anatomy*
        Leeds School of Medicine and Surgery*
        Royal Manchester School of Medicine and Surgery*
        Newcastle on Tyne School of Medicine and Surgery (renamed in 1852, Newcastle on Tyne College of Medicine in connection with the University of Durham)
        Sheffield Medical Institution
        York School of Medicine

        Minto House Dispensary, Edinburgh+
        Royal College of Surgeons of Edinburgh*+
        Queen's College, Edinburgh+(a)
        University of Edinburgh*
        Andersonian Institute, Glasgow

        Royal Belfast Academical Institution+
        Cork School of Anatomy, Medicine and Surgery+

Cork Recognized School of Medicine
Cork North Infirmary
Apothecaries Hall of Ireland (became the Medical School of the Catholic University of Ireland in 1854)*+
School of Medicine, Park Street, Dublin (closed 1849)+
Richmond Hospital School of Anatomy, Medicine and Surgery, Dublin (became Carmichael School in 1852)*
School of Physic in Ireland*
Original School of Medicine, Peter Street, Dublin*
Theatre of Anatomy and School of Surgery, Peter Street, Dublin (closed 1841)+

University of Malta

1840   Physicians of St Marylebone Infirmary

Dublin School of Anatomy, Surgery and Medicine, Digges Street (closed 1857)*+
Jervis Street Hospital, Dublin
Mercers' Hospital, Dublin*
St Vincent's Hospital, Dublin

1841   General Hospital, Birmingham

City of Dublin Hospital
Meath Hospital, Dublin
Royal College of Surgeons in Ireland*+
Military Hospital in the Island of Ceylon

1842   Queen's County Infirmary, Maryborough, Ireland

1843   Bristol Infirmary
St Peter's Hospital, Bristol

Cork South Infirmary
Coombe Lying-in Hospital, Dublin

1844   Manchester Union Hospital

1845   Fever Hospital and Infirmary, Liverpool
Liverpool Infirmary School of Medicine
Manchester Royal Infirmary

Royal Infirmary, Edinburgh

Dr Steeven's Hospital, Dublin

Medical College of Bengal

1846   Royal Naval College at Haslar
        Leeds General Infirmary
        Leicester Infirmary

        University of McGill College, Montreal

1847   Royal College of Chemistry

1848   Medical School of King's College and University of Aberdeen

1849   Nottingham General Hospital

1850   Glasgow Royal Infirmary

1851   Northampton General Infirmary

        Queen's University in Ireland

1852   Sydenham College, Birmingham
        School of Medicine in Chatham Street, Manchester

        University of Glasgow

1853   St Lawrence School of Medicine, Montreal

1854   St Mary's Hospital, Paddington

        Bedford General Infirmary and Fever Hospital+

1855   Grant Medical College, Bombay

1856   Brompton Hospital for Consumption and Diseases of the
        Chest
        Newcastle on Tyne Infirmary

(a) In Edinburgh, a considerable group of extra-academical teachers developed during the early ninteenth century. Several were approved, individually, by the University of London and the Secretary of State. A group of them worked together and apparently called themselves, for a while, Queen's College. Later, some of that group went back to being individually approved teachers. Some form of loose association of these teachers continued through most of the century, and they did not merge into an extra-academical school of medicine of the Royal Colleges, until 1895. While no successful London graduate appears to have been produced by any of these individuals or groups before 1858, one successful candidate for a degree is recorded as having been trained by the Royal College of Surgeons of Edinburgh, and one by Surgeons' Hall, Edinburgh. It is unclear whether the expression, 'the Hall', simply meant the headquarters of the Royal College of Surgeons, or was shorthand for the organization of extra-academical teachers. The old Surgeons' Hall stood in Surgeons' Square, which has been described as 'both the birthplace and the nursery of the extra-mural or extra-academical school of medicine.' (*See* A. Logan Turner, *Story of a Great Hospital. The Royal Infirmary of Edinburgh 1729–1929* (1937), pp. 140, 184.) So far as the University of London is concerned, if Surgeons' Hall was in some way a separate institution from the Royal College then 27 medical schools produced London graduates; if not, then the figure was only 26.

Sources

Specific references in the notes to each chapter comprise a guide to relevant secondary literature. Selected portions of the manuscript material in the collections listed below were examined. In addition, papers privately held by Mr D.C. Holland were used.

Windsor: *Royal Archives*
Baring Bros: *Northbrook Mss*
British Library: *Napier* and *Peel Mss*
Chatsworth: *Devonshire Mss*
Gray's Inn: *Pension Records*
Greater London Record Office: *Liberation Society Records*
Guildhall Library, Corporation of London: *Records of Society of Apothecaries*
House of Lords Record Office: *Shaw Lefevre Mss*
Inner Temple: *Bench Table Orders*
King's College, London: *Council Minutes;* and in the private papers series in the Library Mss collection, the *Daniell Mss*
Lincoln's Inn: *Black Books*
Middle Temple: *Minutes of Parliament*
National Library of Ireland: *Monteagle Mss*
National Library of Wales: *Nassau Senior Mss*
Public Record Office: *Home Office, Treasury, Treasury Solicitor, Granville and Russell Mss*
Royal Astronomical Society: *Minutes*
Royal College of Physicians: *College Records* and *Diary of Sir James Clark*
Royal College of Surgeons: *Minutes of Council*
Royal Society: *Herschell* and *Lubbock Mss*
Society of Apothecaries: *Society Records*
Southampton University: *Melbourne (Broadlands) Mss*
Trinity College, Cambridge: *Whewell Mss*
University College London: *College Records* and *Brougham Mss*

University of London: *University Records, Airy* and *Overstone Mss*
Wellcome Institute, Contemporary Medical Archives Centre: *Ashton-Underwood Mss*

Notes

ABBREVIATIONS
RA   Royal Archives
BL   British Library
DNB   *Dictionary of National Biography*
HO   Home Office
LMG   *London Medical Gazette*
NLI   National Library of Ireland
PP   Parliamentary Papers
PRO   Public Record Office
RCP   Royal College of Physicians
RCS   Royal College of Surgeons
SM   Senate Minutes
T   Treasury
TS   Treasury Solicitor
UCL   University College London
UL   University of London

INTRODUCTION
1 H. Hale Bellot, *University College London 1826–1926* (London, 1929), and 'The University of London' in *Victoria County History of Middlesex* I (1969): F.J.C. Hearnshaw, *Centenary History of King's College, London, 1828–1928* (London, 1929); G. Huelin, *King's College, London, 1828–1978* (London, 1978); Negley Harte, *The University of London, 1836–1986* (London, 1986); Negley Harte and John North, *The World of University College* (London, 1978, 1991); Sheldon Rothblatt, 'London: a metropolitan university?' in Thomas Bender (ed.), *The University and the City: From Medieval Origins to the Present* (Oxford, 1988).
2 S.W.F. Holloway, 'Medical education in England, 1830–1858: a sociological analysis,' in *History*, xlix, 167, Oct 1964, pp. 299–324.
3 Parl Deb 3s, xxvii, debate of 26 March 1835.
4 Brougham Mss, 38156, Russell to Brougham, 22 Dec 1836.
5 A.B. Kriegel (ed.), *The Holland House Diaries, 1831–1840* (London, 1977), pp. 303, 305–6; Lytton Strachey and Roger Fulford (eds) *The Greville Memoirs* III (London, 1938), pp. 204–6.
6 Lubbock Mss, R40, Spring Rice to Lubbock, 24 Sep 1835. A similar letter to Airy is printed in Harte, *University of London*, pp. 81–2.

7 For the early charters of the University, see *University of London: The Historical Record, 1836–1912* (London, 1912).

8 Hearnshaw, *Centenary History*, p. 132; Bellot, *Vic. Hist.*, pp. 317–8.

9 F.M.L. Thompson (ed.), *The University of London and the World of Learning, 1836–1986* (London, 1990). See also F.G. Brook, 'The University of London 1820–60, with special reference to its influence on the development of higher education,' London, PhD thesis, 1958.

10 For a history of the early struggles to establish Convocation, drawn largely from published sources, see P. Dunsheath and M. Miller, *Convocation in the University of London: The First Hundred Years* (London, 1958).

1 THE SEARCH FOR A FRAMEWORK

1 Kriegel, *Holland House Diaries*, pp. 305–6.

2 Select Committee on Medical Education, PP 1834, xiii.

3 Hale Bellot, *University College*, p. 233.

4 *LMG*, 20 Jul 1833, 20 Apr 1834: *Athenaeum*, Dec 1833: Parl Deb 3s xxvii 289–99, 26 Mar 1835.

5 RA MP 85/59.

6 Edwin Lee, a witness before the Select Committee on Medical Registration in 1847, PP 1847–48, xv, Question 5262, stated: 'It was . . . the original intention of the Government, instead of granting a Charter to the London University, to form a general examining Board; that, I believe, was proposed by Mr Warburton in 1834 or 1836.' For more evidence of Warburton's willingness in late 1834 and early 1835 to contemplate an independent set of examiners, see Edward Edwards, *Remarks on the Ministerial Plan of a Central University Examining Board* (London, 29 Feb 1836).

7 HO 72/3, Tooke to Goulburn, 6 Apr 1835.

8 *LMG*, 8 Aug 1835.

9 NLI 555, Letter Book, 27 Jan 1836.

10 *Irish Quarterly Review*, xxvii, Oct 1857.

11 *Eclectic Review*, May 1851, p. 518. See also numerous letters in the Monteagle Mss, and the UCL Council Minutes.

William Tooke, 1777–1863, Solicitor, MP Truro, 1833–7, Founding Member of UCL Council, 1826, Treasurer to 1841; published *University of London: statement of facts as to Charter* (1835).

John Romilly, 1802–1874, second son of Sir Samuel Romilly; barrister, MP Bridport, 1832–5, 1846–7, Devonport, 1847–52, Solicitor General, 1848, Attorney General, 1850, Master of the Rolls 1851–73, raised to peerage, 1865. The last Master of the Rolls to sit in the Commons. Interestingly enough, so formidable a proponent of the concerns of UCL was married to the second daughter of William Otter, first Principal of King's College, later Bishop of Chichester and a fellow of the University of London.

12 NLI 551, Spring Rice to Tooke, 19 Jul 1835.

13 Parl Deb 3s xxix 1249–50, 30 Jul 1835.

14 Whewell Mss, Add Mss a 62/28, Monteagle to Whewell, 28 Jun 1854.
15 UCL Council Minutes, 22 Aug 1835.
16 UCL Council Minutes, 22 Aug 1835.
17 NLI 551, Spring Rice to Romilly, 22 Nov 1835; UCL Council Minutes, 24 Nov 1835.
18 NLI 551, Spring Rice to Tooke, 8 Dec 1835; UCL Council Minutes, 5 Nov 1836.
19 *LMG*, 5 Dec 1835.

2 MEDICAL DEADLOCK

 1 UCL Council Minutes, 4 Jun 1836.
 2 Charles Singer and S.W.F. Holloway, 'Early medical education in relation to the pre-history of London University,' in *Medical History*, vol. 4, p. 15.
 3 Charles Newman, *The Evolution of Medical Education in the Nineteenth Century* (London, 1957), and Singer and Holloway, 'Early medical education,' *passim*.
 4 Zachary Cope, Kt., *The Royal College of Surgeons of England* (London, 1959), p. 158; HO49/8, Fox Maule to Attorney General, 16 Dec 1835.
 5 Sir George Clark, *A History of the Royal College of Physicians of London* 2 (London, 1966), p. 694.
 6 NLI 553, Spring Rice to Halford, 5 and 13 Feb 1836.
 7 *LMG*, 20 Feb 1836.
 8 *LMG*, 23 Apr 1836.
 9 Clark, *College of Physicians*, 2, 694–5. *LMG*, 14 May 1836. Two years later, the Earl of Burlington met Sir Henry Halford at a dinner, and recorded that Halford

> talked to me about the London University. It appears that he proposed that the College of Physicians should have the power of granting degrees in Medicine to candidates receiving certificates from the University. He repeated a vast number of his own Latin verses, and seems to be something of an old twaddle.

Devonshire Mss, Diary of Earl of Burlington, 17 Feb 1838 (Hereinafter, 'Burlington, Diary'.)
10 Clark, *College of Physicians*, 2, 694–5. Sir Henry Holland's Journal, Sep 1836.
11 UCL Council Minutes, 4 Jun 1836.
12 Lubbock Mss B603, Burrows to Lubbock, 25 Jan 1841; Sir Henry Holland's Journal, Sep 1836 and Aug 1838.
13 RCS Minutes of Council, 7 Dec 1835 and 14 Jan 1836; Clark, *College of Physicians*, 2, 669: *LMG*, 20 Aug 1836.
14 UCL Council Minutes, 4 Jun 1836.
15 *London Medical and Surgical Journal*, 24 Dec 1836.
16 UCL Council Minutes, 30 Jan 1836; UCL College Corresp 3615, draft,

Warburton to Spring Rice, Feb 1836; *LMG*, 20 Feb 1836, Warburton's letter to Edinburgh Town Council.
17 UCL Council Minutes, 30 Jan 1836, and College Correspondence 3615.

3 CHOOSING THE SENATORS

1 NLI 13382 MF8432, Melbourne to Spring Rice, 8 Sep 1836.
2 NLI 551, Spring Rice to Warburton, Aug 1835.
3 The full text is reproduced in Harte, *University of London*, pp. 81–2.
4 Faraday's invitation is printed in F.A.J.L. James, *Correspondence of Michael Faraday 1832–1840*, II (London, 1993).
5 NLI 555, letter from Allen, via Lord John Russell, recommending Sir Stephen Hammick, 8 Dec 1835; and letter from Sir George Phillips, Bt, to Spring Rice, recommending Dr Roget, 15 Dec 1835.
6 RA MP 20/131, Burlington to Melbourne, 17 Feb 1836; NLI 553, Spring Rice to Burlington, 15 Feb 1836; HO 117/4, Russell to Burlington, 1 Dec 1836.
7 NLI 13382, Senior to Spring Rice, 16/17 Feb 1836: UCL, Brougham Mss 38156, Russell to Brougham, 22 Dec 1836.
8 PRO 30/22/2D/247–8, Henslow to Russell, 24 Dec 1836.
9 PRO 30/22/2D/283, nd Spring Rice to Russell; NLI 551, Dr Davy to Spring Rice, recommending Jerrard, Dec 1835.
10 NLI 542, Spring Rice to Otter, 16 Aug 1836; NLI 13382 MF8432 Russell to Spring Rice, 30 Oct 1836.
11 *LMG*, 23 Jul, 20 Aug 1836.
12 *LMG*, 4 Jun, 23 Jul 1836.
13 NLI 13382 MF8432, Melbourne to Spring Rice, 8 Sep 1836.
14 *LMG*, 31 Dec 1836.
15 C.R.B. Barrett, *History of the Society of Apothecaries* (London, 1905), Ch. 23. See also Ch. 16 of the unpublished Mss of the History of the Society by Edgar Ashton-Underwood, in the Contemporary Medical Archives Centre at the Wellcome Institute for the History of Medicine, PP/EAU/F39.
16 *LMG*, 31 Dec 1836, 14 Jan 1837; Lubbock Mss R136, Roget to Lubbock, 24 Dec 1836.
17 PP 1842, xxiii, HC 542, Burlington to Goulburn, 8 Dec 1841.
18 PRO 30/22/2D, Warburton to Russell, 17 Dec 1836.
19 NLI 542, Spring Rice to Russell, 18 Dec 1836.
20 PRO 30/22/2D/212–13, Warburton to Russell, 17 Dec 1836.

4 THE TEAM ASSEMBLED

1 W.M. Torrens, *Memoirs of William Lamb, 2nd Viscount Melbourne* ii (London, 1878), p. 158, 'Private and confidential circular, Sept 8, 1835.'
2 Melbourne (Broadlands) Mss, MEL/RU/281, 18 Dec 1836.
3 NLI 13381 MF8431, reproduced in Torrens, above, and in Harte, *University of London*, p. 74; HO 72/3.
4 PP 1836 HC 604 xlvii, 43.

5 RA MP 13/53, Russell to Melbourne, 7 Oct 1836.

6 Melbourne (Broadlands) Mss, MEL/RU/273, Melbourne to Russell, 16 Oct 1836.

7 NLI 13382, Russell to Spring Rice, 30 Oct 1836.

8 NLI 13347, Empson to Spring Rice, 4 Feb 1837.

9 Russell's letter to Burlington was dated 1 Dec, and Burlington's reply was dated 9 Dec. The *Morning Chronicle* carried them on 12 Dec and *The Times* on 13 Dec 1836.

10 *Morning Post*, 13 Dec 1836.

11 *Times*, 13 Dec 1836.

12 *Lancet*, 24 Dec 1836.

13 *Times*, 16 Dec 1836.

14 *Times*, 21 Dec 1836.

15 *Lancet*, 24 Dec 1836.

16 UCL Council Minutes, 7 Dec 1836.

17 PRO 30/22/2D/297–8, Brougham to Russell, nd Nov 1836.

18 PRO 30/22/2D/229–30, Brougham to Russell, 21 Dec 1836.

19 Brougham Mss, 38156, 14427, 38162, 14428, 38166, Russell to Brougham, 22 Dec 1836, 3 Jan, 15 Aug, 3 Oct, 28 Nov 1837.

20 Burlington, Diary, 22 Jan 1838.

21 PRO 30/22/2D/234, Sheepshanks to Russell, 21 Dec 1836.

22 Anthony Hyman, *Charles Babbage, Pioneer of the Computer* (Oxford, 1982), p. 221.

23 NLI 13347, Empson to Spring Rice, 4 Feb 1837; Airy Mss, Lubbock to Airy, 28 Jan 1837.

24 BL Add Mss 34618, Empson to Napier, 27 Feb 1837. It is not clear whether this dinner was the same as one which Airy notes as having preceded the first meeting of the Senate, and which he attended: see Sir George Biddell Airy (ed. Wilfrid Airy), *Autobiography* (Cambridge, 1896), p. 131.

5 AN OLIGARCHICAL TENDENCY

1 HO 72/3, Maltby to Russell, 19 Oct 1837; Herschell Mss, H.l.79, Airy to Herschell, 19 Jan 1839.

2 PP xxiii, 421, HC 542, 1842, Burlington to Goulburn, 8 Dec 1841. See also, Lubbock Mss, J48, Jerrard to Lubbock, 12 Feb 1837, and BL Add Mss 40570, Jerrard to Bishop of Norwich, 14 Jul 1845.

3 Hearnshaw, *Centenary History*, p. 124.

4 Lubbock Mss, A141, Airy to Lubbock, 15 Feb 1839.

5 Arnold to Edward Stanley, Bishop of Norwich, 7 Jun 1838, printed in A.P. Stanley, *The Life and Correspondence of Thomas Arnold, D.D.* (London, 1844), pp. 448–9.

6 Leonard Jenyns, *Memoir of the Rev John Stevens Henslow* (London, 1862), pp. 161–2.

7 Lubbock Mss, A127, A134, Airy to Lubbock, 4 Jan, 9 Apr 1838.

8 Lotte and Joseph Hamburger, *Troubled Lives: John and Sarah Austin* (Toronto, 1985).

9 R.C. Maulitz, 'Metropolitan medicine and the man-midwife: the early life and letters of Charles Locock,' *Medical History*, 1982, 26: 25–46. D.L. Moore, *Ada, Countess of Lovelace, Byron's Legitimate Daughter* (London, 1977), p. 200.

10 *Lancet*, 4 Feb 1865.

6 THOSE WHO SERVED

1 Statistics have been taken or compiled from various documents in the University's archives.

2 Burlington, Diary, 9 Mar 1840; Whewell Mss, Add Mss c88/22, Burlington to Whewell, 9 Mar 1840.

3 Burlington, Diary, 25 Jul 1856.

4 Devonshire Mss, 116.3, Lubbock to Burlington, 20 May 1842; Lubbock Mss C86, Burlington to Lubbock, 30 May 1842.

5 Lubbock Mss C87, Burlington to Lubbock, 11 Jun 1842.

6 Devonshire Mss 116.4, Lefevre to Burlington, 8 Jun 1842.

7 Airy Mss, Airy to Lubbock, 13 Dec 1838.

8 See, e.g., Herschell Mss H.1.79, Airy to Herschell, 19 Jun 1839.

9 UL ST/2/2/1, Meeting of l6 May 1837.

10 Shaw Lefevre Mss, House of Lords Record Office, Burlington to Lefevre, 7 Jun 1842.

11 UL/RO/2/10, 14.

12 See correspondence of C.T. Beke and Bialloblotzky, 5 Jul 1848, 4 Jan 1849, 26 May 1849, published in pamphlet form, and C.T. Beke, *Dr Bialloblotzky's Journey to Discover the Source of the Nile*, 11 Jan 1850.

13 Minutes of the Royal Astronomical Society, vol. 17, p. 103.

7 CURRICULUM, REGISTRAR, CHARTER

1 Thompson, *University of London and World of Learning*, p. 62.

2 NLI 13382, Senior to Spring Rice, 16 Feb 1836.

3 Arnold to Burlington, 26 May 1837, in UL ST 3/2/1, Minutes of Faculty of Arts, 31 May 1837. In the remainder of this chapter, no references are given for the sources of excerpts from letters, etc., reproduced in the minutes of the Senate or the Faculty of Arts.

4 Augustus de Morgan, *Thoughts Suggested by the Establishment of the University of London* (London, 1837), p. 22.

5 UL J Sed (BP4), *Pamphlets Relating to the University of London*, Vol. III, which includes W. Parish Robertson, *Analysis of the Code Universitaire of France*, and *Analysis of the Statutes of the University of Bonn* (London, 1838), and J. Berridge, *Analysis and Abstract, with Reference to the University of Gottingen, of the Laws for Students and of the Mss Relating to Faculties*, nd.

6 See, *inter alia*, Airy Mss, letters between Airy and Lubbock, 8 Feb to 26 Mar, 1839, and again in Oct 1839 to Feb 1840.

7 UL [QML Additions] 370 (BP1), de Morgan to Lubbock, 4 Dec 1838. Handwritten version in Lubbock Mss, D82.

8 L.P. Le Quesne, 'Medicine', in Thompson, *University of London and World of Learning*, p. 131.

9 Lubbock Mss D80, de Morgan to Lubbock, 4 Apr 1838; P109, Peacock to Lubbock, 22 Sep 1838; D7 Daniell to Lubbock, 29 Nov 1838.

10 Comments on proposals for the Arts and Medical degrees were invited from a range of people in UCL, King's and the London medical schools. *See* UL J Sed (BP4), *Pamphlets Relating to the University of London*, Vol. III, which includes *Letters on the Proof Report of the Committee of the Faculty of Medicine*, and *Letters Relating to the Examinations for the Degree in Arts, 1838, to the Lord Bishop of Durham*.

11 Airy Mss, Airy to Lubbock, 15 Feb 1839.

12 NLI 13382 MFP8432, Russell to Spring Rice, 19 Dec 1836; 13347, Empson to Spring Rice, 4 Feb 1837; Lubbock Mss R136, Roget to Lubbock, 24 Dec 1836.

13 NLI 542, Spring Rice to Russell, 18 Dec 1836.

14 PRO 30/22/2D/200, 212–13, Warburton to Russell, 16 and 17 Dec 1836; NLI 542, Spring Rice to Russell, 18 Dec 1836; 13382, Russell to Spring Rice, 19 Dec 1836, 4 Jan 1837; 13347, Empson to Spring Rice, 4 Feb 1837: Brougham Mss 14421, 14427, 38157–8, Russell to Brougham, 3, 10, 15, 20 Jan 1837; Lubbock Mss C332, 344, 350, Coates to Lubbock, 22 Dec 1835, 15 Mar 1837, 10 Feb 1838.

15 PRO 30/22/2D/264–5, Burlington to Russell, 23 and 29 Dec 1836.

16 PRO 30/22/2D/200, 212–13, Warburton to Russell, 16 and 17 Dec 1836.

17 NLI 542, Spring Rice to Russell, 18 Dec 1836; 13382, Russell to Spring Rice, 4 Jan 1837.

18 Airy Mss, Lubbock to Airy, 28 Jan 1837.

19 Airy Mss, Lubbock to Airy, 14 and 16 Mar 1837; Memorandum dated 15 Apr 1837; Airy to Lubbock, 15 Mar 1837.

20 *London Medical and Surgical Journal, (Ryan)*, 11 Mar 1837.

21 L.S. Jacyna (ed.); *A Tale of Three Cities. The Correspondence of William Sharpey and Allen Thomson* (London, 1989), p. 11, Sharpey to Thomson, 22 Mar 1837.

22 *London Medical and Surgical Journal (Ryan)*, 22 Apr 1837.

23 Daniell Mss, Otter to Daniell, nd.; Lubbock Mss D6, Daniell to Lubbock – a formal statement of his candidacy, dated 4 Mar 1838.

24 Russell's memo of proposals made to a delegation on 13 Jul 1838, printed in SM 18 Jul 1838: Brougham Mss, 38162, Russell to Brougham, 15 Aug 1837.

25 Brougham Mss, 38156, Russell to Brougham, 22 Dec 1836; NLI 13382, Russell to Spring Rice, 4 Jan 1837.

26 Brougham Mss, 38166, Russell to Brougham, 28 Nov 1837.

27 Airy Mss, Jerrard to Airy, 29 Jan 1838.
28 Airy Mss, Roget to Burlington, 30 May 1838.

8 DR ARNOLD AND THE SCRIPTURAL EXAMINATION

1 A.P. Stanley, *The Life and Correspondence of Thomas Arnold, D.D.*, 2 (London, 8th edn, 1858), p. 8.

2 NLI 551, Spring Rice to Arnold, 29 Sep 1835; 533/MF 8411, Spring Rice to Whateley, 15 Nov 1838; Stanley, *Life and Correspondence*, 2, p. 8.

3 Stanley, *Life and Correspondence*, 2, p. 8; letters to Hawkins, 4 Nov, Coleridge, 18 Nov 1835, Platt, 5 Feb 1836, Crabb Robinson, 15 Mar 1837. T. Sadler (ed.), *Diary, Reminiscences and Correspondence of Henry Crabb Robinson*, 2 (London, 1872), pp. 168–9, 172, 184, Arnold to Crabb Robinson, 22 Feb 1836, 3 Feb 1837.

4 Stanley, *Life and Correspondence*, 2, pp. 74–8, Arnold to Otter, 30 Apr 1837.

5 Stanley, *Life and Correspondence*, 2, p. 75, Arnold to Otter, 30 Apr 1837: Sadler; *Diary of Crabb Robinson*, 2, p. 184, Arnold to Crabb Robinson, 3 Feb 1837.

6 Burlington, Diary, 25 May 1838; Airy Mss, Lubbock to Airy, 27 Sep 1838; Lubbock Mss R242, Rothman to Lubbock, 15 May 1840. PP 1836, xiii, Evidence to the Select Committee appointed 'to examine the State, Funds and Management of the Diocesan, Royal and other schools of Public Education in Ireland; as also into the System of Education pursued therin.,' 28 and 29 Mar 1836. Airy, *Autobiography*, p. 136, referred to Jerrard as 'the principal representative on the religious side.'

7 BL Add Mss 40570, Jerrard to Bishop of Norwich, 9 Jul 1845, enclosed with Jerrard to Peel, 14 Jul 1845.

8 UL RC/1/1 – from a paper by Jerrard in support of a Notice of Motion to extend the Scriptural Examination to all candidates for the BA, Jul 1845.

9 Stanley, *Life and Correspondence*, 2, pp. 82, 84, Arnold to Empson, 18 and 28 Nov 1837.

10 The letter was dated 1 Feb 1838, and appeared in the *Globe* on 7 February – the very day of the fateful meeting. It appeared over the signature 'A Friend to Religious Liberty.' A copy is included in UL RC/1/1. See, also, Whately to Arnold, 5 Jan 1838, in Nassau Senior Mss C863, reproduced in E. Jane Whateley, *Life and Correspondence of Richard Whateley, D.D.*, 1 (London, 1866), pp. 408–13.

11 Lord Cockburn, *Life of Lord Jeffrey*, 2 (Edinburgh, 1852), p. 295, Jeffrey to Empson, 26 Nov 1837.

12 Burlington, Diary, 26 Jan and 1 Feb 1838.

13 Stanley, *Life and Correspondence*, 2, p. 91, Arnold to Hawkins, 23 Jan 1838.

14 Nassau Senior Mss, C583, Senior to Whateley, 19 Dec 1837.

15 SM 10 Jan 1838.

16 SM 31 Jan 1838. Airy Mss, which also contains a group of relevant and interesting exchanges between Airy and Jerrard, Nov 1837 to Feb 1838.

17 Lubbock Mss H367, Hewett to Lubbock, 1 Feb 1838.
18 UL RC/1/1, Proof of a twelve page document prepared by Jerrard for the Senate in 1846.
19 Airy Mss, Pye Smith to Jerrard, 1 Jan 1838.
20 UL RC/1/1, for this and the two following extracts.
21 BM Add Mss 34618 fol 538, Empson to Napier, 11 Feb 1838.
22 NLI 13390, Empson to Spring Rice 18 [?] Feb 1838. The new Bishop of Norwich's son, A.P. Stanley, was to be Arnold's biographer.
23 Devonshire Mss 3605.6, Bishop of Norwich to Burlington, 1 Feb 1838.
24 Lubbock Mss W80, Warburton to Lubbock, 12 Feb 1838.
25 Stanley, *Life and Correspondence*, 2, pp. 94–5, Arnold to Pasley, 16 Feb 1838.
26 Stanley, *Life and Correspondence*, 2. pp. 126–27.
27 Lubbock Mss R43, Spring Rice to Lubbock, 10 Nov 1838; NLI 533 MF P8411, Spring Rice to Whateley, 15 Nov 1838.
28 Burlington, Diary, 7 Feb 1838; UL RC/1/1; Stanley, *Life and Correspondence*, 2, pp. 94–5, Arnold to Pasley, 16 Feb 1838.

9 ENTER ROTHMAN: EXIT SOMERVILLE

1 Lubbock Mss A109, Airy to Lubbock 20 Mar 1837; E115, Empson to Lubbock, nd.
2 Burlington, Diary, 3, 14 and 21 Feb 1838.
3 Lubbock Mss A133, Airy to Lubbock, 16 Mar 1838; Airy Mss, Rothman to Airy, 7 Oct 1837, 19 and nd Mar 1838.
4 Lubbock Mss M145, Moore to Lubbock, 27 Feb 1838.
5 Lubbock Mss R182–3, 185, Rothman to Lubbock, nd 1837, 2 Apr 1838, nd 1838; Airy Mss, Rothman to Airy, 7 Oct 1837, 19 Mar and nd 1838; Burlington, Diary, 4 Apr 1838.
6 Burlington, Diary, 7 Apr 1838.
7 Brougham Mss, 42872, 15950, Somerville to Brougham, 28 Sep 1832, 20 Jul 1836.
8 Burlington, Diary, 25 and 26 Jan 1838.
9 Ruth Richardson, *Death, Dissection and the Destitute* (London, 1987), p. 237. For another study, see M. Durey, *Bodysnatchers and Benthamites* (London, 1976).
10 Richardson, *Death, Dissection*, pp. 237, 245.
11 Burlington, Diary, 25 and 26 Jan 1838.
12 Burlington, Diary, 30 Jan 1838.
13 Devonshire Mss, 3605.8, 3605.9, Russell to Burlington, 4 Feb 1838; Burlington, Diary, 3, 5, 6 Feb 1838.
14 Devonshire Mss, 3605.10, Russell to Burlington, 9 Feb 1838; BL Add Mss 34618 fol 538, Empson to Napier, 11 Feb 1838.
15 Devonshire Mss, 3605.10, Russell to Burlington, 9 Feb 1838.
16 Burlington, Diary, 9 Feb 1838.
17 Burlington, Diary, 17 Feb 1838.

18 Devonshire Mss, 3605.12, Russell to Burlington, 19 May 1838.
19 Burlington Diary, 18–31 May 1838; Airy Mss, Roget to Burlington, 30 May 1838; Lubbock Mss C47, Burlington to Lubbock, 28 May 1838.
20 Devonshire Mss, 3605.4, Warburton to Russell, 14 Jun 1838. See also Burlington, Diary, 8–15 Jun 1838.
21 Devonshire Mss, 3605.13, Russell to Burlington, 14 Jun 1838; Burlington, Diary, 15 June 1838.
22 HC Jnl, 14/15 Jun 1838.
23 Quoted in *The Times*, 23 Jun 1838.
24 Burlington, Diary, 9 and 13 Jul 1838; *The Times*, 16 Jul 1838, quoting the *Court Circular*.
25 *The Times*, 17 Jul 1838, quoting the *Literary Gazette*, and a letter to *The Times*, in the issue of 18 Jul 1838.

10 EXAMINATIONS AND FAULTLINES

1 Lubbock Mss A127, A132, Airy to Lubbock, 4 Jan and 15 Mar 1838.
2 PP HC542, Burlington to Goulburn, 8 Dec 1841.
3 Airy Mss, Lubbock to Airy, 16 Mar 1838; Burlington, Diary, 17 Mar 1838.
4 SM 9 May 1838.
5 Airy Mss, Lubbock to Airy, 30 Mar 1838; Faculty of Arts, Minutes, 4 Apr 1838.
6 BL Add Mss 37190 fol 517, Rothman to Babbage, 13 Aug 1838.
7 Lubbock Mss H402, Hodgkin to Lubbock, 29 Apr 1839.
8 Lubbock Mss H403, Hodgkin to Lubbock, 29 May 1839.
9 Lubbock Mss C269, Clark to Lubbock, nd 1839; W83 Warburton to Lubbock, 12 Jun 1839.
10 Lubbock Mss R138, Roget to Lubbock, 4 Jul 1838.
11 NLI 13390, Burlington to Spring Rice, 1 Jul 1838.
12 Lubbock Mss R138, 139, 141, Roget to Lubbock, 4 Jul, 16 Nov, 4 Dec 1838; R192, Rothman to Lubbock, 4 Dec 1838. Clark made his displeasure known to Lubbock in four undated letters in 1839 – C266–9.
13 HO 44/31, Lubbock to Russell, 5 Dec 1838.
14 Lubbock Mss R375, Russell to Lubbock, 7 Dec 1838; *see also* NLI 1339, Lubbock to Spring Rice, 28 Nov and 9 Dec 1838, 533, Spring Rice to Russell, nd [Dec 1838].
15 Airy Mss, Lubbock to Airy, 11 Dec 1838.
16 Burlington, Diary, 16 Jun 1839.
17 Lubbock Mss R44, Spring Rice to Lubbock, 20 Nov 1838; R375, Russell to Lubbock, 7 Dec 1838.
18 Airy Mss, Airy to Spring Rice, 14 Jul 1838.
19 Lubbock Mss A140, Airy to Lubbock, 13 Dec 1838.
20 Lubbock Mss C50, Burlington to Lubbock, 8 Jan 1839.
21 Lubbock Mss C257, Clark to Lubbock, 30 Dec 1838.
22 Herschell Mss HS1.79; Airy Mss, Airy to Herschell, 19 Jun 1839.

23 Lubbock Mss R380, Russell to Lubbock, 23 May 1839; W83, Warburton to Lubbock 12 Jun 1839; Herschell Mss HS14.436 and 437, Russell to Herschell, 31 May, Herschell to Russell, 5 Jun 1839.
24 Lubbock Mss C262, Clark to Lubbock, 1 Jun 1839.
25 Burlington, Diary, 28 Jun and 17 Jul 1839.
26 UL RO 1/2/1, Rothman to Rev J. Romilly, 28 Feb 1840.
27 Burlington, Diary, 27 Jan 1840; UL RO 1/2/2, Rothman to Empson, 11 Mar, Rothman to Phillipps, 16 Mar 1840.
28 Burlington, Diary, 17 Feb 1840.
29 Burlington, Diary, 11 and 18 Mar 1840.
30 Burlington, Diary, 20 and 25 Mar 1840.
31 Burlington, Diary, 25 Mar 1840.
32 Burlington, Diary, 6 Apr 1840.

11 TOWARDS STALEMATE

1 HO 44/36, Burlington to Normanby, 17 Oct 1840.
2 Lubbock Mss C75, Burlington to Lubbock, 1 Dec 1841.
3 Parl Deb, 3rd ser, liii, 1319–24; Mirror of Parliament, 2nd ser, IV, 2870–6.
4 UL RO 1/2/2, Rothman to Baring and Russell, 20, 21, 22 Jul 1840. For a survey of Wakley's influence, see Mary Bostetter, 'The Journalism of Thomas Wakley,' in Joel H. Wiener (ed.), *Innovators and Preachers, The Role of the Editor in Victorian England* (London, 1985).
5 Parl Deb, 3rd ser, l, 591–4.
6 The sequence of demands for documents can be followed most readily in the Journals of the House of Commons. The most relevant documents are PP 1840, xl, HC598, and PP 1842, xxxiii, HC 542. For the correspondence in 1840, see UL RO 1/2/2, Rothman to Baring, 15 May, Lubbock to Baring, 18 May, Rothman to Normanby, 29 May; Lubbock Mss C56, Burlington to Lubbock, 15 May.
7 Lubbock Mss R155, Roget to Lubbock, 3 Jun 1840.
8 Lubbock Mss R156, Roget to Lubbock, 29 Jun 1840.
9 The debate took place on 24 and 27 Jul 1840. See Mirror of Parliament, 2nd ser, VI, 4926–7, 4994–6; Parl Deb, 3rd ser, lv, 1054–7.
10 Lubbock Mss C271, Clark to Lubbock, 29 Apr 1840: and see several of Burlington's letters to Lubbock later in the year.
11 HO 44/36, Lubbock to Normanby, 1 Oct 1840.
12 HO 44/36, Burlington to Normanby, 17 Oct 1840.
13 Fox Maule became 2nd Baron Panmure and succeeded as 11th Earl of Dalhousie.
14 HO 44/36, Gordon to Fox Maule, 1 Nov 1840.
15 Lubbock Mss C61, Burlington to Lubbock, 27 Nov 1840. For official correspondence see HO 44/36, T13, and UL RO 1/2/2: some letters were reproduced in Senate minutes.
16 HO 44/36, Copy of 'Memorandum by Mr Fox Maule.'

17 T/13/320, Trevelyan to Fox Maule, 10 Feb 1841.
18 Lubbock Mss C65, Burlington to Lubbock, 25 Jan 1841.
19 T/13/328, Gordon to Fox Maule, 31 Mar 1841.
20 HO 45/78, Normanby to Monteagle, 1 Apr 1841.
21 RCP, Sir James Clark's Diary, pp. 111–14: BL Add Mss 34618 fol 54, Empson to Napier, 27 Feb 1837.
22 The relevant standard work is Newman, *The Evolution of Medical Education in the 19th Century* (London, 1957).
23 UL RC 20/2/6, 13 Jul 1840.
24 Burlington, Diary, 29 Jun 1840.
25 *DNB*. J.F. Clarke, *Autobiographical Recollections of the Medical Profession* (London, 1874), ch. xxiii.
26 Lubbock Mss C14, Carlisle to Lubbock, 14 Jul 1840.
27 Lubbock Mss C16, Carlisle to Lubbock, 29 Jul 1840.
28 Newman, *Evolution of Medical Education*, p. 155.
29 G.N. Clark and A.M. Cooke, *History of the Royal College of Physicians of London*, II, pp. 701–3, III, p. 1137.
30 The report is printed in SM 27 Jan 1841.
31 Lubbock Mss C272, Clark to Lubbock, 19 Jan 1841.
32 Lubbock Mss H297, Hawkins to Lubbock, 5 Feb 1841.
33 UL RO 1/2/2, Lubbock to Hawkins, 15 Jan 1841.
34 SM 27 Jan 1841, Hawkins to Lubbock, 16 Jan 1841.
35 Lubbock Mss B603, Burrows to Lubbock, 25 Jan 1841.
36 UL RO 1/2/2, Rothman to Hawkins, 8 Feb 1841.
37 SM 24 Feb 1841, Halford to Lubbock, 14 Feb 1841; Clark, *History of RCP*, II pp 695–6.
38 *Provincial Medical and Surgical Journal*, 10 Apr 1841.
39 *Quarterly Review*, lxvii, 75–6.
40 Lubbock Mss C85, Burlington to Lubbock, 2 Apr 1842.
41 *Provincial Medical and Surgical Journal*, 10 Apr 1841.
42 Airy Mss include a copy of the article, printed by the University's printer and headed *UNIVERSITY OF LONDON*. Immediately underneath the title is written, unmistakably in Airy's hand, 'Drs Jerrard and Roget?'
43 Lubbock Mss R50, Monteagle to Lubbock, 23 Apr 1841; C67, 68, Burlington to Lubbock, 5 and 25 May 1841; Burlington, Diary, 29 May 1841.
44 Monteagle's *Report Respecting the University of London*, dated 23 Jul 1841, is in HO 45/78.
45 HO 45/78, Burlington to Normanby, 27 Jul 1841.
46 Lubbock Mss C69 and 70, Burlington to Lubbock, 4 and 18 Aug 1841.

12   OFFICIAL INDIFFERENCE: INTERNAL ASSESSMENT
1 SM 8 Dec 1841, Goulburn to Lubbock, 25 Nov 1841.
2 Lubbock Mss C72, 73, 75, Burlington to Lubbock, 16 Oct, 4 Nov, 1 Dec 1841.

3 Airy Mss, Lubbock to Airy, 4 Dec 1841.

4 Lubbock Mss R265, Rothman to Lubbock, 24 Sep 1841.

5 Devonshire Mss 116.0, Graham to Burlington, 4 Dec 1841.

6 Burlington, Diary, 7 Dec 1841.

7 PP xxxiii, HC 542/1842.

8 Burlington, Diary, 9 Dec 1841. For Burlington's letter to Goulburn, dated 8 Dec, *see* HC 542/1842. That paper also contains the replies of examiners to the request for details of their efforts, which were submitted in December 1841 and January 1842. The writer was not a little astonished and delighted to read the examiners' statements, as they reiterated almost exactly, in spirit and even in practical detail, the answers given in a similar exercise conducted among faculty of the University of California, under budgetary threat, in the late 1960s!

9 HC 542/1842, Goulburn to Burlington, 23 Dec 1841.

10 Devonshire Mss, 116.2, Graham to Burlington, 18 Feb 1842.

11 Lubbock Mss C83, Burlington to Lubbock, 8 Feb 1842. Both men took exception to Warburton's 'conduct in bargaining' with Rothman.

12 Lubbock Mss C85, Burlington to Lubbock, 2 Apr 1842; Burlington, Diary, 25 May 1842.

13 SM 17 Aug 1842, Hawkins to Rothman, 1 Aug 1842.

14 *Lancet*, 11 Mar 1848.

15 Newman, *Evolution of Medical Education*, p. 158.

16 Burlington, Diary, 1 and 4 Jun 1842.

17 Lubbock Mss B457, Brodie to Lubbock, 13 Jun 1842.

18 Sir James Clark, *Remarks on Medical Reform in a Letter addressed to the Rt Hon. Sir James Graham, Bart.* (London, 1842). Burlington, Diary, 23 and 27 Jun 1842.

19 Devonshire Mss, 116.3, Lubbock to Burlington, 20 May 1842.

20 Lubbock Mss C86, 87, Burlington to Lubbock, 30 May, 11 Jun 1842.

21 HO 43/62/400, Graham to Secretary, UL, 11 Jul 1842; HO 45/78, Rothman to Phillipps, 12 Jul 1842; UL RO 1/2/6, Rothman to Manners Sutton, 24 Sep 1844. The petition about the Court of Arches was presented by Lord John Russell – House of Commons Jnl and Parl Deb 3s vol 69 col 1095, 30 May 1843; Appendix 680 to Rpt of Sel Cmte on Public Petitions, 9 Jun 1843. For the memorial, see SM 9 Apr 1845, and Billing's evidence to the Select Committee on Medical Registration and Medical Law Amendment, PP 1847–8, xv HC 210, 702, Evid. 4356–71.

22 Nassau Senior Mss, C114.

23 Hodgkin's proposals are contained in 'Outlines of a plan for the future constitution of the University of London,' Airy Mss.

24 Clark, *Remarks on Medical Reform*, p. 17.

25 Airy Mss, Airy to Lubbock, 2 Apr, Lubbock to Airy, 3 Apr 1840.

13   A NEW ROUND OF CONTROVERSY

1 Airy Mss, Burlington to Airy, 14 Mar 1847.

2 Airy Mss, Burlington to Airy, 20 Aug 1847.

3 I.G.Jones, 'The Liberation Society and Welsh politics 1844–1868,' in *Welsh History Review*, i, 2, 1961, p. 202.

4 John Vincent, *The Formation of the Liberal Party 1857–1868* (London, 1966), p. 68.

5 BL Add Mss 40570 fol 350–5, Jerrard to Norwich, 9 Jul, Jerrard to Peel 14 Jul 1845.

6 Burlington, Diary, 15 Jul 1846.

7 PRO 30/22/6D, Warburton to Russell, 10 Mar 1847; *see also* Burlington, Diary, 11 Mar 1847.

8 Airy Mss, Jerrard to Airy, 7 Jun 1847.

9 The main source for this episode is correspondence in the Airy Mss at UL between Airy, Jerrard, Warburton and Burlington in the period June to August, 1847, and between Airy, Lefevre, Burlington and Jerrard in May and June 1849. *See also* Burlington, Diary, 16 Jun 1847; Senate Minutes; and Airy's *Autobiography*, pp. 180, 186–7.

10 1 Vic c56.

11 Minutes of the Middle Temple Parliament, 3 Nov 1843: the Order for the dispensation was moved by Sir William Owen, Bt, who changed his name to Barlow in 1844, on inheriting family estates in Pembroke. UL RO/1/2/6, Rothman to Thackwell, 24 Sep 1844; UL RO 1/2/7, Rothman to House of Commons, 7 Apr 1845.

12 *See* fn 21 to Ch. XII.

13 For Army and Navy, *see London University Magazine* vol. 1, No. 5, Sep 1856, p. 262; for Poor Law, *see* UL RO/1/2/7, Rothman to House of Commons, 7 Apr 1845.

14 SM 9 Apr 1845.

15 *Eclectic Review*, Jul 1852, p. 94. For evidence of the constant and prominent roles of Bacot and Ridout in the Society of Apothecaries, see the minutes of the Parliament Committee of the Society in the Guildhall Library, Ms 8212.

16 *Lancet*, 11 Mar 1848, p. 290.

17 *See* e.g. Burlington, Diary, 9 May, 1845, 2 Jun 1847.

18 Airy, *Autobiography*, p. 180.

19 Airy Mss, Airy to Burlington, 15 Mar 1847.

20 Burlington, Diary, 26 May 1847.

21 UL RO 1/2/9, Rothman to Senior, 16 and 20 Nov 1847.

14 THE BEGINNINGS OF GRADUATE PARTICIPATION

1 UCL Annual Reports.

2 C.J. Foster, *The University of London A Parliamentary Constituency* (London, 1851), p. 3.

3 Lincoln's Inn, *Black Books*, vol. 24, pp. 12–13, 30 Jun 1841.

4 Brougham Mss, 26905, Wood to Brougham, 24 Jun 1841.

5 Lincoln's Inn, *Black Books*, vol. 24, pp. 252–3, 15 Jun 1843.

6 Lincoln's Inn, *Black Books*, vol. 24, pp. 263–4, 422–30, 437–8, 441, 478, 483: 29 Jun 1843, 22 Nov, 2 and 16 Dec 1844, 7 and 21 Feb 1845.

7 Lincoln's Inn, *Black Books*, vol. 25, pp. 36, 100–02, 163, 214–6, 267–8: 8 Jul 1845, 12 Jan, 13 May, 22 Jul, 9 Dec 1846, 11 Jan 1847.

8 Inner Temple, Bench Table Orders, 26 Jan and 11 Feb 1846.

9 The Return, requested by Christie on 9 Feb 1846, is in PP 1846, xxiii: A Statement of the Regulations of the four Inns of Court having the Power to call to the Bar, with the date of each Regulation, and the Authority by which it was made; and specifying any Distinction made betwen the Members of the Universities of Oxford and Cambridge and others. *See, also*, Gray's Inn, G(b)1, 29 Jan 1846, Thesiger to Greene.

10 PP 1846, x, HC 686. The evidence of Amos and Empson throws interesting light on several aspects of the University's involvement with professional education and on the attitudes of senators. Thus, Amos, Evid. 1384: the members of the University 'attend as their avocations permit . . . there is too little responsibility there . . . because gratuitous services to the public are apt to give place to private avocations.' Empson, Evid. 622, on the unattractiveness of the University's qualifications in Law: 'there is nothing to be got from the London University. The feeling is "why should we come to be examined by you, when all you can give us is a degree, but which degree we can make no use of."' And Empson again, Evid. 615, contrasting the behaviour of the University's medical and law faculties, to the detriment of the latter: 'I never was more struck in my life than with the difference I saw between two professions; in the one case the profession united for the improvement of the education of their members, and a perfect indifference in the others.'

11 Lincoln's Inn, *Black Books*, vol. 25, p. 302, 16 Apr 1847.

12 UCL, College Correspondence, John Storrar, 1846–47.

13 UL RO/1/2/7, Rothman to Manson, 8 Mar 1845.

14 *Lancet*, 19 Apr 1845, p. 448.

15 UL/RO/1/2/7, Moore to Tyler Smith, 24 Aug 1845.

16 UL RO/1/2/7, Browne to Rothman, 5 Dec, Rothman to Browne, 16 Dec 1845; SM 10 Dec 1845.

17 *Lancet*, 27 Mar 1847.

18 Parl Deb 3s, vol. 92, cols 790–1, 14 May 1847.

19 PP 1847, ix; 1847–8, xv.

20 PP 1847–8, xv, Appendix 11 to Report of Select Committee on Medical Registration.

21 PP 1847–8, xv, Evid. 4648, 30 Jun 1848, to Select Committee on Medical Registration.

22 *Lancet*, 8 May 1858; W.H. Allchin, *An Account of the Reconstruction of the University of London*, Part I, (London, 1905), p. 14.

23 *Lancet*, 25 May 1850, p. 645; Dunsheath and Miller, *Convocation in the University of London*, p. 6. The lack of precision, in this and many later contexts, is partly due to the regrettable disappearance of the papers of

the Graduates Committee. They were handed to Convocation at its first meeting, on 4 May 1858, and were then described as 'containing a record of the struggle now brought to a successful issue.' *See* Allchin, *Reconstruction of the University of London*, Part I, note to p. 14. There are brief references to the papers in Chapter 2 of the book by Dunsheath and Miller, which was published in 1958.

24 SM 22 Mar 1848. The letter was undated.
25 Burlington, Diary, 13 Apr 1848.
26 *Lancet*, 11 Mar, 3, 10 and 17 Jun 1848.

15 THE SUPPLEMENTARY CHARTER

1 Burlington, Diary, 30 Jun 1847, 21 Jun 1848.
2 PRO 30/22/7C, Grey to Russell, 3 Jul 1848. The recently created See of Manchester was headed by James Prince Lee, formerly Headmaster of King Edward VI's School at Birmingham. Sir Thomas Wyse, who had shown an intense interest in education, especially in Ireland, was currently Secretary to the Board of Control for India, but had lost his seat in the Commons when seeking re-election in 1847. He was appointed British Minister in Athens in January 1849. Herschell was a famous astronomer. Dr Herries may well have been a prominent figure, possibly in education, who has not been recorded in the biographical dictionaries. But if he was John Charles Herries, the veteran Tory politician and minister, now seventy years of age and sitting as MP for Stamford, he was a peculiar choice on Burlington's part, and one unlikely to be accepted by Russell and Grey.
3 UCL Council Minutes, 6 May, 3 Jun 1848; SM 7 and 21 Jun 1848.
4 PP 1847–8, xv, Evid. of Billing, Hodgkin, Barnes and Storrar.
5 Burlington, Diary, 28 Jun 1848.
6 UL RC1/2/6. *See also* HO 45/78A, Foster to Grey, 31 Jul 1848; Foster to Waddington, 23 Aug 1848.
7 HO 45/78A, Foster and Barnes to Grey, 8 and 26 Dec 1848, 14 Jan 1849; Foster to Waddington, 14 Dec 1848.
8 SM 28 Feb 1849. Barnes and Foster to Grey, 26 Dec 1848; 14 Jan 1849.
9 SM 7 Feb 1849.
10 UCL Council Minutes, 10 Feb, 3 Mar 1849.
11 UCL College Correspondence, Foster to Atkinson, 21 Dec 1848, 8 Jan 1849.
12 UCL College Correspondence, Foster to Atkinson, 8 Mar 1849.
13 Dunsheath and Miller, *Convocation*, p. 10. Full text of proposals in SM 4 Apr 1849.
14 HO 45/2660, Bp of Norwich to Grey, 7 Apr 18. Memorial received 9 Apr 1849. Letter of John Ridout, dated Apr 1849.
15 HO 45/2660, Grey's memo on Norwich to Grey, 7 Apr 1849.
16 HO 45/2660, Burlington to Waddington, 16 and 27 Feb 1849; Coulson to Home Office, 10 May 1849.
17 HO 45/2660, and UL RO/1/2/11, Vice-Chancellor to Grey, 4 May 1849;

HO 45/2660, Rothman to Waddington, 25 May; Grey to Law Officers, 26 May 1849.

18 UCL Council Minutes, 19 May and 2 Jun 1849. SM 23 May and 20 Jun 1849. HO 45/4869, Correspondence re Medical Bill, 15–16 Mar 1853.

19 SM 18 Jul, 1 Aug and 7 Nov 1849, letters from Foster to Senate, 16 and 20 Jul, 15 Aug 1849, Barnes and Foster to Senate, 15 Aug 1849.

16   AN UNRIPENESS OF TIME

1 PRO 30/29/18/14, Grote to Granville, 27 Jan 1858.

2 UCL College Correspondence, John Storrar, 1846–7; *The Times*, 12 Mar 1886; Dunsheath and Millar, *Convocation in the University of London*, pp. 34–7, 173–4.

3 Herschell Mss HS18.56, Warburton to Herschell, nd but clearly Feb/Mar 1850. *See also* Warburton's letter of 27 Feb and 4 Mar. Warburton had been conducting, by correspondence, a mathematical discussion with Herschell since 1847, and continued to do so until his death eleven years later.

4 Parl Deb 3s, vol. 122, col. 5, 4 Jun 1852.

5 UCL College Correspondence, E.W. Field to [?] Atkinson, 22 Apr 1848. UCL Council Minutes, 6 May 1848.

6 Gray's Inn, G(b)10, Rothman to Griffith, 29 Oct 1850; UL RO 1/2/13, Printed UL paper headed 'Admission of graduates to the Inns of Court,' dated 3 (or 8) Jun 1851.

7 *Lancet*, 11 May 1850, p. 568.

8 *Lancet*, 25 May 1850, p. 644, Letter dated 13 May 1850.

9 HO 45/3107, Barnes and Osler to Grey, 9 Mar 1850; Osler to Grey, 12 Mar 1850; Homerton, Spring Hill, Airedale and Highbury Colleges to HO, 25 Apr–24 May 1850; Lefevre to Grey, 22 Aug 1850. HO 45/2660, Atkinson to Grey, 9 Apr 1850; Stepney College to Grey, 26 Apr 1850.

10 HO 45/3107, Lefevre to Grey, 22 Aug 1850.

11 *Lancet*, 11 May 1850, p. 568.

12 Among new members of the Graduates Committee at this time were William Withey Gull, who would be one of the first two London graduates appointed to the Senate, and Walter Bagehot.

13 Overstone Mss, 804/1084/1–2, Warburton to Overstone, 5 Feb 1854.

14 HO 45/6434, Fowler to Grey, 28 Jun 1851, Burlington to Grey, 4 Jul 1851.

15 E.L. Woodward, *The Age of Reform, 1815–1870* (London, 1936), p. 503.

16 HO 45/6434, Fowler to Grey, 16 Dec 1851.

17   A PARLIAMENTARY CONSTITUENCY?

1 UL RC1/2/i,ii, Memorial to Foster, 6 May 1863.

2 *Canterbury Times*, NZ, 26 Nov 1896.

3 Brougham Mss 36569, Foster to Brougham, 26 Jun 1852. Foster was seeeking Brougham's support for his application for the Equity Readership at Lincoln's Inn.

4 For Foster's career in Britain, see David M. Thompson, 'The Liberation Society 1844–1868,' in Patricia Hollis, *Pressure from Without in Early Victorian England* (London, 1974), ch. 9; W.H. Mackintosh, *Disestablishment and Liberation: The Movement for the Separation of the Anglican Church from State Control* (London, 1972), pp. 53–9, 69, 78–9, 84–5, 105, 122, 168; John Vincent, *The Formation of the Liberal Party 1857–1868* (London, 1966), pp. 68–75; I.G. Jones, 'The Liberation Society and Welsh politics 1844–1868,' in *Welsh History Review*, vol. 1, no. 2, 1961, pp. 193–224; R.C. Machin, *Politics and the Churches in Great Britain 1832 to 1868* (Oxford, 1977), *passim*.

5 Greater London Record Office, A/LIB/1 and 2; *Nonconformist*, 8 Feb, 10 May 1854.

6 UL RO 1/2/14, Rothman to Shaen, 19 Feb 1852. The letter is printed in SM for 3 Mar 1852. *Eclectic Review*, NS III, pp. 516–17, Apr 1852.

7 UL RC1/2/i,ii.

8 *Eclectic Review*, NS III, pp. 516–17.

9 The statements from colleges were printed in SM: the resolution of the UCL AGM, and the college memorials which reached the Home Office, are in HO 45/4223; but the resolution of the Trustees of Manchester New College of 29 Jan 1852 is in HO 45/6434. UCL Correspondence, Foster - Foster to Atkinson, 28 Jan and 7 Feb 1852.

10 HO 45/6434, Lefevre to Walpole, 5 Mar 1852; Waddington to Lefevre, 9 Mar 1852.

11 HO 45/6434, Shaen to Walpole, 10 Mar 1852.

12 The documents were presented to the Commons on 29 Jun 1852 and ordered to be printed on the following day: PP 1852, xl. Copies of extracts of all communications respecting the organization of the University of London, since the year 1840, between the Home Office and the Senate of the University, any of the affiliated colleges, and the Committee of Graduates respectively; and of such of the minutes of the Senate of the University of London, and of committees appointed by the Senate, as relate to the admission of graduates to form an integral portion of the corporate body of the University (in continuation of PP No. 598 of Session 1840).

13 *Eclectic Review*, NS III, pp. 516–17.

14 Dunsheath and Miller, *Convocation in the University of London*, p. 16.

15 UL RC 1/2/f.

16 D.P. O'Brien, *Correspondence of Lord Overstone* ii (1971), p. 553, Senior to Overstone, 11 Nov 1852. O'Brien quotes Allchin, *Account of the Reconstruction of the University of London*, i (1905), p. 250, claiming that Overstone was a member of the select committee; but that was not so.

17 *Eclectic Review*, NS I, pp. 517–34, May 1851; II, pp. 516–17, Apr, 1852; IV, pp. 91–104, Jul 1852.

18 *Lancet*, 17 Apr 1852.

19 *Lancet*, 8 May 1852.

20 UL RC1/2/i,ii.

21 *Lancet*, 8 May 1852, quoting a recent speech by Graham at Carlisle.

22 Parl Deb 3s, 121, cols 442–3, 10 May 1852. Derby's comments, on the same lines, were reported to the Senate by Foster, Barnes and Shaen in a letter dated 12 May, printed in SM of 16 Jun 1852.

18   THE TOMLINSON FACTOR

1 *Lancet*, 26 Jun 1852.

2 Brougham Mss 36570, Foster to Brougham, 28 June 1852.

3 PP 1852, xl. *See* fn 12, ch. XVII.

4 *Lancet*, 7 May 1853, reporting the AGM of the graduates, held on 3 May 1853.

5 The meeting was reported, quite fully, in the *Lancet* of 4 Dec 1852.

6 UL RC1/2/i,ii, Draft statement enclosed in a printed *Memorial to Foster*, 6 May 1863. For the Militia Bill, see Parl Deb 3s, vol. 122 cols 183–4, 7 June 1852. The bill became the Militia Act, 1852, 15 and 16 Vic c 50. For Charitable Trusts Bills, 1852 and 1853, see HO 45/4223, Shaen to Walpole, 24 Apr 1852; a petition of UCL, praying 'That the Charitable Trusts Bill may be so framed as to place the University of London and its Colleges upon an Equality with the Universities of Oxford, Cambridge and Durham,' House of Lords Journal, 23 June 1853; and Parl Deb 3s, vol. 129, cols 1158, 1490–5, 2 and 8 Aug 1853. The exemption of London, along with the other English universities, from the application of the Act was generally accepted, but in the case of London there was confusion over the affiliated colleges. Thornely tried to have them, as well as the University, excluded, but his amendment was defeated on third reading. The Charitable Trusts Bill reached the statute book in 1853 as 16 and 17 Vic c 137.

7 Lancet, 19 Mar 1853.

8 O'Brien, *Correspondence of Lord Overstone* i, p. 293 fn 3.

9 UL RO 1/2/14, Rothman to Tomlinson, 18 May 1852.

10 HO 45/6434, Case and Opinion, 18 May 1852.

11 UL RC44/18.

12 UL RC44/19.

13 From the Opinion of Willes, dated 23 Aug 1853, printed in SM 30 Nov 1853.

14 HO/45/6434, Waddington's memo to Palmerston, Nov/Dec 1853.

15 HO 45/4869, 25 Apr 1853, Foster and Shaen to Rothman.

16 UL RO 1/2/15, Rothman to Foster and Shaen, 28 Apr 1853; HO 45/4869, Foster and Shaen to Rothman, 25 and 28 Apr, Foster and Shaen to Palmerston, 25 and 29 Apr 1853.

17 *Lancet*, 7 May 1853.

18 *Lancet*, 14 and 28 May 1853.

19 The letters are printed in SM, and copies are in HO 45/6434, 27 May and 14 Jun 1853; HO 45/4869, Atkinson to Palmerston, 6 Jun 1853.

20 HO 49/9, Waddington to Reynolds, 27 May 1853.

21 HO 45/6434, Burlington to Palmerston, 21 Apr and 17 Jun 1853.

22 HO 45/6434, enclosed with Reynolds to Waddington, 2 Sep 1853.

23 UL RO 1/2/15, Rothman to Foster, 11 Nov 1853.

24 HO 45/6434, Foster to Palmerston, c15 Nov 1853.

25 Dunsheath and Miller, *Convocation in the University of London*, p. 17; [Willes' Opinion].

26 HO 45/6434, Memos, 20 and 25 Nov 1853. The year of the first memo is wrongly given as 1859.

27 HO 45/6434, amended draft, Waddington to Burlington, 8 Dec 1853.

28 Arthur Gordon, Baron Stanmore, *Correspondence of Lord Aberdeen*, vol. 12: Gordon's Journal, 22 Nov 1853, Russell to Aberdeen 27 Dec, Aberdeen to Russell 31 Dec 1853; James B. Conacher, *The Aberdeen Coalition: a Study in Mid-nineteenth Century Party Politics* (Cambridge, 1968). pp. 217–18, 231, 295; A Bill further to amend the Laws relating to the Representation of the People in England and Wales, PP 1854, v, Bill 17, 16 Feb 1854.

29 Overstone Mss, 804/1084/1–2, Warburton to Overstone, 5 Feb 1854.

30 HO 45/6434, Shaen to Palmerston, 15 Mar, and Palmerston to Burlington, 28 Mar 1854; Clay to Grey, 1 Jun 1855.

31 Burlington, Diary, 9 May 1855.

32 HO 45/6434, Rothman to Fitzroy, 26 Aug 1854. For Fitzroy's letter of 22 July, *see* SM 1 Nov 1854.

33 HO 45/6434, Shaw Lefevre to Palmerston, 10 Feb 1854.

19   MEDICAL EQUALITY

 1 HO 45/4869, Correspondence re Medical Bill and Durham University, 15–16 Mar 1853.

 2 Medical Graduates (University of London) Act, 17 and 18 Vic c 114.

 3 Parl Deb 3s, vol. 135, col. 690.

 4 *Lancet*, 3 Jun 1854.

 5 Newman, *Evolution of Medical Education*, pp. 172–5: UCL Council Minutes, Apr–Aug 1853; UC RO 1/2/15, Rothman to Waddington, 28 Apr 1853; SM 20 and 27 Apr 1853; Parl Deb 3s, vol. 127, cols 1091–2.

 6 UCL Council Minutes, 23 Jul 1853; *Lancet*, 12 May 1855.

 7 UL RO 1/2/16, Moore to Messrs Few and Co., 15 Mar; invitation to medical senators, 21 Apr 1854. Newman, *Evolution of Medical Education*, pp. 173–4. For the text of the two versions of the Registration Bill, see PP 1854, vol. iii.

 8 *Lancet*, 1 Nov 1856.

 9 SM 14 and 21 Jun 1854. The letter to Palmerston, printed in SM for 21 Jun, was dated 19 Jun 1854.

10 Care and Treatment of Lunatics Act, 16 and 17 Vic c 96; Lunatic Asylums Act, 16 and 17 Vic c 97; Vaccination Act, 16 and 17 Vic c 100; *Lancet*, 3 Jun 1854.

11 RCP Ms 2108, 18 May 1854; Z. Cope, *The Royal College of Surgeons*, p. 158. For the original and two amended versions of the Medical Graduates

(University of London) Bill, see PP 1854, vol. iii. For the debates on the Bill in both Houses, see Parl Deb 3s, vol. 135, cols 94–111, 690–2, 893–6, 1064–7, 1477–8.

12 HC Journal, 7 Jul 1854.

13 Newman, *Evolution of Medical Education*, p. 174; Parl Deb 3s vol. 135, cols 690–2.

14 Nearly 200 MPs voted in the first two, crucial, divisions on 12 July, and three-quarters of them were Liberals, Liberal-Conservatives, Whigs and Radicals. The voting was, broadly speaking, pro or anti-Government, but there was some notable cross-voting, much of it due to the opposition of MPs of all parties, from Scottish and Irish constituencies, to the exclusion of their countries' universities from the Bill. A high proportion of the 20-odd Liberals who opposed the Bill's progress were from Ireland or Scotland. The 50 or so Conservatives who voted split 2 to 1 against the Bill; no Scottish and only one Irish Tory supported it. Many of the majority of the Conservatives from English and Welsh constituencies who voted against the Bill were fervent Anglicans, particularly hostile to any official encouragement of Roman Catholic education. If the special nationalistic aspects of the Bill are discounted, the numbers voting would seem to support the notion that the University of London had very few friends among, and aroused little interest or sympathy from, rank-and-file Conservatives.

15 The vote is not recorded in Hansard, but appears in the printed volume of Divisions, 1854, in the House of Commons Library.

16 ULRO 1/2/16, Rothman to O'Meara, 21 Jul 1854.

17 PRO 30/22/11D/173–4, Monteagle to Russell, [26] Jul 1854. Monteagle's memory was at fault in attributing any vote to Molesworth. Hamilton and Napier were opposed to going into committee. Goulburn voted to go into committee, but also voted in favour of the chairman reporting progress.

18 Full division lists for the House of Lords were not printed until 1857: before then only some lists were kept, and this one was not among them. The teller for the ayes was Monteagle, and for the noes was Lord Wynford. *See* J.C. Sainty and D. Dewar, *Divisions in the House of Lords. An Analytical List 1685 to 1857*, House of Lords Record Office Occasional Publications, No. 2, 1976.

19 Parl Deb 3s vol. 135, cols 1284–6.

20 *See* Newman, *Evolution of Medical Education*, pp. 175–93, for an essential summary.

21 Dunsheath and Miller, *Convocation in the University of London*, pp. 34–7.

20   THE INSISTENCE OF SIR GEORGE GREY

1 *Lancet*, 12 May 1855.

2 HO 45/6434, Shaen to Grey, 22 Mar 1855.

3 HO 45/6434, Burlington to Grey, 11 May 1855.

4 HO 45/6434, Memo: Grey to Waddington, 15 May 1855.

5 F.M.G. Willson, *A Strong Supporting Cast, The Shaw Lefevres 1789–1936* (London, 1993), ch. 15.

6 HO 45/6434, Waddington to Grey, nd but clearly May/Jun 1855. UL RO 1/2/17, Rothman to Waddington, 25 May 1855.

7 HO 49/10, Massey to Reynolds, 25 Jul 1856.

8 HO 45/6434, Clay to Grey, 1 Jun 1855.

9 HO 45/6434, Shaw Lefevre to Grey, 16 Jun 1855. This may well have been the high-water mark of the *anti-graduate* feeling recalled by Grote in 1858 – *see* Note 1 to ch. 14.

10 HO 45/6434 Lewis to Grey, 21 Jul; Grey to Waddington, 14 Aug 1855.

11 HO 45/6434 Grey to Burlington, 18 Aug 1855.

12 The letters of 19 and 28 Jan and 6 Feb are printed in SM for 20 Feb, and in the *Lancet* of 10 May 1856.

13 *Lancet*, 10 May 1856.

14 SM 14 May 1856, Grey to Burlington, 6 May 1856.

15 UL RO 1/2/18, Vice-Chancellor to Foster, 6 May 1856. The *Lancet*'s report of the graduates' dinner was badly confused and claimed that the Senate 'had transmitted to the Home Secretary a Draft Charter.'

16 Reynolds to Registrar, 12 Dec 1856, in SM for 17 Dec.

17 Brougham Mss 20187, 20188, Heaviside to Brougham, 25 Apr and 9 May 1856.

18 Burlington Diary, 21 May 1856.

19 Vance M.D. Hall, 'The contribution of the physiologist, William Benjamin Carpenter (1813–1885) to the development of the principles of the correlation of forces and the conservation of energy', in *Medical History*, 1979, 23, 129–55.

20 Brougham Mss 20190, Heaviside to Brougham, 24 May 1856.

21 Devonshire Mss 4.37, Burlington to Grey, 13 Aug 1856; UL RC 1/2/i, ii, Memorial to Foster, 6 May 1863; Greater London Record Office A/LIB/2, Minutes of Executive Committee of Liberation Society, 5 Jan 1857.

22 Devonshire Mss 4.37, Burlington to Grey, 13 Aug 1856.

23 *See* Note 2 to ch. 16.

24 Dunsheath and Miller, *Convocation in the University of London*, pp. 173–4.

25 Devonshire Mss 4.39, Grey to Burlington, 18 Aug 1856.

26 Palmerston (Broadlands) Mss, GC/BU/618, Burlington to Palmerston, 13 Aug 1856; Devonshire Mss 4.38, Palmerston to Burlington, 15 Aug 1856; 4.39, Grey to Burlington, 18 Aug 1856.

27 Devonshire Mss 4.37, Burlington to Grey, 13 Aug 1856.

28 Devonshire Mss 4.39, Grey to Burlington, 18 Aug 1856.

29 Devonshire Mss 4.40, Burlington to Grey, 1 Sep 1856. This is a draft letter which continues: 'He also seems to me disposed to take a moderate and reasonable view of the questions which must soon be decided – that of the future position of . . . ' and then stops.

30 Brougham Mss 5910, Shaw Lefevre to Brougham, 2 Dec 1856.

31 Willson, *A Strong Supporting Cast*, p. 147.

32 *Lancet*, 1 Nov and 27 Dec 1856.

33 *DNB*, Stanley, Edward Henry (1826–1893).

34 SM, 14 May 1856.

35 SM, 18 Jun 1856. White's letter to Carpenter was dated 23 May.

36 Northbrook Mss, Vol. iv, N4.13, Shaw Lefevre to Grey, 30 Jun 1856.

37 UL RC 19/1, Opinion dated 3 Jul 1856.

21   NEW PERSPECTIVES

1 This and the following extract are from UL RC 2/1, *The Proposed Abandonment of the College Test in the Case of Candidates for Degrees in Arts and Laws in the University of London. Statement of Facts and Arguments*. Graduates Committee, 1 June 1857.

2 Dr Robert Barnes, quoted in Dunsheath and Miller, *Convocation in the University of London*, p. 24. *Lancet*, 2 May 1857.

3 While the full texts of the various arguments were printed in SM, an excellent summary is to be found in Allchin, *Reconstruction of the University of London*, Part 1.

4 *See* ch. 1, and Whewell Mss, Add Mss a62/28, Monteagle to Whewell, 28 Jun 1854.

5 *See* chs 4 and 10.

6 SM 1 Feb, 5 Apr, 7 Jun, 1 Nov 1854.

7 TS 42/3, Home Office Registers, 5/6 May 1856; SM 14 May 1856, Grey to Burlington, 6 May 1856.

8 TS 42/3, Home Office Registers, 25/26 May 1856; HO 49/10, Waddington to Reynolds, 5 May 1856.

9 TS 2/56, Goldfinch to Foster, 27 Nov 1856.

10 TS 2/56, Reynolds to Lefevre, 28 Nov 1856.

11 HO 45/6434, Foster to Grey, 19 Jan 1857.

12 UL RC 2/1, p. 2.

13 *University of London Magazine*, Jan 1857.

14 Dunsheath and Miller, *Convocation in the University of London*. p. 22.

15 *Lancet*, leaders of 2 May, 20 June, 4 Jul, 1 and 8 Aug 1857.

16 UL ST3/2/6.

17 Dunsheath and Miller, *Convocation in the University of London*, p. 23.

18 Dunsheath and Miller, *Convocation in the University of London*, p. 25.

19 *Lancet*, 20 Jun 1857.

20 HO 49/10, Massey to Reynolds, 7 Aug 1857.

21 Report included in SM 22 Jul 1857.

22 HO 49/10, Massey to Reynolds, 7 and 13 Aug 1857.

23 HO 49/10, Waddington to Reynolds, 9 Oct, 15 Dec 1857.

24 Dunsheath and Miller, *Convocation in the University of London*, pp. 27–28; *London Quarterly Review*, Nov 1857.

25 SM, 6 Jan 1858.

26 PRO 30/29/18/14, Grote to Granville, 27 Jan 1858.

22 RETROSPECT

  1 PRO 30/29/18/14, Grote to Granville, 27 Jan 1858.
  2 PRO 30/29/18/14, Granville to Mrs Grote, 8 Aug 1858. Nassau Senior's
    records of his meetings, then and later, were to be published in four
    volumes between 1868 and 1878: *Journals, Conversations and Essays
    Relating to Ireland* (1868), *Journals kept in France and Italy* (1871),
    Correspondence and Conversations of S. Tocqueville (1872), *Conversations
    with M. Thiers, M. Guizot, and other distinguished persons during the
    Second Empire* (1878).

Index